Athens and Wittenberg

Studies in Medieval and Reformation Traditions

VOLUME 234

The titles published in this series are listed at *brill.com/smrt*

Athens and Wittenberg

Poetry, Philosophy, and Luther's Legacy

Edited by

James A. Kellerman
R. Alden Smith
Carl P.E. Springer

Technical Editor

Eric Hutchinson

BRILL

LEIDEN | BOSTON

Cover illustration: Martin Luther as Augustine Monk. Engraving by Lucas Cranach the Elder, 1520. Image in public domain.

The Library of Congress Cataloging-in-Publication Data is available online at https://catalog.loc.gov

Typeface for the Latin, Greek, and Cyrillic scripts: "Brill". See and download: brill.com/brill-typeface.

ISSN 1573-4188
ISBN 978-90-04-20670-0 (hardback)
ISBN 978-90-04-20671-7 (e-book)

This book is printed on acid-free paper and produced in a sustainable manner.

Printed by Printforce, United Kingdom

Contents

PART 2
The Reformation of Hymnody and Liturgy

PART 3
Lutheran Readings of Philosophy and Poetry

Preface

This volume represents the fruit of many rich conversations, collaborations and symposia (in the literal sense of that word) in connection with the now biennual conferences on some aspect of Luther and the legacy of the ancient Greco-Roman world. John Nordling was, along with Jon Bruss and Carl P.E. Springer, the instituter and promoter of that conference, and John remains its organizer. Yet this collection is much more than merely a collection of the fruits of those conferences. While it does include some papers whose prototypes were presented there in much shorter versions, it also includes papers that were solicited separately. In addition to the scholars who contributed the fruits of their research to the pages following, there are many other people who helped make this project a success, and here we should like to name a few.

We should like to begin by thanking the participants of all the conferences, whether they are represented in this volume or not. The contributors' friendship and rich conversations with them have afforded this volume its particular richness. We also wish to thank the administration of Concordia Theological Seminary, Fort Wayne, by whose generosity and through whose leadership Luther studies have been greatly advanced; in particular, we would here mention President Lawrence Rast, Provost Charles Gieschen, and Professor Cameron MacKenzie. We would here mention others, too, who in various ways made this volume possible, including Rachel Donnelly, David Jacks, Ella Liu, Cynthia Liu, Cameron Mackenzie, Kara Mertz, Grace Miller, Sara Nordling, Eva Parmenter, LeeAnn Rondot, Bailey Sloan, and Jamie Wheeler. We should be remiss not also to mention the assistance of Timothy Heckenlively, Jeff Hunt, Thelma Mathews, and Diane Smith.

Finally, we should like to thank the anonymous reviewers, whose criticism greatly improved this volume. We are also beholden to the fine editors at Brill and their staff, among whom we particularly wish to thank Ivo Romein, Arjan van Dijk, and Christopher Ocker, editor of *Studies in Medieval and Reformation Traditions*. That said, of course, the editors of this volume are responsible for its shortcomings, shortcomings that we hope are surpassed by the valuable insights the individual contributions have to offer.

J.A.K, R.A.S, C.P.E.S.
June, 2022

Illustrations

Figures

Examples

Abbreviations

CR	*Corpus Reformatorum*. Volumes 1–28: *Philippi Melanchthonis Opera quae supersunt omnia*. Edited by C.G. Bretschneider and H.E. Bindseil. Halle: C.A. Schwetschke, 1834–60. Volumes 29–87: *Ioannis Calvini Opera quae supersunt omnia*. Edited by W. Baum., E. Cunitz, and E. Reuss. Braunschweig: C.A. Schwetschke et filius, 1863–1900. Volumes 88–: *Huldreich Zwinglis Sämtliche Werke*. Edited by Emil Egli et al. Leipzig: Hinsius, 1905–.
ESV	*The Holy Bible: English Standard Version*. Crossway Bible, 2001.
FC SD	Formula of Concord, Solid Declaration
LCL	Loeb Classical Library
LS	Charlton T. Lewis and Charles Short, *A Latin Dictionary* (Oxford: Oxford University Press, 1879).
LW	*Luther's Works: American Edition*. Volumes 1–30: Edited by Jaroslav Pelikan. St. Louis: Concordia Publishing House, 1955–76. Volumes 31–55: Edited by Helmut Lehmann. Philadelphia/Minneapolis: Muhlenberg/Fortress, 1957–1986. Volumes 56–82: Edited by Christopher Boyd Brown and Benjamin T.G. Mayes. St. Louis: Concordia Publishing House, 2009–.
OCD	*Oxford Classical Dictionary*. Third Edition. Oxford: Clarendon Press, 1996.
Sehling	Sehling, Emil. *Die evangelischen Kirchenordnungen des XVI. Jahrhunderts*. Volumes 1–9, 11–20, 24 in 23 physical volumes to date. Leipzig: O.R. Reisland, 1902–13; Tübingen: J.C.B. Mohr/Paul Siebeck, 1955–.
WA	*D. Martin Luthers Werke: Kritische Gesamtausgabe*. 73 volumes in 85. Weimar: H. Böhlau, 1883–.
WA Br	*D. Martin Luthers Werke: Briefwechsel*. 18 volumes. Weimar: H. Böhlau, 1930–.
WA DB	*D. Martin Luthers Werke: Deutsche Bibel*. 12 volumes in 15. Weimar: H. Böhlau, 1906–.
WA TR	*D. Martin Luthers Werke: Tischreden*. 6 volumes. Weimar: H. Böhlau, 1912–1921.

Classical Authors and Works

Cic.		M. Tullius Cicero [= Cicero]
	Brut.	*Brutus*
	Cael.	*pro Caelio*
	Pis.	*in Pisonem*
	Sest.	*pro Sestio*
	Tusc.	*Tusculanae disputationes*
Ov.		P. Ovidius Naso [= Ovid]
	Ep.	*Epistulae* (*Heroides*)
Sal.		G. Sallustius Crispus [= Sallust]
	Cat.	*Catalina*
Suet.		C. Suetonius Tranquillus [= Seuteonius]
	Jul.	*Julius*
Virg.		P. Vergilius Maro [= Virgil]
	A.	*Aeneid*
	Ecl.	*Eclogues*

Notes on Contributors

Joseph Herl
is professor of music at Concordia University, Nebraska and research professor in the School of Music, University of Illinois at Urbana-Champaign.

Jane Schatkin Hettrick
is Professor Emeritus of Music, Rider University, Lawrenceville, NJ and Director of Parish Music, Redeemer Lutheran Church, Bayside, New York City.

E.J. Hutchinson
is Associate Professor of Classics and Director of the Collegiate Scholars Program at Hillsdale College in Hillsdale, Michigan.

James A. Kellerman
is Associate Professor of Theology at Concordia Lutheran Theological Seminary in St. Catharines, Ontario.

Jack D. Kilcrease
is Associate Professor of Historical and Systematic Theology at Christ School of Theology, Institute of Lutheran Theology, Brookings, South Dakota.

E. Christian Kopff
is Professor Emeritus, University of Colorado Boulder.

John G. Nordling
is Professor of Exegetical Theology at Concordia Theological Seminary in Fort Wayne, Indiana.

Piergiacomo Petrioli
is Professor of Renaissance Art History for Geo University of Oregon Program in Siena and for Springhill College Program in Bologna.

Eric G. Phillips
is the Pastor of Concordia Lutheran Church in Nashville, Tennessee.

Richard J. Serina, Jr
is Associate Executive Director of the Lutheran Church—Missouri Synod's Commission on Theology and Church Relations.

R. Alden Smith
whose expertise lies in Augustan poetry, is Professor of Classics at Baylor University.

Carl P.E. Springer
is SunTrust Chair of Excellence in the Humanities and Professor in the Department of Modern and Classical Languages and Literatures, University of Tennessee Chattanooga.

Manfred Svensson
is Professor of Philosophy at the Universidad de los Andes, Chile.

William P. Weaver
is a Professor of Literature in the Honors College at Baylor University, in Waco, TX.

Daniel Zager
is Associate Dean of Sibley Music Library and Associate Professor of Musicology at the Eastman School of Music, University of Rochester.

Introduction: Martin Luther: From Classical Formation to Reformation

James Kellerman, R. Alden Smith and *Carl P.E. Springer*

That the legacy of Martin Luther looms large in the history of Christianity is beyond dispute. That this legacy has been analyzed and evaluated extensively by countless theologians and historians over the last five centuries is equally indisputable.[1] Jaroslav Pelikan used to quip that more has been written about Luther than any other figure in the history of the Christian church except for Jesus Christ himself.[2] Pelikan himself, of course, did his own part to contribute to the enormous body of scholarship devoted to the 16th-century reformer. There is, however, at least one aspect of Luther's legacy that has not received as much scholarly attention as that of others, at least until fairly recently, and that is the close relationship of his reformation of the church with the Greco-Roman cultural tradition.

The title of this volume plays on Tertullian's famous rhetorical question: "What does Athens have to do with Jerusalem?" In the past, the answer to

1 Research on Luther's life increased greatly in anticipation of the five-hundred-year anniversary of the Reformation. The recent work of Lyndal Roper, *Martin Luther: Renegade and Prophet* (London: The Bodley Head, 2016) which came out precisely on schedule for that anniversary (2016) is the most significant recent work, comprehensive in scope and, in spite its provocative subtitle, thoughtful and judicious in approach. Other important works include *The Cambridge Companion to Martin Luther*, ed. Donald K. McKim (Cambridge, UK: Cambridge University Press, 2003), in which Albrecht Beutel's article (tr. Katharina Gustavs), 2–19 is, among other articles, a vital tool for understanding the background of Luther's life experience. The most exhaustive biography of Luther available in English is the three-volume work by Martin Brecht originally published in German by Calwer Verlag in 1981–87: Martin Brecht, *Martin Luther*, tr. James L. Schaaf (Minneapolis: Fortress Press, 1985–93). Bernard Lohse's *Martin Luther: An Introduction to his Life and Works*, tr. Robert C. Schultz (Edinburgh: T. & T. Clark, 1987) is also an invaluable resource, particularly as it is laid out in an easy to use frequently subdivided manner. Other important contributions include that of Richard Marius, *Martin Luther: The Christian Between Life and Death* (Cambridge, MA: The Belknap Press of Harvard University Press, 1999) as well as the "gold standard" of Luther biographies, namely that of Hieko A. Oberman's *Luther: Man Between God and the Devil*, tr. Eileen Walliser-Schwarzbart (New Haven: Yale University Press, 1989). H.G. Haile, *Luther: A Biography* (London: Sheldon Press, 1980) is somewhat dated, but nevertheless still interesting. More up to date and filled with valuable insights is Scott H. Hendrix, *Martin Luther: Visionary Reformer* (New Haven: Yale University Press, 2015).

2 See, e.g., Jaroslav Pelikan, *The Melody of Theology: A Philosophical Dictionary* (Cambridge, Mass. and London: Harvard University Press, 1988), 154.

 | DOI:10.1163/9789004206717_002

Tertullian's question as applied to Luther's Wittenberg would often have been, to put it crassly, "not much."[3] It is not all that surprising that this particular aspect of Luther and his legacy should have so often been overlooked or minimized. For one thing, many scholars of the reformation, especially in the 19th century, have been at considerable pains to emphasize Luther's revolutionary uniqueness rather than his indebtedness to the past. Even today, Luther is probably still more often regarded as a rebel against tradition rather than a devotee of antiquity.[4] In fact, Luther has been credited—or blamed—for just about everything that has happened in the five hundred years that have passed since he wrote the 95 Theses.[5] Whether it be rugged individualism, the nation-state, the Protestant work-ethic, the Nazis, or even Donald Trump, the ultimate responsibility for a whole host of modern phenomena has been laid at Luther's door at one time or another.

3 There have, of course, been many Christians over the centuries who have not regarded the Greco-Roman classics as completely antithetical to Christianity. Paul's sweeping command in Philippians 4:8 could be read as suggesting that followers of Jesus should think not only about the Holy Scriptures or the truths of Christianity, but about "whatever is true, whatever is noble, whatever is right, whatever is pure, whatever is lovely, whatever is admirable," in short, anything that is "excellent or praiseworthy." From Basil of Caesarea to John Henry Newman and beyond, there is a long line of Christian thinkers who have considered the classics to be worth of inclusion among those things that are considered "excellent or praiseworthy." In one of his Latin letters, C.S. Lewis goes so far as to venture the opinion that young people should become pagans before Christians: *Fere auserim dicere "Primo faciamus juniores bonos Paganos et postea faciamus Christianos"* ("I would almost dare to say 'First let us make the younger generation good pagans and afterwards let us make them Christians'") Martin Moynihan, tr. and ed., *The Latin Letters of C.S. Lewis* (South Bend: St. Augustine's Press, 1998), 93.

4 See, e.g., the subtitle of Heinz Schilling's recent biography, *Martin Luther: Rebel in an Age of Upheaval*, tr. Rona Johnston Gordon (Oxford: Oxford University Press, 2017).

5 For some ways in which Luther has been misunderstood, see James R. Payton, Jr., *Getting the Reformation Wrong: Correcting Some Misunderstandings* (Downers Grove, Illinois: IVP Academic, 2010), 80–88. Payton notes that even in Luther's day he was misunderstood, such as when the humanists regarded him as an ally or the peasants thought of him as a German hero or a revolutionary—and later as part of the old guard. Luther has also been blamed for creating a subservient, anti-Semitic Germany that is the direct ancestor of Nazi Germany. But as Uwe Siemon-Netto has pointed out (*The Fabricated Luther: Refuting Nazi Connections and Other Modern Myths*, 2nd Edition [St. Louis: Concordia Publishing House, 2007]), Luther's true political legacy may be found in the work of the anti-Nazi mayor of Leipzig, Carl Goerdeler, and the Lutheran-organized protests in Leipzig that led to the collapse of East Germany. Steven Ozment concurs, noting that the "ugly German" phenomenon of the twentieth century derives from the romanticism and millennialism found in Luther's foes rather than from Luther's more conservative approach to politics; Steven Ozment, *Protestants: The Birth of a Revolution* (New York: Image Books, 1991), 147.

If it is not at all clear that Luther is really responsible for all of the things for which he has been blamed or praised in the years that followed his reformation, there are some aspects of his legacy that are incontrovertible. One of the most obvious examples of his influence is the emergence over the last centuries of a large number of institutions (including schools, universities, hospitals, charitable foundations, and church bodies) that have called themselves "Lutheran." The church bodies have disagreed on any number of issues, but they have all acknowledged Luther as their eponymous founder.[6] One can question to what degree various Lutherans have the right to call themselves Luther's spiritual heirs. After all, it was a point debated already in the generation after Luther's death, when some of his followers such as Nikolaus von Amsdorf and Matthias Flacius found themselves at odds with Luther's friend and colleague, Philip Melanchthon.[7] But it is fair to say that all "Lutherans" have seen themselves as embracing the values of the Reformer in some way or other, however they define them. Even more broadly, Luther can also be credited with influencing the growth of Protestantism in general. While other Protestant churches may rightly credit other individuals such as Ulrich Zwingli, John Calvin, or Thomas Cranmer rather than Luther as the fathers of their churches, they nonetheless share some of his fundamental ideas (such as justification by faith and the supreme authority of the Scriptures). Certainly, these churches have drawn inspiration and encouragement from Luther's success in reforming the church in Electoral Saxony.[8]

---

6 FC SD VII:34 speaks of Luther as the chief teacher among those who subscribe to the Augsburg Confession and directs its readers to his writings to understand better what that confession means.

7 On the origin of the conflict, see Robert Kolb, *Nikolaus von Amsdorf: Champion of Martin Luther's Reformation* (St. Louis: Concordia Publishing House, 2019), 47–85. The chief catalyst of the conflict would seem to have lain in the manner in which the heirs of Luther were to respond to the Augsburg Interim, a series of conditions imposed by Emperor Charles V on the Lutheran territories that he had conquered. Almost all Lutherans rejected the Augsburg Interim, and Melanchthon and others posited a counter-proposal (the Leipzig Proposal, sometimes pejoratively called the Leipzig Interim), a document which Amsdorf and his allies thought conceded too much to Rome. The bitterness of the fight over this matter spilled over into other theological issues (such as the doctrine of original sin).

8 The corollary to this truth is that Luther's legacy led to division within the church, first as he stood against the pope and his allies, and then as he stood against fellow Reformers, especially those who disagreed with him on baptism and the Lord's Supper. This corollary should not be overstated, however, since the growing fissures in the late medieval church may have made institutional unity impossible to maintain in the long run. It should not be forgotten that Rome had broken with the East nearly half a millennium before Luther, and that the Waldensian and Hussite churches had existed for a century by Luther's day. Moreover, while on paper (such as in the bull *Unam Sanctam*) the pope had established himself at the center

Luther's reform agenda was not entirely original, to be sure, but his criticism of a corrupt church hierarchy and his sharply focused theology met the needs of his changing times perfectly. Even though Luther did not organize his thoughts into an abstract systematic theology (like Melanchthon or Calvin), he had a unique ability to combine his reading of the Scriptures with contemporary concerns. Furthermore, Luther developed his ideas over time—not entirely negating previous insights, but adding further nuances.[9] For example, in his early controversies with Rome he stressed that faith was necessary for the sacraments to be beneficial and spoke little about what the Lord's Supper was. But as time progressed and the real presence of Christ in the sacrament began to be questioned by other reformers, Luther responded by shifting his attention from the words "for you" in the words of institution to the word "is."[10] Much scholarly ink has been spilt exploring the development of these and others of Luther's theological ideas and their impact on the doctrine and practice of the church in his own time and subsequently.

Luther's ideas would never have had such an impact were it not for his astonishing ability to express them in words that were both powerful and persuasive, making adroit use of the latest communication technology of his age, namely, the printing press. This aspect of his legacy, too, has been widely acknowledged and thoroughly studied.[11] He had an uncanny way with words which he used to communicate effectively not only with learned international scholars but also with ordinary Germans. His Small Catechism, one of the briefest in use in Christendom, has been memorized by millions of young Lutherans over the years.[12] In his translation of the Bible, Luther combined his keen ear for the rhythms of spoken German with investigations into the technical terms used by craftsmen—asking jewelers and smiths and butchers how

---

of at least western Christendom, the reality was quite different, as demonstrated by the Avignon captivity of the papacy (1309–76) and the Western Schism (1378–1417).

9 Cf. his warning of how the world resembles a drunken peasant who may be helped up from one side of the horse only to fall off the other side. According to the metaphor, the world falls from an error on one extreme to an error on the other extreme, all the while remaining in the devil's service. WA TR 1:288.9–11 (No. 631); *LW* 54:111.

10 In addition, he explored in greater detail the personal union of the two natures in Christ so as to be able to explain better Christ's presence in the sacrament. See Bernhard Lohse, *Martin Luther's Theology: Its Historical and Systematic Development*, tr. and ed. Roy A. Harrisville (Minneapolis: Fortress Press, 1999), 128–129, 169–71.

11 For more on this point, see Elizabeth Eisenstein, *The Printing Press as an Agent of Change* (Cambridge: Cambridge University Press, 1979) and, most recently, Andrew Pettegree, *Brand Luther* (New York: Penguin Books, 2016).

12 See Albrecht Peters's monumental *Commentary on Luther's Catechisms*, tr. Holger K. Sonntag, Thomas H. Trapp, and Daniel Thies, ed. Charles P. Schaum, 5 volumes (St. Louis: Concordia Publishing House, 2009–13).

they would describe particular items—so that the entire Bible would sound as if it had been written originally in German.[13] He was not the first to pioneer a sort of standard German, since the formal court language of chancellery German already existed, but he removed some of its overly formal expressions and wrote in a style that would be understood throughout all of Germany with its various dialects for years to come.[14]

If much previous scholarship has tended to focus on Luther's legacy in terms of its undeniable impact on the dramatically changed church (and world) that emerged in the centuries following his reformation, more recently Luther scholars have begun to focus more intensely on his debt to the past and his demonstrable interest in preserving, not disrupting, cultural continuity. Today it is just as common for serious students of Luther to consider him as much a product of the late Middle Ages as someone who set out to "change the world," as though he were only a harbinger of modernity.[15] Luther scholarship now very often focuses on his rootedness in the world of patristic and medieval theology, especially the Augustinian tradition, his debt to other previous would-be reformers of the church such as Jan Hus, as well as his fervent belief in the reality of the supernatural in general and the devil in particular, a world-view that he shared with many of his late medieval contemporaries but far fewer post-Enlightenment thinkers.[16]

Recent scholarship has also begun to demonstrate that Luther was just as interested as any of his contemporaries, whether north or south of the Alps, in returning *ad fontes*, *sc*. to the literary and linguistic sources of the

---

13 Otto Mann, *Deutsche Literaturgeschichte* (Gütersloh: Verlagsgruppe Bertelsmann GmbH, 1969), 98. Luther could at times be more literal and at times freer in his translation—as long as the meaning was clearly presented; see Brecht 2:50.

14 Brecht, 2:48–49. At times the literary value of Luther's German Bible has been underappreciated, such as in the two centuries following his death when classical models were all the rage. However, since then authors as diverse as Herder, Schiller, Goethe, and Nietzsche have rediscovered Luther's crisp German style and imitated it (see Mann, *Deutsche Literaturgeschichte*, 99–100).

15 This last phrase forms part of the dramatic subtitle of Eric Metaxas's recent biography: *Martin Luther: The Man Who Rediscovered the Gospel and Changed the World* (New York: Viking, 2017).

16 For more on Luther's knowledge of the church fathers, see Rudolf Mau, "Die Kirchenväter in Luthers früher Exegese des Galaterbriefs," in *Auctoritas Patrum II: Neue Beiträge zur Rezeption der Kirchenväter im 15. und 16. Jahrhundert*, ed. Leif Grane, Alfred Schindler, and Markus Wriedt (Mainz: Philipp von Zabern, 1993), 117–127. Of the patristic theologians, Luther knew Augustine the best. He was himself, of course, an Augustinian friar. For further background, see Eric Saak, *High Way to Heaven: The Augustinian Platform Between Reform and Reformation, 1292–1524* (Leiden: Brill, 2002) and *Luther and the Reformation of the Later Middle Ages* (Cambridge: Cambridge University Press, 2017).

Greco-Roman past.[17] As Lewis Spitz, Helmar Junghans, and others have convincingly argued,[18] Luther should not be excluded from the company of other humanists (e.g., Petrarch or Poggio) whose names are more often connected with the revival of the Greco-Roman linguistic and literary tradition during the early modern period. Despite differences in theological perspectives and literary styles between so-called "Renaissance humanists" and what we may describe as "Reformation humanists," or "Biblical humanists," these latter have made equally important contributions to the perpetuation of the study of the classics.[19] There is a long and influential tradition of classical education in Lutheran schools and universities (one thinks of Johann Sturm's famous gymnasium in Strasbourg) that can be traced directly or indirectly back to the Wittenberg reformation.[20]

Now, it is not at all self-evident that Luther, the polemical preacher, the doughty champion of the German language, the fierce foe of rationality, Aristotle, and Rome should be properly considered a serious devotee of the classics.[21] After all, we know that "the father of the German language," as Luther has been described, was as responsible as any of his fellow reformers for moving away from the use of Latin in the liturgy. It is also the case that Luther's own commitment to the classics has often been overshadowed by the prodigious linguistic gifts and pedagogical achievements of his learned colleague,

17 For a good definition of Renaissance humanism, see Paul Oskar Kristeller, *Renaissance Thought: The Classic, Scholastic, and Humanist Strains* (New York, 1955), p. 10: "The *studia humanitatis* came to stand for a clearly defined cycle of scholarly disciplines, namely grammar, rhetoric, history, poetry, and moral philosophy, and the study of each of these subjects was understood to include the reading and interpretation of its standard ancient writers in Latin and, to a lesser extent, in Greek."

18 See Helmar Junghans, *Der Junge Luther und die Humanisten* (Göttingen: Vandenhoeck & Ruprecht, 1985), and Lewis Spitz, "Luther and Humanism," in *Luther and Learning: The Wittenberg University Luther Symposium*, 69–94. Ed. Marilyn Harran (Selinsgrove, London, and Toronto: Susquehanna University Press, 1985).

19 See, e.g., *Die Musen im Reformationszeitalter*, ed. Walther Ludwig (Leipzig: Evangelische Verlagsanstalt, 2001), and Wilfried Stroh, *Latein ist tot, es lebe Latein* (Berlin: Ullstein, 2007). For the term "biblical humanism," see E.G. Schwiebert, *Luther and His Times* (St. Louis: Concordia Publishing House, 1950), Chapter 9.

20 See Carl P.E. Springer, *Cicero in Heaven: The Roman Rhetor and Luther's Reformation* (Leiden: Brill, 2017), 101–86, for a historical overview of the important role played in Lutheran education by Cicero in particular and the classics in general. On Johann Sturm, see Lewis W. Spitz and Barbara Sher Tinsley, *Johann Sturm on Education: The Reformation and Humanist Learning* (St. Louis: Concordia Publishing House, 1995).

21 On Luther's antipathy to some aspects of Aristotle's thought, see Theodor Dieter, *Der junge Luther und Aristoteles: Eine historisch-systematische Untersuchung zum Verhältnis von Theologie und Philosophie* (Berlin and New York: de Gruyter, 2001).

Philip Melanchthon.[22] In addition, there is his famous controversy with the famed humanist Erasmus with whom Luther waged a monumental battle of words. At issue was the question of free will. Luther's determined opposition to Erasmus in this particular controversy is still taken to mean that he pretty much opposed the humanism of his age in all other respects as well.[23]

Erasmus contributed to the notion that Luther was opposed entirely to the literary humanism he himself represented. He once declared that "wherever Lutheranism reigns, literature perishes."[24] While Erasmus was one of the first to suggest Luther's enmity to humanism and ancient literature, he was certainly not the last. In his *Literature and the American College*, Irving Babbit maintained that Luther saw "the study of the pagan classics, except within the narrowest bounds, as pernicious."[25] More recently, Louis Markos has claimed that "much Christian (especially evangelical) suspicion surrounding the study of the Greeks and Romans can be traced back to the father of Reformed theology: Martin Luther."[26] According to this point of view, Luther is a vulgar, pious, audacious philistine, not a learned, urbane intellectual steeped in Greco-Roman philosophy and literature. Nietzsche, himself a Lutheran pastor's son, dubbed Luther a "northern barbarian of the intellect."[27] Contributing to this perception, or better, misperception, is that Luther himself would frequently represent himself as a "barbarian," a commoner descended from peasant stock, a plain-speaker who eschewed any sort of rhetorical finesse. He regularly depreciated his own abilities in Greek and Latin, especially in comparison with his colleague, Melanchthon.

But it would be a mistake to take Luther's expressions of humility in this regard entirely seriously, just as it would also be a mistake to try to capture the essence of this complicated man in a single category. Luther hated Rome, but

22 For the lasting impact of Melanchthon's pedagogical work, see Asaph Ben-Tov, *Lutheran Humanists and Greek Antiquity: Melanchthonian Scholarship between History and Pedagogy* (Leiden: Brill, 2009). It is unlikely that the *praeceptor Germaniae*, as Melanchthon is sometimes described, would have been able to accomplish nearly as much as he did in this regard without Luther's enthusiastic endorsement and support.

23 See Michael Massing, *Fatal Discord: Erasmus, Luther, and the Fight for the Western Mind* (New York: HarperCollins, 2018).

24 See Carl P.E. Springer, *Luther's Aesop* (Kirksville: Truman State University Press, 2011), 3.

25 See Springer, *Luther's Aesop*, 3.

26 Louis Markos, *From Achilles to Christ: Why Christians Should Read the Pagan Classics* (Wheaton: IVP Academic, 2007), 11.

27 The descriptive phrase *"Ein nordischer Barbar des Geistes"* appears in *Jenseits von Gut und Böse* III, 46 (see Springer, *Luther's Aesop*, 6).

he also loved it. He used Aristotelian reason even as he deplored its use in matters of faith. He was bilingual, as fluent in Latin as his native tongue.[28]

Luther's education throughout his school and university days was in Latin, and by all accounts he took his schooling very seriously. After attending school first in Mansfeld and then in Magdeburg, Luther transferred to St. George's school in Eisenach.[29] To do so, he had to leave his immediate family, staying with relatives beginning in 1498.[30] In two years, Luther commenced his university studies at Erfurt where in preparation for the study of law he enjoyed a broad liberal arts education that heavily focused on the works of Aristotle, especially logic and metaphysics.[31] At the age of twenty-two, he attained to the masters-level.[32] Even after his dramatic decision to enter the monastery in Erfurt in 1505, we learn that the only two books that he took with him contained not patristic commentaries or sermons but the works of Virgil and Plautus. While there he prayed and worshipped exclusively in Latin. He would probably have memorized the entire Vulgate by the time he left. In 1510 or 1511, though having to endure harsh conditions en route, Luther made a pilgrimage to Rome. Not only the churches and catacombs of the "eternal city" but pagan monuments such as the Pantheon and the Colosseum also made an indelible impression on him.[33] Luther was awarded his doctorate when he was 29.

At the University of Wittenberg where Dr. Luther was to serve as a professor and academic administrator for the rest of his life, he insisted that Aristotle's works on rhetoric, poetics, and logic continue to be studied in the schools. Even though he learned ancient Greek much later in life than Latin, Luther learned enough to be able to translate the New Testament from Greek into German in 1522.[34] He considered Aesop's fables to be second only to the Bible, especially useful in the instruction of children. He "loved" Terence and Cicero and

28 Birgit Stolt, *Martin Luthers Rhetorik des Herzens* (Tübingen, Mohr Siebeck, 2000).

29 Brecht, *Martin Luther*, 1:15–17; Roper, *Martin Luther*, 35–37.

30 Brecht, *Martin Luther*, 1:17–21; Roper, *Martin Luther*, 37; 41–42.

31 Brecht, *Martin Luther*, 1:32–33. Brecht notes that the curriculum in the liberal arts was firmly set across universities, thus ensuring a relatively consistent education. That said, Aristotle could be taught from more than one perspective, and Luther was exposed to the Occamist critique of Aristotle at Erfurt. In the end Luther would borrow much from both Aristotle and the Occamists, while being critical of them; see Brecht, *Martin Luther*, 1:36–38. See also Klaus-Bernward Springer, "Luther als Student der Artes und stundentisches Leben in Erfurt im Spätmittelalter und zu Beginn der Frühen Neuzeit," *Mitteilungen des Vereins für die Geschichte und Altertumskunde von Erfurt* 72 (2011): 72–97.

32 Roper, *Martin Luther*, 46 notes that we do not know the exact date but says "around 1505."

33 On the Rome journey, see now Carl P.E. Springer, *Luther's Rome, Rome's Luther* (Minneapolis: Fortress Press, 2021), Chapter One.

34 See Carl P.E. Springer, *Luther's Rome, Rome's Luther* (Minneapolis: Fortress, 2021), 61–109.

even wished that the latter could find a place in heaven. He wrote many of his treatises and disputations in Latin, including the famous 95 Theses. His university lectures were delivered in Latin for the most part. He even wrote poetry in Latin. Many of his letters are in Latin, including one in which he explains why he is reluctant to write in Latin—in Latin! The final written words of Luther mention Virgil and Cicero and include a citation from Statius:

> Virgilium in *Bucolicis* nemo potest intelligere, nisi fuerit quinque annis pastor. Virgilium in *Georgicis* nemo potest intelligere, nisi fuerit quinque annis agricola. Ciceronem in *Epistolis* nemo integre intelligit, nisi viginti annis sit versatus in republica aliqua insigni. Scripturas sanctas sciat se nemo degustasse satis, nisi centum annis cum Prophetis, ut Elia et Elisaeo, Joanne Baptista, Christo et Apostolis Ecclesias gubernarit. Hanc tu ne *Aeneida* tenta, sed vestigia pronus adora. Wir sind Bettler, Hoc est verum.
>
> [No one, unless he has been a shepherd for five years, can understand Virgil[35] in his *Eclogues*. No one, unless he has been a farmer for five years, can understand Virgil in his *Georgics*. No one can understand Cicero in his *Epistles* unless he has been active in important matters of state for twenty years. Let no one think that he has sufficiently digested the Holy Scriptures unless he has governed churches for a hundred years together with the prophets, such as Elijah and Elisha, John the Baptist, Christ and the Apostles. Do not try (to challenge) this divine *Aeneid* but, bowed down, humbly adore its footprints. We are beggars. That is true.][36]

So, it is this Luther, the erudite lover of the Latin language, the keen student of Greek and Roman history, literature, and rhetoric, the unwavering advocate for the continued value of ancient authors like Aesop and Cicero for the education of future Lutherans, who will be considered in the following pages. His devotion to the classics will not be regarded as a passing fancy or a youthful

---

35 Because the great Roman epic poet was known chiefly as "Virgil" during the time of the Reformation, this volume has adopted that particular spelling except where a quoted author spells it as "Vergil."

36 Heinrich Bornkamm, *Luther's World of Thought*, tr. Martin H. Bertram (St. Louis: Concordia Publishing House, 1958), 291. See also R.A. Smith, "*Deipnosophistae* Reformed: Classical Intertexts in Luther's *Tischreden*," *Logia* 21 (2012): 19–23, as well as Carl P.E. Springer, "Arms and the Theologian: Martin Luther's *Adversus Armatum Virum Cochlaeum*," *International Journal of the Classical Tradition* 10 (2003): 41.

indiscretion incidental to his mature theology, but formative, thoroughgoing, and influential.[37]

Since 2010, scholars with an interest in furthering our understanding of this neglected aspect of Luther's legacy have held a biennial conference in order to explore this issue more fully. Two recent conferences (held at Concordia Theological Seminary in 2016 and 2018) have focused on topics related to poetry and philosophy, considered broadly.[38] The essays assembled in this volume represent scholarly fruits related to both conferences. The various authors consider Luther's and his followers' appropriation of the classics for themselves and future generations in a wide variety of ways. Given the far-ranging scholarly contributions included here, it would be impossible to imagine that all of them share a common hermeneutic. It could be said, however, that taken together they do represent an interesting contribution to a growing field sometimes termed "reception studies."[39]

The study of reception acknowledges first and foremost the power of seminal, primary texts within a long literary tradition. Authors standing at the head of the Greco-Roman cultural tradition like Plato and Aristotle, Cicero and Virgil, could not be ignored by Luther and his followers. These authors and their texts, emerging from the same ancient Mediterranean world of thought that produced the Bible, played an indispensable role in the intellectual formation of reformers like Luther, making it nearly impossible to forget or ignore them, even in later years. As a lover of paradox like the Lutheran philosopher Johann Georg Hamann might have put it, every great book reads us as much as we read it. They question us as much as we question them—the same kind of dialogue that occurs on a grander scale between God and humans in the Scriptures.[40]

---

37 Even as thoughtful a Luther scholar as Jaroslav Pelikan has contributed to the notion that Luther was little more than a dabbler in the Greco-Roman cultural tradition who "had also read around in the classics" (*LW* 1:x).

38 Proceedings of previous conferences have been published. These include: "Lutheranism and the Classics," a special issue of *Logia: A Journal of Lutheran Theology* (ed. Jon Bruss and Carl Springer) 21.2 (2012); *Ad Fontes Witebergenses: Select Proceedings of "Lutheranism and the Classics II: Reading the Church Fathers,"* ed. James Kellerman and Carl Springer (Fort Wayne: Lutheran Legacy Press, 2014); and *Ad Fontes Witebergenses: Select Proceedings of "Lutheranism and the Classics III: Lutherans Read History,"* ed. James A. Kellerman, E.J. Hutchinson, and Joshua J. Hayes (Minneapolis: Lutheran Press, 2017).

39 For one of the best known articulations of this theory, see Hans Robert Jauss, *Toward an Aesthetic of Reception*, tr. Timothy Bahti (Minneapolis: University of Minnesota Press, 1982).

40 See Oswald Bayer, *A Contemporary in Dissent: Johann Georg Hamann as a Radical Enlightener*, translated by Roy Harrisville and Mark Mattes (Grand Rapids: Eerdmans, 2012).

At the same time, the intertextual nature of reception means that we must not discount the importance of readers for authors. Even the most significant of authors in the past would cease to exist without readers, as Roland Barthes has observed.[41] "Reception" is a somewhat misleading term since the classical past was never simply "received" by Luther and Lutherans. It was transformed by them. Perhaps "reciprocal creation" would be a more accurate descriptor.[42] The way in which the reformers read the classics shaped the way in which their own epigoni and then *their* followers read the same texts ever thereafter, and so on. The "vibrancy" of intertextuality, as Alden Smith has explained, consists in its ever "redefining and increased depth." The result is "an ever-widening literary heritage that produces literature increasingly enriched by the tradition itself."[43] Kierkegaard read Luther; Luther read Augustine; Augustine read Cicero; Cicero read Plato.

Our volume begins with essays that explore the use that Luther himself made of classical poets and philosophers. It has long been recognized that Luther appreciated the poetry of Virgil, crediting him for his success in writing German chorales. Yet if Virgil is Luther's most-quoted ancient poet, that does not mean that he neglected others. Somewhat surprisingly, he seems to have made ample use of Ovid and Martial, even if the sophisticated author of *Ars amatoria* or the Roman devotee of Epicurus would not appeal in every respect to Luther. Alden Smith demonstrates that Luther found wisdom in poets such as Horace and Ovid, although their lifestyles and world-views did not necessarily align perfectly with his own. Luther praises Christian poets such as Sedulius and wishes they were read more, but this does not mean that he neglected the pagan poets of antiquity.

And yet there are limits to Luther's veneration of pagan poets. He seems to have known Catullus but can only bring himself to mention or allude to him three times. John Nordling asks why this is the case, since he quotes Aristotle, Cicero, and Virgil hundreds of times. Nordling concludes that Catullus does not meet Luther's standard as a serious literary author. It is not that he denies Catullus's poetic skill, but rather that he deems that his message is not the sort to be included in the schoolboys' canon. Luther, however, was more than a consumer of poetry; he was a poet in his own right. As Carl P.E. Springer demonstrates by examining two of Luther's poems written in elegiac couplets,

---

41 For a recent consideration, see Laura Seymour, *An Analysis of Roland Barthes's The Death of the Author* (London: Macat International Limited, 2018).

42 For the terms "transformation" or "reciprocal creation," see Patrick Baker, Johannes Helmrath, and Craig Kallendorf, eds., *Beyond Reception: Renaissance Humanism and the Transformation of Classical Antiquity* (Berlin: De Gruyter, 2019), 4.

43 Alden Smith, *Poetic Allusion and Poetic Embrace in Ovid and Virgil* (Ann Arbor: University of Michigan Press, 1997), 3.

Luther did not share the Renaissance interest in creating light-hearted, trifling ditties, but wrote poems that combined artistic sensitivity with theological depth.

Alongside ancient poets, and sometimes even in conjunction with them, Luther was interested in the philosophers of antiquity, often considering how their work could inform his own study of theology. From an early period, Christian theologians tended to side with the Stoics rather than the Epicureans. At first glance, the Reformation seems to do the same, with the Stoic doctrine of fate being more amenable to the biblical doctrine of the bondage of the will than the Epicurean notion of chance is. Luther, however, was an eclectic philosopher, as Springer points out in his second article in this collection. Thus, Luther rendered Psalm 127 as a Latin poem that took on the ideas of the Epicurean poet Martial, thereby showing both continuity and disagreement with Epicurean ideas. Although Luther did not countenance the vulgar pursuit of pleasure, he was no dour puritan, as the Stoics were, but shared a *joie de vivre* with the Epicureans, no matter how much he disagreed with their atheistic outlook.

Philosophers not only impart new knowledge to their pupils, but they also develop a deep relationship, whether through their writings or in person, with their students that often lasts long after the period of formal education has come to an end. In his contribution on Aristotle and Cicero in the *Tischreden*, Alden Smith discusses how Greek philosophers are refined through the filter of Cicero's own philosophical adaptations and rhetorical flair in such a way as both to incorporate the best ideas of the Greeks and to correct notions that are not entirely compatible with the gospel.

If Luther could take a mildly Epicurean approach to life with non-Epicurean goals in mind, one should not be surprised to see Luther use a scholastic device to undo scholasticism. Unfortunately, because many scholars see the Reformation as creating a clean break from the past, they overlook Luther's continued use of disputation, says Richard J. Serina, Jr. Although this form of debate is grounded in Aristotelian philosophy, Luther saw no reason to abandon it and used disputation ably to undo Aristotle's undeserved influence on scholastic theology. Serina argues that if we understand the purpose of the form of disputation, we might well come to a different conclusion about the content of the Heidelberg Disputation in particular. The Heidelberg Disputation was not meant to encapsulate all of Luther's theology, let alone introduce a new "theology of the cross." Rather it built on previous disputations about grace, works, and the law. Thus, scholars would do better to look back toward previous such debates in Wittenberg rather than to look to later writings of Luther to understand the Heidelberg Disputation's particular intent.

Up until this point we have considered only Luther's appropriation of late Renaissance culture with its rediscovery of the classical world, but Piergiacomo Petrioli considers how late Renaissance culture may have appropriated Luther (or at least his image) for a fresco created in Bologna in 1511, when Luther stayed in a monastery there on his return from Rome. The fresco reflects contemporary turmoil, both within the Augustinian order and in the Bolognese government.

While the first section of this book is devoted to Luther's relationship with classical poets and philosophers, the second section turns to considerations of how the hymnody and liturgy were reformed in Luther's day and thereafter. We saw earlier that Luther appreciated the content of Virgil. Yet Luther's particular use of him as a stylist has been overlooked, principally with regard to Luther's composition of his German chorales. E. Christian Kopff argues that Luther learned from the poet how to align metrical ictus and word accent—and when not to, as exemplified in his Sanctus for the German mass.

In addition, Luther also translated some Latin hymnody into the vernacular. Perhaps the best example is his translation of Ambrose's hymn, *Veni redemptor gentium*. Although Luther's version, *Nu kom der heyden Heyland*, is largely a faithful rendition of the Latin original, there are some subtle variations in the translation. Eric Phillips argues that these were not haphazard or due to the difficulty of translating from one language to another but rather divulge Luther's theological concerns.

Later Lutherans would imitate their denominational founder in translating Latin hymns into the vernacular and writing new chorales in German. For centuries Lutheran chorales, with their beautiful poetry and rich, biblical thought, have shaped Lutheran piety and taught the Lutheran faith. However, Joseph Herl notes that there was another source by which Lutheran schoolchildren in the first century of the Reformation learned the faith: Latin liturgical music sung in chapel services. Herl examines the practice of the school in Naumburg, where the older children participated in the largely Latin Vespers every day and the mixed German and Latin Matins five days a week. There they sang sequences, introits, responsories, canticles, and other liturgical songs in Latin. These elements were taken from the medieval church, but carefully purged of false doctrine and scripturally verified.

That works in Latin continued to be sung in church and school is not particularly remarkable, especially when one considers that Luther himself valued motets and other works of Latin polyphony. As Daniel Zager argues, Luther did not want his German chorales to replace Latin polyphony altogether, any more than he expected his German mass to lead to the abolishment of his Latin mass. Luther appreciated the beautiful music of polyphony to such an extent that he asked Ludwig Senfl for a motet—and received two. Zager examines the connection between Luther and Senfl.

Eric Hutchinson's contribution compares three classicizing Latin poetic paraphrases of Psalm 1, those of Helius Eobanus Hessus (whose *Psalterium Davidis* was well loved by Luther), George Buchanan, and Theodore Beza, highlighting the poems' expansions upon the biblical base-text (*amplificatio*), as well their use of allusion. These Psalm paraphrases represent a lively tradition that crossed confessional boundaries, for Hessus's influence is discernible in the works of both Buchanan and Beza. Luther's love for the music of language was carried forward in Protestant Europe more broadly.

Yet the Protestants were not the only beneficiaries of Luther's high esteem for music and his musicality. Following his lead, early Lutherans cherished older Latin music alongside the newer German chorales. Two centuries later Roman Catholics were returning the favor. As Jane Schatkin Hettrick demonstrates, late eighteenth-century Viennese church music had fallen on hard times. If the music was not overly theatrical, the texts were filled with Enlightenment sentiment bereft of Christian substance. As an antidote to both these issues, the Austrians imported Lutheran chorales into their churches. Although these chorales were not always warmly received by parishioners, many did become accepted and cherished.

In the final section of this book we consider later Lutheran readings of philosophy and poetry. William Weaver explores how a revolution in theology accompanied a revolution in literary criticism. In pre-Reformation times, both Scripture and the classics suffered at the hands of commentators who tended to showcase their own ideas rather than explicate the actual texts. Philip Melanchthon invented an anti-commentary of sorts: he created an index of the topics in the *Georgics* as well as the rhetorical devices employed in that work. Rather than make an exhaustive list, he indexed enough to allow students to discover more of the same phenomena on their own as they interacted with the text. As a result, an entirely new approach to literature developed in succeeding years.

But did the Reformation innovate to such a degree that it obliterated any positive legacy from medieval thought? A common charge laid against Luther and against Protestants in general is that they embraced nominalism and John Duns Scotus's rejection of the analogy of being, both of which caused a fateful turn in intellectual history that has led to the modern secular world. Jack Kilcrease, however, demonstrates that few of the Reformers were nominalists—and none agreed with Scotus's rejection of the analogy of being.

In fact, Aristotle remained of great interest among the early Protestants, who wrote over fifty commentaries on his *Nicomachean Ethics* alone in the sixteenth and seventeenth centuries. Manfred Svensson looks at the way these commentaries attempted to correct Aristotle in the light of Christian doctrine. He addresses the nature and extent of these corrections, the way in which they intersect with philosophical criticism, and the degree to which confessional loyalties are relevant to the kinds of criticism that each commentator raises.

This volume fittingly concludes with John Nordling's examination of the legacy of the teachers by whom one has been taught in person. Long after Cicero had entered middle age, he praised and defended one of his early teachers, Archias, when Gratius brought a suit against him for political motivations. Nordling finds parallels with Luther's warm regard for his mentor, Johannes von Staupitz. Like Cicero, Luther and many Lutherans after him have found poetry and philosophy infinitely rewarding, no matter the circumstances in which they have found themselves (*Pro Archia* 16).

We proposed at the opening of this chapter that, in many ways, as its title suggests, this volume seeks to show that for Luther the "Athens" of his own education and its manifestation in the rediscovery of classical texts, which activity had commenced at the beginning of the Renaissance, has very much to do with the "Jerusalem" of the Church and, especially, of that of the Reformation. As Carl P.E. Springer has amply shown, there was an abiding tension in Luther's relationship with Rome, where Rome can be seen both as a symbol of the ancient culture that produced and transmitted classical texts and, qua the seat of the Church's power, as the Jerusalem of its time. That tension is stretched upon an intertextual frame that can be seen in the writings of, about and derived from Luther. The intertextuality of which we speak is one created by Luther's own and others' allusions to the works of antiquity, particularly Latin literature, that reveal how those texts shaped Luther's own thought and continue to shape the thought of Christian humanism. The intelligent, well-educated and thoroughly bilingual Luther, using both Latin and German, understood that tension—indeed he exploited it for his own and the Church's rich intellectual and spiritual advancement. It is not merely the occurrence of Latin and German side by side in the *Tischreden*, Latin and German quotations of Dr. Luther that likely reflect is own bilingual dinner conversation, but even his reported final words, that rhetorically emphasize that tension. In fact, we are not "beggars" before the *Aeneid* or classical literature, though Luther hyperbolically proclaims it to be the truth. We are, however, along with Luther truly heirs of both and, in that sense, it is most assuredly true that we remain in their debt. And in Luther's, as well.

PART 1

Luther and Classical Poets and Philosophers

CHAPTER 1

Naso erat magister? Virgil and Other Classical Poets in Luther's *Tischreden*

R. Alden Smith

Well into the compendium of *bons mots* and learned banter that forms *Table Talk*, Martin Luther offers a timeless observation about married couples:

> Es ist ein groß Ding, wenn einer ein Mägdlin immerbar kann lieb haben, denn der Teufel läßt es selten zu; sind sie von einander, so kann ers nicht leiden; sind sie den einander, so leidet ers abermals nicht. Wie man pflegt zu sagen: *nec tecum vivere possum, nec sine te*.[1]

> It is a great thing if a married couple can have love continually, for the devil permits this but rarely. Say they are apart, then he cannot bear it; say they are together, once again he does not bear that. As one tends to say, "I can live neither with you nor without you."

This citation might well seem, at first blush, a less-than-sweet sentiment on the part of Martin Luther, albeit the passage itself contains an amusing reference to what "one tends to say" about husbands, wives, and domestic relations. Though we can leave the verity of Luther's appraisal for the individual reader to aver or repudiate, this essay opens by pointing out that the source of this material is surprisingly not the poet that Luther most often cited, Virgil. He was, for Luther, *der Dichter* and thus, when one finds a citation such as this, one might immediately think of a Maronian source as it is Virgil that Martin Luther knew and esteemed most highly among the ancient poets.[2] Yet that is not the case here, however frequent it may be elsewhere.

To take a trivial example of Luther's preference for Virgil, the reformer cites a less than often quoted pair of lines from the fourth book of the *Aeneid* merely

1 WA TR 6:264 (No. 6910). All translations are my own, rendered in coordination with my students Cynthia Liu, Jamie Wheeler, and Joseph Lloyd, all of whom are here thanked for their assistance and friendship.

2 Carl P.E. Springer, "Martin's Martial: Reconsidering Luther's Relationship with the Classics," *International Journal of the Classical Tradition* 14, no. 1 (2007): 23.

 | DOI:10.1163/9789004206717_003

to show how children look like their parents: *Si mihi parvulus Aeneas luderet in aula, Qui te tantum ore referret,*[3] which itself would seem to be a slight error in memory (and in in dactylic hexameter) on Dr. Luther's part of the original:

> saltem si qua mihi de te suscepta fuisset
> ante fugam suboles, *si quis mihi paruulus aula*
> *luderet Aeneas, qui te tamen ore referret,*
> non equidem omnino capta ac deserta uiderer.
>
> *A.* 4.327–30

> At least, if before your flight a child had been born to me from you, *if in my hall some "Aeneas junior" were playing, who by his face nonetheless might evoke your memory,* I should indeed not seem to have been entirely vanquished and abandoned.

Even for a slight matter, such as genetic similarity, Luther thought that Virgil was precisely the poet to address the issue. Thus, it is a bit surprising that for domestic relations—and the *Aeneid*'s fourth book has plenty of purple passages to suggest the struggle that occurs in relationships—Luther does not quote Virgil for his quip about being able to live in harmony.

Nor does he even turn for that clever remark to Horace, who elsewhere in *Table Talk* is used, albeit obliquely, as an example of poetry worth teaching in schools, though he is ranked well behind Prudentius:

> Doctor Martinus Luther lobte die hymnos und geistlichen Gesänge und Gedichte Prudentii, daß er der beste und christlichste Poet wäre, und wenn er zur Zeit Virgilii wäre gewest, so wäre er über Horatium gelobt worden, den doch Virgilius gelobet hat. "Ich wollt sehr gern, daß Prudentii Carmen, Gesänge und Vers in Schulen gelesen würden; aber die Schulen sahen ist an, heidnisch zu warden...."[4]

> Dr. Martin Luther loved the hymns and spiritual poems of Prudentius. Luther held that he was the best Christian poet and that, had he lived in the time of Virgil, he would have been beloved beyond Horace, whom Virgil certainly praised. Luther said, "I wish very much that the poetry and verse of Prudentius would be read in schools, but schools have nowadays become heathenish ..."

---

3 WA TR 4:393 (No. 4593).

4 WA TR 4:96 (No. 4042).

Here Luther is described as imagining that, had Prudentius lived in Virgil's time, he would have outstripped Horace. The clear implication is that Virgil is left aside because Virgil is in fact better than them both—that is the idea behind *den **doch** Virgilius gelobet hat.* Luther's "heathenish" remark suggests that Horace, at least, was still being read in the schools of his time. However heathenish that may have been, certainly Horace was studied while Prudentius apparently was not.

Getting back to our earlier citation, Luther curiously does not mention which poet it is who said, *nec tecum nec sine te.* Rather, he simply states, "as one tends to say (*wie man pflegt zu sagen*)." He trots out this quote like a sweet treat, one with the right ingredients in its context but sans apposite attribution as to its origin. Nevertheless, even pagan poets are normally cited by name in *Tischreden.* Beyond Horace, other poets are extolled by Luther, though the power of the Bible is consistently touted, as well:

> Biblia esse Dei scripturam et non hominis, Dei librum et non hominis probatur hoc argumento, quia omnia, quae sunt et ut sunt in mundo, id est, wie es gehet und stehet in mundo, ea omnia scripta sunt in Genesi per Mosen, das nicht anders geht noch steht, den wie es Gott geschaffen hat. Ad haec Iulius Caesar, Augustus, Alexander, regnum Aegyptiorum, Babyloniorum, Persarum, Graecorum, Romanorum sind hinweg, qui tamen omnes voluerunt hunc librum delere et perdere atque hoc unice studuerunt, ut hic liber deleretur, sed non potuerunt; mansit incolumis contra omnium ipsorum voluntatem ... Homerus, Virgilius esto sint vetusti libri, sed nihil ad biblia.[5]
>
> That the Bible is the writing of God and not of men, and that it is the book of God and not of men is proved by this argument: because all things that exist, and how they exist in the world—that is, how it goes and how it stands in the world—all that is written in Genesis by Moses, that it exists and stands not otherwise than how God created it. Additionally, Julius Caesar, Augustus, Alexander the Great, the kingdom of the Egyptians, Babylonians, Persians, Greeks, and Romans are gone, who yet wished to obliterate and destroy this book; and only this did they desire that this book would be obliterated but they also were unable to do so; it remained safe contrary to the desire of all ... Let Homer exist, Virgil exist, let the old books exist, but they are nothing compared to the Bible.

5 WA TR 1:380–81 (No. 799).

Perhaps it should not be surprising that the father of the Reformation should extol the Bible over Homer and Virgil or any other book. After all, he had risked his life for the authority of holy writ, narrowly escaping what amounted to a death sentence at the Worms Reichstag in 1521. His famous utterance upon that occasion—even if historians continue to debate its authenticity[6]—resonates with the situation of one of Virgil's characters from the *Eclogues*. Thus, Luther's *Hier stehe ich, ich kann nicht anders* might be compared to Tityrus's description, presented to his fellow goatherd Meliboeus in the first *Eclogue*, of the situation he found himself in at Rome when he was standing before the young ruler, Octavian:

> quid *facerem*? neque seruitio me exire licebat
> nec tam praesentis *alibi* cognoscere diuos.
> *hic* illum uidi iuuenem …
>
> *Ecl.* 1.40

> What *could I do*? It was neither possible for me to leave nor to acknowledge *in another place* gods that were so very present. *Here* I saw that youth …

This situation is not specifically the same—after all, "Here I stand; what could I do elsewhere" is not precisely "I can do no other"—yet the notion of the weaker party standing boldly before a potentate and making his claim does offer an interesting parallel. Whether Luther had the first *Eclogue* in mind or not, or whether he even actually did say, "Here I stand, I can do no other," we shall perhaps never know. Yet given another famous quote, *Wir sind Bettler*, attributed to Luther in his final days, and in the context of demonstrating great respect to the Bible and the *Aeneid*, the notion that Virgil might have provided an inspirational model at least does not seem to be utterly impossible.[7]

After all, Luther freely grants that honor can be found in pagan literature:

---

6 Cf. Gerhard Besier, "Myth Creation and Projections: From the Luther Myth to the Luther Campaign" in *Kirchliche Zeitgeschichte* 26, no. 2 (2013): 422–36; also Timothy F. Lull and Derek R. Nelson, *Resilient Reformer: The Life and Thought of Martin Luther* (Augsburg Fortress, Publishers: Minneapolis, MN, 2015), 130 n. 35.

7 WA TR 5:318 (No. 5677): *Hanc tu ne divinam Aeneida tenta, sed vestigia pronus adora. Wir sein pettler. Hoc est verum.*

> Gloria est quaerenda in Virgilio, Achille, Terentio, non in sacris literis, denn Christus sagt: "Sanctificetur nomen tuum, non: Magnificetur vel celebretur". So will er das wort brauchen: "Sanctum".[8]

> Glory ought to be sought in Virgil, Achilles, Terence, not in sacred writings, for Christ says: Let your name be holy. He could have said: let it be magnified, or: let it be celebrated. Accordingly, he wants a (particular) word to be used: Holy.

Luther qualifies such honor, of course, for he wishes to contrast the vanity of honor *honoris causa* with the notion of human agency seeking God's glory, not that of humankind.[9] This principle Luther demonstrates in his brief exegesis of Judges:

> Nos videmus in iudicibus, quos Deus Israeli salvatores excitavit ... confidens in Deum promissorem, invocate enim ipsum: Adiuva me, Deus, etc. Und wenn sie ir sache haben aufgericht, dicunt: Tu, Domine, dedisti mihi victoriam, und werffens unserem Herrn Gott wider in den himel hin auff.[10]

> We see in Judges those whom the God of Israel called forth as heroes ... as I am confident in God who keeps his promises, [I charge you to] call yet upon him: "Help me, God, etc." And when it happens that they have the matter justified, they say: "You, lord, gave me victory," and they lift our Lord God again on high.

Elsewhere, too, Luther is quite wary of the vainglory and corruption that can spring from honor given too lavishly. He cites another poet and writer of epistles, Peter Blois, to that effect:

> Dignitas magistratus est valde necessaria ordinatio in politia, ideo Deus pro illis orandus est; facillime enim corrumpi possunt. Nam honores mutant mores nunquam in meliores, et facile efficerentur tyranni. Nam ille, qui sine lege imperat, est belua; homo cum lege imperans est Deus, qui est autor legis.[11]

---

8 WA TR 4:676 (No. 5127).

9 Cf. Springer, "Martin's Martial," 50.

10 WA TR 1:368 (No. 768).

11 WA TR 5:496 (No. 6118).

> The magistracy is a strong, necessary institution in politics. Therefore, we ought to pray to God for them, for they are easily corrupted. Honors alter a man's character, never for the better, and easily are men made into tyrants. For he who rules without law is a beast; the man who rules with law is [in a manner of speaking] God, who is the author of law.

Let us now return to Virgil, who was indeed the most important poet of antiquity for Luther. That this is the case can even be seen when he is bringing down curses upon his contemporaries. In an interesting "tell-all" section of *Table Talk*, Luther pronounces a curse upon his Catholic counterpuncher, Erasmus, doing so, notably, not *auf deutsch* but *auf lateinisch*.

> "Ich will den Spruch Jesaiä von Basiliskeneiern wider ihn anziehen und brauchen, derselbige schickt und reimet sich fein auf Erasmum." Darnach sagt er diese zween Verse, die er desselben Tags im Bette gemacht hatte von Erasmo:
> Qui Satanam non odit, amet tua carmina, Erasme,
> Atque idem iungat Furias et mulgeat Orcum.[12]

> "I want to quote and put to use against him that saying of Isaiah about basilisk eggs, which applies well to Erasmus." Next he says these two verses, which in bed he had made the same day about Erasmus:
> "He who does not hate Satan, let him love your songs, Erasmus,
> And let the same man join the Furies, and let him milk Orcus."

The reason that this pronouncement is in Latin is not simply because Luther desires to give it the feeling of an "official" curse as, for example, an author such as J.K. Rowling frequently does in the *Harry Potter* series. Rather it is in Latin because its model is drawn from Latin.[13] It is a clear adaptation of another, again perhaps less-than-well-known, line from Virgil:

> qui Bauium non odit, amet tua carmina, Maeui,
> atque idem iungat uulpes et mulgeat hircos.
> *Ecl.* 3.90f.

12 WA TR 1:340 (No. 699). Cf. WA TR 1:195 (No. 446). The reference is to Isaiah 59:5, "basilisk eggs" is translated as "adders' eggs" or "vipers' eggs" in modern English translations.

13 Cf. Carl P.E. Springer, "Arms and the Theologian: Martin Luther's *Adversum Armatum Virum Cocleum*," *International Journal of the Classical Tradition* 10 (2003–04).

> Whoever does not hate Bavius, let him love your songs, Maevius,
> And let this same one join wolves [to his car] and milk he-goats.

Here Menalcas responds to his fellow goatherd Damoetus in a singing competition that comprises the entirety of the third Eclogue. Whoever it is who is enamored of the shoddy poetry of Bavius or Maevius is in danger of being subject to the rustic curse of having his cart drawn by wolves, the shepherd's nightmare, or vainly trying to obtain milk from male goats. Thus, Erasmus is cast via the allusion similarly as a hack writer, and Erasmus's reader, having yoked madness to his cart, is allusively doomed to derive his sustenance from Hell (Orcus) itself.

Lest we go too far in this Virgilian direction, however, let us turn to two further examples of Luther's citations of poets in *Table Talk*. Elsewhere in that collection Luther speaks about the corruption of the papal office in his day, citing half of an elegiac couplet—clearly not the work of Virgil, who wrote exclusively in dactylic hexameter. This citation, oddly enough, would turn out to be one that would stay with Luther even to the grave:

> Magna et insolentissima papae avaritia fuit, und der Teuffel hat im eben Rom darzu erwelet, illum locum ad avaritiam. Ideo veteres dixerunt: Roma, Radix Omnium Malorum Avaritia. Et ego in vetustissimo libro inveni hunc versum: Versus amor mundi caput est et bestia terrae.[14]

> The avarice of the Pope was great and most insolent, and the Devil has therefore chosen Rome itself "as a place for avarice." Therefore, the ancients have said, "Rome is avarice, it is the root of all wickedness." I have also found in a very old book the following verse:
>
> Versus Amor, Mundi Caput est, et Bestia Terræ.
>
> That is (when the word Amor is turned and read backward, then it is Roma), Rome, the head of the world, the beast of the earth.

Interestingly enough, this verse would be combined with an apt refrain to form Martin Luther's epitaph, one that was specifically requested, so says one source at least (a letter of 1537 from a friend to Luther's nemesis Johann Eck[15]). There the correspondent to Eck divulges the final charge of Luther to his close confidants about the care of his family, and, according to Eck's correspondent, he prescribes a specific epitaph, one that includes this citation from the

14 WA TR 3:567 (No. 3724).
15 J. Pflug, *Correspondance* (Leiden: E.J. Brill, 1982), 52.

"old book." The resultant epitaph seems to be a blend of the citation of Ovid's *Epistula Heroidum* 15.169 with a new verse that aptly summarizes Luther's life:

> Ipse sibi hoc epitaphium prospexit:
> "Versus amor mundi caput est et bestia terrae.
> Vivus eram pestis, mortuus ero mors tua, papa."
>
> He himself foresaw this epitaph for himself:
> Amor turned round is the world's head, the beast of the earth.
> I was when alive a plague, and now that I'm dead, I will be your death, Pope.

Amor "turned round," that is to say, with its spelling reversed, is *Roma*, the greatest city in the world. Here we can envision and perhaps even share a grin with the dying Luther looking ahead to his legacy, especially in the immediate wake of the Reformation. But where does the idea behind the verse come from, both the borrowed line and the unique combination of it with a line featuring Luther both alive and after his death? Answers can be found in Luther's engagement with classical texts.

Luther's grasp of classical literature is not an uncommon topic of discussion; as Carl Springer has noted, Luther believed that classical literature was "valuable for Christians to read," both because of these books' purpose as "a useful propaedeutic to Scripture study, but also because of the wise instruction they offered." Luther also proposed that beyond its own inherent value, classical literature was in fact "essential: 'These languages are the scabbard which sheathes the blade of the Spirit; they are the shrine in which this precious jewel is encased.'"[16]

The high regard with which Luther held the classics only lends support to the claim that his knowledge of the field must have been far reaching. This having been said, his epitaph can by no means be as clear as some allusions that are in fact near citations—as we shall see in a moment in the case of *nec sine nec tecum te possum uiuere* with which we opened this chapter. Here, however, a couplet from Ovid would seem to offer at least a basis for Luther's combination of ideas:

> aut si uersus amor tuus est in taedia nostri,
> quam sine te cogis uiuere, coge mori!
>
> OVID, *Ep.*, 3.140

16 Carl P.E. Springer, *Luther's Aesop* (Kirksville, Missouri: Truman State University Press, 2011), 11.

> Or if your love is turned into hatred for us—I, whom you compel to live without you—compel me to die!

At first blush this seems quite an improbable allusion. Yet the Mavius/Baevius adaptation of *Eclogue* 3 is itself, if we are honest, also a bit improbable, as that couplet is not drawn from a purple passage. Operating on just such a tenuous assumption, let us consider the Ovidian Urtext, for it offers a very interesting commentary on Luther's life and work. While his dying words speak of us as all beggars before the *Aeneid*, this brief record of his legacy would seem to be far cleverer yet, compelling the reader to ponder Briseis's words to Achilles: she would rather die than live without the one she loves. Mapping that kind of devotion onto Luther's life in the triumphant vaunt "***uiuus** eram pestis, mortuus ero **mors** tua, papa*" turns it around so that Luther reverses the pathetic tone of Briseis's claim upon Achilles. Instead, Luther seems to say "I am no Briseis—rather, as I was in life the scourge, so in death shall I be the ruin of the papacy." It is not that he would rather die than lose his love; conversely, it is in dying that he shall seek to save his love, the Church, by continuing to vex the papacy. Lurking behind all this bravado may be, therefore—if in fact Luther knew his *Heroides* as well as he knew his *Eclogues* or his *Amores*—a sincere expression of his steadfast devotion both to the Church *qua ecclesia* and, behind the Church, to God Himself.

We have now come full circle, and thus let us consider afresh what we only brush-stroked at this study's outset, namely the question of who it is that Luther is alluding to when he offers his conjugal advice: it is Ovid. While the tentative connection of *Heroides* 3 to Luther's epitaph may, of course, be debated, there can be no doubt in the case of the near citation from *Table Talk* 6920, even if one acknowledges that Martial had, too, adapted Ovid's original verse for his own purposes in his twelfth book of *Epigrams* (12.46). Yet Ovid was behind it all, and is possibly even behind Luther's less-than-famous epitaph.

To conclude, let us consider Ovid as an important poet for Luther, if not quite alongside Virgil, at least not far from him. Just as in the Augustan Age when Ovid was by far the more prolific poet, easily twice as prolific as Virgil, somehow Virgil managed to get all the "credit"; the same could be said in the way that Luther appropriated both poets. Though Ovid is cited verbatim in *Table Talk*, and may even have gently informed the reformer's epitaph, he is alluded to all too often *sine nomine*; Virgil, by contrast, winds up on Luther's lips when he is dying, and he is the one remembered. Other poets are adapted, contrasted, alluded to, but rarely with Virgilian force, Virgilian authority. Thus, though in Luther's *Table Talk*, Virgil, rightly or wrongly, too often seems to claim center stage, nonetheless *Naso* was, to some extent, Luther's *magister*, as well.

CHAPTER 2

Nugatory Nonsense: Why Luther Rarely Cites Catullus

John G. Nordling

Carl P.E. Springer has demonstrated convincingly that Luther was familiar with a wide variety of classical authors, recommended some of these for continued use in the Lutheran schools, and enjoyed a close relationship with classical literature overall.[1] This means, practically speaking, that Luther was a superb Latinist in his own right[2] and wrote Latin verse compellingly—as seen, for example, in those two splendid Latin epigrams Luther wrote late in life in imitation of the Roman poet Martial.[3] Some Luther scholars, to be sure, have maintained, rather condescendingly, that Luther merely "read around" in the classics[4] or that Luther did not know much more about the classics than any "well-educated medieval person" in the secondary schools.[5] In addition to correcting such misimpressions, Springer identifies which classical authors in particular influenced Luther—namely, Aristotle (to whom Luther refers or from whose works he quotes some 700 times), Cicero (more than 300 times), and Virgil (more than 250 times).[6] Then follow in order Horace (some 200 times),

1 See especially, Carl P.E. Springer, "Martin's Martial: Reconsidering Luther's Relationship with the Classics," *International Journal of the Classical Tradition* 14, no. 1/2 (Summer 2007): 23–50.

2 E.g., Preserved Smith, *The Life and Letters of Martin Luther* (New York: Barnes & Noble, Inc., 1911), 333; Roland H. Bainton, *Here I Stand: a Life of Martin Luther* (Nashville: Abingdon Press, 1950), 18; E.G. Schwiebert, *Luther and His Times: the Reformation from a New Perspective* (St. Louis: Concordia, 1950), 110–17; Timothy F. Lull, "Luther's Writings," in *The Cambridge Companion to Martin Luther*, Donald K. McKim, ed. (Cambridge: Cambridge University Press, 2003), 39.

3 The titles of the two poems are "Anti-Martial Poem from Psalm 127 [*carmen antimartiale ex psalmo 127*]" (in Springer, "Martin's Martial," 24–25), and "Sarcasm against Epicurus [*sarcasmus in Epicurum*]" (in Springer, "Martin's Martial," 26–27). See also Carl P.E. Springer, "Luther Between Stoics and Epicureans," chapter 4 in this volume.

4 So Jaroslav Pelikan (*LW* 1:x) in Springer, "Martin's Martial," 28 n. 8.

5 So Lewis W. Spitz ("Luther and Humanism," in *Luther and Learning: the Wittenberg University Luther Symposium 1983*, Marilyn J. Harran, ed. [Selinsgrove: Susquehanna University Press; London and Toronto: Associated University Presses, 1985], 83), cited in Springer, "Martin's Martial," 29 n. 11.

6 So Springer, "Martin's Martial," 31–32. These numbers are based, apparently, on Springer's own enumerations of the Luther references contained in the WA indices. Springer expands

 | DOI:10.1163/9789004206717_004

Terence (just under 200 times), Ovid, the elder Pliny, Plato, and Aesop—the last four names cited by Luther roughly 100 times.[7] We need not rehearse the totality of Springer's enumerations here;[8] rather I shall focus upon the Roman poet Gaius Valerius Catullus whom, according to Springer, Luther supposedly referred to, or quoted, "in the single digits."[9] In this chapter, I shall account for the very few places where Luther cites Catullus, comment upon the nature of those citations, and attempt to explain why Luther cites Catullus so rarely. It shall become clear that both Catullus and Luther possessed radically different reasons for producing poetry: Catullus drew on Alexandrian themes to reflect the vitality of a young, impressionable pagan; Luther used even so unlikely a tool as coarse invective in his poetry to serve didactic purposes related to the Christian gospel.

Luther mentions Catullus twice by name explicitly, and twice alludes to poetry that can with some confidence be attributed to Catullus—for a total of three attestations.[10] Furthermore, while Catullus apparently made a small impression on Luther when measured against the hundreds of references one finds in Aristotle, Cicero, and Virgil, nevertheless Luther reveals his own knowledge of Catullus and, if we examine the three citations more carefully,

---

on the observations of Spitz ("Luther and Humanism," 78) who merely provides a list in the order of frequency of classical authors whom Luther cites.

7 Springer, "Martin's Martial," 32.

8 In addition to the previous citations listed, Springer provides classical authors whom Luther cited or alluded to 50, 40, 30, and 20 times, as well as references "in the single digits." See Springer, "Martin's Martial," 32–33.

9 So Springer, "Martin's Martial," 32. The authors whom Springer places into "the single digits" category are (in order of frequency) Herodotus, Lucan, Democritus, Manilius, Xenophon, the Younger Pliny, Tacitus, **Catullus**, Varro, Menander, Vegetius, Aristophanes, Lucretius, Parmenides, Zeno, Valerius Flaccus, Stesichorus, Statius, Apuleius, and others. Interestingly, Luther appears to have been "almost completely unaware of the Greek tragedians" (Springer, "Martin's Martial," 33 n. 23).

10 For the two places where Luther cites Catullus's name see WA TR 4:75 (No. 4012) and WA 56:489.1–2. In the latter citation Luther cites both Catullus's name and alludes to his poetry (Catullus 64.406). In a third passage Luther's Latin diction seems to resemble a line of Catullan poetry—namely, "all things are unpleasant [*omnia sunt ingrata*]. There is nothing that has been done kindly [*nihil est fecisse benigne*]" (WA 20:159), to which cf. "all this wins no thanks [*omnia sunt ingrata*]; to have acted kindly is nothing [*nihil fecisse benignest*]" (Catullus 73.3; transl. by Francis Warre Cornish, in G.P. Goold, ed., *Catullus, Tibullus, Pervigilium Veneris*, LCL [Cambridge, MA: Harvard University Press; and London, UK: William Heinemann Ltd., 1988], 152). Interestingly, the editors of the Weimar edition (WA 20:159) fail to cite the Catullan source in the apparatus; however, the editors of the American Edition of *Luther's Works* do state that "some" attribute these words to Catullus *Carmina* LXXXIII (obviously in error for LXXIII). See *LW* 15:145 n. 2.

we may determine what Luther thought about Catullus and understand more clearly why Luther cites him so rarely.

It is generally believed that Gaius Valerius Catullus was born in 84 BC and died young, in about 54 BC.[11] He came from a prominent family in Verona, in Cisalpine Gaul, a tract of northern Italy that had been governed by Julius Caesar. We know from Suetonius (*Jul.* 73) that Catullus's father entertained Caesar when he was governor, and from so small a detail it can be surmised that Catullus came from wealth. He describes his family's lavish estate at Sirmio on Lake Garda in poem 31. Still, Catullus did not much like Caesar: he mocks him openly in three poems (see 11.10; 57.2; 93.1), apparently with impunity. Catullus takes aim at the leading powerbrokers and luminaries of the day: Furius and Aurelius, who competed with Catullus in trysts with girls, and sometimes boys as well;[12] Lesbia's notorious brother, the politician P. Clodius Pulcher;[13] Mamurra, the corrupt billionaire prodigy of Caesar and Pompey, whom Catullus dubs "Mentula" ("the Prick," 94.1–2);[14] M. Caelius Rufus, whose strongly smelling arm-pits frightened the girls away (69.5–7);[15] and Caesar himself, as we have seen, who apparently liked Catullus despite his offensive attacks. Then Catullus wrote 26 poems (out of 116 total) about one Lesbia, likely the sister of P. Clodius Pulcher, already mentioned. She did not hesitate, Cicero states, to cheat on her husband Q. Metellus Celer (who died 59 BC), and was ten years older than Catullus, who maintains a perpetually youthful demeanor in all the

---

11 For the dating of Catullus's life see C.J. Fordyce, *Catullus: A Commentary* (Oxford and New York: Oxford University Press, 1961; reprinted, 2006), ix; C.J. Fordyce, "Catullus, Gaius Valerius," *OCD*, 303; Kenneth Quinn, *Catullus: The Poems*, 2nd ed. (New York: St. Martin's Press, 1973), xiv–xv; John Godwin, *Catullus: The Shorter Poems* (Warminster: Aris & Phillips, Ltd., 1999), 2.

12 For example, "O Aurelius ... 'tis you I fear, you and your penis [*verum a te metuo tuoque pene*], so ready to molest good boys and bad alike [*infesto pueris bonis malisque*]" (poem 15.2, 9–10). For similar conceits involving one of the other of the pair, or both, see 11.1–20; 16.1–2; 21.1–4; 23.1, 24; 26.1.

13 "Lesbius is a pretty boy [*Lesbius est pulcher*]; why not? Since Lesbia likes him better than you, Catullus, with all your kin. But let this pretty boy [*hic pulcher*] sell Catullus and all his kin if he can find three acquaintances to vouch for him" (Catullus 79.1–4). Cf. Quinn, *Catullus: The Poems*, 414: "The pun in line 1 makes it tolerably certain that the victim of this lampoon is Clodia's [that is, Lesbia's] infamous brother, P. Clodius Pulcher, for whom, if Cicero's repeated insinuations are to be taken seriously, she had a more than sisterly affection ([Cicero] *Cael.* 32, 36 and 78; *Pis.* 28; *Sest.* 16, etc)."

14 See also poems 29.3; 57.2; 105.1.

15 This is probably the Caelius addressed in poem 58.1 and 100.1, and possibly also the Rufus mentioned in poems 69.2 and 77.1. So Kenneth Quinn, *Catullus: An Interpretation* (New York: Barnes and Noble, 1973), 48.

poems.[16] In the Lesbia poems Catullus reveals every possible emotion associated with love affairs: the joy of falling in love apparently for the first time, jealousy toward rivals, resentment toward Lesbia for not returning his favors, hope that Lesbia might come around in the end, anguish when she does not, and the half-hearted resolve to get on with life after been crushed by a woman who all but treats him as her pet dog.[17]

So Luther, as stated earlier, twice mentions Catullus by name, and twice cites a line of poetry that confidently can be attributed to Catullus. Let us begin with one of the latter passages first—namely, the bit of Catullus Luther cites (without mentioning Catullus's name) in a series of lectures Luther delivered on Ecclesiastes in 1526.[18] Luther regarded Ecclesiastes as the second book of biblical wisdom,[19] and writes the following about the purpose of wisdom for a Christian:

> While in the first book [i.e. Proverbs] Solomon teaches obedience in the face of mad lust and desire, so in this book [Ecclesiastes] he teaches that men are to be patient and steadfast in obedience, in the face of unpleasantness and temptation [*Anfechtung*], and ever to wait out the brief hour in peace and joy. What they cannot keep or alter, they are to let go; it will all work out.[20]

Catullus came to Luther's mind while expounding upon Ecclesiastes 9:3, which reads: "This is an evil in all that is done under the sun, that the same event happens to all. Also, the hearts of the children of man are full of evil, and madness is in their hearts while they live, and after that they go to the dead" (ESV). On

16 Catullus mentions Lesbia's name 15 times in 13 poems (5.1; 7.2; 43.7; 51.7; 58.1, 2; 72.1; 75.1; 79.1; 83.1; 86.5; 87.2; 92.1, 2; 107.4), and alludes to her in 13 additional poems—namely, 2, 3, 8, 11, 13, 36, 37, 68, 70, 76, 85, 104, and 109. See the chart in Quinn, *Catullus: The Poems*, xvi.

17 "Catullus berates his puppy instinct: Don't keep following her around!" So Daniel H. Garrison, *The Student's Catullus*. 2nd ed., Oklahoma Series in Classical Culture, vol. 5 (Norman: University of Oklahoma Press, 1995), 98 (on Poem 8.9–10). For the sundry details of Catullus's life revealed in this paragraph see Fordyce, "Catullus, Gaius Valerius," 216; Quinn, *Catullus: An Interpretation*, 54–70; Quinn, *Catullus: The Poems*, xi–xxxix.

18 They were lectures delivered in the school at Wittenberg, published later in 1532 by friends based on Rörer's lecture notes and others who attended the lectures. For the details of publication see WA 20: 1–6; *LW* 15:ix–x.

19 Proverbs is first, in his opinion. See WA DB 1011:8; *LW* 35:260.

20 *LW* 35:260; the translation is based on the German text in WA, DB 1011:9–10.

this passage, which may be taken as representative of the Preacher's[21] generally sober perspectives on life "under the sun," Luther observes:

> This is another Solomonic extravagance ... Therefore this must be understood as applying to the world, not to God. Those who live righteously are despised in the presence of the world and within the world. But in the presence of God they are well off, as he said earlier (cf. 7:18): "He who fears God will be well off." The world, however, gives the same reward to the good and to the evil.[22]

At this point the quotation from Catullus 73.3 occurs ("all things are unpleasing [and] to have acted kindly is nothing"),[23] Luther used only the first line of Catullus's elegiac couplet, which in its complete form is a dark saying, to be sure:

> Omnia sunt ingrata, nihil fecisse benigne
> Prodest, immo etiam taedet obestque magis.
> CATULLUS 73.3–4

> All things are unpleasing [and] to have acted kindly is of no advantage,
> Nay rather, it is wearisome and more harmful.

One may well wonder what Catullus meant by it originally, and why Luther chose these seemingly obscure lines—when he could have cited much brighter, more vibrant, and suggestive themes, as our earlier survey of Catullus's life and poetry might suggest.

---

21 The English title of this scriptural book goes back to Eccl 1:1: "The words of the *Preacher*, son of David, king in Jerusalem ..." (ESV; added emphasis). The Hebrew term for "preacher" (*qoheleth*) is related to that for "assembly" (see Ex 16:3; Num 16:3). Possibly the Preacher (whose work is described in Eccl 12:9–10) also held an office in the assembly. The Septuagint word for preacher is ἐκκλησιαστής, from which most English titles of the book are taken, and from which such English words as "ecclesiastical" are derived. See the text note for Eccl 1:1 in Robert G. Hoerber, general editor, *Concordia Self-Study Bible: New International Version* (St. Louis: Concordia, 1986), 994.

22 WA 20:159.7–12; in *LW* 15:145.

23 My translation, with some dependence upon the translation of Francis Warre Cornish in Goold, *Catullus, Tibullus, Pervigilium Veneris*, 153. The version of the text provided here is based on *V*, a lost archetype of probably the late 12th-century known to have been at Verona (hence the designation *V*) in the early fifteenth century. See G.P. Goold, "Reviser's Preface (1987)," in *Catullus, Tibullus, Pervigilium Veneris*, ix.

In the opinion of Thomson, poem 73 is "the most emotionally charged"[24] of Catullus's poems. Catullus complains that he has never been so vexed or troubled by anyone as bitterly as "him who but now held me for his one and only friend [*quam modo qui me unum atque unicum amicum habuit*]" (73.6). Experienced Latinists will note the five disruptive elisions at the end of the line—so many, in fact, that here diaeresis cannot occur, making it Catullus's longest pentameter.[25] The overall effect is to slow the line down and make it unbearably heavy, clumsy, and difficult to pronounce: a "harsh, slurred rush of words," is what Quinn calls it.[26] Catullus fails to reveal the identity of the false "friend" who does him wrong, but scholars have tried to group poem 73 with complaints Catullus makes elsewhere of other named assailants who, in their diverse ways, harm the poet grievously: Alfenus, "ungrateful and false to your faithful comrades" (30.1ff); Lesbia again, for whom a "lethargy" has crept into Catullus's inmost joints and casts all joys from his heart (76.21–22); Rufus, whom Catullus, his friend, had "trusted in vain and to no purpose" (77.1); and the pervert Gellius whom Catullus berates for having made a pass at Lesbia:

> I was hoping, O Gellius, that you would be true to me in this miserable, this ruinous love affair of mine—not on the ground that I knew you, or thought that you were truly honorable or could restrain your mind from baseness or villainy—but because I saw that she, whose mighty love was consuming me, was neither a mother nor sister of yours [*sed neque quod matrem nec germanam esse videbam / hanc tibi, cuius me magnus edebat amor*].
>
> CATULLUS 91.1–6[27]

---

24 D.F.S. Thomson, *Catullus* (Toronto: University of Toronto Press, 1997), 496.

25 Garrison, *Student's Catullus*, 153. Both Fordyce (*Catullus: A Commentary*, 365) and Thomson (*Catullus*, 497) suppose that the phrase *unum atque unicum* has an archaic ring to it. The second line of an elegiac couplet consists of the duplication of the so-called *hemiepes* ("half verse"), separated by diaeresis (the break in the line [||] caused by the coincidence of the end of a foot with the end of a word). But in Catullus 73.6 the normal diaeresis cannot occur on account of the five elisions indicated below. The line cannot be scanned in the usual manner; thus:

— U U — — — U U — — U U X

quam modo qui me‿unum‿atque‿unicum‿amicum‿habuit.

On the elegiac couplet in both Greek and Latin literature see James W. Halporn, Martin Ostwald, and Thomas G. Rosenmeyer, *The Meters of Greek and Latin Poetry*. Revised edition (Norman: University of Oklahoma Press, 1980), 12–13, 71–72.

26 Quinn, *Catullus: The Poems*, 404. On the difficulty of the line see also Garrison, *Student's Catullus*, 153; Godwin, *Catullus: The Shorter Poems*, 188.

27 My translation, with acknowledgement of debt to the translation of Francis Warre Cornish in Goold, *Catullus, Tibullus, Pervigilium Veneris*, 165–67.

Gellius had clearly harmed Catullus by carrying on an affair with Lesbia;[28] but the poet more than gets back at him by making the claim that he had not suspected Gellius of going after Lesbia because his mother and sister were not involved. Catullus intimates here that Gellius sleeps with his mother and sister! This Gellius is probably the younger L. Gellius Poplicola, usually identified as the Gellius of poems 74, 80, 88, 89, 90, 91, and 116.[29] If the identity holds, "[The elder] L. Gellius ... was almost certain that his son had been guilty of very serious crimes [*gravissima crimina*], namely adultery with his stepmother and plotting his father's murder [*in novercam commissum stuprum et parricidium cogitatum*]" before the senate (Valerius Maximus *Factorum et dictorum memorabilium libri novem* 5.9.1).[30] The picture Catullus paints of Gellius in poem 91—that of an incestuous pervert, who nonetheless has had his way with Lesbia—corresponds to what can be pieced together of the historical L. Gellius Poplicola.

Was Luther aware of the subtle relationships that exist between Catullus 73 and the other poems documented immediately above? I doubt Luther read the Catullan corpus all that carefully—perhaps for fun, or to possess some sense of the debauchery of the pagan mind (about which I will enter into greater detail below). In my opinion, however, Luther would not have read Catullus as a subject of serious, theological inquiry—the way, by contrast, he *did* read the works of Aristotle, Cicero, and Virgil. Nevertheless, Catullus's dark epigram came to Luther while producing serious theology on the Ecclesiastic theme that the world gives the same reward—death—to the righteous as well as to the wicked. Scripture is dark on the futility of life lived "under the sun," and Luther splices in a similarly dark epigram from Catullus on how a supposed friend had done him grievous wrong. Luther's citing of Catullus here shows how the reformer used even a seemingly unrelated snatch of pagan poetry

28 This much is intimated by how the poem concludes: "And although I was connected with you by much familiar friendship, I had not thought that that was reason enough for you. You thought it enough: so much delight do you take in any fault in which there is something of dishonor [*tantum tibi gaudium in omni / culpast, in quacumque est aliquid sceleris*]" (91.7–10). Translated by Francis Warre Cornish in Goold, *Catullus, Tibullus, Pervigilium Veneris*, 167.

29 See Garrison, *Student Catullus*, 168. Also, Fordyce, *Catullus: A Commentary*, 403.

30 Even though the younger L. Gellius had engaged in such serious crimes, the elder Gellius did not rush to punish straightaway but took the entire senate into his confidence and allowed his son to defend himself. After a thorough investigation the younger Gellius was acquitted by a vote of the council. For the text and translation of this curious passage see D.R. Shackleton Bailey, ed. and trans., *Valerius Maximus, Memorable Doings and Sayings*, LCL (Cambridge, MA and London, UK: Harvard University Press, 2000), 536–39.

to elucidate a point of biblical theology—in this case, the futility of life lived "under the sun."

In a second passage, Luther cites a line of Catullus in the course of one of his more famous lectures on Romans, a portion of which he delivered to students in Wittenberg in the summer of 1516.[31] Catullus 64.405 appears toward the end of a veritable catena of passages meant to cast light on Paul's injunction "not in orgies and drunkenness [μὴ κώμοις καὶ μέθαις], not in sexual immorality and sensuality, not in quarreling and jealousy" (Rom 13:13 ESV)—as if the additional passages were needed to underscore the sort of dissolute behavior it was that Paul marks and condemns. After pointing out that there was an ancient god of drunkenness named Comus that the Greeks devoted themselves to more assiduously than even the inebriated Germans did, Luther mentions texts whose pertinence to Paul's "drunken bouts" are generally valid, if imprecise: 2 Cor 6:6 (for a positive example of purity), Jerome's handling of "the six vices,"[32] Suetonius's *Lives of the Caesars* (where debauchery runs rampant nearly everywhere), a portion of Juvenal's *Satires* 6.292,[33] and finally a phrase in 1 Pet 4:4—namely, "the same flood of debauchery [τὴν αὐτὴν τῆς ἀσωτίας ἀνάχυσιν]" (ESV). What struck Luther about this Petrine picture of pagan excess, apparently, was the state of confusion that reigned everywhere in Rome, which Luther follows Peter in calling Babylon:[34]

> Nor was blessed Peter silent about the wantonness of the same city [*eiusdem urbis luxuriem*], but he also called it a "mixing with wantonness and vileness [*luxurie Confusionem seu colluviem*]."[35] Indeed, because of this he does not hesitate to call this city a Babylon, because all things there

31 To be precise, Luther lectured on Romans in Wittenberg from spring 1515 to fall 1516, but this portion of his lectures (Rom 9:1–16:27) was delivered in summer 1516. He had the printer make copies of the Vulgate text of Scripture with ample space between the lines and generous margins. He made notes on his copy and dictated these to the students. See the editor's comments in WA 56:XII–XIII; *LW* 25:x. The composite student notes on Luther's Romans lectures are contained in WA 57.

32 Possibly a reference to Eph. 5:5, perhaps Jerome citing Origen (see Ronald E. Heine, *The Commentaries of Origen and Jerome on St. Paul's Epistle to the Ephesians* [Oxford University Press, 2002], 213), either in his commentary or in the Apology against Rufinus.

33 "A stronger enemy, namely, luxury, has come to lodge with us and takes vengeance upon a conquered world." As translated in *LW* 25:481.

34 Further on Luther's reference to Rome as Babylon, cf. Carl P.E. Springer, *Rome's Luther, Luther's Rome* (Minneapolis: Fortress Press, 2020): 133.

35 Luther apparently paraphrases 1 Pet 4:4 here, departing significantly from the Vulgate version.

were confused [*Quod omnia ibi essent Confusa*], as also Catullus testifies [*etiam Catullo teste*] …

WA 56:488–89

Then occurs the line from Catullus 64.405, whose thought is completed by the subsequent line:

omnia fanda nefanda malo permixta furore
iustificam nobis mentem avertere deorum.

… then all right and wrong, mixed together in impious madness,
turned from us the righteous will of the gods.

The Catullan lines serve Luther's purposes here because the "mixing together of right and wrong" (*fanda nefanda … permixta*) corresponds reasonably well with the idea of "confusion" that the scriptural citations—and Luther's comments thereon—have established in the Romans commentary to this point.[36] Catullus's "mixing together of right and wrong" occurs nearly at the end of Catullus 64, the longest poem in the corpus, which is the epyllion celebrating the legendary marriage of Peleus and Thetis. The legendary tale takes one back to the days of yore, before religion was despised, when "the heavenly ones" (*caelicolae*) were wont to visit the pious homes of heroes, and even show themselves to mortal company (64.382–86). But the Catullan picture ends with images of bloodshed, of a father desiring the death of his son "that he might without hindrance enjoy the flower of a young bride" (64.402), and of an impious mother "lying beneath" (*substerens*, 64.403) her unassuming son—that is, allowing herself to be sexually penetrated by him (64.404).[37] Then occur the

36 In addition to the words *confusionem* and *confusa*, Luther plays in this section upon *luxuriem, luxuriam*, and *colluviem* which possess the sense of "reveling" or "an outpouring of prodigality"—as he himself points out in WA 56:489.15–16. And the word ἀνάχυσις—εως, f. in 1 Pet 4:4, a *hapax-legomenon* in the New Testament, means literally a "pouring out," then a "wide stream" (from ἀναχέω, "to pour out"), as in "the pouring out of the sea" (ἀνάχυσις θαλάττης, Maximus of Tyre 38.3e). See BDAG, s.v. ἀνάχυσις—εως, f.

37 Quinn suggests (*Catullus: The Poems*, 350) that the father's enjoyment of his son's pretty young wife without hindrance from the son may allude to Catiline's allegedly incestuous marriage to Orestilla, said to be the daughter of Catiline's former mistress (Sallust *Cat.* 15). So he murdered his legitimate son to marry his own daughter by a former mistress. For the mother's sleeping with her son Quinn suggests (*Catullus: The Poems*, 350) that Gellius and his mother are meant (see note 28 above). It could be neither Oedipus nor Jocasta, who both acted in ignorance.

final four lines of the poem, the first of which I repeat here to demonstrate the context wherein it occurs:

> ... **then all right and wrong, mixed together in impious madness,**
> turned from us the righteous will of the gods.
> Wherefore they deign not to visit such companies [*tales ... coetus*],
> nor endure the touch of clear daylight.
> CATULLUS 64.405–8

Again, it seems difficult to determine whether Luther cited Catullus in the bolded portion because he was aware of, or all that interested in, how the line functioned in Catullus 64 originally. Indeed, he may have been aware of the Catullan connections, simply because Luther read Latin avidly, no doubt enjoying the poetry of Catullus as well as other Latin authors. However, I think the Catullan associations took a back seat in the reformer's mind to the picture of pagan excess and profligacy that Luther attempts to establish at this portion of his Romans commentary. Catullus 64.405 is just one of several passages establishing the debauchery and wickedness of ancient Rome, and essentially indistinguishable from the other passages in that regard.

In a third passage, Luther lumps Catullus together with some poets whose books should not be read in the schools on account of the "obscene and ridiculous things" they contain:

> Afterwards he [Luther] said that it was especially imperative that the books of Juvenal, Martial, Catullus, and the Priapeia of Virgil should be removed from the schools, because they write such obscene and ridiculous things [*tam obscoena et ludicra*] that they are not able to be read without causing harm [*ut non possent sine damno legi*].[38]

As is well known, Luther was in favor of completely overhauling the monastically-oriented schools of his day[39] by ridding them of Aristotle's dialectic, disputations, and canon law, and instead reintroducing rhetoric, grammar, ancient languages and, above all, the Bible. Now schools would educate

---

38 WA TR 4:75 (No. 4012). Cited in Springer, "Martin's Martial," 44 n. 68; and Carl P.E. Springer, "Luther's Latin Poetry and Scatology," *Lutheran Quarterly* 23, no. 4 (Winter 2009): 385 n. 21.

39 For Luther's educational reforms in general see Smith, *Life and Letters of Martin Luther*, 85, 185–87, 233–34; Bainton, *Here I Stand*, 262; and James M. Kittelson, "Luther the Educational Reformer," in *Luther and Learning: the Wittenberg University Luther Symposium 1983*, ed. Marilyn J. Harran (Selinsgrove: Susquehanna University Press; London and Toronto: Associated University Presses, 1985), 95–114.

increasing numbers of students—girls as well as boys—in the useful arts, and in the Christian religion.[40] Latin played a role in the reforms, of course, though the reformers would have prized salutary texts conveying only the best, and ignoring the worst, of the classical tradition. The passage before us states that, in Luther's opinion, Juvenal, Martial, Catullus, and the Priapeia of Virgil did not make the cut.[41] Not that Luther refrained from such forbidden fruit himself; plenty of circumstantial evidence suggests that Luther drank deeply from the tainted wells and was capable of imitating in his poetry the less-than-salutary themes of the ancients. Nevertheless, it seems fair to conclude that the reformer desired to guard his students' chastity against such pernicious influences as we have glimpsed for ourselves in the poetry of Catullus. Catullus, to be sure, could carry on with a kind of "moral earnestness" that Garrison at least has noticed;[42] but Catullan art usually requires the poet (and complicit readers) to renounce moral scruple and even trounce it with a kind of perverse glee. However, my "usually" cannot mean that Catullus was immoral "all the time"; hence, I would like to conclude this chapter by demonstrating both the moral earnestness of which Catullus could be capable, pagan though he was, and, paradoxically, the coarseness of Luther who used even vulgar poetic invective to achieve his aims.

Catullus's unnamed brother died somewhere near Troy and the poet apparently stopped by his graveside to make an offering and prepare splendid elegiac couplets in the manner of a Hellenistic grave epigram:

> Multas per gentes et multa per aequora vectus
> advenio has miseras, frater, ad inferias,
> ut te postremo donarem munere mortis
> et mutam nequiquam alloquerer cinerem ...
>
> CATULLUS 101.1–4

---

40 For the visitations used to achieve such ends see Smith, *Life and Letters of Martin Luther*, 233; Kittelson, "Luther the Educational Reformer," 101; and John G. Nordling, "The Catechism: The Heart of the Reformation," *Logia* 16, no. 4 (2007): 5–13, especially 6–7.

41 Technically speaking, the Priape(i)a were poems in honor of Priapus, the Roman god of male fertility, whose depictions invariably feature emaciated bodies connected to enormous phalli. The collection of priapic poems is distinguished by its "extreme obscenity, genuine wit, fierce mockery of the ridiculous or grotesque, clever use of verbal borrowings and parody, amusing tension between the sophistication of the literary form and the crudity of the subject-matter, and elegant variations on a number of recurrent themes," Lindsay Cameron Watson, "Priape(i)a," *OCD*, 1244. See also Robert Christopher Towneley Parker, "Priapus," in *OCD*, 1245.

42 E.g., Catullus "remains emotionally sympathetic and morally earnest, more traditional than decadent in his beliefs." So Garrison, *Student's Catullus*, x.

Borne over many nations and over many seas
  I arrive, O brother, to these sorrowful obsequies,
to present you with that final gift the dead receive
  and to address—in vain!—[your] mute ash … (my translation)

Fordyce supposes[43] that Catullus stopped at his brother's grave in 57 BC whilst on the way to Bithynia to join there the staff of the praetor C. Memmius, a provincial administrator.[44] The "final gift the dead receive" likely consisted of offerings of milk, wine, honey, and flowers which family members proffered to the *dis manibus* out of a sense of duty;[45] fortune had taken his unnamed brother away from Catullus,[46] and the poet's apparently genuine sadness is reflected in the poem's ponderous, though stately, meter—especially in the fourth line whose heavy elision again obscures the diaeresis that is supposed to occur in the middle of a dactylic pentameter line. Much else could be said about the poem, but what should be recognized here is Catullus's unfeigned earnestness: his brother's death has affected him deeply, nor is there any evidence

---

43 Fordyce, *Catullus: A Commentary*, 388.

44 See Quinn, *Catullus: The Poems*, 123. Thomson (*Catullus*, 536) supposes that Catullus made his visit in 56 BC, upon his *return* from Bithynia—rather than in 57, upon his way there. It seems impossible to provide a solution to the conundrum here. For the desire of Catullus (and other Roman gallants) to strike it rich while on service to some provincial praetor see poem 10.6–12. Most did not get rich there—especially when one had such a "beast" (*irrumator*, 10.12) for a praetor. ("Beast" is the translation Francis Warre Cornish preferred [in Goold, *Catullus, Tibullus, Pervigilium Veneris*, 12] for a word too obscene to translate.) On the rituals themselves to which Catullus's portrayal of his brother's death corresponds see Andrew Feldherr, "*Non inter nota sepulcra*: Catullus 101 and Roman Funerary Ritual," in *Catullus*, ed. Julia H. Gaisser, Oxford Readings in Classical Studies (New York: Oxford University Press Inc., 2007), 399–426.

45 So Quinn, *Catullus: The Poems*, 442; Godwin, *Catullus: The Shorter Poems*, 213. The *Di Manes* were chthonic deities sometimes thought to represent souls of deceased loved ones. Many a grave inscription bore the caption D[is] M[anibus] ("to the spirits of the dead"), which could refer to the departed spirit, ghost, or shade of a person. See Charlton T. Lewis, *A Latin Dictionary* (Oxford: Oxford University Press, 1879; reprint, 1996), 1108, s.v., *Manes, -ium*, m. Feldherr argues ("Catullus 101 and Roman Funerary Ritual," 402–3), however, that at the time of the funeral Catullus's brother had not yet become one of the *di manes* but actually was in a kind of liminal state between life and death. Therefore, the offerings made to the dead were slightly different: salt, cereals, beans, wine, milk, and violets. See Feldherr, "Catullus 101 and Roman Funerary Ritual," 404. Further on *di manes*, cf. Charles W. King, *The Ancient Roman Afterlife:* Di Manes, *Belief, and the Cult of the Dead* (Austin, TX: University of Texas Press, 2020), 1–29 et *passim*.

46 "Since fortune has taken you away from me [*quandoquidem fortuna mihi tete abstulit ipsum*] …" (Catullus 101.5; my translation). The noun *frater* ("brother") occurs three times in the poem (101.2, 6, 10), and the related adjective *fraterno* ("a brother's") occurs in line 9.

of the "obscene and ridiculous things" Luther complains about above. In this respect the Catullan dirge seems akin to a pair of elegiac couplets Luther wrote as the epitaph for his daughter Magdalena's tomb:

> Dormio cum sanctis hic Magdalena, Lutheri
>   Filia, et hoc strato tecta quiesco meo;
> Filia mortis eram, peccati semine nata.
>   Sanguine sed vivo, Christe, redempta tuo.
>
> I, Magdalena, daughter of Luther, sleep here with the saints,
>   and rest covered by this my bed;
> I was a daughter of death, born of the seed of sin.
>   But I live, O Christ, redeemed by Thy blood.[47]

Luther's poem is unabashedly Christian, testifying to his daughter Magdalena's victory over death by Christ's redemptive blood; Catullus's poem is just as unmistakably pagan, testifying to that poet's sense of futility: "his [Catullus's] words are vain because he can have no answer."[48]

Aside from such obvious differences, however, the two poems actually have much in common. Both are epitaphs written in elegiac couplets, of course, a convention that was in popular usage since the middle of the sixth-century BC;[49] more importantly, both poems share a kind of melancholy reverence for the dearly departed that brooks no levity. Thus, we know how keenly Luther felt about his daughter's death, despite his strong faith in the resurrection of the dead.[50]

---

47 The Latin version appears twice in WA TR 5:185–86 (No. 5490), as well as four distinct German translations of the Latin. The English translation appears in Carl P.E. Springer, "Death and Life after Death in Martin Luther's Latin Elegies," *Acta conventus neo-latini upsaliensis: Proceedings of the Fourteenth International Congress of Neo-Latin Studies* (*Uppsala 2009*) (Leiden, Boston: Brill 2012), 1052 n. 13.

48 Fordyce, *Catullus: A Commentary*, 389 (on *nequiquam*, 101.4).

49 On the elegiac couplet see note 25 above. For the origin of the elegiac couplet among the Greeks in the seventh century BC see Martin Litchfield West, "Elegaic Poetry, Greek," *OCD*, 517.

50 "When she had died, he [Luther] said: 'I am joyful in spirit, but as far as my flesh is concerned, I am very sad. The flesh will not adapt to this. Separation vexes us above all measure. It is strange that I know that she surely is at peace and that she is very well off where she is and nonetheless to grieve so [*et tamen sic dolere*]!'" (WA TR 5:193 [No. 5498]). For the English translation see Springer, "Death and Life after Death," 1053 n. 14.

On the other hand, several of Luther's Latin poems fail to say anything at all, even indirectly, about life after death,[51] and even employ terminology associated with "pagan descriptions of [the] infernal topography."[52] One of my favorite Luther poems in this regard is a sharp (though probably humorous) blast against the pagan philosopher Epicurus who taught that there is no life after death:

> Vivas ut tua sus tuusque porcus
> Et tandem moriare porcus et sus.
> Sic, sic itur ad insulas beatas,
> Aeterno quibus igne carcer ardet
> Et tales coquit ustulatque porcos.

> May you live like your sow and your pig,
> And finally die a pig and a sow.
> This, this is how you'll make your way to the blessed isles,
> Where a prison burns with eternal fire,
> And cooks and roasts such pigs as these![53]

Note that this splendid poem is composed in the phalaecean or hendecasyllabic meter. Catullus wrote two thirds of his polymetric poems (poems 1–60) in hendecasyllables;[54] and though it seems a stretch to suggest that Luther wrote

---

51 For example, "Just as there is nothing more certain than fate [*fato*], so, too, nothing is less certain than the hour [*hora*] when your fates will arrive" (translated in Springer, "Death and Life after Death," 1053 n. 15); and, "Luther, himself glass, gives a glass to glassy Jonas [*dat vitrum vitro Ionae vitrum ipse Lutherus*], so that both recognize that they resemble fragile glass" (WA 35:602; translated in Springer, "Death and Life after Death," 1054 n. 17).

52 So Springer ("Death and Life after Death," 1055) on a pair of slightly damaged dactylic hexameters Luther penned against Erasmus (the second line does not quite scan correctly):

> *Qui Satanam non odit, amet tua carmina, Erasme,*
> *Atque idem iungat Furias atque mulgeat Orcos.*
> WA TR 1:399 [NO. 823]

> He who does not hate Satan should love your poems, O Erasmus,
> and let the same yoke the furies and appease the infernal regions! (my translation).

Further on this couplet, cf. A. Smith, "*Naso erat magister?* Virgil and Other Classical Poets in Luther's *Tischreden,*" which appears in this volume.

53 WA TR 5:358–59 (No. 5794). In Springer, "Death and Life after Death," 1056 n. 22. This is just lines 6–10 of Luther's *Sarcasmus in Epicurum* ("Sarcasm against Epicurus"), the entire poem of which appears (and is translated) in Springer, "Martin's Martial," 26–27 n. 4.

54 Fordyce, *Catullus: A Commentary*, 83; Godwin, *Catullus: The Shorter Poems*, 14.

this blast against Epicurus in hendecasyllables because Catullus did so,[55] we must nevertheless recognize that hendecasyllables were perceived by the ancients to be a meter of invective.[56] Now the very sound of this Luther poem, with its seething sibilants, breathes out hostility against the "piggish" Epicurus and his followers: *vivaṣ ut tua ṣuṣ tuuṣque porcuṣ*. According to Luther's schematization of spiritual reality, the gospel of Christ is intended for all. Yet unbelievers and purveyors of the flesh nevertheless need the Law to help them recognize their selfishness and self-chosen idols. Here Luther's sarcasm against Epicurean pig-headedness approaches that of some deranged Old Testament prophet[57]—or even the violent response of Jesus Christ who fashioned a whip out of cords to drive the money-changers out of the temple in a frenzy.[58] Perhaps Luther lets his hendecasyllables fly because he wants to suggest that he has lost patience; yet, if this is the case, he has nonetheless not lost his sense of humor, as the poem is at the same time uproariously funny. Luther peppers his castigations of Epicurus with a derogatory usage of the word "pig": *porcis* (line 2), *porcus* (lines 10 and 11), *porcos* (14). Luther says in so many words that anyone who prefers the porcine philosophy of Epicurus to Christ and the gospel is a damned pig, and such pigs from Epicurus's trough will pay the penalty by being "cooked to a crisp."[59] If the image elicits a hearty chuckle, we should recognize that Luther's primary role model, Jesus Christ, of all people, could raise a laugh—even when (or perhaps especially when)—he was laying down the law. When Jesus says, for example, that it is not that which enters a man that defiles the man, but rather that which goes into his stomach—and flows out into the latrine (εἰς τὸν ἀφεδρῶνα ἐκπορεύεται, Mark 7:19)—he could be making a crude joke. But that possibility is completely lost on readers who rely on English translations (which invariably sanitize the text here).[60]

---

55 Springer argues ("Martin's Martial," 26), in fact, that Luther models his anti-Epicurus epigram upon Martial 10.47 (for the Latin poem and translation of which see Springer, "Martin's Martial," 25 n. 3). Springer is of course completely correct in this identification.

56 Cf., for example, Catullus's threat to Asinius Marrucinus, the napkin thief: "wherefore, either watch out for 300 hendecasyllabes [*quare aut hendcasyllabos trecentos/ expecta*], or send me back my napkin ..." (Catullus 12.10–11; my translation). Elsewhere the poet bids personified hendecasyllables to gang up on an "impudent hussy" who takes Catullus for a fool: "Come hither, hendecasyllables [*adeste, hendecasyllabi*], all of you there are, from every quarter, all of you there are. An impudent hussy [*moecha turpis*] takes me for a fool, and says, if you please, that she'll not return my tablets. Let's go after her, and demand them back [*persequamur eam, et reflagitemus*]" (Catullus 42.1–6; my translation).

57 E.g., Isa 1:10–15; Amos 4:1; 5:21–25.

58 John 2:15; cf. Matt 21:12–13; Mark 11:15–17; Luke 19:45–46.

59 So Springer, "Death and Life after Death," 1056.

60 Some translations do render this phrase in a more literal manner: "and goes out into the sewer" (NRSV); "and so passes out into the drain" (NEB); "and passes into the latrine" (NAB); "and goeth out into the draught" (KJV). But most translations sanitize the expression: "and

To conclude: Luther's three all-too-brief citations of Catullan poetry do not indicate that Luther rarely read Catullus or did not appreciate Catullan art. Indeed, Luther read Catullus deeply, just as he read all other Latin authors of his own and prior ages. Luther was a Latinist through and through, and so at home in the rich Latinity that runs as a scarlet thread through Western literature from antiquity into his own day and age. Why then did Luther not cite Catullus more frequently? Possibly because Luther did not take Catullus's poetry all that seriously. Catullus referred to his own poetry as *nugae*—"nugatory nonsense."[61] So in comparison to Aristotle, Cicero, and Virgil—authors that plainly influenced Luther's theology more profoundly—Catullus scarcely registers. Still, cite Catullus Luther did, albeit infrequently. Those three citations indicate at the very least that Luther not only knew who Catullus was, but that he read Catullus's fine work, reflected on his poetry and, quite probably, enjoyed Catullus.

---

is eliminated" (NKJV); "and so passes on" (RSV); "and then out of his body" (NIV); "and then out of your body" (TNIV); "and so passes out of the body" (NET); "and then goes on out of the body" (TEV); "but only passes through the digestive system" (Living).

61 "To you, Cornelius: for you used to think that my trifles [*nugas*] were worth something long ago" (Catullus 1:3–4; translated by Cornish, in Goold, *Catullus, Tibullus, Pervigilium Veneris*, 3).

CHAPTER 3

"Pious Mirth": Listening to Martin Luther's Latin Poetry

Carl P.E. Springer

> "*Requiescat in pace*," he said. "*Sit tibi terra levis. Requiem aeternam dona ei, Domine.*" You see, when it is a matter of death and one speaks to the dead or of the dead, that is when Latin regains its power; it is the official language in such situations, and then one can observe what a special relationship it has with death. But it isn't a result of humanistic *courtoisie* that one speaks Latin, in order to honor death; when we talk about death that is not a time for refined Latin, you see. No, it comes from a completely different spirit, a completely opposite spirit, one could probably say. This is sacred Latin, the monks' dialect, the Middle Ages, which means a ponderous, monotonic, underworldly song....[1]

∴

There are many Latin poems written in the sixteenth century that are light in tone, highly refined, politely superficial, that breathe, as Thomas Mann suggests, the air of "humanistic courtesy." There are poems about kisses or a chess game or an erotic conquest. There are countless celebratory odes written to commemorate a wedding or the birth of a child or a coronation. Sometimes

---

1 *"Requiescat in pace," sagte er. "Sit tibi terra levis. Requiem aeternam dona ei, Domine." Siehst du, wenn es sich um den Tod handelt und man zu Toten spricht oder von Toten, so tritt auch wieder das Latein in Kraft, das ist die offizielle Sprache in solchen Fällen, da merkt man, was für eine besondere Sache es mit dem Tode ist. Aber es ist nicht aus humanistischer* Courtoisie, *dass man Lateinisch redet zu seinen Ehren, die Totensprache ist kein Bildungslatein, verstehst du, sondern von einem ganz anderen Geist, einem ganz entgegengesetzten, kann man wohl sagen. Das ist Sakrallatein, Mönchsdialekt, Mittelalter, so ein dumpfer, eintöniger, unterirdischer Gesang gewissermassen.* The quotation comes from Thomas Mann's *Zauberberg* (Frankfurt: Fischer, 2004), 405. Unless otherwise noted, translations here and elsewhere in this chapter are my own or provided by Rachel Donnelly and Jamie Wheeler, research assistants at Baylor University.

 | DOI:10.1163/9789004206717_005

there is an exotic air about these literary *nugae*, evocative of a distant, long vanished Arcadia situated somewhere in the ancient world where satyrs once pursued nymphs.[2] Sometimes they are virtuosic. The entire point seems for the poet to meet a challenge of some sort. Is it really possible to write a Latin poem, as Girolamo Fracastoro did, about the origins of syphilis?[3] These are the Neo-Latin poems of the humanists that have so often attracted the attention of classically trained scholars. This is not surprising. Ever since the Enlightenment, the classics have been understood to be more or less synonymous with light-hearted pagan enjoyment, playful elegance, and this-worldliness.[4]

It would be a mistake, however, to assume that sixteenth-century humanists only wrote incidental poetry on trivial subjects. Many, for instance, set out to paraphrase the psalms and other portions of Scripture in Latin verse. Helius Eobanus Hessus, the *rex poetarum*, as Luther called him, turned the Psalms into Latin elegiac distichs. Neo-Latin poets produced a number of biblical epics (e.g., Marco Girolamo Vida's *Christiad*) and countless epyllia. Christ's descent into hell was a favorite subject for shorter epics during this period.[5] Erasmus wrote a *Carmen heroicum de solemnitate paschali atque de tryumphali Christi resurgentis pompa eius ad inferos*.[6] And these poets often contemplated the sober mystery of death.[7] Funeral elegies, whether in the form of epitaphs, dirges (*epicedia*), or songs of comfort (*consolationes*), were as ubiquitous, it would seem, as the funerals of humanists themselves.[8]

---

2 For a discussion of Neo-Latin pastoral poetry, see David Marsh's essay in *Brill's Encyclopaedia of the Neo-Latin World* (Leiden: E.J. Brill, 2014), 425–36.

3 Francis Cairns, "Fracastoro's *Syphilis*, the Argonautic Tradition, and the Aetiology of Syphilis," *Humanistica Lovaniensia* 43 (1994): 246–61.

4 Peter Gay makes this point in *The Enlightenment: The Rise of Modern Paganism* (New York: Knopf, 1966).

5 See Ralf Georg Czapla, *Das Bibelepos in der Frühen Neuzeit: Zur deutschen Geschichte einer europäischen Gattung* (Berlin/Boston: De Gruyter, 2015), 709–16.

6 See my "Macarius Mutius' *De Triumpho Christi:* Christian Epic Theory and Practice in the Late Quattrocento," *Acta Conventus Neo-Latini Torontonensis* (Binghamton, NY: SUNY-Binghamton Press, 1991), 745.

7 See K.O. Conrady, *Lateinische Dichtungstradition und deutsche Lyrik des 17. Jahrhunderts* (Bonn: Bouvier, 1962), 277: *Die neulateinische Lyrik des 16. wie die deutsche Lyrik des 17. Jahrhunderts meditieren mit gleicher Anstrengung und in thematisch wenig unterschiedener Weise über Zeit und Vergänglichkeit, über die Wandelbarkeit der Dinge und über das Mysterium des Todes* ("The neo-Latin lyric of the sixteenth century, like the German lyric of the seventeenth, meditates, with the same effort and in a thematically not dissimilar way, upon time and transience, upon the mutability of things and upon the mystery of death").

8 See Susanna de Beer, "Elegiac Poetry," *Brill's Encyclopaedia of the Neo-Latin World* (Leiden: E.J. Brill, 2014), 396, on the poems which were written on the occasion of Erasmus's death and published in 1536.

What all these Neo-Latin poems have in common, whether they are grand epics or mere *nugae*, and regardless of their various content, is that they turn away from the accentual, end-rhymed verse of the Middle Ages and instead return to the quantitative meter and largely unrhymed verse of the classical Latin poets. As the humanists reimagined the world the ancient Greeks and Romans inhabited, they conceived of it as altogether different from and superior to the Middle Ages, not only in terms of art and architecture (compare St. Peter's Basilica in Rome with Chartres Cathedral) but also the Latin language. The utilitarian, unadorned style of Aquinas's prose was unceremoniously rejected in favor of Cicero and Quintilian by Renaissance and Reformation humanists alike. Lorenzo Valla describes "monastic Latin" as the language spoken by "a stupid, fat, and heavy clergyman who spouts forth these opinions and these words while intoxicated by the heat of wine."[9] The scholastic Latin which the humanists had learned in school and the medieval hymns which they had once sung in church they now deplored. Not Bernard of Clairvaux or Jacopone da Todi but Virgil and Martial were the new poetic authorities. The Latin poetry of the humanists sounded less like *Dies irae, dies illa / Solvet saecla in favilla / Teste David cum Sibylla* (attributed to Thomas of Celano; 13th c.) than *Arma virumque cano Troiae qui primus ab oris* (the opening words of Virgil's *Aeneid*).

Now, Luther certainly was not a typical humanist (Petrarch, Erasmus, or even his colleague at Wittenberg, Philip Melanchthon, come more readily to mind). But despite his deep differences with Erasmus and other humanists on the question of human freedom, we must consider Luther a humanist, too, insofar as he sincerely shared their deep commitment to returning to the languages and literature of the ancient Greeks and Romans. The only books that he took with him when he entered the cloister in Erfurt were copies of Virgil and Plautus.[10] While not himself a strict Ciceronian, Luther loved "the dear man" Cicero and even went so far as to hope that there might be a place for him in heaven.[11] Like other humanists, he complained about the deficiencies of medieval Latin:

9 Wilfried Stroh, *Latein ist tot, es lebe Latein* (Berlin: Ullstein, 2007), 167.

10 WA TR 1:44.

11 *Er hat fleissig geerbeit, ut sciret, quid esset Deus, et eo pervenit etiam, ut unum tantum Deum esse statueret. Wolan, Deus est iustus iudex. Er wirds wol mit den selben leuten machen, denn das auch Cicero so ser solt verdampt sein als Caiphas, das gleube ich nicht; wie der tzu unterst in der hell sitzt, wirt Cicero im paradeis sein* ("He [Cicero] worked sedulously to find out what God is, and he even got to the point where he could establish that there is only one God. Very well then, God is a just judge. He will treat such people well, because

> So in the monastery, all the fathers read *mumpsimus* instead of *sumpsimus*. When a younger monk tried to correct them, they said: "You young whippersnapper; are you going to set us straight? We have read *mumpsimus* for such a long time; it must remain *mumpsimus*."

Luther dismissed such obscurantism with a vulgarity: "That's the kind of *Bescheisserei* that they engaged in."[12] And, like other northern reformers (Erasmus, Beza, Melanchthon), Luther, too, wrote Neo-Latin poems. Some thirty in all have come down to us.[13]

It was not inevitable that Luther would write Latin poetry in the classical style. His colleague Karlstadt was unimpressed with classical learning in general and criticized Lutheran humanists for using "worldly-wise" language that was "courtly" and "cosmetic."[14] All of the reformers wrote Latin prose, but not necessarily verse. Calvin wrote only one Latin poem that we know of (*Epinicion Christo Cantatum*; CR 33:425–28). Unlike Latin prose, Latin verse had relatively little practical utility in the sixteenth century. One could say with some justification that Luther *had* to use Latin prose to write theological treatises, give lectures, and write letters, if he was to be taken seriously as an academic or have a larger influence as a theologian. But why would this busy reformer have permitted himself to take so much time from his crowded schedule to compose Latin verse (a time-consuming process even for accomplished poets)?

One answer is that writing Latin poetry may have helped to make clear Luther's solidarity with other humanists who also enjoyed writing Latin poetry. Early on in his career Luther seems to have been quite interested in demonstrating to learned readers his dedication to humanist principles, his

---

I do not believe that Cicero should be as severely condemned as Caiaphas; as he sits in the lowest part of hell, Cicero will be in paradise," WA 5:413).

12 *Ita in monasterio omnes patres legerunt mumpsimus pro sumpsimus; iunior frater ex grammatica aliquando reprehendens, dixerunt reliqui: Du junger lecker, wiltu uns straffen? Wir haben also lange mumpsimus gelesen; es sol und muss mumpsimus heissen und bleiben … Solche Beschisserei ist mit ihnen gewesen* (WA TR 5:685–86 [No. 6479]).

13 We still await a thorough analysis of Luther's Latin poetry. Udo Frings, *Martinus Lutherus—Poeta Latinus* (Aachen: Hauptabteilung Erziehung und Schule im Bischöflichen Generalvikariat, 1983), is all too brief (46 pages). O. Albrecht's discussion of Luther's Latin verse in WA 35:596–606, is helpful but does not go into depth. "The necessary observations" of Georg Schleusner, *D. Martin Luthers Dichtungen in gebundener Rede mit den nötigen Anmerkungen* (Wittenberg: P. Wunschmanns Verlag, 1892) are minimalistic. Georg Bäsecke, *Luther als Dichter* = Hallische Universitätsreden 65 (Halle: Niemeyer, 1935), concentrates on Luther's German poetry.

14 Calvin Pater, *Karlstadt as the Father of the Baptist Movement: The Emergence of Lay Protestantism* (Toronto: University of Toronto Press, 1984), 65.

interest in returning *ad fontes*. In 1523, he turned, for instance, to the first lines of Virgil's *Aeneid* when he wanted to attack his annoying adversary, Johann Cochlaeus.[15] But he could have demonstrated the same intention by writing Latin prose in the Ciceronian style, not Latin verse. And Luther's interest in writing Latin verse was certainly not confined to his earlier years when he was in more frequent contact with humanists like Erasmus. His longest Latin poems were written quite late in his life; he used one of Martial's best known epigrams (10.47) to set Psalm 128 to Latin verse in 1543, just a few years before his death.[16]

Another explanation for why Luther wrote Latin poetry in the classical style is that he may have wished thereby to demonstrate that the Wittenberg reformation was not to be confused with reform movements (e.g., the Anabaptists) that made their indifference to the classics manifestly clear and whose anti-intellectual disregard for traditional education in the liberal arts Luther and his colleague Melanchthon vigorously opposed. Not only as a young professor at Wittenberg, but throughout the course of his academic career, Luther continued to support with great enthusiasm the study of the classics in general and Latin in particular. His own personal commitment to writing Latin poetry would have made it clear that he was entirely serious about the benefits of an education grounded in the languages and literatures of the ancient Greeks and Romans.[17]

Perhaps the best answer to the question of why Luther would have written Latin poetry is that he simply enjoyed doing so. We know that Luther relished reading and listening to poetry: "For I do admit that I am one of those whom poems move more forcefully, delight more intensely, and stick with more persistently than prose, yes, even if the prose is written by Cicero himself and Demosthenes" (WA Br 8:107). And even though he himself may have deprecated his poetic abilities,[18] there were others who thought that he was good at writing poetry. Melanchthon tells us that Luther excelled in composing verses

15 See my "Arms and the Theologian: *Adversus Armatum Virum Cochlaeum*," *International Journal of the Classical Tradition* 10 (2003): 38–53. Luther credited his success in writing German hymns to Virgil: *Der Poet Virgilius hat mir solches gelehret, der also seine Carmina und Wort auf die Geschichte, die er beschreibt, so künstlich applicieren kann* ("The poet Virgil has taught me such, who can so artistically apply his *carmina* and word to the story that he describes," WA 19:50).

16 See my "Martin's Martial: Reconsidering Luther's Relationship with the Classics," *International Journal of the Classical Tradition* 14 (2007): 23–50. See also chapter 4 of this volume.

17 On this point, see my *Cicero in Heaven: The Roman Rhetor and Luther's Reformation* (Leiden and Boston: Brill, 2017), ch. 3.

18 *Nam poetae nolo ullo modo comparari, sicut nec debeo neque possum* ("For I do not wish in any way to be compared to a poet, as I neither ought nor can," WA Br 5:549).

as a schoolboy.[19] Indeed, some of the Latin poems that we have from his pen are quite complicated. In one poem, for instance, he uses various forms of the Latin word *merda* 12 times, a very sophisticated example of a figure of speech called *polyptoton*.[20]

If Luther appreciated the ludic qualities of verse, its capacity to delight the reader and listener (and the author), we should not thereby assume that his Latin poetry must somehow be less than serious. The figure of *polyptoton* in *Dysenteria Lutheri adversus merdipoetam Lemchen* is not used simply to delight Luther's readers, but also to remind them of one of the fundamental principles of Lutheran theology, justification by faith and not by good works (cf. Phil 3:8). The Latin word for "good works" (*merita*) sounds quite similar to *merda*. The pun makes a profound theological point—playfully. Luther's poetic mirth is "pious," like that of the angels in Catherine Winkworth's translation of the final stanza of Luther's famous Christmas hymn, "From Heaven Above."[21] Luther knew that there was more to being a poet than simply mastering the formal elements of art for art's sake.[22] His Latin poems were not merely diversions or distractions, any more than his German chorales were, but were intimately involved in the theological principles for which he cared so deeply.

In this connection, there are two Latin poems of Luther's to which I want to call attention. The first is his verse paraphrase of Psalm 118:17. In it Luther declares that he will not die, despite his not infrequent brushes with mortality, but continue to live and go on preaching the Gospel:

Non moriar, sed vivus ero vivusque manebo

---

19 *Et in scribenda soluta oratione et in versibus ceteros adolescentes, qui una discebant, facile vicit* ("He easily outdid the other youths who studied together with him, both in the writing of prose and verse," Frings, *Martinus Lutherus—Poeta Latinus*, 3). On Melanchthon's eulogistic biography of Luther, see Harald Weinacht, ed., *Melanchthon und Luther: Merkmal einer Kirchenreform: Martin Luthers Lebensbeschreibung durch Philipp Melanchthon* (Zurich: TVZ, 2008).

20 A famous example of *polyptoton* in the English language can be found in the Gettysburg Address: "Government of the people, by the people, for the people." Substitute "poop" for "people" and you get some idea of the effect Luther's poem must have had! For further discussion of this poem, see my "Luther's Latin Poetry and Scatology," *Lutheran Quarterly* 23 (2009): 373–87. For the text of the poem, see WA TR 4:89–90 (No. 4032).

21 "Glory to God in highest Heaven / Who unto man His Son has given / While angels sing with pious mirth / A glad New Year to all the earth." From Catherine Winkworth's *Lyra Germanica: Hymns for the Sundays and Chief Festivals of the Church Year* (London: Longman, Brown, Green, and Longmans, 1855), 14. See also my discussion in "Pious Mirth: Poetry and Theology in Luke 2:13–14," *Faith-Life* 86:4 (2013): 2–10.

22 *Non est esse poetam nosse quantitatem syllabarum* ("To know the quantities of syllables is not to be a poet," WA TR 5:326 (No. 5709).

Et narrabo mei facta stupenda Dei.
Seu vivam, seu non vivam, tamen undique vivam.
Vita mea est Christus, quid mihi mors noceat?

I will not die but I will be alive and remain alive,
And I will tell the amazing deeds of my God.
Whether I live or do not live, nonetheless I will live in every respect.
My life is Christ, how could death harm me?[23]

Life and death are in a fierce struggle here. The key words follow each other in close succession in the first line: *Non moriar, sed vivus*. *Moriar* comes first, to be sure, but it is quickly overtaken and overwhelmed by the repeated *vivus*. Luther could be thinking here of dangerous illnesses he suffered or perilous situations in which he kept finding himself. It often appeared to Luther and those around him that he was about to die. But he had not, yet, and, as he avers here, he will not. He will remain living.

Now what does life mean for Luther? What does it mean to be *vivus?* The poet quickly makes that clear in the next line. He will not simply keep on breathing, "remaining," literally (*manebo*), but he will continue to "tell" (*narrabo*). His new lease on life means that he will be able to carry on with his ministry of teaching and preaching the gospel. Notice that he encloses the amazing deeds which he is going to tell between the adjective in the genitive case, *mei* ("of my"), and the noun in the genitive case that it modifies, *Dei* ("God"). These are God's deeds, not Luther's, to be sure. God does it all, *sola gratia*. But Luther is going to be the one telling God's deeds.

It avails the reader to "listen" carefully to the sound of Luther's verse. To appreciate poetry, one must pay attention not just to what is said but how it sounds. The sound affirms the sense, heightens the impact of the meaning of the words. Notice the rhyme in the second line, not an end rhyme, but an internal rhyme on *mei* and *Dei*, the two critical words at the end of the two halves of this line. They go together like "Jill" and "hill" in the familiar childhood poem.

Rhyme consists of two elements: first, there must be a common phonological element to the two words that are being rhymed. In the case of the nursery poem "-ill" is common to both rhymed words. And, secondly, there must be a phonological difference; at the beginning of the rhymed words in question, the first sound is J, but the second sound is H. Likewise, in these Latin verses the rhymed words are *mei* with an M, and *Dei* with a D. *Mei* refers to Luther,

23 WA 35:606.

the one who is going to die, if not now, then eventually; *Dei* refers to God, the one who is keeping him alive to preach the everlasting Gospel. The two are different, of course: God does not get sick; God does not worry about dying. Yet, nevertheless Luther and God share something vitally important: Luther will live eternally just as God does, thanks to the everlasting Gospel. Thus, fittingly, Luther and God rhyme.

The second distich takes the idea of ongoing life much further than the Psalm verse does. Even when Luther does die, as he now admits that he will, he will nonetheless continue to live *undique* ("in every respect"), because Christ is his life. Luther echoes the words of Paul in Philippians 1:21: "For me to live is Christ...." *Vivam* ("I will live") is repeated three times in one line. This figure (*epiphora* or *epistrophe*) achieves its effect in a way that is quite different from *polyptoton*. The inflected endings do not change at all. But it is the repetition without variation that makes the figure all the more emphatic. The repetition of *vivam ... vivam ... vivam* sounds like a bell, ringing the same powerful peal, one after the other, tolling not death but life.

Death is a reality. It is the second word in the poem, and it is the second to the last word in the poem. It frames the poem. Death is the reason for the poem; it is the embracing context. "In the midst of earthly life, snares of death surround us." But despite its apparent ubiquity, finality, and power, death has lost its ability to hurt Christians, as the Apostle declares (1 Cor 15:55): "O death, where is your sting?" Or, as Luther puts it in his Easter chorale, "Christ Lay in Death's Strong Bands" (*Christ lag in Todesbanden*): *da bleybt nichts denn tods gestalt, / Die stachel hat er verloren.*[24] The last words of the Latin poem strike an equally triumphant note: *Quid mihi mors noceat?* "How may death harm me?"

Let us consider, too, another example of Luther's poetry. Luther wrote A Latin epitaph for his daughter Magdalena, his own version of "Death and the Maiden":[25]

Dormio cum sanctis hic Magdalena Lutheri
  Filia et hoc strato tecta quiesco meo.
Filia mortis eram, peccati semine nata,
  Sanguine sed vivo, Christe, redempta tuo.

I sleep here with the saints, Magdalena, daughter of Luther,

24 "There remains nothing but death's guise, it has lost its sting," WA 35:606.

25 *Der Tod und das Mädchen* is the title of a short German poem by the pietist poet Matthias Claudius (1740–1851), set to memorable music by Franz Schubert.

> And I take my rest covered in this my bed;
> I was a daughter of death, born of the seed of sin,
> But I live, redeemed by your blood, O Christ.[26]

The deep tenderness of Luther's feelings for his daughter is evident in his use of gentle, even euphemistic, terms for death in the first two lines.[27] He describes Magdalena as though she were simply sleeping or quietly resting in a bed. He avoids such predictable words as "death" or "coffin" or "grave" that must surely have been on his mind as he wrote these lines. Magdalena is *tecta*, "covered." That could refer to a wool blanket or a comfortable quilt. She has been tucked in for the last time. Like Jairus's daughter, Luther's child is not dead but sleeping (Mark 5:39).

Still, death cannot (and should not) be completely euphemized. *Tecta* could also refer to the earth that Luther may have helped to shovel into her grave. "Dust thou art and unto dust shalt thou return" (Gen 3:19). Magdalena is a daughter of dust. Adam, whose name has something to do with earth, the man by whom sin entered into the world and death by sin, is her father. So, that also makes her, as Luther puts it here, "a daughter of death." She is Luther's daughter, to be sure, but she has another powerful filial relationship, too.

There is a Latin saying that suggests one should say only good things about the dead: *de mortuis nihil nisi bonum*. But Luther ignores this polite bit of worldly etiquette. His beloved daughter was a sinner, *peccati semine nata*. Luther suffers from no illusions about who his daughter was. She was, after all, his daughter! Just like her father, she was *simul iustus et peccator*. He does not talk here about what a good girl she was, or how innocent she was when she left this world at age 13. She is a sinner, and sinners need redemption. If by Adam's offence death reigned because of one, "much more they which receive abundance of grace and of the gift of righteousness shall reign in life by one, Jesus Christ" (Rom 5:17). Even after death, Magdalena will live because her sins have been forgiven through the redemptive blood of Christ, shed for her and for many for the forgiveness of sins. What is expressed here is not an empty wish on Luther's part for some kind of vague continued spiritual existence for his daughter after death. His hope and hers for eternal life are inextricably connected with her faith in the one to whom Luther imagines that she is speaking:

---

26 WA TR 5:185–87 (No. 5490). For other examples, see Grazyna Urban-Godziek, "Patrum erga filiam amor luctuosus. L'espressione funebre dell'amore familiare nella poesia di Giovanni Pontano e Jan Kochanowski. Paralleli e ispirazioni," *Studi Slavistici* 3 (2006): 65–80.

27 See also Luther's moving expression of his own mixed and powerful feelings in WA TR 5:192–93 (No. 5497).

Christe, God's son, sent into the world to redeem it "from all sins, from *death*, and from the power of the Devil."[28]

Notice that it is Magdalena who is speaking in this poem. This, too, is an oft-used poetic figure, called *prosopopoeia*. Luther is the one speaking, really, of course, but he imagines his dead daughter speaking. Is that just an exercise of poetic fancy? I think not. You cannot talk if you are dead. As Isaiah says grimly (38:18): "For Sheol does not thank you; death does not praise you." But Luther's dead daughter, like Abel, through faith "still speaks" (Heb 11:4). *Vivo* ("I live"), she declares from the coffin. Magdalena is Christ's own, and that is why after death she lives "with him in his kingdom," serving "him in everlasting righteousness, innocence, and blessedness."[29]

How then shall we consider these two Latin poems written by Luther in the classical style on the subject of death? On the one hand, like other humanists, Luther must have enjoyed writing Latin poetry. He seems to have taken positive delight in using the unique capacity of poetry to create an elegant auditory experience that no doubt was as satisfying to himself as his well-educated readers. On the other hand, it is also clear that it was not just his fascination with the literary challenge that drew Luther to the composition of Latin verse. Neither death nor life after death were incidental topics for him.[30] Like Thomas Mann, Luther seems to have found the Latin language exceptionally well suited to one of the most profound of all possible poetic themes, death, and also that of life after death. Yet despite what Mann and others may assume about humanistic Latin and its incompatibility with serious subjects such as death, it seems that Luther wanted to use Latin verse in the classicizing style of the humanists, not in the manner of medieval Latin, to deal with the most pressing issues of his life. Thus he could be a Latin poet both in unmistakably classical and, at the same time, biblical terms.

---

28 From Luther's Small Catechism, as translated in *Lutheran Service Book* (St. Louis: Concordia Publishing House, 2006), 323.

29 From Luther's Small Catechism, as translated in *Lutheran Service Book*, 323. Some of the discussion of these two poems is drawn from my "Death and Life after Death in Martin Luther's Latin Elegies," in the *Acta Conventus Neo-Latini Upsaliensis*, ed. Astrid Steiner-Weber (Leiden: E.J. Brill, 2012), 1049–59.

30 "His greatest terror, one that came on him periodically as a horror of darkness, was the fear of death"; Richard Marius, *Martin Luther: The Christian between God and Death* (Cambridge, MA and London: Harvard University Press, 1999), xiii–xiv. Here as elsewhere in his study, there is an important kernel of truth in what Marius has to say, in spite of his exaggerations.

CHAPTER 4

Luther between Stoics and Epicureans

Carl P.E. Springer

Philosophy is the study of wisdom, and theology is the study of God. To judge from their etymologies alone, the two words must have something in common. In the late Middle Ages, it would have been hard to distinguish entirely between them. Was Thomas Aquinas a philosopher or a theologian? If wisdom is the same as Christ, as early Christians believed (on the basis of their reading of the books of Proverbs and the Wisdom of Solomon), and Christ is God as confessed in the ancient creeds, how exactly would the studious love of wisdom differ from the loving study of God? If their definitions are similar, so are their purposes. As practiced by the ancient Greeks and Romans, philosophy was a way for mortals to live their lives in preparation for dying. It was not purely an exercise in knowing for the sake of knowing. Philosophy was knowledge applied to life. Nor for medieval theologians was it enough simply to study God. The purpose of theology was to lead its students to God, not only to know him, but to live accordingly, that is to say, wisely. Since the Enlightenment, the two disciplines have come to be more sharply differentiated, especially as philosophy grew to be more often associated with the idea that truth could be pursued unfettered from a given metaphysical worldview (or as theologians might say, unmoored from the ground of its being), committed only to a rigorous adherence to a particular intellectual methodology.

It is no surprise, therefore, that the theologian Martin Luther should have been so familiar with the philosophers of ancient Greece and Rome. In the course of his education, especially as he was preparing for his master's and doctoral degrees and beginning his professorial career, he would have become thoroughly familiar with many of their ideas and their works. His nickname in college was *philosophus*.[1] As a late medieval academic it would have been impossible for him not to have been engaged, as he was, with Aristotle, the great Greek philosopher who was so important for the scholastic theologians of the late Middle Ages.[2] Any young man attending the University of Erfurt

1 Carl P.E. Springer, *Cicero in Heaven: The Roman Rhetor and Luther's Reformation* (Leiden: Brill, 2017), 124.

2 On Luther and Aristotle, see Theodor Dieter, *Der junge Luther und Aristoteles: Eine historisch-systematische Untersuchung zum Verhältnis von Theologie und Philosophie* (Berlin/New York: De Gruyter, 2001).

 | DOI:10.1163/9789004206717_006

at Luther's time, when Northern Humanism was in its flower, would have come to grips with Plato, the teacher of Aristotle, who influenced important Christian thinkers from Augustine to C.S. Lewis.[3] Nevertheless, it is surprising that throughout the course of his life, even after he had long ago emphatically repudiated them, Luther never ceased to argue with pagan philosophers.[4] He continued not only to find fault with their methodologies and conclusions but also to appreciate their insights when they coincided with those of the Gospel. And he himself used masterfully the traditional tools of philosophy, reason and dialectic, against whose misuse he so often railed, in the service of his own theology.

Even more surprising, perhaps, is that the ancient philosophy with which he seems to have become more and more engaged as he got older was that of Epicurus.[5] The Stoics and the Epicureans were philosophical schools that appeared on the Greek scene somewhat later than Plato and Aristotle, during the Hellenistic period, beginning in the fourth century BC. One of the central questions that interested practitioners of both philosophies was the problem of individual human happiness. How can we be truly happy? In a time of political turmoil and war, how can human beings manage to live their lives in a state of unruffled peace of mind, *ataraxia*?[6]

In response to these concerns, the Stoics, who believed in fate and endless repetition, suggested that we should simply embrace whatever is given to us to endure. Regardless, therefore, of whether one was a slave or a master, rich or poor, involved in politics or not, in love or celibate, every human being was capable of achieving *autarcheia*, self-sufficiency, and could as a result be happy, knowing that there is nothing we can do (or that anyone can do to us) that will change our fixed destinies. The Epicurean answer to the question of how one can achieve *ataraxia* was somewhat different. Their goal in life was to avoid the caprices of fortune, less predictable than fate but equally beyond humans' control, equally deterministic, although with effects random, not planned. One should steer clear of politics. Happiness is more attainable in the privacy of one's garden than in the public forum. One should also never fall in love.

3 Amy Nelson Burnett, *Debating the Sacraments: Print and Authority in the Early Reformation* (Oxford: Oxford University Press, 2019), 55–56.

4 For Luther's ambivalence about philosophy see the essays collected in Jennifer Dragseth, ed. *The Devil's Whore: Reason and Philosophy in the Lutheran Tradition* (Minneapolis: Fortress, 2011).

5 Gottfried Maron, *Martin Luther und Epikur: Ein Beitrag zum Verständnis des alten Luther* = Berichte aus den Sitzungen der Joachim Jungius—Gesellschaft der Wissenschaften E.V., Hamburg 6 (1988), Heft 1.

6 See William O. Stephens, *Stoic Ethics: Epictetus and Happiness as Freedom* (London: Bloomsbury, 2007) and Julia Annas, "Epicurus on Pleasure and Happiness," *Philosophical Topics* 15 (1987): 5–21.

The soul is more likely to remain unperturbed by friends than by lovers. Most important of all, unlike the Stoics who stressed the importance of duty, the Epicureans suggested that the goal of life was to pursue pleasure, true, lasting pleasure achieved not through excess, as they have often been misunderstood as promoting, but through moderation.

The early church saw many similarities between Pauline and Stoic teachings, especially those of Seneca (in fact it was commonly believed that the Apostle exchanged letters with the Roman Stoic),[7] but they practically dismissed Epicurus from consideration. His works were mostly lost. Only one or two manuscripts of Lucretius, the great Roman popularizer of Epicurus's philosophy, survived the Middle Ages.[8] The Reformers did not differ greatly from the Church Fathers in this regard.

There are a number of points of similarity between Luther's theology and that of Stoicism which have often been cited. One need only think of Luther's position on the bondage of the will. Stoic views on fate and the value of accepting one's destiny without complaint were certainly more compatible with his theology than the Epicurean doctrine of chance. Marjorie O'Rourke Boyle has pointed out the importance of paradox for both the Stoic philosophers and Luther's theology.[9] Elizabeth Agnew Cochran has studied the connection between "Protestant virtue" and "Stoic ethics."[10] Andries Raath has written an article on the "Stoic Roots of Early Reformational Resistance Theory."[11] By the same token, Luther's hearty disagreement with Epicureanism is well known and has been frequently studied. Luther famously associated Epicurus with Erasmus (in "The Bondage of the Will") and implied that his followers were cynical relativists who did not really believe in God or the afterlife.[12]

Accordingly, one way (the usual one) to explain why Luther took Epicureans and not Stoics so to task in his later years is simply that he continued to be so emphatically opposed to them. But such an unsubtle explanation may not do full justice to a complex question such as this one. It should not simply be assumed from the fact that Jesus rails so often against the scribes and the

7 See the essays collected in J. Dodson and D. Briones, eds., *Paul and Seneca in Dialogue* (Leiden: Brill, 2017).

8 David Butterfield, *The Early Textual History of Lucretius' De rerum natura* (Cambridge: Cambridge University Press, 2013).

9 Marjorie O'Rourke Boyle, "Stoic Luther: Paradoxical Sin and Necessity," *Archiv für Reformationsgeschichte* 73 (1982): 69–93.

10 Elizabeth Agnew Cochran, *Protestant Virtue and Stoic Ethics* (London: Bloomsbury; T & T Clark, 2018).

11 Andries Raath, "Stoic Roots of Early Reformational Resistance Theory," *Studia Historiae Ecclesiasticae* 35 (2009): 303–22.

12 See Volker Leppin and Kirsi Stjerna, *The Bondage of the Will, 1525* (Minneapolis: Fortress Press, 2016).

Pharisees in the Gospels that he had little in common with them or that he was more favorably inclined to the Sadducees whom he mentions less frequently. In fact, it is the adversaries whom one takes most seriously with whom one engages most vigorously. I suggest that Luther continued to argue with the Epicureans till the end of his life because he took them seriously, and he took them seriously because some, although by no means all, of their philosophical views actually coincided with his own.

To illustrate this, let us consider a poem that Luther wrote late in life, the year before he died, in response to a much earlier poem of Martial's, a Roman poet of the first century who wrote a famous epigram in Latin espousing an Epicurean view of life. Luther's poem is second, following Martial's original:

> Vitam quae faciant beatiorem,
> iucundissime Martialis, haec sunt:
> res non parta labore, sed relicta;
> non ingratus ager, focus perennis;
> lis numquam, toga rara, mens quieta;
> vires ingenuae, salubre corpus;
> prudens simplicitas, pares amici;
> convictus facilis, sine arte mensa;
> nox non ebria, sed soluta curis;
> non tristis torus et tamen pudicus;
> somnus qui faciat breves tenebras:
> quod sis esse velis nihilque malis;
> summum nec metuas diem nec optes.
>
> EPIGRAM 10.47

> ["Most delightful Martialis, the elements of a happy life are as follows: money not worked for but inherited; land not unproductive; a fire all the year round; lawsuits never, a gown rarely worn, a mind at peace; a gentleman's strength, a healthy body; guilelessness not naïve, friends of like degree, easy company, a table without frills; a night not drunken but free of cares; a marriage bed not austere and yet modest; sleep to make the dark hours short; wish to be what you are, wish nothing better; don't fear your last day, nor yet pray for it."][13]

---

13 I use D.R. Shackleton Bailey's edition and translation of the poem from the Loeb edition of Martial's epigrams (vol. 2; Cambridge, Mass. and London, 1993), 366–69. The "gown" (*toga*) was associated with civic duties as opposed to less formal clothing worn when relaxing at home.

Let us contrast this with Luther's Christianization of this same theme:

Vitam quae faciunt beatiorem,
O charissime christiane, sunt haec:
Aeternum Dominum Deum timere
Mandatique sui vias amare.
Sit victus manuum labore partus.
Sic vivis bene, sic agis beatus.
Uxor prole tuam domum beabit
Laetis ut generosa vitis uvis.
Ad mensam tibi filii sedebunt,
Ut pinguis tenerae novellae olivae.
Sic fidus benedicitur maritus
In casto Domini timore vivens.
Donet te benedictione semper
Ex Zion Dominus Hierusalemque.
Florentem faciat bonis videre,
Ut natos videas et inde natos.
Et pacem super Israel per aevum.
Hic dicat pius omnis Amen, Amen.[14]

Carmen antimartiale ex psalmo 127

["These are the things, O most dear Christian, which make for a happier life: fearing the eternal Lord God and loving the ways of his command. Let your food be gained by the work of your hands; this is how you live well; this is how you are happy. Your wife will bless your house with offspring like an abundant vine with happy grapes. Your sons will sit at your table like the fat shoots of a tender olive. Thus the faithful husband is blessed who lives in the chaste fear of the Lord. May the Lord bless you always from Zion and Jerusalem. May he make you see her flower with good things, so that you may see your sons and their sons. And may he bestow peace upon Israel forever. Let all the faithful say Amen here. Amen."][15]

14 I use the text of Luther's poem as it appears in WA TR 5:359 (No. 5795a). English translations here and elsewhere are my own, unless otherwise indicated.

15 For a fuller discussion, see my "Martin's Martial: Reconsidering Luther's Relationship with the Classics," *The International Journal of the Classical Tradition* 14 (2007): 23–50.

There can be no question that Luther is using this famous Latin poem, written by a follower of Epicurus, to take issue with Epicurean ideology. After all, his is a biblical poem, based on Psalm 128, entitled *Carmen Anti-Martiale*. The differences are obvious. For Luther, there is an eternal Lord God, one instead of many, who is not detached from human affairs, like the carefree gods of Epicurus, but who gives a blessed life to those who love his commands. Luther's view of human labor is much more positive (*sit victus manuum labore partus*) than Martial's (*res non parta labore sed relicta*).[16] Also, it is easy to see that the family is of greater importance to Luther's view of happiness; wife *and* children are gathered together at the table of his blessed man. Martial mentions the "marriage bed" in his poem but he himself was probably never married.[17] Finally, it is clear that Luther does not attribute human happiness to our own merits or sense of moderation but to the gracious blessing of God, who will give us peace forever.

It is important for us to understand that Luther's corrective psalmodic epigram participates in a time-honored form of poetic apologetic, going back as far as the fourth century, practiced by the earliest Christian Latin poets. Its purpose would seem to be what the Germans call *Kontrastimitation*. In other words, Luther expected that his learned readers (most doubtless quite familiar with Martial's famous epigram) would appreciate the challenge of searching out the differences between the epigram and the psalm.

Having noted these differences, however, we must not overlook some obvious points of commonality. This is after all, not a poem *contra* Martial, a complete refutation or repudiation, but rather a complementary piece, an *anti-Martiale* poem, as it is entitled. That means it is Luther's response to Martial, if you will, just as in Greek drama an *anti*strophe answers a strophe, expanding on a notion, exploring another dimension, but not necessarily repudiating it entirely.[18] What do the poems have in common? In the first place, obviously, Luther's poem is written in Martial's language and meter, Latin hendecasyllables,

---

16 Luther makes this point in one of his *Tischreden: Res non parta labore ist unrecht, quia Deus praecipit laborare in sudore vultus etc.* (WA TR 5:326 [No. 5709]). ["Property gained without working is not right, because God orders us to work in the sweat of the brow, etc."]

17 See J.P. Sullivan, *Martial: The Unexpected Classic. A Literary and Historical Study* (Cambridge: Cambridge University Press, 1991), 25–26 on whether Martial was ever married. See also Patricia Watson, "Martial's Marriage: A New Approach," *Rheinisches Museum* 146 (2003): 38–48.

18 I owe this insight to Alden Smith, to whom, along with other members of the audience at "Lutheranism and the Classics V" who raised questions and offered suggestions for improvement, I here express my gratitude.

a common meter used for short and pithy epigrams. Luther's first line is practically the same as Martial's, while the second line addresses the reader in the vocative, just like Martial's. The poems have the same acoustical footprint. Also, both poems share a common theme. Luther's and Martial's poems are about how best to live a happy life, and both authors suggest that the recipe to happiness is not wealth or worldly success but contentedness. Not riches or power but the everyday simple pleasures of the dining table and the bedroom in the company of others make for the happy life.[19] Finally, both poems have a similar character and purpose. They are not simply witty or sardonic (although Luther and Martial both wrote such epigrams), but earnest in tone and didactic in intent.

It is not surprising that Luther should have been as interested in the question of happiness, the *vita beata*, as the Epicureans and the Stoics ever were. The reason why God sent his son to the world was, as Luther puts it in his explanation to the second article, "that I may be his own and live under Him in His kingdom and serve Him in everlasting righteousness, innocence, and *blessedness*."[20] This everlasting blessedness is not only to be realized in heaven but begins also here on earth. Yes, Luther was deeply concerned with the ultimate issues of salvation, life and death, judgment and redemption, God and the devil. But such existential preoccupations did not prevent him from also paying attention to other, more quotidian, considerations: how families, governments, schools, and the like should be constituted here on earth in order to help Christians live safe, constructive, and, yes, happy lives this side of eternity. These concerns seem to have become even more pressing for Luther later in life, once he had children of his own and began to be involved in their rearing and education.[21]

The significance of Luther's poem may become clearer if we ask a fundamental question based on a different set of assumptions than the ones posited in the first paragraph of this chapter. Let us assume that there is nothing at all in common between philosophy and theology, between Athens and Jerusalem (as Tertullian famously put it),[22] and let us assume that the principle of *sola*

19 On *prudens simplicitas*, see Gregor Damschen and Andreas Heil, *Epigrammaton liber decimus. Das zehnte Epigrammbuch. Text, Übersetzung, Interpretationen. Mit einer Einleitung, Martial-Bibliographie und einem rezeptionsgeschichtlichen Anhang* = Studien zur klassischen Philologie 148 (Frankfurt: Peter Lang, 2004), 184.

20 From Luther's Small Catechism, as translated in *Lutheran Service Book* (St. Louis: Concordia Publishing House, 2006), 323.

21 I make this point in *Luther's Aesop* (Kirksville, MO: Truman State University Press, 2011), passim.

22 *De praescriptione haereticorum* 7.9 (Corpus Christianorum Series Latina 1:192).

scriptura means that one should only read the Bible and nothing else, because, after all, it is the only text that is necessary for salvation. If so, our subsequent question would be to ask why instead of writing this poem, Luther did not simply reprint Psalm 127 in the Hebrew original or reproduce his own German translation already in circulation. Or alternatively, why did he not put this and other poems by Martial and his fellow pagan poets on some sort of index of prohibited books?

One possible answer as to why Luther did not pursue options such as these was because he hoped or even expected that his Lutheran readers would already be familiar with Martial's popular pagan poem. The idea that any good Christian should be blissfully ignorant of the pagan classics would have made no more sense to Luther than it did to C.S. Lewis. In a letter he wrote in Latin to a Catholic priest after WWII in which he recommends the study of the classics as a valuable propaedeutic, Lewis writes: *Fere auserim dicere "Primo faciamus juniores bonos Paganos et postea faciamus Christianos."* "I would almost dare to say 'First let us make the younger generation good pagans and afterwards let us make them Christians.'"[23] Luther himself believed that the good common sense of Aesop's pagan fables was second only to the Bible and valued the outstanding ethical teachings and personal example of Cicero so highly that he wished he might be given a place in heaven.[24] Both pagan authors were to be read by Lutheran children in school.[25] Like the Old Testament laws, Martial's epigram has its valid, albeit limited, function, to serve as a "schoolmaster to bring us to Christ" (Gal. 3:24). The latter did not come to do away with the Law but to fulfill it. The ethical principles to be found in Cicero's *De officiis* are not so different as one might suppose, *mutatis mutandis*, from those of the "Table of Duties" in Luther's *Small Catechism*.

There is another assumption and another question to be considered here. If we take it for granted that Luther's main interest lay in communicating the Gospel as efficiently as possible to the largest possible audience, then it makes little sense indeed for him to have used Latin poetry instead of German prose, as he does in this little poem, to express his views on the happy life. It is true that more people were able to understand Latin in his day than now, but German would certainly have been much more accessible to the great

23 Martin Moynihan, ed., *The Latin Letters of C.S. Lewis* (South Bend, IN: St. Augustine's Press, 1988), 92–93.

24 See my *Cicero in Heaven: The Roman Rhetor and Luther's Reformation* (Leiden: Brill, 2017).

25 On the importance of *De officiis* for Melanchthon, see Anne Eusterschulte, "Zur Rezeption von 'De officiis' bei Philipp Melanchthon und im Kreis seiner Schüler," 323–62 in *Cicero in der frühen Neuzeit*, eds. Anne Eusterschulte and Günter Frank (Stuttgart-Bad Cannstatt: frommann-holzboog, 2018).

majority of Luther's fellow countrymen at this time. Also, if we are to think practically, in terms of his own workload, Luther was very busy indeed with numerous pressing ecclesiastical matters late in his life, and it clearly takes a much longer time to write a poem than to express the same ideas in prose. If all of this is true, why would the Reformer "waste" valuable time composing Latin hendecasyllables? In answering this question, we must remind ourselves that efficiency, that preoccupying concern of our own commercial age, was by no means the only consideration Luther had in mind, late in life or earlier. Indeed, it seems clear that he read and wrote Latin poetry, among other reasons, simply because it gave him pleasure to do so. Perhaps that is still the best reason for reading and writing poetry.[26]

One final, clarifying, question: if Luther was more indebted to the Stoics than to the Epicureans, why did he not simply draw on the philosophical tenets of the Roman philosopher Seneca, with whose Stoic ideas on the subject of how best to live one's life Luther was quite familiar, rather than the Epicurean Martial? The answer to this question, I suggest, is that Luther's moral philosophy in general and his views on the subject of the happy life in particular were actually more closely aligned with the pleasure-loving Epicureans than the stern-minded Stoics.

"Pleasure" was not a negative word for Luther. In Psalm 1, the blessed man takes "delight" (*Lust* is how Luther translates the Hebrew) in the Law of the Lord, on which he meditates day and night. The believer's life is characterized by God-pleasing pleasure. Just think of the obvious pleasure Luther personally took in music.[27] This theologian/philosopher wrote popular poetry which he set to music, and he himself played the lute. Why? Because it made him and others happy. The German adjective describing "the prince of this world" in Luther's famous hymn, *Ein' feste Burg*, is *sauer* ("sour"). Luther knew the devil as "the creator of saddening cares and disquieting worries," but he also knew that he could easily be put to flight by sweet music, which was second only to theology in Luther's mind, thanks in large part to this unusual power.[28] Like

26 None of this is to suggest that Andrew Pettegree's insights about Luther's engagement with the "business" aspects of the Reformation, especially when it came to the printing of his works (see *Brand Luther*, New York: Penguin, 2015), are invalid. Luther was very much interested in the practical aspects of the publishing business and not at all opposed in principle to efficiency or unaware of marketing considerations. These were not, however, his only (or primary) concerns.

27 See Miikka E. Anttila, *Luther's Theology of Music: Spiritual Beauty and Pleasure* (Berlin: De Gruyter, 2013).

28 See Robin Leaver, *Luther's Liturgical Music* (Grand Rapids, MI: Eerdmans, 2007), 93.

music, pleasurable activities such as dancing and even drinking (in moderation, of course) could also be put to good use in dispelling the isolating attacks of the gloomy tempter. For someone with a "melancholic head," which, as Luther colorfully puts it, Satan may use as "his bathtub," it is not a good idea to be alone or to have "an empty stomach."[29]

Real, lasting pleasure is to be found in the company of others. This is a fundamental doctrine of the Epicureans, and it is a common theme in both Martial's and Luther's epigrams. Over time, it seems, Luther grew to hate the idea of monastic isolation more and more. Far from bringing the believer closer to God, as had so often been supposed, ascetic deprivations of any kind, including the company of friends and family, were more likely to give the devil even greater opportunity for *Anfechtungen* or, as Luther rendered the notion of temptation in his version of the Lord's Prayer, *Versuchung*.[30] Iconic pictures of Luther from later centuries, like that of Gustav Adolph Spangenberg in 1875, feature him in the midst of his family, surrounded by his loved ones, lute in hand. In Spangenberg's portrayal, Philip Melanchthon is included in the Luther family, even though he is not a blood relative. Luther was not a loner, unlike Jerome in his monastic cell, or the bachelor Erasmus, but a social being who cherished his association with wife, children, and friends. He loved to compliment his friends, to challenge them to do better, to write them poems such as these, and above all to have them sit around the table with him. (The Latin word for "table," *mensa*, occurs in both Martial's and Luther's epigrams.) We have six stout volumes of his *Table Talks* which give the reader a rather good idea of how much pleasure he derived from eating and drinking and talking in the company of his friends. His wife, Katie, sometimes joined them. He teased her, too.

To be sure, Luther was not an epicure, in the vulgar sense of the word. He certainly did not precipitate the Reformation so that he might have an excuse to forsake his monastic vows and to marry and have children. Though he personally enjoyed beer, he abhorred drunkenness in general. He praised sex as a God-given gift, but railed against lasciviousness. He was also no particular fan of the poet Martial, whose obscene verse he expressly recommended against

29 WA TR 2:64 (No. 1349). (See also WA TR 1:122–23 [No. 294] and WA TR 2:33 [No. 1299].) For more on Luther's attitude toward the devil and his *tentationes*, see my "The Uses of *Tentatio*: Satan, Luther, and Theological Maturation," 27–46 in *The Hermeneutics of Hell: Devilish Visions and Visions of the Devil in World Literature* (Cham: Palgrave Macmillan, 2017).

30 For more on this subject, see Paul Bühler, *Die Anfechtung bei Martin Luther* (Zürich: Zwingli-Verlag, 1942).

teaching in Lutheran schools. But Luther did indulge in Epicurean moral doctrines where they might coincide with biblical ideas, and he expressed that coincidence in beautiful, memorable language that harks back, if not to Epicurus himself, at least to one of that philosopher's finest poetic representatives, Martial. "Eat, drink, for tomorrow we may die" is how St. Paul pithily characterized that school of thought (1 Cor. 15:32). To this point of view Luther's philosophical and theological answer might well be, "Eat and drink, for we have been made alive."

CHAPTER 5

Philtered Philosophy: Aristotle and Cicero in Luther's *Tischreden*

R. Alden Smith

> And although we see that the heathen philosophers now and then discoursed touching God and his wisdom very pertinently, so that some have made prophets of Socrates, of Xenophon, of Plato, etc., yet, because they knew not that God sent his Son Christ to save sinners, such fair, glorious, and wise-seeming speeches and disputations are nothing but mere blindness and ignorance.
>
> HAZLITT trans.[1]

This opening quotation amply reveals Luther's *men / de* ("on the one hand, on the other hand") relationship to the ancient philosophers in the *Tischreden*. Put positively, while Platonic and Aristotelian philosophical systems certainly do not dominate Luther's thought, from time to time elements of both are clearly important for him; they are not merely to be refuted. As Carl Springer has noted, Luther had, after all, begun his career as a young professor at Wittenberg lecturing on, not complaining about, Aristotle four times per week.[2] Earlier on, when circa 1505 Luther had gained his Master's degree in philosophy at the University of Erfurt, he was thoroughly steeped in Aristotelian philosophy.[3] Yet, as Roper notes, at that point, "nothing indicated the course that Luther's thinking would later take."[4] Thus it happened that Luther slowly began to resist Aristotle's dominance in the Academy of his day, particularly as he withdrew his allegiance from papal authority.[5]

---

1 Cf. WA TR 6:118 (No. 6682). All translations in this article are my own or, as indicated passim, that of William Hazlitt, *The Table Talk of Martin Luther* (George Bell & Sons: London, 1884).

2 Carl Springer, *Luther's Aesop* (Kirksville, MO: Truman State University Press, 2011), 23.

3 Lyndal Roper, *Martin Luther: Renegade and Prophet* (New York: Random House, 2017): 32.

4 Roper, *Martin Luther*, 32.

5 Springer, *Luther's Aesop*, 23.

 | DOI:10.1163/9789004206717_007

Nevertheless, *Table Talk* records Luther's wariness about Greek philosophers and reveals his whelmed attitude toward their often overblown status, as we see in the opening quotation. Luther notes, too, that the influence of philosophy has even cleverly infiltrated and led astray the school education of his day:

> Ego maxime optarem, ut Prudentii carmen in scholis praelegeretur, sed scholae iam in dies incipiunt profanari, et sacrae litterae iterum expelluntur ex illis [oder mit der Philosophie vermischt und verfälscht].
> WA TR 4:96 [No. 4042]

> I would especially wish that the poem of Prudentius were read in schools, but schools nowadays are beginning to become heathen, and Holy Writ is banished from them [or filtered and sophisticated through philosophy].

This resistance to philosophy that had begun to arise in Luther's time itself stemmed from a dichotomy of thought that was happening not only in Luther's mind, particularly when he taught in Wittenberg, but around him as well. Roper has called the sum of the ideas resisted the *via antiqua*, a blend of "old school" scholastic learning of the Middle Ages, when Greek originals were known only through Latin compendia. With fresh Renaissance learning, a new way developed, which began slowly in various studia that sprouted up first in Italy and soon throughout northern Europe.[6] Meanwhile, this fresh approach was baptized into Reformation thought, where it saw a downplaying of ancient "pagan" philosophy, which had made (and was still making) quite a comeback in the Renaissance, of course.[7]

Thus, in certain academic circles—those of reformed thinking—a "via moderna," as Roper calls it, came into being, as articulated by Johannes Lang, prior of the Monastery of Erfurt. Lang proposed this in 1516, early on in his administrative responsibilities in that monastery, stating that students nowadays "are all excited and enthusiastic about the lectures on the Bible and the early Fathers, whereas the study of the scholastic doctors (as they are called) attract maybe two or three students" (*sacram bibliam antiquosque scriptores*

6 Roper, *Martin Luther*, 31–33; Jeffrey M. Hunt, R.A. Smith, and Fabio Stok, *Classics from Papyrus to the Internet: An Introduction to Transmission and Reception* (Austin: University of Texas Press, 2017), 161; Heiko Oberman, *Luther: Mensch zwischen Gott und Teufel* (Berlin: Severin and Seidler, 1982), 169.

7 Hunt et al., *Classics from Papyrus to the Internet*, 132–35; 194f.

complures et anhelant et laetanter audiunt, dum scholastici doctores [quod appellant] vix aut duos aut treis habent auditores).[8]

Nevertheless, as Springer has deftly shown, not all pagans fare as badly in the *Tischreden* as Aristotle and his gaggle of Greeklings.[9] Indeed, Luther goes so far as to admit that he favors Cicero, touting his preference for *De officiis* to Aristotle's *Ethics*:[10]

> Mirari non possum, cur nunc laudent adeo Aristotelis philosophiam et non magis Ciceronis, viri qui in negotiis maxime conversatus est, quod Officia eius testantur …
>
> WA TR 2:456 [No. 2412a]

> I cannot be surprised at why they now so praise Aristotle's philosophy and not more that of Cicero, a man who was especially engaged in business, to which his *De officiis* amply testifies …

There are two further examples of a similar ilk. The first scolds Aristotle as asinine:

> Officia Ciceronis multum praestant Ethicis Aristotelis, et Cicero, homo plenus curarum et onerum civilium, tamen longe excellit otiosum asinum Aristotelem, qui abundabat pecunia et otio.
>
> WA TR 2:456 [2412b]

> Cicero's *De officiis* far outstrips Aristotle's *Ethics*, and Cicero was a man full of concerns and the burdens of state; he nevertheless far excels the otiose and even asinine Aristotle, who had much more money and free time.

Elsewhere Luther is less abrasive, but his preference for Cicero is clear:

> Cicero ubertrifft Aristotelem weit in Philosophia und mit Lehren. Officia Ciceronis sind viel besser, denn Ethica Aristotelis. Und nachdem Cicero in großen Sorgen …
>
> WA TR 2:457 [2412b]

---

8 Text and translation from Kenneth Hagen, "An Addition to the Letters of John Lang: Introduction and Translation," *Archiv für Reformationsgeschichte* 60 (1969): 28, 30.

9 Carl P.E. Springer, *Cicero in Heaven: The Roman Rhetor and Luther's Reformation* (Leiden: Brill, 2018).

10 Cf. Carl P.E. Springer, *Luther's Rome, Rome's Luther* (Minneapolis: Fortress Press, 2020): 53–57; 63–66.

Cicero far outstrips Aristotle in philosophy and teaching. Cicero's *De officiis* is much better than Aristotle's *Ethics*. And Cicero was once in the midst of great cares ...

Why does Luther prefer Cicero? Part of the reason Luther tells us fairly openly: even though he was a man of action and in serving the state had little time in comparison to Aristotle to formulate his philosophical system, nevertheless Cicero raises the God question with greater candor than his Greek predecessor. Aristotle may define the problem, but Cicero solves it—from a pagan perspective, of course, and thus only obliquely. Most of all, Cicero does so eloquently and Luther, following Seneca, believes sincerely that eloquence is of high value:

Tardiloquentia est convenientissima homini praedicatori. Quae praemeditatius et accuratius proponere potest suas contiones. Et Seneca de Cicerone scribit, quod ipse fuerit tardiloquus et emphaticus ...

WA TR 4:420 [No. 4657]

Slow and deliberate speech best befits the preacher; This quality can advance his sermon more effectually and accurately. And Seneca writes about Cicero, that he was slow of speech and emphatic ...

For Luther, Cicero is the best of the ancient philosophers. This is in part because his filtering and distillation of Greek philosophy in fact refined it and allowed him to offer a philosophical mélange that was, generally speaking, more compatible with Christianity. Yet it is also true, and perhaps especially so, because Cicero was eloquent in his exposition. Homiletics was not Luther's specialty, per se, but he understood the value of that part of theological discipline. And, under the spell of Cicero, having drunk of his rhetorical philter, so to speak, Luther, like Cicero came to look down upon the Greeks a bit, seeing them as clever but impractical. One can't be entirely sure why this is the case, of course, but it is certainly clear that Cicero comes off better than his Greek forebears.

Even if Luther's indebtedness to Aristotle is more than he is willing to admit, he is nevertheless quick to lump Aristotle in with other philosophers:

Aristoteles est prorsus Epicurus. Non credit Deum curare res humanas, vel si credit, tum cogitat Deum sic gubernare mundum, wie ein schlaffrige magd ein kind wieget. Aber Cicero ist viel weiter komen.

WA TR 5:155 [No.5440]

> Aristotle is altogether an Epicurean; he does not believe that God cares for human affairs. Then he thinks that God so governs the world like a sleepy maid rocks a child. But Cicero has come much further.

Luther is, of course, playfully unfair here. Leaving the obvious and no doubt purposeful philosophical anachronism aside, Aristotle, for whatever he might be faulted, was certainly not a proponent of hedonism, even the subsequent qualified hedonism of Epicurus. Yet Luther's characterization is important: philosophy is generally deficient for understanding God or grasping human depravity.

Still, pan Aristotle here as he may, Luther has to admit that others find that philosopher to be a powerful theological influence. At Cologne, Luther writes, Aristotle was seen as a true authority:

> Superioribus temporibus infelicissima fuerunt studia, ubi neglecta theologia omnibusque artibus ingenuis optima ingenia argutiis sophisticis vexabantur. Aristotelem ita in pretio habebant, ut Coloniae eum, qui Aristotelem negaret, pro summo haeretico damnarent, cum tamen Aristotelem non intelligerent, qui quidem recte scripsit de rebus, sine quibus nemo verba et φράσιν Aristotelis intelligere potest.
>
> WA TR 5:684 [No.6478]

> In earlier times, studies were very unfortunate, when theology was neglected and the best talents were being harassed by all the ingenious, slick and sophistic arts. They were holding Aristotle in such regard, that they would condemn at Cologne anyone who contradicted him, doing so on the high charge of heresy; nonetheless, they did not understand Aristotle, who indeed wrote justly about things, without which no one is capable of understanding the words and *la mode de parlance* of Aristotle.

Thomas Aquinas, too, Luther notes disdainfully, finds Aristotelian logic an asset to interpreting Scripture:

> Gratianus ... videns praesentem statum papae omnia in illius arbitrium conclusit. Habet optima argumenta, optimas conclusiones, sed tandem concludit: Sed hoc est contra concilium, ergo papae oboediendum. Similiter facit Thomas, qui, cum optimos scripturae locos tractavit, tandem concludit cum sententia Aristotelis.... Papa voluit Decretale haberi aequale euangelistarum et apostolorum scriptis. Omnium canonum et

> distinctionum status est: Papa vult esse dominus rerum et ecclesiarum, dominus dominantium. Pfu dich wol an!
>
> WA TR 5:686 [No.6480]

> Gratianus, seeing the present status of the pope concluded that all things are within the pope's realm to judge. He has the "best" arguments, the "best" conclusions, but nevertheless he concludes: "But this is against the council, and therefore the Pope must be obeyed." Thomas Aquinas does the same thing; although he has drawn upon the best passages of the Scripture, he concludes with the sentiment of Aristotle.... The pope wished that his decree be regarded equal to the writings of the evangelists or of the apostles ... the pope wishes to be lord of all authorities, whether secular or ecclesiastical. Shame on you!

Clearly Aristotelian "authority" is, in Luther's eyes, far from an asset. Here he goes so far as to liken the papist Thomas to the pope himself, basing that comparison on the pope's evocation of his own decrees to Thomas's evocation of Aristotelian philosophical (and thus reasoned) supremacy. The comparison is, of course, not fully congruent, as Aquinas looks beyond his own writing and reasoning to support his claim. Nevertheless, both the pope and Aquinas, Luther points out, have placed reason or philosophy over Scripture, and this is for Luther an unholy inversion of authority. Aristotle is, therefore, guilty more by association here than by any particular thing he happened to have written. He is a victim of his own popularity both in the Renaissance, as at Cologne, and in the late Middle Ages, in Thomas Aquinas.

Luther's resistance to philosophy is broad-ranging and is certainly not confined to Aristotle. For example, through Bonaventure's adaptation of Plato, Luther playfully criticizes both the saint and the Academy's founder at once:

> Speculativa scientia theologorum est simpliciter vana. Bonauenturam ea de re legi, aber er hett mich schir toll[11] gemacht, quod cupiebam sentire unionem Dei cum anima mea (de qua nugatur) unione intellectus et voluntatis. Sunt mere fanatici spiritus. Hoc autem est vera speculativa, quae plus est practica: Crede in Christum et fac, quod debes. Sic mystica

11 Hazlitt renders *toll* as "deaf," but in Luther's time had the sense of *unsinnig* or *rasend*, so "crazy" might here be a more accurate translation. The subsequent causal clause introduced by *quod* explains why reading Bonaventure nearly made Luther *toll*: it is because he wanted to feel the union of God with his soul through the union of his intellect and will. I here thank my co-editor James Kellerman for his observations on this passage.

> theologia Dionisii sunt merissimae nugae; sicut enim Plato nugatur: Omnia sunt non ens et omnia sunt ens, und lests so hangen.
>
> WA TR 1:302–3 [No.644]

> The school divines, with their speculations in holy writ, deal in pure vanities, in mere imaginings derived from human reason. Bonaventura, who is full of them, made me almost deaf. I sought to learn in his book, how God and my soul had become reconciled, but got no information from him. They talk much of the union of the will and the understanding, but 'tis all idle fantasy. The right, practical divinity is this: Believe in Christ, and do thy duty in that state of life to which God has called thee. In like manner, the Mystical divinity of Dionysius is a mere fable and lie. With Plato he chatters: *Omnia sunt non ens, et omnia sunt ens*—(all is something, and all is nothing)—and so leaves things hanging.
>
> HAZLITT trans.

Here Hazlitt's paraphrastic translation catches the vitriol of the passage well. Luther's denigration of Catholic theologians and, behind them, the great minds of Hellas shows a debt to Cicero's words similar sentiments about effete actions but thoughtfulness of Greek philosophers:

> Chartae quoque quae illam pristinam severitatem continebant obsoleverunt; neque solum apud nos qui hanc sectam rationemque vitae re magis quam verbis secuti sumus sed etiam apud Graecos, doctissimos homines quibus, cum facere non possent, loqui tamen et scribere honeste et magnifice licebat, alia quaedam mutatis Graeciae temporibus praecepta exstiterunt. Itaque alii voluptatis causa omnia sapientes facere dixerunt, neque ab hac orationis turpitudine eruditi homines refugerunt; alii cum voluptate dignitatem coniungendam putaverunt, ut res maxime inter se repugnantis dicendi facultate coniungerent; illud unum derectum iter ad laudem cum labore qui probaverunt, prope soli iam in scholis sunt relicti.
>
> CIC., *Cael.* 40.3–41.7

> The pages also that recorded that old-fashioned austerity have become obsolete; nor has that been the case only among us who have followed this path and rule of life more in deeds than in words, but even among the Greeks, most learned men, for whom, although they could not do anything, nevertheless were able to write honorably and magnificently, certain other precepts have arisen, now that the times have changed for Greece. Therefore, some have said that the wise do everything for the

> sake of pleasure, nor have learned men fled from the baseness of such statement; others have thought that virtue must be combined with pleasure, so that by the cleverness of their speech they unite things that are incompatible per se. Those who have approved of that single direct road to praise joined together with hard work, have now almost been left behind by themselves in the schools.

Cicero's attitude is not unlike Luther's, for it is paradoxically a Greek formulation: "on the one hand (*men*) and on the other hand (*de*)." On the one hand, Cicero laments the lack of old-fashioned education and, incumbent upon it, a newfound decadence among the Roman youth, which, of course, he is busy both maligning and simultaneously defending in the *Pro Caelio*. On the other hand, the Greeks, for all their good thoughts, were not men of action; that fell to the Romans. So, on the one hand, it is too bad no one studies the great thoughts of the Greeks; on the other, they were no good at translating those thoughts into anything practical anyway. There is, therefore, a playful quality to Cicero's lament, and we shall return to that quality later, for we find a similar playfulness, of course, quite frequently in the *Tischreden*.

Elsewhere in the *Tischreden*, Luther's circumspection about philosophy is contextualized in terms of where philosophy, broadly speaking, fits into the human intellectual experience. Yet it is not so much that philosophy simply comes off badly as it is that it is subject to Luther's biblical ordering of the universe, which includes the universe of ideas. Luther does not here pound philosophy as a kind of whipping boy. Rather, he allows philosophy to have its say, but only in subordination to the God-centered view of life. Accordingly, philosophy cannot be seen merely as a balm for the vexed soul but rather as an actor on a stage, and a comedic stage, at that. This is not simply a case of Luther poking fun at philosophy; it is his contextualization of it, his prioritization of Jesus Christ over human reason and, with it, over all things.

Thus it is that Luther has, if we may say so, some fun at philosophy's, and in other cases, specifically at Aristotle's expense. Some of the fun, on the one hand, we saw earlier comes when Luther is purposely mapping Aristotle errantly onto the landscape of Greek philosophy, calling the founder of the Peripatos an "Epicurean." On the other hand, some of that fun comes via a somewhat unwieldy comparison that follows upon that very Epicurean passage cited earlier:

> Aber Cicero ist viel weiter komen. Credo, quod collegerit, quidquid invenerit boni in omnibus Graecis scriptoribus. Nam hoc est optimum

> argumentum, quod me multum saepe movit, quod ex generatione specierum probat esse Deum: Ein ku gebür allzeit ein ku, ein pferd ein pferd etc.; kein ku gebür ein pferd nec equus vaccam, kein stigliß den zeissen. Ergo necesse est esse aliquid, quod ita gubernet omnia.
>
> WA TR 5:155 [No. 5540]

> Cicero got much further [than Aristotle]. I believe that [Cicero] collected whatever he found to be good in all the Greek writers. This is the best argument, which has often moved me much, because he proves there is a god based on the birth of living creatures. A cow always produces a cow; a horse, a horse, etc. No cow gives birth to a horse, nor a horse a cow, nor a goldfinch a mouse. Therefore, it is necessary that there be something that thus governs everything.

Cicero expounds, Luther says here, the "God argument" better than Aristotle, and in fact better than Greek philosophy in general. Thus, Cicero escapes a negative brushstroke, as Luther's selective application of his thought permits the distillation of the best, or at least most applicable, bits of Greek philosophy through that Roman writer. Cicero provides Luther not simply with a filter through which to reinterpret Plato and to castigate Aristotle and the "other Epicureans," but a kind of potion-like "philter" whereby he can, through a type of rhetorical alchemy, winsomely represent the essential Christian message. Cicero is seen as sensible and stylistically apt; his eloquence influences Luther's rhetorical flourishes and that orator's reasoned assessment of philosophical issues offers Luther a positive approach to moral and spiritual arguments.

Yet another passage from Cicero points up such criticism in a manner not unlike Luther, whose playful tone we have seen both mocking Aristotle as asinine and simultaneously speaking of his "Epicurean" charm. Cicero admits that he once nearly fell victim to the magnetism of even the man who was, for a season, his political archrival:

> Me ipsum, me, inquam, quondam paene ille decepit, cum et civis mihi bonus et optimi cuiusque cupidus et firmus amicus ac fidelis videretur; cuius ego facinora oculis prius quam opinione, manibus ante quam suspicione deprendi.
>
> CIC., *Pro Cael.*, 14.10–13

> I myself, yes, I say, even I was once nearly taken in by him when I regarded him to be a good citizen, zealous for every "best" man, and I regarded him

> to be a firm and faithful friend. I grasped his crimes by seeing them more than just opinion, and I grasped them more with my hands then by mere suspicion of them.

When Cicero describes the enticements of Catiline, he admits that even he himself was tempted by Catiline's charms. We shall never know to what degree Cicero is merely waxing rhetorical in his defense and to what degree he might have found his arch enemy of 63 BC a legitimately intriguing character. But it is clear here that Cicero can, in a sense, subject himself playfully to criticism.

And it is that same playful tone, even as we saw earlier, that Luther uses to subject Aristotle to Cicero. Yet that is not all, for Luther will even turn that playfulness upon himself when comparing the rhetorical sway of Melanchthon, Carlstadt, and Erasmus with his own:

> Anno 1536. Den 1. Augusti, schrieb D.M. Luther auf seinen Tisch: "Res et verba Philippus; verba sine re Erasmus; res sine verbis Lutherus; nec res nec verba Carolostadius; das ist, was Philippus schreibet, das hat Hände und Füße, die Materie ist gut, so sind die Wort auch gut; Erasmus macht viel Wörte, es ist aber nichts dahinter; Lutherus hat wol gute Materia, aber die Worte sind nicht gut; Carlstadt hat weder gute Materie noch gute Wort."
>
> WA TR 3:461 [No.3619]

> In the year 1536 on the first of August, Doctor Martin Luther wrote at his desk as follows: *Res et verba Philippus; verba sine re Erasmus; res sine verbis Lutherus: nec res, nec verba Carolostadius*; that is, what Philip Melanchthon writes has hands and feet; the material is good, and so are the words; Erasmus of Rotterdam writes many words, but it is to no purpose; Luther has really good material, but his words are not good: Carlstadt has neither good words nor good material.

When it comes to "that 'Epicurean' Aristotle," it is not a grain of salt that is required, but something a bit more. Rather, it is a wry smile, even a chuckle that expresses appreciation for the comedic side of serious rhetoric. That is the kind of rhetoric that Cicero displays in the *Pro Caelio*. And it is that very kind, too, that Luther marshals in the service of the King of kings throughout the *Tischreden*.[12]

---

12 I should like to thank Rachel Donnelly, Ella Liu, Eva Parmenter, Josiah Stephens and Jamie Wheeler for their assistance with this project.

FIGURE 5.1 Hans Holbein the Younger, Woodcut, 1519. Luther as *Hercules Germanicus* with club and lionskin. Luther is depicted triumphing over Aristotle, Thomas Aquinas, William of Ockham, Peter Lombard and Jacob van Hoogstraaten. Roper, *Martin Luther*, 159 (with 448n62) notes that at this early point in the Reformation, "Luther's main antagonists were thought to be the scholastic philosophers and opponents of humanism." Further, cf. David Paisey and Giulia Bartrum, "Hans Holbein and Miles Coverdale: A New Woodcut, *Print Quarterly* 26 (2009): 227–53.

CHAPTER 6

A Debatable Theology: Medieval Disputation, the Wittenberg Reformation, and Luther's Heidelberg Theses

Richard J. Serina, Jr.

Medieval intellectual life revolved around the disputation. Disputations were held in universities and monasteries, for bachelors in the arts through doctors in higher faculties, and across all academic fields—theology, law, even medicine.[1] Two important features led to the emergence of the theological disputation in the Middle Ages. The first was the use of Aristotelian logic, in particular the subset of logic known as dialectic.[2] Logic had been a part of the medieval curriculum, including the works of Aristotle, but took precedence with the fresh translation into Latin of the so-called *Logica nova*, or New Logic. Logic had a place in the medieval trivium because of the sixth-century thinker Boethius, who in addition to his own writings on logic, translated Aristotle's *On Categories* and *On Interpretation*, as well as Porphyry's *Isagoge*, into Latin. Together, these came to be called the *Logica vetus*, or Old Logic. The *Logica nova* included Aristotle's *Topics, Prior Analytics, Posterior Analytics*, and *Sophistical Reflection*, rounding out the canonical version of Aristotle's *Organon*. Aristotelian logic provided formal rules for making an argument, but it was the specific form of dialectic that had the greatest impact on medieval disputation. Dialectic is best defined as a dialogue or discussion where truth is sought through question and answer, thesis and antithesis, problem and solution, or—as the famous medieval text of Peter Abelard put it—*Sic et Non*. Using dialectic, medieval scholastics could resolve theological problems by contrasting their ideas with other proposed solutions.[3]

1 Brian Lawn, *The Rise and Decline of the Scholastic 'Quaestio Disputata': With Special Emphasis on Its Use in the Teaching of Medicine and Sciences* (Leiden: Brill, 1993), 18–38, deals with how the disputation influenced the sciences.

2 On these developments, see Alex J. Novikoff, *The Medieval Culture of Disputation: Pedagogy, Practice, and Performance* (Philadelphia: University of Pennsylvania Press, 2013), 63–66, 108–14; and John Marenbon, *Later Medieval Philosophy (1150–1350)* (London: Routledge, 1987), 35–49.

3 On medieval logic in general, see the treatments in E.J. Ashworth, *Language and Logic in the Post-Medieval Period* (Boston: Reidel, 1974), and Alexander Broadie, *Introduction to Medieval Logic* (Oxford: Clarendon Press, 1987).

 | DOI:10.1163/9789004206717_008

The second element contributing to the development of the disputation was the *quaestio*, or a disputed topic in theology. This primarily began in the study of Scripture by asking a question about a specific biblical text or gloss of the text.[4] It would eventually furnish the subject matter for disputations in all academic disciplines, enabling the organization of specific theological topics, or *loci*, for analysis, whether it was in Peter Abelard's *Sic et Non*, Peter Lombard's *Sentences*, or Gratian of Bologna's collection of canon law, the *Concordance of Discordant Canons*. Ultimately, Aristotelian dialectic and the disputed question in theology supplied the method and the subject matter for the practice of disputation in the universities of the twelfth century and would shape its practice for the next four centuries.[5]

What was that practice? What did a medieval debate look like? While the particulars changed depending on the occasion for the disputation, the most common type followed a framework not dissimilar from modern debate. A *magister*, or teacher, presided over the debate. He would usually put forward a disputed question, accompanied by his own proposed solution to the question, called *propositiones*, or theses. One of his students would take the position of the *respondens*, or respondent, in the debate, while another would take the role of *opponens*, or opponent. It was the respondent's responsibility to defend the theses of the magister. He did not have to agree with the theses or even prove them: he simply had to defend them. The opponent, on the other hand, had to establish why the theses were wrong and to substitute his own resolution to the disputed question. Afterwards—sometimes immediately, sometimes days later—the magister would render his *determinatio*, or judgment of the debate. The magister would thus judge one disputant the winner; the winner would then go on to substantiate further the position that he had set forward in his theses.[6] By the fourteenth century, a student might attend disputations his first two years in the school of arts, participate in the debates for another two years, and then finally be allowed by his magister to render a *determinatio* in his fifth year.[7] After that he would become a master of arts, and if he proceeded to the theology faculty he would have to supervise his own

4 For the origins of the *quaestio* in medieval exegesis, see Beryl Smalley, *The Study of the Bible in the Middle Ages* (Notre Dame, IN: University of Notre Dame Press, 1964), 66–82.

5 Lawn, *Rise and Decline*, 6–17.

6 There is a lack of documentary evidence describing actual disputations in the Middle Ages, and there were no manuals with prescribed rules. For the above, see Schubert's summary in Anselm Schubert, "Libertas Disputandi: Luther und die Leipziger Disputation als akademisches Streitgespräch," *Zeitschrift für Theologie und Kirche* 105 (2008): 414–19. See also the discussions in Novikoff, *Medieval Culture of Disputation*, 141–7, and Marenbon, *Later Medieval Philosophy*, 19–20.

7 William J. Courtenay, *Schools and Scholars in Fourteenth-Century England* (Princeton: Princeton University Press, 1987), 33.

disputations for a year on the way to his doctorate.[8] This meant a medieval doctor of theology—indeed, a doctor of theology just like Luther—had been thoroughly saturated in the logic and practice of disputation.

While disputations tended to follow this formula, they were not formulaic. There were different types of disputations that served different functions within the medieval university. The primary kind most closely resembled what was just described: the private (*privata*) or circular (*circularis*) disputation. This was a required part of the curriculum in the school of arts and in the higher faculties, including theology. The magister had to supervise disputations at regular intervals, often on a weekly basis, that were restricted to his own pupils. A similar version was the solemn (*solemnis*) or ordinary (*ordinaria*) disputation. These disputations followed the same pattern but were open to students and masters from other faculties as well. There was also the *disputatio de quolibet*, a public event that broke from the traditional form. In this instance, the magister would open the debate not only to other faculties but to the community at large. Clerics, prelates, and civic leaders attended. The magister proposed the *quaestio*, offered his theses, and defended them in response to objections from the gathered audience.[9] Later in the Middle Ages, celebratory graduation or promotion (*pro gradu*) disputations were held, where masters or doctors taking the next degree would have to preside over a disputation in connection with their graduation ceremony. These last disputations would play an instrumental role in the articulation of Reformation theology at Wittenberg.

The role that disputations played in medieval university theology was to provide a legitimate search for truth on the part of the participants. To a certain extent, they were observed simply for the sake of academic exercise (*exercitii causa*) in order to receive a degree. More than that, however, the participants genuinely believed that through this ongoing practice of debate—using logic and dialectic, addressing disputed questions and proposing solutions, and objecting and responding—they would gain a greater grasp of truth.[10] These were not monologues or lectures; they were dialogues about

8 Courtenay, *Schools and Scholars*, 41.

9 On these, see Novikoff, *Medieval Culture of Disputation*, 133–47; Lawn, *Rise and Decline*, 12–15; and Marenbon, *Late Medieval Philosophy*, 27–34.

10 Schwarz and Leppin maintain that Luther and his colleagues shifted the focus of the disputation from this notion of an academic exercise to a search for truth (*inquirendae veritatis causa*); see Reinhard Schwarz, "Disputationen," in *Lutherhandbuch*, ed. Albrecht Beutel, 2nd ed. (Tübingen: Mohr Siebeck, 2010), 374, and Leppin, "Zuspitzung und Warheitsanspruch: Disputationen in den Anfängen der Wittenberger reformatischen Bewegung," in *Reformation und Rationalität*, ed. Herman Selderhuis and Ernst-Joachim Waschke (Göttingen: Vandenhoeck & Ruprecht, 2015), 55. But for my opinion I follow Novikoff, *Medieval Culture of Disputation*, 169–71, and Ernst Wolf, "Zur

contested theological questions governed by the rules of Aristotelian logic and dialectic. Of course, this method would come under fire in the century prior to the Reformation. Nominalism and voluntarism began chipping away at certain features of it beginning in the fourteenth century.[11] Humanists targeted it, too. Francesco Petrarch wrote of his "aversion to the logicians," and Lorenzo Valla argued for the superiority of Ciceronian rhetoric to scholastic logic.[12] By the time Luther began criticizing scholastic theology and theologians in 1515, widespread humanist and Augustinian curricular reforms had begun in Wittenberg and elsewhere.[13]

For all the conflict in the academic communities of the late Middle Ages, however, the medieval practice of disputation remained ensconced in educational life as the presumed method to obtain truth. Nominalists like Ockham recorded their *quodlibeta*, and Erasmus praised the practice alongside other methods: "Hilary thunders against heretics, Augustine disputes, Jerome

---

wissenschaftsgeschichtlichen Bedeutung der Disputationen und der Wittenberger Universität im 16. Jahrhundert," in *Peregrinatio: Studien zur reformatorischen Theologie, zum Kirchenrecht und zur Sozialethik*, ed. Ernst Wolf, 2 vols. (Munich: Ch. Kaiser, 1965), 1:48, who is forced to admit it through gritted teeth.

11 The primary target of the nominalists and voluntarists was Aristotelian realism among the Thomistic scholastics, but their arguments furnished Luther and his colleagues with much of the ammunition they needed to criticize both the Thomistic conclusions and confidence in their logic-heavy methodology. For the nominalist and voluntarists, see Heiko Oberman, *The Harvest of Medieval Theology: Gabriel Biel and Late Medieval Nominalism* (Durham, NC: The Labyrinth Press, 1983), and Francis Oakley, *Omnipotence, Covenant and Order: An Excursion in the History of Ideas from Abelard to Leibniz* (Ithaca, NY: Cornell University Press, 1984). For Luther and Aquinas, see Dennis Janz, *Luther on Thomas Aquinas: The Angelic Doctor in the Thought of the Reformer* (Stuttgart: Franz Steiner Verlag Wiesbaden, 1989), and O.H. Pesch, *Martin Luther, Thomas von Aquin und die reformatische Kritik an der Scholastik: Zur Geschichte und Wirkungsgeschichte eines Mißverständnisses mit weltgeschichlichen Folgen* (Hamburg: Joachim Jungius-Gesellschaft der Wissenschaften, 1994).

12 On these and other related arguments, see James A. Overfield, *Humanism and Scholasticism in Late Medieval Germany* (Princeton: Princeton University Press, 1985), and Erika Rummel, *The Humanistic-Scholastic Debate in the Renaissance and Reformation* (Cambridge, MA: Harvard University Press, 1995), 1–18, and 183–86 for the humanist criticism of dialectic in theology.

13 On the conflict between the respective theological *viae*, or curricular approaches to theology, at the time of the Reformation, see Leif Grane, *Contra Gabrielem: Luthers Auseinandersetzung mit Gabriel Biel in der Disputatio Contra Scholasticam Theologiam 1517* (Copenhagen: Gyldendal, 1962), and Heiko Oberman, *Masters of the Reformation: The Emergence of a New Intellectual Climate in Europe*, trans. Dennis Martin (Cambridge: Cambridge University Press, 1981), 3–110, but see especially Heiko A. Oberman, "Headwaters of the Reformation: Initia Lutheri—Initia Reformationis," in *Luther and the Dawn of the Modern Era*, ed. Heiko Oberman (Leiden: Brill, 1974), 40–88.

contends in dialogues, Prudentius wars in various forms of verse, Thomas and Scotus fight with the help of dialectic and philosophy. All have the same purpose but each uses a different method. Variety is not condemned as long as the same goal is sought."[14] The method may have been academic disputation, but the goal was always the discovery of truth. And, most importantly, medieval disputants believed they could arrive at that truth not by the single exegesis of a passage or a single resolution to a disputed question but by the process of proposition, objection, response, and judgment, and then running it back and doing it again.

1 Academic Disputation and the Wittenberg Reformation

Little work has been done on the role medieval disputation played in the articulation of early Reformation theology. Most scholarship regrettably seems only to begin with Wittenberg and pays far less attention to its medieval context.[15] Nevertheless, for all the changes occurring on the eve of the Reformation, this medieval culture of academic disputation neither waned nor ceased but directly impacted Luther personally and, more broadly, Wittenberg and the early Reformation. Despite its relative newness as an institution and its connection with the Reformation to come, Wittenberg was essentially a medieval university, and that meant academic life there revolved around disputations.[16] The Theology Faculty Statutes of 1508 provided for three different types of disputations.[17] The first was the weekly circular *disputatio*. It constituted a

---

14 Erasmus, *Colloquies*, 633; quoted in Mishtooni Bose, "The Issue of Theological Style in Late Medieval Disputations," in *Medieval Forms of Argument: Disputation and Debate*, ed. Georgina Donavin, Carol Poster, and Richard Utz (Eugene, OR: Wipf & Stock, 2002), 2.

15 One exception is David Luy's entry in the *Oxford Encyclopedia of Martin Luther*, which takes into account many of the same studies. See David Luy, "Disputations," in *The Oxford Encyclopedia of Martin Luther*, ed. Derek R. Nelson and Paul R. Hinlicky, 3 vols. (Oxford: Oxford University Press, 2017), 518–50. This chapter shares the same view on medieval disputation as Luy, but goes farther than him in suggesting how formative the disputation culture was for early Reformation theology.

16 On the university's academic culture, see Jonathan Mumme, "The University of Wittenberg," in *Martin Luther in Context*, ed. David M. Whitford (Cambridge: Cambridge University Press, 2018), 38–46.

17 Wolf, "Zur wissenschaftsgeschichtlichen Bedeutung," 38–51, as well as the shorter summary in Christine Helmer, *The Trinity and Martin Luther: A Study on the Relationship between Genre, Language and the Trinity in Luther's Works (1523–1546)* (Mainz: Verlag Philipp von Zabern, 1999), 47–50. For a recent treatment of this based upon the best documentary evidence, see Henning Bühmann, "The Wittenberg Disputation Culture and the Leipzig Debate," in *Luther at Leipzig: Martin Luther, the Leipzig Debate, and the*

regular part of academic instruction, typically three hours on Friday morning. The magister presided during the term and the bachelors during vacation, and students were required to participate in a certain number of disputations to earn their degree. The second was the public, or solemn, *disputatio*. Faculty were required to hold one per year. These were presumably no different than the public debates of the medieval variety, with the magister presenting his theses and serving as respondent. The third was the graduation, or *pro gradu*, disputation. Like its earlier analogue, this was primarily ceremonial. The candidate for the degree would serve as respondent. It would last three hours for the bachelor, a day for the license to teach (*licentia docendi*), and two days for the doctorate, with a second disputation at the ceremony itself. The course for Luther's doctorate in 1512 deviated somewhat from these, but the principal pieces were there: private disputation, public address, and a public disputation.[18]

As doctor of theology and professor of Bible, Luther involved himself intimately in these disputations, and out of them emerged some of the more pivotal contributions to the start of the Reformation. Wittenberg had been in the throes of curricular reform, as scholars like Luther and his mentor and predecessor at Wittenberg, Johannes von Staupitz, advocated for humanist and Augustinian ideas over against Thomistic and nominalist positions. They wanted more Bible, church fathers, and ancient rhetoric, and less Aristotle, logic, and medieval scholastic commentary. For one example, note Luther's oft-cited comment from a 1516 letter: "Our theology and St. Augustine are progressing well and with God's help rule at our University. Aristotle is gradually falling from his throne, and his final doom is only a matter of time.... Indeed no one can expect to have any students if he does not want to teach this theology, that is, lecture on the Bible or on St. Augustine or another teacher of ecclesiastical eminence."[19]

Luther and his growing circle of Augustinian- and humanist-influenced colleagues criticized late medieval scholastic theology for its views on grace, nature, reason, faith, and a host of other positions, and provided a fresh—if not altogether new—alternative. Yet, alongside Luther's biblical lectures, the

---

Sixteenth-Century Reformations, ed. Mickey L. Mattox, Richard J. Serina Jr., and Jonathan Mumme (Leiden: Brill, 2019), 61–92.

18 Martin Brecht, *Martin Luther*, trans. James L. Schaaf (Minneapolis: Fortress, 1985), 1:125–28, and Ernst Schwiebert, *Luther and His Times: The Reformation from a New Perspective* (St. Louis: Concordia Publishing House, 1950), 193–96. See also Richard J. Serina, Jr., "Luther's Doctorate and the Start of the Reformation," *Lutheran Forum* 56, no. 3 (2017): 53–57.

19 *LW* 48:42.

means for engaging those positions was the same as it was for their scholastic opponents: the disputation. In 1516, for instance, a master's candidate named Bartholomäus Bernhardi presented a set of three theses debating the natural powers of man apart from grace on the occasion of his promotion. The theses directly reflect Luther's own lectures on Romans, which Bernhardi would have attended. They voiced Luther's opposition to Thomistic and nominalist notions of free will and expressed a conscious reliance upon the arguments of Augustine.[20] A year later, Luther's colleague, Andreas Bodenstein von Karlstadt, published a set of 151 theses protesting indulgences, in the process decrying the *mala mixtura* of Aristotle and theology in a way that evokes Luther's own arguments.[21] Luther himself composed a set of theses for debate at the September 1517 promotion disputation for Franz Günther to bachelor of Bible. The resulting *Theses against Scholastic Theology* pitted Augustine against the nominalist Gabriel Biel on the ability to love God and keep the commandments.[22] And it was at his own September 1519 disputation for promotion to bachelor of Bible that Philip Melanchthon unveiled a set of theses on the sufficiency of Scripture that many now equate with the original formulation of *sola scriptura*.[23]

Though these are normally treated as part of the early Wittenberg Reformation, they were nonetheless concrete examples of interscholastic debate between medieval schools of theology on contested questions that entered the public realm through, of all things, university disputation.[24] Of course, that is to say nothing yet of the most notable disputations and theses:

20 Jens-Martin Kruse, *Universitätstheologie und Kirchenreform: Die Anfänge der Reformation in Wittenberg 1516–1522* (Mainz: Verlag Philipp von Zabern, 2002), 78–82, and Martin Brecht, *Martin Luther: His Road to the Reformation, 1483–1521*, trans. James L. Schaaf (Minneapolis: Fortress Press, 1985), 1:166–67.

21 Leppin, "Zuspitzung und Warheitsanspruch," 51, and Brecht, *Martin Luther*, 1:170.

22 Brecht, *Martin Luther*, 1:172, and Theodor Dieter, "Martin Luther and Scholasticism," in *Remembering the Reformation: Martin Luther and Catholic Theology*, ed. Declan Marmion, Salvador Ryan and Gesa E. Thiessen (Minneapolis: Fortress Press, 2017), 55–74. Dieter notes that the theses did not even receive their current title until the Erlangen edition; prior to that, they were simply identified by the name of Gunter as respondent, or described as a debate over nature and grace.

23 Schwarz, "Disputationen," 374. See also Volker Leppin, "Die Genese des reformatischen Schriftprinzips: Beobachtungen zu Luthers Auseinandersetzung mit Johannes Eck bis zur Leipziger Disputation," in *Reformatorische Theologie und Autoritäten: Studien zur Genese des Schriftprinzips beim jungen Luther*, ed. Volker Leppin (Tübingen: Mohr Siebeck, 2015), 138–39 for Melanchthon.

24 For a differentiation of disputations and theses during this period and their goals, see Volker Leppin, "Disputation als Medium der Theologie- und Kirchenreform in der Reformation: Zur Transformation eines akademischen Mediums," in *Lehren und Lernen*

the *Ninety-Five Theses* of October 1517, the Heidelberg Disputation of 1518, and the Leipzig Disputation of 1519. We know the impact of the *Ninety-Five Theses*, even if we do not know when or how they were distributed, or for what purpose.[25] We do know, however, the implications of the Leipzig Disputation of 1519, which was the first disputation for which we have protocols recording exactly what arguments were set forth and debated during the proceedings.[26] We also know that Luther's ultimate conclusion there—that pope and council can err, but Scripture alone is infallible—led to the resumption of heresy charges against him and to his eventual excommunication.[27] But this culture of disputation provides a different insight into the theses Luther composed for debate at Heidelberg and raises important questions about the historical significance of the *theologia crucis* that twentieth-century Lutheran theology found in those theses.[28]

2 Heidelberg in the Context of Academic Disputation

No one looks to the indulgence theses or the protocols of the Leipzig Debate—or for that matter the other examples of disputations and theses cited above—as definitive expressions of Reformation or Lutheran theology, yet Heidelberg is treated differently, as the Heidelberg Disputation has become functional shorthand for the "Theology of the Cross." In fact, one will strain to find entries in theological or historical reference works on the Heidelberg Disputation. In reference works, the actual disputation is normally found as a mere keyword in entries titled "Theology of the Cross." The theses are cast as expressions of

---

im Zeitalter der Reformation: Methoden und Funkionen, ed. Gerlinde Huber-Rebenich (Tübingen: J.C.B. Mohr, 2012), 115–25.

25 For the debate on the posting of the theses, see Kurt Aland, *95 Theses: With Pertinent Documents from the History of the Reformation* (St. Louis: Concordia Publishing House, 1967); Erwin Iserloh, *The Theses Were Not Posted: Luther between Reform and Reformation*, trans. Martin E. Marty (Boston: Beacon Press, 1968), and, more recently, Volker Leppin and Timothy J. Wengert, "Sources for and against the Posting of the *Ninety-Five Theses*," *Lutheran Quarterly* 29 no. 4 (2015): 373–98.

26 It is interesting that Leipzig was the first disputation to have official protocols, or record of the proceedings, per agreement between the disputants. On this, see especially Schubert, "Libertas Disputandi."

27 On the fallout, see Brecht, *Martin Luther*, 1:322–48.

28 For a possible—but somewhat conjectural—explanation of the historical reasons behind the development of the theology of the cross in the early twentieth century, see James Stayer, *Martin Luther, German Saviour: German Evangelical Theological Factions and the Interpretation of Luther, 1917–1933* (Montreal: McGill-Queen's University Press, 2000), 48–78, especially 60–63.

a new, distinctly Reformational, even Lutheran vision for theology, with a line directly connecting Heidelberg in 1518 to Luther's 1525 *Bondage of the Will* and his biblical lectures of the 1530s, in order to substantiate this vision.[29] While this essay cannot address the content of the theology of the cross or the Heidelberg Theses, placing the theses in their context as an academic disputation will shed important light on how to understand their historical significance.

First, while it is customary to speak of the Heidelberg Disputation as occurring at a chapter meeting of the Saxon-Thuringian province of Luther's religious order, the Augustine Hermits (sc. the "Order of the Eremites of Saint Augustine," [OESA]), it was actually an academic disputation conducted at the University of Heidelberg.[30] Though the Augustinians technically sponsored the disputation, it was hosted by the school of arts and incorporated faculty and students from Heidelberg and elsewhere.[31] The disputation was consequently an interscholastic debate between rival schools of theology in the late medieval university, and thus it was a place for schools to debate their material differences on contested theological subjects.[32]

Second, we cannot even be sure of what role Luther played in the debate at Heidelberg, for the record of what happened there is scant. The most widely influential account, that of Luther's contemporary Martin Frecht, was not written until 1556—nearly forty years after the disputation itself—and was not discovered until 1934.[33] Frecht seemingly overstates his point that the theses represented Luther's "entire theology" (*seine ganze Theologie*). Further

29 The most representative examples remain Walter von Loewenich, *Luther's Theology of the Cross*, trans. Herbert J.A. Bouman (Minneapolis: Augsburg, 1976), and Gerhard O. Forde, *On Being a Theologian of the Cross: Reflections on Luther's Heidelberg Disputation, 1518* (Grand Rapids, MI: Eerdmans, 1997). For a statement that reflects the current consensus in Luther scholarship, see Robert Kolb, "Luther's Theology of the Cross Fifteen Years after Heidelberg: Lectures on the Psalms of Ascent," *The Journal of Ecclesiastical History* 61, no. 1 (2010): 69–85, especially 84.

30 Bühmann, "Wittenberg Disputation Culture," 77 n. 66, suggests that the theological and philosophical theses may have been debated at different meetings on consecutive days—the theological to the Augustinians, the philosophical in the broader university forum—but there is no evidence of this, even if there may be precedent for it.

31 Hans Scheible, "Die Universität Heidelberg und Luthers Disputation," in *Melanchthon und die Reformation: Forschungsbeiträge*, ed. Rudolf May and Rolf Decot (Mainz: Verlag Philipp von Zabern, 1996), 371–91. Also, see Brecht, *Martin Luther*, 1:213–15.

32 Leppin, in fact claims this was the primary goal of disputation for Luther: to distinguish between schools of theology, "Zuspitzung und Warheitsanspruch," 50.

33 Scheible, "Die Universität Heidelberg," 375, 383–84. The letter is printed in Walter von Freidensburg, "Ein Brief an Matthäus Nägelin von Strassburg vom 22. Juni 1556," *Zeitschrift für die Geschichte des Oberrheins* 86 (1934): 387–92.

reservations remain about the accuracy of Frecht's recollection and its relation to other accounts. It appears certain that Luther presided over the disputation as director of his order's program of study and wrote the theses for Wittenberg Augustinian Leonhard Beier. When the disputation was held on April 26, Luther presumably presided as magister, but not as respondent who would have been tasked with substantiating his own theses. That duty in fact fell to Leonhard Beier.[34] The disputation was as much about Beier as Luther, and that means Heidelberg did not provide Luther the theological or ecclesiastical platform a public disputation like the medieval *quodlibet* would have.

Lastly, if the report of Martin Bucer (then a student at Heidelberg) is to be believed, Luther's proposal for a new "theology of the cross" did not factor centrally into the debate. Earlier scholars discredited Bucer's report because they did not believe the young Dominican with Erasmian tendencies understood the argument of the theses. But Thomas Kaufmann argues that, on the contrary, Bucer recounted the theses correctly and that past scholarship itself had understood the debate wrongly by focusing on the *theologia crucis* rather than the more characteristic Wittenberg emphasis on Augustinian views of grace and works.[35] For instance, Bucer's account does not even mention theological Theses 17 through 24, in which Luther explains his theology of the cross. Bucer was not taken by Luther's new method for theology as much as Luther's description of the law in Thesis 1: "The law of God, the most salutary doctrine of life, cannot advance man on his way to righteousness, but rather hinders him."[36] This new view of the law astounded Bucer during the disputation, as it encompassed Wittenberg's characteristic Augustinian theology of grace and works over against scholastic notions of those same doctrines.[37]

The placement of the Heidelberg Theses in the context of medieval academic disputation offers us a view of that document that is less a distinctively Lutheran or Protestant view of theology than an ongoing interscholastic debate over specific, material doctrines. Luther and his colleagues addressed such doctrines chiefly on the basis of St. Paul and Augustine. Heidelberg may not have been the start of a new theological platform so much as it was the

34 Schwartz, "Disputationen," 378.

35 Thomas Kaufmann, "Bucers Bericht von der Heidelberger Disputation," *Archiv für Reformationgeschichte* 82 (1991): 147–70. Kaufmann includes numerous examples of the scholarly critique of Bucer at 149–50.

36 *LW* 31:39.

37 In this connection it is worth noting that Luther cites Augustine twice in his proof for Thesis 1, and continues to cite him through subsequent proofs (Theses 5, 13, 14, 15, 26), yet not a single citation of the church father most pivotal for the movement in Wittenberg is found in the proofs for the more celebrated Theses 17–24.

fruition of a conversation taking place in Wittenberg going as far back as 1516 or even earlier.[38] The disputation had more to do with what came before it in Wittenberg than what came after it in Luther's corpus. In that case, instead of a single "theology of the cross" beginning at Heidelberg and running through the remainder of Luther's career, it could be more accurate to speak of something like multiple *theologies* of the cross.

The first of these ends rather than begins with Heidelberg and in some sense punctuates the interscholastic debates revolving around Wittenberg and precipitating the indulgence controversy, then dissipates when debates over papal authority and justification come to the fore.[39] The second relates to Luther's diatribe against the perceived skepticism of Erasmus in *Bondage of the Will*, where he distinguishes between God preached and God not preached in a way strikingly similar to his Eucharistic arguments against Oecolampadius and Zwingli, as well as his emphasis upon the external Word over against "fanatics" like Karlstadt or Anabaptist practice.[40] A third would then appear in his understanding of the "Hidden God" in the 1530s, with its characteristic emphasis upon enduring suffering, possibly explained by Luther's own perception of his reform efforts as a failure.[41] Thus, it is anachronistic to speak of a single theology of the cross beginning with Heidelberg and spanning the majority of Luther's theological career, even if one were to argue that it changes guises over

38 For whatever novelty his position on a theology of the cross may have entailed, it had its own precursor within the late medieval Augustinian tradition. See the discussion of Augustinian Jordan Quidlenberg's theology of the cross in Eric Leland Saak, *Luther and the Reformation of the Later Middle Ages* (Cambridge: Cambridge University Press, 2017), 44–45.

39 Interestingly, there are references aplenty to something like a "theology of the cross" in the year immediately preceding the Heidelberg Disputation, including Luther's response to Eck's *Obeliski* (WA 1:290–91), the lectures on Hebrews (WA 57:79), and the *Resolutiones* to the indulgence theses (WA 1:614). His use of a theology of the cross to criticize the theology of indulgences can even be traced back to a February 1517 sermon (WA 1:509.35–510.8). On this, see David Bagchi, "Luther's Ninety-Five Theses and the Contemporary Criticism of Indulgences," in *Promissory Notes on the Treasury of Merits: Indulgences in Late Medieval Europe*, ed. R.N. Swanson (Leiden: Brill, 2006), 334.

40 For one example of parallel language in Luther's sacramental writings, see Luther's "That These Words of Christ, 'This Is My Body,' etc., Still Stand Firm Against the Fanatics," *LW* 37:68–69.

41 E.g., Luther's sermon on cross and suffering at Coburg delivered before the presentation of the Augsburg Confession, *LW* 51:197–208. On Luther's later view of the reform movement, see the classic Gerald Strauss, "Success and Failure in the German Reformation," *Past & Present* 67 (1975): 30–63. See also Gerald Strauss, *Luther's House of Learning: Indoctrination of the Young in the German Reformation* (Baltimore: Johns Hopkins University Press, 1978), 268–308, and Mark U. Edwards, *Luther's Last Battles* (Ithaca, N.Y.: Cornell University Press, 1984).

time due to shifting circumstances and language (in which case it becomes a rather unhelpful unifying concept since it is not identifiable as a single concept at all).

Ultimately, Heidelberg provides but one example of how the culture of medieval disputation may help us better contextualize the early Reformation. Medieval disputations were self-contained, internal dialogues over contested questions in the study of theology. These were the same topics debated in different formats and different venues, from Wittenberg to Paris, from Oxford to Rome, from the twelfth century to the sixteenth century, from classrooms to monasteries and city halls. Disputations were not programs or platforms but perennial discussions. They assumed a recurring process of question and proposition, objection and response that would lead to the acquisition of theological truth but not in a single disputation and not in a single set of disputation theses—even that of Heidelberg. Reading the Heidelberg Disputation in this sense does not allow us to establish Heidelberg as a paradigm for Lutheran theology to come but rather to take it as the summary statement of an inter-scholastic debate that had been going on in Wittenberg since Luther's arrival. This debate involved questions about free will, nature, grace, reason, Aristotle, Augustine, St. Paul, and any number of academic matters that would give shape to the early Reformation.

CHAPTER 7

A Painted Record of Martin Luther in Renaissance Bologna

Piergiacomo Petrioli

A beautiful Italian Renaissance fresco painting, dated at the beginning of the sixteenth century, in the Gothic church of Santa Maria della Misericordia of Bologna, testifies to a particular event that occurred in early sixteenth-century Bologna. In it, Saint Augustine is depicted surrounded by four Augustinian friars. Though some of the figures have been variously identified,[1] the present article will suggest that the figures in the fresco are portraits of relevant personalities of the Augustinian order of that time. To do so, we shall put the work in its proper religious and historical context of Bologna in that period, thereby suggesting the milieu and patronage of that unique picture. Perhaps most importantly, the youngest of the pictured friars looks very similar to other portraits of the young Martin Luther.[2]

The twenty-seven-year-old Martin Luther arrived in Bologna when he was en route to Rome in December of 1510.[3] Then an Augustinian friar based at the monastery in Erfurt, Luther was travelling south, as a *socius itinerarius* (or junior companion) of the senior friar, or *litis procurator*, who was in charge of discussions about a theological controversy.[4] The expert theologian on the journey was the Dutch doctor Johan van Mechelen from Osbach (before 1500–sixteenth century).[5] These two men were charged by Johann von Staupitz (*c.*1460–1524),

---

1 Elisa Gamberini identifies the two friars on the right as the prior of the monastery, Nicola da Carignano and the blind preacher, Nicola (Elisa Gamberini, "Il complesso di Santa Maria della Misericordia di Bologna attraverso i suoi documenti," *I quaderni del m.æ.s. = Journal of Mediæ Ætatis Sodalicium*, no. 10 [November 2007]: 141–61).

2 Marco Poli and Simona Costato, "Martin Lutero in un affresco alla Misericordia? Ipotesi per una ricerca storico-artistica," *Strenna Storica Bolognese*, 47 (1997): 427.

3 About the date of the travel, see: Franz Posset, "Luther's Journey to Rome 1511–12," *Luther Digest* (2012): 9–14. Hans Schneider, *Martin Luthers Reise nach Rom neu datiert und neu gedeutet*, Studien zur Wissenschaft und zur Religionsgeschichte (Berlin: De Gruyter, 2011), 78. For the most recent, very rich discussion of Luther's journey, cf. Carl P.E. Springer, *Luther's Rome, Rome's Luther* (Minneapolis: Fortress Press, 2021) 1–42 *et passim*; on the date of the trip, 1–4.

4 Posset, "Luther's Journey to Rome," 14.

5 Posset, "Luther's Journey to Rome," 15–18; Schneider, "Martin Luthers Reise nach Rom neu datiert und neu gedeutet," 16. Johan van Mechelen is the name of Luther's companion,

 | DOI:10.1163/9789004206717_009

vicar General of the Augustinian friars in Germany, to speak with the prior general of the Augustinian order, Giles of Viterbo (1469–1532), about the controversy concerning the order in Germany, the so called *Contentio Staupitii* or "Controversy of the German Observantines."[6] Later, in his *Table Talk*, Luther would say that his personal goal for his trip to Rome was to be able to make a full confession about the sins of his childhood years and thus to become fully pious, for his theology at that time regarded such an act as an important step on the road to purification. The results for Christianity, of course, would prove to be radically different from what the young Luther found in the city or even the unformed theology that he brought with him.[7] The two friars left Wittenberg (or Erfurt) to Nuremberg, crossed the Alps through the Septimer Pass to Chiavenna, and from Milan they arrived in Bologna in wintertime.[8] Having set out on their return journey in January 1511, Luther and van Mechelen spent several weeks in the northern Italian town of Bologna, staying at Santa Maria della Misericordia, an Augustinian monastery there (figure 7.1).[9]

---

considered correct by the most recent scholars. There are two earlier hypotheses about the identity of Luther's companion: Anton Kresz from Nuremberg has been suggested; he was also an Augustinian friar, a scholar and someone well versed in the practices of the Curia in Rome; the other suggestion is that the figure is Johan Nathin, the theologian and former teacher of Luther (Lyndal Roper, *Der Mensch Martin Luther—Die Biographie* [Frankfurt am Main: Fischer, 2016]), 90–92.

6 About the controversy within the Augustinian order, see: Theodor Kolde, "Innere Bewegungen unter den deutschen Augustinern und Luther Romreise," *Zeitschrift für Kirkengeschichte*, 2 (1977): 460–480; Herbert Jedin, "Die römischen Augustinerquellen zu Luthers Frühzeit," *Archiv für Reformationsgeschichte*, 25 (1928): 256–270; Franz Posset, *The Front-Runner of the Catholic Reformation: The Life and Works of Johann von Staupitz* (London: Routledge, 2017), ch. 3; Schneider, "Martin Luthers Reise nach Rom neu datiert und neu gedeutet," 38–95.

7 Martin Luther, WA TR 3:432 (No. 3582b) and 5:656–57 (No. 6427). Volker Leppin, "*Salve, Sancta Roma* Luthers Erinnerungen an seine Romreise," *Martin Luther in Rom: die Ewige Stadt als kosmopolitisches Zentrum und ihre Wahrnehmung*, ed. Michael Matheus, Arnold Nesselreth, and Martin Wallraff (Berlin: De Gruyter, 2017), 35, 41–42; Waltraut Schwarz, *Bologna ja Bologna nein: La città nella letteratura tedesca dal medioevo ad oggi* (Bologna: Cappelli, 1975), 30.

8 An accurate description of the Italian itinerary of Luther is that of Emilio Comba, "Luther a Rome," *Revue de Théologie et de Philosophie et Compte-rendu des Principales Publications Scientifiques* 33 (1900): 228–46. See also: Adolf Hausrath, *Martin Luthers Romfahrt nach einem gleichzeitigen Pilgerbuche* (Berlin: Grote, 1894); Heinrich Bömer, *Luthers Romfahrt* (Leipzig: Deichert, 1914); Reinould Weijenborg, "Neuentdeckte Dokumente im Zusammenhang mit Luthers Romreise," *Antonianum* 33 (1957): 147–202; Schneider, "Martin Luthers Reise nach Rom neu datiert und neu gedeutet"; Hans Schneider, "Luthers Romreise," *Martin Luther in Rom: die Ewige Stadt als kosmopolitisches Zentrum und ihre Wahrnehmung* (Berlin: De Gruyter, 2017), 12–21.

9 Schwarz, *Bologna ja Bologna nein*, 40; Marco Poli and Simona Costato, "Martin Lutero in un affresco," 427; Giovanni Sassu, "Appunti per uno studio del Sant'Agostino e quattro monaci nella chiesa della Misericordia," *Strenna Storica Bolognese*, 47 (1997): 439.

Pope Julius II, during those same weeks, also happened to be in Bologna with his entire papal court, having arrived on September 20th of the previous year.[10] He was in fact celebrating his triumph as the conqueror of Bologna, which status he had achieved by defeating the lord of the town, Giovanni II Bentivoglio (*c.*1463–1506). To evidence his control over the town to the Bolognese community, in 1506 he commissioned a colossal bronze statue of himself from the best sculptor of the period, Michelangelo. That Florentine prodigy set up his workshop just behind the main church of San Petronio. By symbolically using the bronze from the large bell of the Bentivoglio palace bell tower, the very construction of which was in fact a sign of Giovanni II's power, Michelangelo would render yet another masterpiece of Renaissance art. The huge portrait of the pope was placed on the central door of the civic church of San Petronio in Piazza Maggiore on February 21, 1508; in it, Julius is portrayed blessing the people of Bologna, but his expression looks severe, even frightful. He is depicted as holding a sword to demonstrate his sovereign sway, evidencing that the whole Bolognese community was subject to him and under the direct authority of the Roman Catholic Church. Unfortunately, this statue was destroyed on December 13, 1511, when Annibale II Bentivoglio (1466–1540) seized his dynasty power again for a while, and Michelangelo's masterpiece was melted down to make a cannon for the duke of Ferrara, Alfonso I d'Este (1476–1534), ironically called "the Giulia."[11]

---

10 Poli and Costato, "Martin Lutero in un affresco," 427; Sassu, "Sant'Agostino e quattro monaci," 432.

11 See Giorgio Vasari, *Life of Michelangelo*: "His Holiness commanded him that he should make a statue of bronze in the likeness of Pope Julius, five *braccia* in height. In this work he showed most beautiful art in the attitude, which had an effect of much majesty and grandeur, and displayed richness and magnificence in the draperies, and in the countenance, spirit, force, resolution, and stern dignity; and it was placed in a niche over the door of S. Petronio [...]. Michelagnolo had the statue finished in clay before the pope departed from Bologna for Rome, and his Holiness, having gone to see it, but not knowing what was to be placed in the left hand, and seeing the right hand raised in a proud gesture, asked whether it was pronouncing a benediction or a curse. Michelagnolo answered that it was admonishing the people of Bologna to mind their behaviour, and asked his Holiness to decide whether he should place a book in the left hand; and he said, 'Put a sword there, for I know nothing of letters.' The Pope left a thousand crowns in the bank of M. Anton Maria da Lignano for the completion of the statue, and at the end of the sixteen months that Michelagnolo toiled over the work it was placed on the frontispiece in the façade of the Church of S. Petronio, as has been related; and we have also spoken of its size. This statue was destroyed by the Bentivogli, and the bronze was sold to Duke Alfonso of Ferrara, who made with it a piece of artillery called La Giulia; saving only the head, which is to be found in his *guardaroba*." (Giorgio Vasari, *Lives of the most eminent Painters, Sculptors and Architects* (1568), trans. G. De Vere [London: Macmillan, 1912–15], 9:26–27). About this lost work see also Norbert Huse, "Ein Bilddokument zu Michelangelos

During that period of time Luther, in fact, would have had the opportunity to admire this bronze monument before its destruction. The German friars would likely also have seen the famous two medieval towers of Bologna and the thirteenth-century palace of King Enzo on the main square and would have had the opportunity to visit the most important churches in town, such as the cathedral of San Pietro, San Petronio, San Domenico (with the magnificent tomb of the founder of the order), as well as those of San Giacomo Maggiore, San Martino, San Francesco and San Bartolomeo.[12] It seems likely, too, that there, for the first time, Luther could have seen the pope in person, maybe as Julius gave a mass in the cathedral of Bologna or perhaps even when he was merely out and about in the town.[13]

During his lifetime, Luther wrote two times about *Bononia*; the first occasion was in 1538, in which he reflected on the rhetorical ability of the local preachers.[14] The second concerned an episode involving the German students at the university, who wrote a letter to the pope asking of him a special exemption (*dispensa*) from the canonical hours of prayer, as they said that the prayer time impinged upon their opportunity to study. The pope answered, *Surge manius et ora citius!* ("Wake up earlier and pray faster!").[15] Without a doubt, the few weeks the young monk spent in Bologna were vital for his personal formation and thought, for while there he could directly consider the context of the important Italian community of his order.

The aforementioned lord (*signore*) of Bologna, Giovanni II Bentivoglio, plays a very important role in this story, as patron of many local artists and close to the Augustinian order. A typical Renaissance Italian lord, he embodied the Renaissance's love of power, on the one hand, and art, on the other, for he was a generous and well-known patron of arts, yet he was also an unscrupulous and Machiavellian politician, under whom Bologna would become one of the richest and most beautiful towns in Italy. A capital of art and culture, Bologna was without doubt one of the prime urban Renaissance centers.[16] Bentivoglio

'Julius II' in Bologna," *Mitteilungen des Kunsthistorischen Institutes in Florenz*, 12, no. 3/4 (December 1966): 355–58; Monika Butzek, *Die kommunalen Repräsentationsstatuen der Päpste des 16. Jahrhunderts in Bologna, Perugia und Rom* (Bock und Herchen: Bad Honnef 1978), 77ff.; Michael Hirst, *Michelangelo: The Achievement of Fame* (New Haven & London: Yale University Press, 2011), 79–84.

12 See Herbert Voßberg, *Im Heiligen Rom: Luthers Reiseeindrücke 1510–1511*, (Berlin: Heinrich Grote, 1966) 28.

13 Herbert Voßberg, *Im Heiligen Rom*, 28–29; Schwarz, *Bologna ja Bologna nein*, 31.

14 Martin Luther, WA TR 4:28–29 (No. 3949).

15 Martin Luther, WA TR 4:654 (No. 5094). The passage is quoted also in Theodor Elze, *Luthers Reise nach Rom* (Berlin: Verlag von Alexander Duncker, 1899): 68.

16 See: Marco Viroli, *I Bentivoglio Signori di Bologna* (Cesena: Il Ponte Vecchio, 2011).

was also very familiar with the Augustinian order; in fact, the family church, San Giacomo Maggiore, was Augustinian and was located in the Bentivoglio district, near their huge palace (today, Verdi Square).[17] The other Augustinian church, Santa Maria della Misericordia, was located just outside the city walls (just beyond the Castiglione Gate) and today lies nearby the park *Giardini Margherita*. It was familiar to the Bentivoglio family and their friends, as well.

The first records concerning Santa Maria della Misericordia date to the beginning of the thirteenth century where it is described as a convent of Cistercian nuns. Later, in 1432, it would become an Olivetan monastery under the auspices of the monastery of San Michele in Bosco, and finally from 1473 to 1757 an Augustinian monastery.[18] When Pope Sixtus IV gave the church to the monks of the Augustinian order, owing to the patronage of the Bentivoglio family and some powerful, aristocratic families linked to them, the monastery was restored and enriched with many important Renaissance artworks. One of the most remarkable artists to work on this church was the local painter Francesco Raibolini, who was known by the appellation Francia (ca. 1447–1517).[19]

At the end of the fifteenth century, another family, the Felicinis, had their personal chapel constructed, commissioning Francia both for its altarpiece (*Madonna with Baby Jesus and Saints Augustine and Sebastian and the Portrait*

17 The magnificent Bentivoglio palace was sacked and totally destroyed when Pope Julius II conquered Bologna. Today the little hill of the park *Giardini del guasto* lies over the ruins of the Renaissance building (*guasto*, in Italian, means "destroyed"). See Carolyn James, "The Palazzo Bentivoglio in 1487," *Mitteilungen des Kunsthistorischen Institutes in Florenz*, 41, no. 1/2 (1997): 188–96; Marco Viroli, *I Bentivoglio Signori di Bologna*, 231–33.

18 Elisa Gamberini, "Il complesso di Santa Maria," 141–61.

19 See Vasari, *Life of Francia*: "The first work that he made was a panel of no great size for Messer Bartolommeo Felicini, who placed it in the Misericordia, a church without Bologna; in which panel there is a Madonna seated on a throne, with many other figures, and the said Messer Bartolommeo portrayed from life. This work, which was wrought in oil with the greatest diligence, was painted by him in the year 1490; and it gave such satisfaction in Bologna, that Messer Giovanni Bentivogli, desiring to honour his own chapel, which was in S. Jacopo in that city, with works by this new painter, commissioned him to paint a panel with the Madonna in the sky, two figures on either side of her, and two angels below sounding instruments; which work was so well executed by Francia, that he won from Messer Giovanni, besides praise, a most honourable present. Wherefore Monsignore de' Bentivogli, impressed by this work, caused him to paint a panel containing the Nativity of Christ, which was much extolled, for the high-altar of the Misericordia; wherein, besides the design, which is not otherwise than beautiful, the invention and the colouring are worthy of nothing but praise. In this work he made a portrait of Monsignore de' Bentivogli from the life (a very good likeness, so it is said by those who knew him), clothed in that very pilgrim's dress in which he returned from Jerusalem." Vasari, *Lives*, 9:24. See also *Il genio di Francesco Francia*, catalogue of the exhibition Bologna 2018 (Venezia: Marsilio, 2018).

of Bartolomeo Felicini) and for the painting on the top of the altarpiece, known as a "cimasa," a *Deposition of Jesus*. A talented goldsmith, Francia painted a carefully wrought jewel on Mary's head; for that reason, this masterpiece is also known as the *Madonna of the Jewel*. Moreover, the noble family Manzoli, which also had ties to the Bentivoglio family, purchased a chapel in the church and commissioned from Francia an altarpiece with *Madonna and Baby Jesus with Saints George, John the Baptist, Augustine, and Stephen*. Add to this that Francia also completed the *Vision of Saint Augustine* for the same church.

Finally, Anton Galeazzo Bentivoglio in 1498, back from a pilgrimage to Jerusalem, commissioned from Francia an altarpiece with the *Adoration of the Magi* to commemorate this crucial event of his spiritual life.[20] The painting at the bottom of an altarpiece, known as the "predella," is by another artist, also very close to the Bentivoglio family, Lorenzo Costa the Elder (1460–1535). For example, in 1490 Costa created the beautiful paintings to decorate the Bentivoglio family chapel in San Giacomo Maggiore, with the *Bentivoglio family praying in front of Virgin Mary* (a real family portrait), *Vision of the Apocalypse*, *The Triumph of Fame*, and *The Triumph of Death*.[21] We should also mention that Santa Maria della Misericordia has connections to Giovanni II Bentivoglio.

In 1996 a fresco painting on the external pilaster in front of the Manzoli family chapel of Santa Maria della Misericordia was restored. This work, albeit quite faded, is of extremely high quality, painted by a talented local artist of the early sixteenth century; it depicts *Saint Augustine on a throne with four monks* (see figure 7.2). In the center on a marble staircase an aged Saint Augustine with a long white beard is seated; he is wearing a miter and a huge red cloak over the traditional black clothes of the Augustinian order and is holding an opened book with writing displayed within it; though it is no longer discernable, it probably revealed a portion of the Augustinian order's rule.

In the foreground there are four Augustinian monks, kneeling in front of the saint, two on the right and two on the left; the two closer to the saint are piously looking at him, and the other two are looking at the viewer. The youngest one, on the left, is crossing his hands in a gesture of humility and devotion; in front of him is the oldest friar with closed eyes. In the background one sees a typical and gentle Italian landscape with hills and trees on the left and, on the right, a town, a river and a building that appears to be a large church in front

---

20 All those paintings are today housed in the Pinacoteca of Bologna. See also *Il genio di Francesco Francia*, passim.

21 See: Anna Ottavi Cavina, "La cappella Bentivoglio," in *Il tempio di San Giacomo Maggiore in Bologna*, ed. Carlo Volpe (Bologna: Padri Agostiniani, 1967), 117–32.

of it. It is worth considering the possibility that this is a rendering of the Santa Maria della Misericordia because at the time that church was not a part of the urban center but, in fact, in the countryside, just outside the city walls, as the walls of Bologna were surrounded by a water channel where today one finds heavily trafficked ring roads.

On the throne of Saint Augustine, the artist pictured monochrome paintings as reliefs; on the left, one can see a naked lad depicted from behind (foreground). That lad is portrayed as standing in front of a young similarly naked young woman. In the background there is a young man on a horse and another faded figure. In the monochrome piece that lies to the right of the portrait one can see two young men on horseback dressed in elegant clothes and feathered hats meeting a bishop, also on a horse, along with another man, perhaps a deacon. There is, too, another naked figure lying on the ground and, in the foreground on the left, another figure still, in this case perhaps a soldier, though that is hard to say with certainty.

My own autopsy has not been able to discern any iconological reference to Saint Augustine's typical representations or hagiography.[22] Even if one were to suspect that some of the images could bear symbolic significance, it is also true that they seem typical of the antiquarian taste of the time and of Costa style, as well and, with regard to the manner of their execution, they approximate the monochrome relief of the altar of the Virgin Mary that is a part of the Manzoli family altarpiece (1490), the work of Renaissance artist Francesco Francia, originally in the Manzoli Chapel of Santa Maria della Misericordia, very close to the location of our painting.[23]

In terms of style, the possible Luther painting appears to be similar to the frescoes of the Santa Cecilia Oratory of 1506, commissioned by Giovanni II Bentivoglio from the masters of Renaissance painting in Bologna: Lorenzo Costa, Francesco Francia, Amico Aspertini, Giovanni Maria Chiodarolo and Cesare Tamaroccio.[24] But we have more than merely stylistic corroboration: Corrado Ricci, in his *Guide of Bologna* of 1886, writes about the fresco painting,

---

22 See Alessandro Cosma, Gianni Pittiglio, *Iconografia agostiniana: Il Quattrocento*, books 1–2 (Roma: Città Nuova Editrice, 2015).

23 See Elisa Coletta, in Cosma and Pittiglio, *Iconografia agostiniana*, 1:322.

24 Costa and Francia worked also for the decoration of the Santa Cecilia Oratory, in 1506, commissioned by Giovanni II Bentivoglio, connected to San Giacomo Maggiore (see Daniela Scaglietti, "La Cappella di Santa Cecilia," in *Il tempio di San Giacomo Maggiore in Bologna*, ed. Carlo Volpe [Bologna: Padri Agostiniani, 1967]: 133–46; Clifford Malcolm Brown, "The Church of Santa Cecilia and the Bentivoglio Chapel in San Giacomo Maggiore in Bologna, with an Appendix containing a catalogue of Isabella d'Este's correspondence concerning Lorenzo Costa and Francesco Francia," *Mitteilungen des Kunsthistorischen Institutes in Florenz*, 13, no. 3/4 [October 1968]: 301–24).

then recently discovered, and attributes this painting to the "Francia workshop" (probably by Tamaroccio).[25] Giovanni Sassu, in his 1997 article on the painting, suggests that Lorenzo Costa the Elder should be identified as the author.[26]

Marco Poli and Simona Costato in their thoughtful essay about the painting, were the first to argue that the young friar on the left side, crossing his arms and kneeling in front of Augustine is, in fact, a portrait of Martin Luther, made when he was in Bologna.[27] Between 1510 and 1511 Nicola da Carignano served as priest to Santa Maria della Misericordia.[28] During that same period of time, the city of Bologna suffered many serious setbacks, including earthquakes (1505 and 1506) and numerous political squabbles.

Yet after 1506, clashes between the followers of the pope and those of the Bentivoglio family, who tried to regain control of the city, created problems for Santa Maria della Misericordia, a place that the Bentivoglio followers considered safe, faithful to their cause.[29] On November 13, 1510, when Bologna was a city assuredly loyal to the papacy, Simone Benadies, vicar of Cardinal Alidosi, ambassador of the pope in Bologna, even gave the monks of the Misericordia an exemption from taxes as recompense for their labor to restore and to enrich the church. Poli and Costato conjecture that the fresco with Saint Augustine and the monks was painted during that period.

Regarding the painting's style, it is quite clear that a date near the beginning of the sixteenth century is accurate, and it was, with all probability, created in 1510–11, precisely when Luther was staying in the Misericordia church on his way to Rome. By comparing the figure of the young monk with Lucas Cranach's portrait of Luther of 1520, which is deemed to be extremely accurate, Poli and Costato believe that the Italian artist indeed portrays Luther, even if there is not any documentary reference.[30] In any case, the young monk depicted by Costa looks strikingly similar to the thirty-seven-year old Luther in Cranach's work (see figures 7.3–7.4, below). One should keep in mind, too, that the man

25 Poli and Costato, "Martin Lutero in un affresco," 427; Sassu, "Sant'Agostino e quattro monaci," 439–43.

26 Sassu, "Sant'Agostino e quattro monaci," 441.

27 Poli and Costato, "Martin Lutero in un affresco," 430.

28 Poli and Costato, "Martin Lutero in un affresco," 434.

29 Poli and Costato, "Martin Lutero in un affresco," 427; Sassu, "Sant'Agostino e quattro monaci," 435.

30 Gamberini points out that from an initial analysis of the documentary fund of the Augustinians in Bologna, there is no specific element that can help to establish either when the fresco was made or which artist made it, or who were the friars portrayed, which still retain very precise physiognomic characteristics. Gamberini, "Il complesso di Santa Maria," 157.

rendered by the German painter is ten years older than the one attributed to Costa. The structure of his facial bones, the intense and penetrating eyes, long pointed nose, the mouth with protruding chin are all the same. Elisa Gamberini also thinks that, in accordance with the record of the contemporary chronicle of Cherubino Granacci, the older monk on the right could be identified as the monastery's friar, Nicola (not to be confused with the priest of the monastery, Nicola da Carignano), who, as noted above, was blind and a very popular local Bolognese preacher (perhaps one of the regional preachers who could have impressed Luther for his powerful eloquence).[31]

The figure of Saint Augustine is also a point of interest; even if, as some have argued, Augustine is portrayed here according to the standard portrait features of his traditional iconography, nonetheless we can find a certain resemblance, too, with portraits of Giles of Viterbo, the prior general of the order who was a well-educated Neoplatonic humanist, philosopher and theologian.[32] If we compare the portrait of Giles in the Sala Regia of the Palazzo dei Priori in Viterbo (17th c.), or the older one by Ippolito Romano, dated 1537, from an altarpiece of the SS. Trinità church in Viterbo where we find a portrait of *Jesus Giving the Keys to Heaven to Saints Peter and Paul* (see figures 7.5–7.7), we can identify the figure of the Misericordia as Saint Augustine with the prior of the order; the expression, the features and facial bones (especially the eyes, the mouth and the long beard) are all very similar.

Regarding the book the saint is holding, it seems to be the very one that Giles used to call the Augustinians back to the rule of Saint Augustine, a new annotated edition of which was published in Venice in 1508, at just the time of this painting; thus, Augustine exhibited quite precisely that new edition of the

---

31 In her article, Gamberini quotes the local chronicle by Cherubino Granacci, which records that on 9 June 1495 a certain friar of the Order of St. Augustine and of the Misericordia, named Nicola, who dwelled on Castiglione Street and was blind from birth, preached with great success to an audience in Saint Petronio church, as the whole city came to listen to him, for he was admired for his profound doctrine; and it was as a "marvel to hear a blind man with so much *gratia* in his preaching," (my rendering of Gamberini, "Il complesso di Santa Maria," 157).

32 Giles of Viterbo, a close friend of Pope Julius II, also takes part in expounding upon the complex program of Raphael's fresco paintings in the Segnatura Room, in the Vatican Palace (1508–12). See: Heinrich Pfeiffer, "La Stanza della Segnatura sullo sfondo delle idee di Egidio da Viterbo," *Sodalizio tra studiosi dell'arte: Colloqui del Sodalizio*, 3 (1970–72): 31–43; Heinrich Pfeiffer, *Zur Ikonographik von Raffaels "Disputa": Egidio da Viterbo und die christlich-platonische Konzeption der Stanza della Segnatura* (Rome: Pontificia Università Gregoriana, 1975); Michael Wernicke, "Egidio da Viterbo: Humanist und Reformer des Augustiner-Eremitenordens," *Martin Luther in Rom: die Ewige Stadt als Kosmopolitisches Zentrum und seine Wahrnehmung*, ed. Michael Matheus, Arnold Nesselrath, Martin Wallraff (Gruyiter: Berlin, 2017), 309–318.

book, and Giles was connected to the founder of the order, as reformer of the Augustinians.[33] Unfortunately, the letters written on the open pages of the volume are faded, and just a few words can be read today on the book: "SCA [...] M," on the top. On the other page, we can identify just an "R," for instance. Only two references with "SCA" can be found in the rule of the Augustinian order, and one of them is the first sentence from chapter 6: *ne ira crescat in odium* ("Let rage not grow into hatred"). This is certainly quite interesting, inasmuch as the chapter in question treats the theme of *Lites aut nullas habeatis* ("Have no quarrels"), which suits perfectly the case of Giles of Viterbo and the mission of Johan van Mechelen and Luther in Italy: one will recall that they were commissioned to smooth out the dispute inside the Augustinian order.

Add to this that in 1506 Giles of Viterbo, during the period the pope was conquering Bologna, was in that selfsame city. Thus, his appearance would have been well known by local people and artists. On this interpretation, the monk behind the proposed Martin Luther figure would be Johan van Mechelen, for at that time he would have been the most important member of the German mission. As Johan van Mechelen was of higher status than Luther in the embassy, it seems likely that if the artist would portray Luther, we can suppose that he would have had to include Johan van Mechelen in his fresco, as well.

What about the other friar on the right, next to friar Nicola? It seems possible that he could be another Nicola, or Nicola da Carignano, the priest of the monastery of Santa Maria della Misericordia, a very important member of the Bolognese Augustinian community, who showed hospitality to the two German monks. If that is the case, we can identify all those in the fresco as Augustinian monks: in the center, Giles of Viterbo, prior of the order; to the left, Johan van Mechelen and Martin Luther, the German guests of Santa Maria della Misericordia; and, on the right, the prior of the monastery, Nicola da Carignano accompanied by the old blind preacher Nicola.

Yet what is the point of such a fresco? We propose that this fresco is related to the mission of the two monks, commissioned probably by the priest of Santa Maria della Misericordia to Costa, in order to recall that relevant event for the Augustinian community of Bologna. The painting is not only celebrating the stay of the two famous German friars at the Misericordia but can be also considered an invitation to settle the controversies within the Augustinian order, under the wise guidance of Giles depicted as the sapient founder of the order. In fact, on one side the German friars are portrayed and, on the other side, the Italian ones, all, with gestures of humility and reverence, are looking at Saint

---

33 Germana Ernst and Simona Foà, "Egidio da Viterbo," *Dizionario Biografico degli Italiani* (Roma: Istituto Treccani, 1993), 42.

Augustine, who has the appearance of Giles of Viterbo; the order finds unity and harmony under his wise and authoritative guidance.

After the Reformation, when Luther was excommunicated from the Roman Catholic Church, the painting, with a portrait celebrating a "heretic" in a church, would no longer have been considered appropriate and, not surprisingly, just a few years later it was covered with a layer of plaster. In fact, the artwork is significantly *not* mentioned in the related pages about the paintings of the Santa Maria della Misericordia in a guide of Bologna of 1560. Thus, that date should be considered a date *ante quem* vis-à-vis the covering over of the fresco.[34] Its survival, however, gives us rich visual insight into a unique moment in time, and today it represents the earliest known portrait of Luther, offering us a signal image of the father of the Reformation preserved within an Italian, Roman Catholic, church.[35]

FIGURE 7.1 Santa Maria della Misericordia, Bologna
PHOTO BY THE AUTHOR

34 Pietro Lamo, *Graticola di Bologna, ossia descrizione delle pitture, sculture e architetture di della città, fatta l'anno 1560* (Bologna: Tipografia Guidi all'Ancora, 1844): 14. Also, Carlo Cesare Malvasia, in his reliable guide of 1755, fails to mention the fresco: Carlo Cesare Malvasia, *Le pitture di Bologna, che nella pretesa, e rimostrata sin'ora da altri maggiore antichità, e impareggiabile eccellenza nella pittura, con manifesta evidenza di fatto, rendono il passeggiere disingannato, ed instrutto* (Bologna: Stamperia Longhi, 1755): 354–56.

35 I am deeply grateful to the editors of this volume for their thoughtful suggestions that have greatly improved this chapter.

FIGURE 7.2 Lorenzo Costa (?), *Saint Augustine and four monks*, ca. 1510, fresco, 90.5 × 43.3 inches (230 × 110 cm), Santa Maria della Misericordia, Bologna
PHOTO BY THE AUTHOR

FIGURE 7.3 Lucas Cranach the Elder, *Martin Luther*, 1520, engraving, 3.9 × 1.7 inches (10 × 14.4 cm), Museum of Fine Arts, Houston
ARTWORK IN THE PUBLIC DOMAIN, WIKIPEDIA

FIGURE 7.4 Lorenzo Costa (?), *Saint Augustine and four monks*, detail, ca. 1510, fresco, 90.5 × 43.3 inches (230 × 110 cm), Santa Maria della Misericordia, Bologna
PHOTO BY THE AUTHOR

FIGURE 7.5 Baldassare Croce, *Giles of Viterbo*, 1588, fresco, 43.3 × 82.6 inches ca. (110 × 210 cm. ca.), Viterbo, Palazzo dei Priori, Sala Regia
ARTWORK IN THE PUBLIC DOMAIN, WIKIPEDIA

FIGURE 7.6 Lorenzo Costa (?), *Saint Augustine and four monks*, detail, ca. 1510, fresco, 90.5 × 43.3 inches (230 × 110 cm), Santa Maria della Misericordia, Bologna
PHOTO BY THE AUTHOR

FIGURE 7.7 Ippolito Romano, *Jesus gives the keys to Saint Peter and Saint Paul*, detail, 1537, oil on wood, Ss.Trinità church, Viterbo
ARTWORK IN THE PUBLIC DOMAIN, WIKIPEDIA

PART 2

The Reformation of Hymnody and Liturgy

CHAPTER 8

What Virgil Taught Martin Luther About Poetry and Music

E. Christian Kopff

Martin Luther (1483–1546) was a Humanist before he became the Reformer, and his classical education influenced him as a theologian and a clergyman. This chapter will explore Virgil's influence on Luther as poet and musician.

Luther received an excellent classical education at the University of Erfurt.[1] He remembered entering the Augustinian monastery in 1505 with only two books, Plautus and Virgil.[2] The indices of the authoritative Weimar Ausgabe of Luther's works list over 250 references to Virgil.[3] Fifty of them appear in his *Table Talk*.[4] Of ancient authors, Luther quotes only Aristotle and Cicero more than Virgil. Luther uses Virgil as a popular source of classical tags and elegant periphrasis throughout his works, even presenting a serious discussion of *fatum* in the *Aeneid* in the major work *De Servo Arbitrio*.[5] Luther goes so far as to credit Virgil as a shaping influence on his creative works, such as the music and poetry he composed for the German liturgy and his chorales, which remain of lasting religious and artistic importance.

When the Elector of Saxony, Frederick the Wise, hid Luther in Wartburg Castle, Luther's colleague Andreas Carlstadt moved to reform the liturgy. On Christmas morning 1521, Carlstadt arrived at All Saints' Church, where he was archdeacon, dressed in layman's clothes. Though he read the mass in Latin, Carlstadt omitted references to the mass as a sacrifice and invited the congregation to the communion table, whether they should prefer the traditional

1 Helmar Junghans, *Der junge Luther und die Humanisten* (Göttingen: Vandenhoeck & Ruprecht, 1985), esp. 71–93.

2 WA TR 1:4 (No. 116); *LW* 54:14.

3 Carl P.E. Springer, "Martin's Martial: Reconsidering Luther's Relationship with the Classics," *International Journal of the Classical Tradition* 14 (2007): 23–50; reference, 32.

4 Lewis W. Spitz, "Luther and Humanism," in *Luther and Learning: The Wittenberg University Luther Symposium*, ed. Marilyn J. Harran (London: Associated University Presses, 1985), 69–94; reference, 78.

5 WA 18:617–18; *LW* 33:41. E. Christian Kopff, "Virgil and Augustine in Luther's *De servo arbitrio*" in *Ad Fontes Witebergenses*, ed. James A. Kellerman and Carl P.E. Springer (Fort Wayne, IN: Lutheran Legacy, 2014), 39–52.

 | DOI:10.1163/9789004206717_010

format or this less formal approach. By New Year's Day every congregation in Wittenberg was doing so.[6]

The Elector Frederick, shocked by the rapidity and violence of the reforms, invited Luther to return to Wittenberg. Luther soon produced a new Latin mass, *Formula Missae*. This *Formula Missae* remained largely traditional in language and form with two major changes: the elimination of the theological error of treating the mass as a sacrifice and the delivery of the hymns, the sermon, and the Words of Institution in German. Luther wanted to preserve the traditional liturgy and yet make essential parts intelligible to ordinary Christians. A complete German service, his *Deutsche Messe*, was celebrated October 29, 1525 and again on Christmas Day.[7]

While composing the German Mass, Luther asked the elector for the help of two chapel musicians, Conrad Ruppsch (d. 1525) and Johann Walter (1496–1570). Walter mentioned the three weeks he spent working with Luther in notes published by Michael Praetorius.[8] Walter was impressed by Luther's mastery of the words and music: "As could be seen *inter alia* from the German Sanctus (*Jesaia dem Propheten das geschah* etc.), how he directed all the notes to the text according to *accent* and *concent* so masterfully and well that I came to ask the Reverend" where he had learned to do so. On the basis of the Latin words *accentus* and *concentus*, I interpret Walter's question to be about the correlation of word accent or emphasis on the correct syllable and the harmony of the music.

> Der *Poët Virgilius* hat mir solches gelehret, der also seine *Carmina* und Wort auf die Geschichte, die er beschreibet, so künstlich *applicиern* kan: Also sol auch die *Musica* alle ihre *Noten* und Gesänge auf den *Text* richten.
>
> WA 19:50

> The poet Virgil taught me such, who can apply so artfully his poems and word to the story he describes. So should the music direct all its notes and singing to the text.[9]

---

6 Martin Brecht, *Martin Luther: Shaping and Defining the Reformation 1521–1532* (Minneapolis: Fortress, 1990), 34.

7 WA Br 3:591; *LW* 53:60.

8 Michael Praetorius, *Syntagmatis Musici Tomus Primus* (Wittenberg: Johannes Richter, 1615), 451–53 = *Syntagma musicum*: Bd. 1: *Musicae artis Analecta* Wittenberg 1614/15, Faksimile-Nachdruck, ed. Wilibald Gurlitt (Basel: Bärenreiter Kassel, 1959), 451–53.

9 Praetorius, *Syntagma musicum*, 453, with original spelling and punctuation.

What trait of Virgilian verse had Luther noticed and employed in his own hymns? To understand this one must grasp the basic form of Virgil's verse, the dactylic hexameter. "Dactylic" refers to the individual *metron* or verse unit or foot consisting either of an initial long syllable followed by two short syllables, a dactyl, or of the metrical equivalent, two long syllables, a spondee. "Hexameter" refers to the six *metra* in the verse. Thus one verse consists of a composition of six *metra*, either dactyls (long, short, short) or spondees (long, long). The sixth *metron*, however, always counts as a spondee, even if the second syllable is short. There is an ictus or stress on the first syllable of each *metron*. Pronouncing Latin involves an interaction of syllable length (or weight) and word accent or stress. If the penult syllable is long, it is stressed. If the penult is short, the antepenult (third syllable from the end) is stressed.

The Roman poets drew these methods from the Greek poets. Roman poets started using Greek meters, including the dactylic hexameter, in the second century BC. Ancient Greek words were pronounced with little or no stress, but with pitch accents, a rise or lowering of tone (or both). The stress accent of Modern Greek is historically influenced by the ancient pitch accent. In ancient Greek verse, however, there was no correlation between the metrical ictus and the pitch of words. As in contemporary and older Greek verse, there was no correlation between verse ictus and word stress or accent in early Roman poetry. This situation changed with Virgil.

A significant factor here is the position of a word-end in the verse. There are certain places in the Virgilian hexameter where we often find word end, or caesura, especially after the first long syllable of the third dactylic *metron* (80% of the verses). There is also one "bridge," a location where there is never word-end, namely after the first long syllable of the fifth *metron*. As a result the first four *metra* of Virgil's dactylic hexameter show considerable variation in the relation between metrical ictus and word accent or stress, but for the last two *metra* there is usually complete agreement in verse ictus and word accent or stress. (The rare exceptions to this rule always have a clear poetic effect.) Therefore, the first four *metra* of Virgil's verse have sixteen different possible variations of dactyls (long, short, short) and spondees (long, long) and Virgil uses all of them, although some are more common than others. The last two *metra* are usually dactyl and spondee, but even when the verse ends in two spondees, word accent or stress and verse ictus agree. There is considerable, although not indefinite, variety in the way Virgil composes the beginnings of his verse, but the overwhelming majority of Virgil's verses end with words in which word accent and metrical ictus agree.

A few examples may give an idea of the texture of Virgil's verse. Agreement of ictus and accent over an entire verse is rare. Ictus and word accent agree in all six *metra* at *A.* 12.176, with two spondees introducing a run of dactyls to emphasize the solemnity and vigor of Aeneas's oath:

> ésto núnc Sol téstis et haéc mihi térra vocánti.
> *A.* 12.176[10]

Another of these relatively rare verses is found in Virgil's first *Eclogue*:

> ímpius haéc tam cúlta novália míles habébit.
> *Ecl.* 1.70

Four of the six *metra* are dactyls and ictus and accent agree in every *metron*. The speaker is a farmer outraged at the unjust loss of his property, which has been given away to soldiers as the spoils of civil war. In fact, lines 70–72 are worth looking at to see how Virgil varies meter and word stress.

> ímpius haéc tam cúlta novália míles habébit
> bárbarus hás segetes. En quó Discórdia cívis
> produxit miseros: his nos consévimus ágros!

The angry indignation of the language of verses 70–71 is reinforced by the frequent dactyls (seven out of a possible ten) and agreement of ictus and accent (11 out of a possible 12). In verse 72 the farmer's angry indignation turns to hopeless acceptance. His despair is reinforced by the three spondees in the first four *metra* and lack of agreement of ictus and accent until line's end.

An example of agreement of ictus and accent (5 times) with, however, the first four *metra*, all spondaic, can be seen in Virgil's description of the blinded Cyclops:

> Mónstr' horrénd' infórm' ingens, cui lúmen adémptum.
> *A.* 3.658

The language, "a frightening, shapeless giant monster, who has lost his eye," is reinforced by four spondees, three with elision. The verse echoes the blinded giant's heavy, slow stumbling steps before dactyls return at the end.

There are many verses where the last two metra are the only ones where ictus and accent agree. The full effect of Virgil's metrical artistry is seen best

10 All Latin quotations of Virgil's works are taken from R.A.B. Mynors, ed., *P. Virgilii Maronis Opera*, Oxford Classical Texts (Oxford: Clarendon Press, 1969). The accent marks (my additions) indicate where metrical ictus and word stress concur.

in longer passages where the predominance of dactyls or spondees and agreement or absence of agreement of ictus and accent change from verse to verse. Let us examine one shorter passage.

> His accénsa super iactátos aéquore tóto
> Tróas, reliquias Danaum atque inmítis Achílli,
> Arcebat longe Latio multósque per ánnos
> Errabant acti fatis maria ómnia círcum.
> Tántae mólis erat Románam cóndere géntem
>
> *A.* 1.29–33

> Angry Juno kept the Trojans far from Latium. They were tossed over all the sea, sole survivors of the Greeks and pitiless Achilles, and for many years they wandered, driven by the fates over all the oceans. So great a task it was to found the Roman race.

The meter reinforces the difficulty of the plight of the survivors of Troy. In lines 31–32 there is only one dactyl in the first four *metra* and no agreement of ictus and accent. In verse 33 spondees still dominate—it is a hard task—but the agreement of ictus and accent gives the verse, as Jackson Knight says, "a strong and triumphant finality."[11] The framing verses 29 and 33 have agreement of ictus and accent in the fourth *metron*, which is less frequent in Virgil than in other Latin poets and is used to frame important passages and underline significant insights and events.[12]

Rarely does Virgil break the pattern of the last two metra, e.g., his description of the storm Juno has roused against the Trojan fleet:

> ... et úndis
> Dát latus; insequitur cumulo praerúptus aquae mons
>
> *A.* 1.104–5

> [The boat] turns its side to the waves and a sheer mountain of water attacks it in a mass.

The line has two agreements of ictus and accent: one to begin the line and one at the expected fifth *metron*. Agreement is missing in the sixth *metron*, which closes with a crash: *aquae mons*, just as at *A.* 5.481 the sacrificed bull falls to

---

11 W.F. Jackson Knight, *Accentual Symmetry in Virgil* (Oxford: Basil Blackwell, 1939), 22.

12 Avery Woodward, "The Fourth Foot in Virgil," *Philological Quarterly* 15 (1936): 126–35; Jackson Knight, *Accentual Symmetry*, 36–84.

the ground with a crash: *stérnitur exanimísque tremens procúmbit humi bos.* "Prostrate the lifeless bull falls to the ground [with a thud]." The thud, however, is in the meter, not the words. Because Virgil creates an expectation of metrical regularity in the last two *metra* throughout the poem, when he violates that regularity, the effect is striking. There are thirty-nine Virgilian hexameters that end with a monosyllable separating ictus and accent. There are eleven in Ovid's much larger corpus; only one in Lucan and four in Statius, whose corpus is as large as Virgil's.

This interaction between variety and contrast in the first four *metra* of each verse and an expected, if not quite inevitable, consistency in the last two *metra* was noticed and analyzed in the twentieth century for the first time.[13]

Or was it the first time it was noticed? It seems to me that best explanation of Luther's enigmatic comment to Walter that "the poet Virgil taught me" to connect word accent or stress and musical beat is that Luther had already noticed the agreement of word accent and metrical ictus in the last *metra* of Virgil's line, his "verse and word" (*Carmina und Wort*). I take Luther's reference to "applying verse and word to the story" to mean that he had noticed that even when metrical ictus and word accent did not agree exactly, the variations were still meaningful.

The most striking and noticeable aspect of Virgil's art of verse, however, is the contrast between the variety in the interaction of metrical ictus and word accent or stress in the first four *metra* of his line and the consistent agreement between ictus and accent at the end of the line, which is more emphatic and significant when accent and ictus agree in the fourth *metron*.

An examination of Luther's chorales and the Sanctus of the German Mass shows Luther varying the relationship of music and word. In such classic chorales as *Ein feste Burg ist unser Gott* and *Vom Himmel hoch*, musical beat and long notes are found in agreement with word accent or stress. The situation is rather different with the Sanctus, *Jesaja dem Propheten das geschah*, where there seems to be no settled agreement of long notes and word accent—the long notes are found with *dass*, *und* and prepositions—until the great threefold Sanctus and then it is clear and emphatic: ***Hei**lig ist **Gott** der **Her**re Zeba**oth*** three times. (*Zebaoth* is correctly stressed on the last syllable as it is in the second stanza of *Ein feste Burg*.)

Luther had observed Virgil's skill in composing so that the metrical beat agreed with the Latin word accent at the end of almost all hexameters and

13 Jackson Knight, *Accentual Symmetry*, 85–107, surveys his own and others' work.

even over entire verses.[14] Luther applied this insight to the relation of musical beat and word stress in German. In his great chorales the musical beat matches and emphasizes the normal word stress. In the Sanctus in his German Mass there is no such consistent agreement of ictus and accent. He stresses connecting words to mirror the awe and even confusion of the human prophet before the Almighty. Only when the seraphs sing the three-fold *Heilig*, do word accent and musical beat come together to emphasize the solemnity of the moment, relating music and word just as Virgil connected *Carmina und Wort* in his dactylic verse.

Luther had noticed this trait in his (obviously oral) reading of Virgil and referred to it in his answer to Walter. Luther read Virgil for content, as his discussion of *fatum* in *De servo arbitrio* amply demonstrates. Yet that is not the only way he read and reflected on that epic poet, for he clearly also noticed a distinctive and important trait of Virgilian verse technique, one that would not receive due attention by modern scholars until the twentieth century. Luther used that observation to create a new German liturgy and alongside it to compose beautiful hymns that are still sung today.

14 L.P. Wilkinson, *Golden Latin Artistry* (Cambridge: Cambridge University Press, 1963), 120–22.

CHAPTER 9

Collaboration over Time: Luther's Adaptation of Ambrose's *Veni Redemptor Gentium*

Eric Phillips

One of the main points of intersection between Lutheranism and the Classics is the translation of classical texts into the vernacular languages that are spoken by Lutherans. The most delicate of these translations is that of poetry. When classical verse is written by no less a figure than St. Ambrose of Milan, a doctor of the Western Church, and the translator in question is Martin Luther himself, it is no surprise perhaps to find that the product is a hymn still sung by Christians in every Advent season. This collaboration that spanned centuries shall be the focus of this study.

The hymn in question is "Savior of the Nations, Come," or in Luther's translation, "*Nu kom der heyden Heyland.*" The introduction to this hymn in volume 53 of the American edition says, "It is a quite literal translation of the '*Veni Redemptor Gentium*' by Ambrose, except in the last stanza where Luther substituted a doxology for the original words."[1] Yet there are some places where Luther's translation changes the idea substantively, and the doxology—while it may be the most obvious deviation—is in fact not one of them. The concluding Ambrosian stanza is also a doxology in Trinitarian form; it addresses Christ primarily (rather than all three Persons of the Trinity equally) and mentions the virgin birth, which is also featured earlier in the hymn, one more time:

Gloria tibi, Domine,
Qui natus es de virgine,
Cum Patre et Sancto Spiritu
In sempiterna gloria.[2]

1 LW 53: 235. The original first stanza of Ambrose's hymn, beginning with *Intende qui regis Israel* was often omitted in the Middle Ages, as it is in Luther's translation. See Carl P.E. Springer, "Ambrose's *Veni Redemptor Gentium:* The Aesthetics of Antiphony," *Jahrbuch für Antike und Christentum* 34 (1991): 76–87.

2 Here and throughout the chapter, the text for *Veni Redemptor Gentium* is the one found in WA 35:149. All translations, unless otherwise noted, are the author's.

 | DOI:10.1163/9789004206717_011

Glory to you, O Lord,
Who were born from a virgin,
With the Father and the Holy Spirit,
In eternal glory.

Luther replaces these words with,

Lob sey Gott dem vatter thon
Lob sey got seym eyngen son
Lob sey got dem heyligen geyst
Ymer unnd ynn ewigkeyt[3]

Praise be made to God the Father
Praise be to God His only Son
Praise be to God the Holy Spirit
Now and in eternity.

Luther thus opts for a generic doxology instead of one recalling the theme of the hymn, but no one who has paid attention to his rendering of stanzas 1–4 could possibly suppose that he had some doctrinal reason for omitting mention of the virgin birth in stanza 8.

This chapter will address four translational deviations that do change the meaning of the hymn: two of these present only subtle changes, while the other two have a greater effect on the hymn's doctrinal content.

The first of the subtle changes comes in stanza 6. Ambrose's version is set forth thus:

Aequalis aeterno Patri,
Carnis tropaeo accingere,
Infirma nostri corporis
Virtute firmans perpetim

Equal to the eternal Father,
Gird on the trophy of flesh,
The weaknesses of our body
Supporting perpetually by Your strength.

3 Here and throughout the chapter, the text for *Nu kom der heyden Heyland* is the one found in WA 35:430–31.

Luther renders these lines as follows:

Der du bist dem vater gleich.
Fur hynnaus den syeg ym fleisch,
Das dein ewig gots gewalt
ynn unns das kranck fleysch enthallt

You are the Equal of the Father.
Complete your victory in the flesh,
That your eternal divine power
May sustain the sick flesh in us.

The original, perhaps showing the influence of the Greek Fathers on Ambrose,[4] comes close to explaining salvation as a direct result of the Incarnation: because the Father's Equal put on our flesh, our flesh is sustained by His strength. The fact that *firmans* is a present-active participle shows that this is an effect accomplished at the same time as, and by means of, the second-person imperative *accingere*, which is the main verb. The only reference to Christ's death and resurrection lies in the word *tropaeo*, since He must win a victory by means of His flesh in order for His flesh to become a trophy.

Considering how indirect this reference is to the cross, and how central the cross was to Luther's theology, one might have expected a significant deviation from Luther here, but his touch is very light. Luther keeps God's power as the acting subject *and* the healing of the flesh as the salvific result, showing that he is comfortable with this Patristic language, and feels no need to add a qualifying statement about forensic justification. He gives Ambrose as much credit as possible by using the word *Syeg* (*Sieg*, victory, a word implied by *tropaeo*, trophy) to refer to the cross and resurrection. This word makes it clear that the victory Christ won was a necessary precondition for this divine strengthening.

4 Since Ambrose became a bishop suddenly, appointed to the position at the will of the Emperors Gratian and Valentinian I when the people of Milan (or an influential faction thereof) unexpectedly asked for him, he began his episcopate with no formal theological education. He had held only secular offices until then. Indeed, he had not even been baptized yet, following a widespread fourth-century custom of delaying baptism out of uncertainty regarding the forgiveness of serious post-baptismal sin. Notably, Ambrose enjoyed an excellent command of Greek from his study of the classics and an impressive determination to make up for lost time. Craig Alan Satterlee writes: "In learning Christian theology Ambrose relied on his knowledge of Greek. His curriculum consisted of the Greek tradition—Origen, Basil, Hippolytus of Rome, Eusebius of Caesarea, Didymus the Blind, Gregory Nazianzus, and Athanasius, as well as Jewish writers such as Philo and Flavius Josephus" (*Ambrose of Milan's Method of Mystagogical Preaching* [Collegeville, MN: The Liturgical Press, 2002], 84).

It cannot be understood, in Luther's version, as a simple effect of the Word assuming human flesh.

The second subtle change comes in stanza 7. Ambrose's Latin reads as follows:

> Praesepe iam fulget tuum,
> Lumenque nox spirat novum
> Quod nulla nox interpolet,
> Fideque iugi luceat
>
> Already your stable shines,
> And night breathes a new light
> That no night may corrupt,
> And that glows with living[5] faith.

Luther translates:

> Dein kryppen glentzt hell und klar.
> Die nacht gybt eyn new liecht dar
> Tunckel muß nicht komen dreyn
> Der glaub bleib ymer ym scheyn
>
> Your crib shines bright and clear.
> The night gives a new light.
> Darkness must not come into it.
> Faith stays ever in the glow.

In the original, faith relates to light (the light of Christ) only insofar as faith displays that light. It does not produce it per se, for it already shines ("already your stable shines."); it does, however, "adorn" it (taking *Fideque iugi* as an ablative of description) or "reveal" it (ablative of means) or at least "shape" its revelation (ablative of manner). In Luther's version faith does none of these things. There, the only relationship between faith and the light of Christ is that "Faith stays ever in the glow," meaning that if it should ever move out of that glow, it could no longer be faith, for it would no longer have a promise to believe. This change is very much in line with Luther's doctrinal emphases. Ambrose has

---

5 Or "perennial." Luther takes this meaning of *iugi* and turns the adjective into an adverb to get *ymer* (*immer*; always, ever).

faith serving the light by adorning it or making it known. Luther has the light serving faith by endowing it with saving content.

Now we move to the two changes that are more obvious, the first of which probably stands out more because of its position in the very first line of the hymn, which is also its title. For Ambrose, this is "*Veni, Redemptor gentium*" ("Come, Redeemer of the nations"). For Luther it is "*Nu kom der heyden Heyland*" ("Now come, Savior of the heathen"), where the word *heyden* (*Heiden*, heathen) has some considerations in its favor. First, it alliterates very nicely with *Heyland* (*Heiland*). Second, although it is technically a rendering of *gentilium* (gentiles) and not *gentium* (nations), it could easily be defended on Old Testament grounds, since in that context "the nations" usually does mean gentiles, i.e. the nations beyond Israel that do not know God.[6] And this makes sense thematically, since the hymn is written and sung from the perspective of an Israel awaiting Christ's *first* Advent, when the *gens Romana,* the *gens Graeca,* the *gens Germana,* and all the recognized *gentes* of Luther's day with the sole exception of the Jews, were all still heathen. All this being said, it remains a strangely distancing translation, especially for Luther. The people who would be singing it in German churches were not heathen, and had not been, even in Saxony, for five or six centuries. Thus, from Luther's vantage point it must have seemed that if Jesus is the Savior of the *nations,* they were still included. If He is the Savior of the *heathen,* this was a line that would have had direct application only to their ancestors.

The notes in the Weimar edition mention three other German translations of *Veni Redemptor gentium* that preceded Luther's. From the twelfth century came the anonymous translation "*Chume erloser der diete, zaiege geburt der maide*" ("Come, Savior of the People, Show the Birth of the Virgin").[7] Two centuries later Heinrich von Laufenberg offered his own translation (1418): "*Kum har, erlöser volkes schar*" ("Come Here, Redeemer of the Host of People").[8] Finally, in 1523, the year before Luther's version was published, a translation by revolutionary reformer Thomas Müntzer, "*O herr, erloser alles volcks*" ("O Lord, Savior of All People").[9] All three of these previous translations render

---

6 E.g. Isaiah 49:6 [ESV]: "It is too light a thing that you should be my servant to raise up the tribes of Jacob and to bring back the preserved of Israel; I will make you as a light for the nations (Hebrew *gôyim,* LXX ἐθνῶν, Vulgate *gentium*) that my salvation may reach to the end of the earth."

7 WA 35:149. My thanks to Matthew Carver for help with the Old German in this chapter.

8 Philipp Wackernagel, *Das deutsche Kirchenlied von der ältesten Zeit bis zu Anfang des XVII. Jahrhunderts* (Leipzig: B.G. Teubner, 1867), 2:580 [Hymn No. 755].

9 WA 35:149. The date of publication of Müntzer's *Deutsches Kirchenamt,* in which the hymn was included, comes from WA 35:75.

gentium with a word also meaning "people." The two current in Luther's day chose *Volk*, which would seem to be a straightforward equivalent to *gens*, and one that would not separate contemporary worshipers from the salvation they were singing about. What motivated this change? It may be that Luther is reacting against Thomas Müntzer's recent translation, because of the meaning that Müntzer likely intended. The primary meaning of *Volk* is indeed "a people, race, or nation," but it can also be used to refer to *the* people, in the sense of the common folk, the segment of society that Müntzer was urging to rise up in arms and set Christian society right. When *Nu kom der heyden Heyland* was published in summer, 1524, Müntzer was at the height of his influence, and the Peasants' Revolt was less than half a year away. In this context, Luther may have found the expected word to be tainted.

In support of this theory, I offer the following examples of Müntzer's use of the word, taken from his anti-Luther treatise "A Highly-Provoked Vindication and a Refutation of the Unspiritual, Soft-Living Flesh in Wittenberg," published in December 1524. In all three excerpts, *das Volk* means the virtuous salt of the earth, those who recognize and desire the truth and must stand up for it against entrenched authorities, whether political or intellectual, who are duplicitous and abuse their positions:

> It is a good old custom that the people (*das Volk*) must be present if someone is to be judged properly by the law of God, Num. 15. Why? So that if the authorities try to give a corrupt judgement (Isaiah 10), the Christians present can object and prevent this happening.[10]
>
> The ambitious biblical scholars ... thirsted for [Jesus'] blood, and would be satisfied with nothing less, for they said, John 11: "If we let him go, then all the people will believe in him; the common man [*das Volk*] will attach himself to him; look, already they are beginning to swarm around him, If we allow him to carry out his mission then we are done for, we will be nothing but poor wretches." In just the same way along came that Caiaphas, Doctor Liar [*Lügner*, a pun on *Luther*] and gave his princes sound advice. He managed it splendidly, saying that he was worried about his fellow countrymen near Allstedt. As the whole land will testify on my account, the honest truth of the matter in this, that among

10 Peter Matheson, ed. and trans., *The Collected Works of Thomas Müntzer* (Edinburgh: T&T Clark, 1988), 334–35; the original German reads: *Darum muß auch aus altem, gutem Brauch das Volk daneben sein, wenn einer recht verrichtet wird nach dem Gesetz Gottes* (*4. Mos. 15*). *Ei warum? Ob die Oberkeit das Urteil wöllte verkehren* (*Jes. 10*), *so sollen die umstehenden Christen das verneinen und nicht leiden* (http://www.mlwerke.de/mu/mu_003.htm).

> the poor thirsty people [*das arme dürstige Volk*] there was such a thirst for truth that every road was crammed with people from far and near, who had come to hear how worship was conducted in Allstedt, with its biblical praise and preaching.[11]
>
> You [Luther] have strengthened the power of the godless evil-doers, so that they could continue on in their old way. Therefore your fate will be that of the fox that has been hunted down; the people [*das Volk*] will go free, and God alone will be their Lord.[12]

Considering that the two translations appeared in such a close span of time and that Luther's was published when the conflict between the two men was coming to a head, it is reasonable to surmise that Luther made his close translation with the object of replacing Müntzer's paraphrase, lest it gain traction with the German people. By using the word *Heyden* instead of the more obvious and relatable *Volk*, Luther rescued the hymn from the social unrest of that period and brought its focus back to its original subject material.[13] The word *Volk*, in mid-1524 with Müntzer's recent appropriation, was open to a wholly different and unsuitable contextualization.

The final significant change appears in the last line of that same opening stanza. Ambrose's Latin version reads:

> Veni, redemptor gentium;
> Ostende partum virginis;
> Miretur omne saeculum.
> Talis decet partus Deum.

11 *The Collected Works of Müntzer*, 338–39; the original German reads: *die ehrgeizigsten Schriftgelehrten ... Ihre Begiere waren zu eitel Totschlagen dürstig, denn sie sagten (Joh. am 11.): »So wir ihn lassen bezähmen, dann werden die Leute alle an ihn glauben. Es wird ihm das Volk anhängen. Sehet, es läuft ihm schon mit großen Haufen zu. Werden wir ihn lassen seine Sache also ausführen, so haben wir verloren, so sein wir arme Leut.« Also kam auch Kaiphas, Doktor Lügner, und gab einen guten Rat seinen Fürsten. Da hat er die Sache wohl ausgerichtet. Er hätte Sorge für seine Landsleute hart bei Allstedt. Es ist nicht anders in der Wahrheit, wie mir das ganze Land Gezeugnis gibt, das arme dürstige Volk begehrte der Wahrheit also fleißig, daß auch alle Straßen voll Leute waren von allen Orten, anzuhören, wie das Amt, die Biblien zu singen und zu predigen, zu Allstedt angerichtet ward* (http://www.mlwerke.de/mu/mu_003.htm).

12 *The Collected Works of Müntzer*, 350; the original German reads: *Damit hast du gestärkt die Gewalt der gottlosen Böswichter, auf daß sie je ja auf ihrem alten Wege bleiben. Darum wird dir's gehen wie einem gefangenen Fuchs. Das Volk wird frei werden, und Gott will allein der Herr darüber sein!* (http://www.mlwerke.de/mu/mu_003.htm).

13 It is interesting to note in this connection that although our English version (*Lutheran Service Book* #332) follows Luther rather than Ambrose on most things, it has gone back to Ambrose on this translation: "Savior of the *Nations*, Come."

Come, Redeemer of the Nations,
Show the birth of the Virgin.[14]
Let all the world marvel.
Such a birth befits God.

Luther's renders these lines:

Nu kom der heyden heyland,
der yungfrawen kynd erkannd,
Das sych wunnder alle welt,
Gott solch gepurt yhm bestelt.

Now come, Savior of the heathen,
Renowned Child of the Virgin,
That all the world might marvel,
God appointed such a birth for Him.

There are two possible reasons why in Luther's version the world might be expected to marvel. The distinction depends on which verb is construed as the one causally preceding the *das* (*dass*): either 1) that the Savior should come as any woman's son ("Now come ... that all the world might marvel that God appointed such a birth for Him"),[15] or 2) that a man should be born from a virgin ("[In order] that all the world might marvel, God appointed such a birth for Him"). In the first case, the marvel would be the humiliation of God, to become a man. In the second case, the marvel would be the glory of this man, to be born in such a miraculous manner.

The standard English translation by William M. Reynolds (1812–76) seems to understand Luther in the first way: "Marvel now, O heav'n and earth, / That the Lord chose such a birth." And this would seem to be the preferred meaning, the more significant one and the one more in line with Luther's doctrinal emphases, but it is not the meaning of the original. Ambrose's Latin is unambiguous: "*Talis decet partus Deum*" ("Such a birth befits God"). Far from expressing wonder that the Eternal Word should become a Man, Ambrose cites the virgin birth as glorious evidence that the man is God. If this seems a strange emphasis, one only need remember that when Ambrose was Bishop of Milan, the Arian controversy had not yet passed into the pages of history. Auxentius, his predecessor in that office, had in fact been an Arian, and one of the most memorable

14 Subjective genitive here: the birth that the Virgin gave.

15 In its construal of the final line, this reading takes *bestelt* (*bestellt*) as a subjunctive with the final "e" elided. Thanks to Matthew Carver for this suggestion.

chapters of Ambrose's career, mentioned by St. Augustine in Book IX of his *Confessions*, involved an extended act of civil disobedience carried out in defiance of the Arian regent Justina, mother of the child-Emperor Valentinian II, who demanded in 385 and 386 that the bishop allow at least one of Milan's churches to be used by her faction.

In 386, as Easter drew near, Ambrose organized a round-the-clock sit-in so that the imperial court would not be able to secure a church for the feast, unless they resorted to violence against the populace. With the people of Milan solidly on his side, Ambrose won this showdown. It was a harrowing experience, though, as Augustine remembered it, and he recalled that *hymn singing* played a significant role in keeping the people's spirits up:

> Only a year or a little more had passed since Justina, mother of the young king Valentinian, was persecuting your servant Ambrose in the interest of her heresy. She had been led into error by the Arians. The devout congregation kept continual guard in the Church, ready to die with the bishop, your servant. There my mother, your handmaid, was a leader in keeping anxious watch and lived in prayer.... That was the time when the decision was taken to introduce hymns and psalms sung after the custom of the eastern Churches, to prevent the people from succumbing to depression and exhaustion.[16]

Veni Redemptor Gentium was probably not one of the hymns employed in this fashion, as Augustine says this was the first time Ambrose had introduced such music, and its Advent/Christmas theme makes it an unlikely composition for Lententide, but the story makes it clear that Ambrose counted hymns among his anti-Arian weapons, and brings home to us the degree to which Arianism was still a living threat, although we, from our historical vantage point, usually think of it as having been defeated at the Council of Constantinople in 381. Since the obvious humanity of Jesus Christ, complete with limitations and weaknesses, was a fact to which the Arians would often appeal when arguing that He could *not* have been consubstantial with the Father, the hymn's original first stanza makes a lot of polemical sense. Yes, He was born of a woman, but the woman was a virgin. "Such a birth befits God."

16 Augustine of Hippo, *Confessions*, trans. Henry Chadwick (Oxford: Oxford University Press, 1991), IX.15 (pp. 164–65).

Luther, however, was not dealing with Arians in 1524.[17] It was but an old controversy to him, without any contemporary manifestation. This probably explains his more ambiguous rendering of the hymn's first stanza, in which it is not clear whether the "heavens and earth" should be marveling at the magnanimous condescension that God displayed in choosing a human birth for his Son, or at the sign of Jesus's divinity that God conveyed by making that birth uniquely miraculous and claiming paternity himself. Perhaps the ambiguity was deliberate, and he intended both reasons at the same time. Whatever the case, the result for English-speaking Lutherans has been a verse that points us firmly in the opposite direction from the one that Ambrose intended.

In sum, the four changes that Luther made in his translation alter the meaning of the original in some meaningful way: 1) a change in stanza 6 that prevents it from being read as if the Incarnation could have accomplished our salvation by itself; 2) a change to stanza 7 so that it says the light of Christ gives life to faith, instead of saying that faith makes the light of Christ visible to the world, or adorns it in some way; 3) a change to the first line of stanza 1 that makes the hymn's focus more historical and less immediate; and 4) a change in the final line of stanza 1 that leads us to think of the humiliation of the Word, rather than the glory of the man. I have argued that the first two changes were theologically motivated, and the last two changes were historically conditioned. In closing, however, I would like also to call attention to a passage Luther did not change.

In *Veni Redemptor Gentium*, stanza 4 runs as follows:

Procedens de thalamo suo,
Pudoris aula regia,
Geminae gigas substantiae
Alacris ut currat viam.

He came out from His chamber,
The kingly hall of chastity,
A Giant of twofold Substance
Eager to run His path.

---

17 He began to speak against the "New Arians" in the 1530s. See Manfred Schulze, "Martin Luther and the Church Fathers," 573–626 in *The Reception of the Church Fathers in the West: From the Carolingians to the Maurists*, vol. 1, ed. Irena Backus (Leiden: E.J. Brill, 1997), 585–86.

The fourth stanza of *Nu kom der heyden Heyland* is rendered thus:

> Er gieng aus der kamer seyn,
> dem könglichen saal so reyn.
> Gott von art vnd mensch eyn hellt
> seyn weg er zu lauffen eyllt.
>
> He came out from His chamber,
> The kingly hall so pure,
> God by nature, and Man, a hero,
> He hastened to run His path.

The third line contains the only significant deviation from the original, save the use of a verb instead of an adjective in line 4. While Luther's line is not as tersely grand as Ambrose's "A giant of twofold substance," the substitution of *Hellt* (*Held*, Hero) for *Gigas* (Giant) is perfect in terms of connotation, and with each syllable being a separate word, the line rolls like a drum.

What makes this rendering even better, though, is the fact that the original alludes closely to Psalm 19:5, reusing many of the words of the Vulgate version,[18] and Luther's translation does exactly the same thing. Luther employs many of the same words from his own translation of the Psalter. In both versions, Jesus does what the sun does in Psalm 19, verse 5: "coming out of his chamber, [He] rejoiceth as a strong man to run a race" (KJV). Thus Ambrose's *procedens de thalamo suo ... Alacris ut currat viam* draws on the Vulgate's Psalm 19:5 (18:6): *procedens de thalamo suo exultavit ut fortis ad currendam viam*, and Luther's *Er gieng aus der kamer seyn ... eyn Hellt seyn weg er zu lauffen eyllt* draws on the Luther Bible's (1524) Psalm 19:5: *Er ...*[19] *gehet ... aus seyner Kamer und ist fro wie eyn Held zu lauffen den Weg.*[20]

Luther's depth of fidelity to Ambrose's original verse emerges very clearly here with his attention not only to Ambrose's words, but his biblical source material, allowing the two major historical church leaders to collaborate, as it were, though separated by more than a millennium. Even the substitution of "Hero" for "Giant" was a choice not determined by mere metrical considerations but rather based on the German translation he had already made of

18 Though Ambrose was writing before his contemporary Jerome made the Vulgate translation, the Gallican Psalter, which is the Vulgate Psalter referred to here, predates Jerome.

19 The *Er* comes from verse 4, and is not restated in verse 5.

20 WA DB 10^{I}:156.

Psalm 19. This stands as an allusive and enduring testimony to Luther's skills as a translator, as much as the other changes testify to his dexterity as a theologian, a dexterity that shines through different languages and interpretive difficulties that face the translator, and especially a translator of poetry. Luther was equal to such challenges, and made his changes advisedly.

CHAPTER 10

The Latin Liturgy and Juvenile Lutheran Instruction in Sixteenth-Century Germany

Joseph Herl

When one thinks of the instruction of children in the teachings of the Lutheran Church, the Bible and the catechism spring to mind immediately. In sixteenth-century Germany, as is widely known, vernacular hymns also played an important part. Less well known is the role played by the Latin liturgy.

On the surface, this seems inexplicable. Did not German Lutherans, in the wake of Luther's translation of the Bible into the common tongue, come to stress the importance of hearing the Gospel in one's own language? And were not liturgies and hymns sung in German so that people could understand what was going on? Yes, and yes, but Lutherans also did not give up the Latin liturgies so quickly. Educated men could speak Latin, and for them the language would have posed no obstacle. And any boy who may have had a professional career in mind—lawyer, theologian, physician, diplomat, government official, or schoolmaster—had to learn to speak and write Latin fluently, for Latin was (if it may be said) the *lingua franca* of Europe at the time.

To this end, Lutherans set up Latin schools for boys in the larger towns. Smaller municipalities had German schools, and there were also German schools for girls, but it was the Latin schools that were the most academically oriented. In these schools, most of the instruction was in the Latin language, and the boys were even required to speak Latin to each other outside of class. Those who flouted this rule were typically whipped or fined.[1]

Of course, it helped if the boys had an incentive to learn the language. Fortunately, Lutherans had just the thing: a mass and daily offices they had inherited in that language from the pre-Reformation church. The boys heard, sang, and led such services, and Luther himself admitted, "For by no means would I have the Latin language completely removed from the divine service, as my chief concern is with the youth."[2] He was afraid that the boys' mastery of

---

1 O. Albrecht, "Bemerkungen zu Medlers Naumburger Kirchenordnung vom Jahre 1537," *Neue Mitteilungen aus dem Gebiet historisch-antiquarischer Forschungen* 19 (1898): 623.

2 *LW* 53:62–63; cf. WA 19:74.

 | DOI:10.1163/9789004206717_012

Latin would suffer if they did not receive daily practice in the language both in church and in school, a concern that was to be echoed many times by Lutheran writers over the next two hundred years. Luther also had another reason for retaining Latin in the services: among the most useful vestiges of the pre-Reformation liturgies, he wrote, were the "fine Latin songs, *de tempore* ... they truly please us from the heart."[3]

1 The Latin School Curriculum in Naumburg

To appreciate the role of the Latin liturgy in forming children's faith, we must first understand its place in the school curriculum. One Latin school typical of its time was in Naumburg, a city in Ernestine Saxony about sixty kilometers southwest of Leipzig. Evangelical preachers had been allowed in Naumburg as early as 1520, and the city called its first Lutheran pastor in 1525; but it was not until 1536, when Dr. Nicolaus Medler was named pastor and superintendent, that the curriculum assumed its shape. The year after his arrival Medler issued the city's first evangelical church and school order for the parish church of St. Wenceslaus.[4] Medler was an experienced teacher as well as a pastor, having taught in the cities of Arnstadt, Eger, Wittenberg, and Hof, and as school rector designed the curriculum for the school in Hof.[5] His order for Naumburg named three teachers for the Latin school: the *magister ludi*, or schoolmaster, the *baccalaureus*, and the cantor. There was also a German school for girls taught by the organist. Notably, the Naumburg church order stands out among sixteenth-century orders in that it specifies that the girls' choir sing on occasion in public church services; in this case, in Sunday Vespers.[6]

3 *LW* 34:59; cf. WA 30:2:352. *De tempore* here means "of" or "pertaining to the time" or "occasion"; that is, related to a specific day or season of the church year.

4 [Carl Felix] Köster, "Die Naumburger Kirchen- und Schulordnung von D. Nicolaus Medler aus dem Jahre 1537," *Neue Mitteilungen aus dem Gebiet historisch-antiquarischer Forschungen* 19 (1898): 497–569, with a 32-page supplement containing the music from the church order following page 636. Printed from a manuscript in the Königliche Öffentliche Bibliothek in Dresden (the present-day Sächsische Landesbibliothek), current shelfmark Mscr.Dresd.K.50. Reprinted from Köster, but without the music, and compared word for word with the original manuscript in Sehling, 2:61–90. Although the date on the order is 1537, there is evidence that the form in which it has come down to us actually dates from five or six years later: see WA 35:291–2.

5 Albrecht, "Bemerkungen," 625.

6 Sehling, 2:71. Girls' choirs were also used in Hof and Joachimsthal. See the discussion in Joseph Herl, *Worship Wars in Early Lutheranism* (Oxford, 2004), 164.

The Latin school was divided into eight classes or grades. This reflected the new humanistic educational philosophy rather than the traditional medieval practice, which tended to use only three or four classes; (the Saxon visitation instructions of 1528, written by Philip Melanchthon, mention only three).[7]

The four lower classes attended twenty-eight hours of instruction per week: six hours on Monday, Tuesday, Thursday, and Friday; and two hours on Wednesday and Saturday (they had the afternoon off). Their curriculum consisted of Latin reading, German reading, *syllabicantium*, and *elementarium*. The school order does not tell us, unfortunately, how the classroom time was organized or exactly what *syllabicantium* and *elementarium* comprised.

We have much more information for the four upper classes. Instruction began at 6:00 AM and continued until mid-afternoon, with a two-hour break from 10:00 to noon. From the class schedule (Table 1) we learn that the scholars spent quite a bit of time with Latin grammar and readings: 18 hours for the upper first class (the oldest boys), 24 hours for the lower first, 16 for the second class, 14 for the third, and 16 for the fourth.[8] Authors covered in the upper classes were Virgil, Cicero, and Terence; the comedies of Terence were memorized and performed. In addition, the first class had declamation and disputation exercises after Vespers and holy days. Other materials were used in the second through fourth classes, including a Latin translation of Luther's catechism, the fables of Aesop, and the distichs (or proverbs) of Cato. The second through fourth classes also had Latin instruction eight times per week (grammar four times and Virgil or other literature four times) in whatever time remained between the end of morning and afternoon church services and the start of the next class.

The requirement that only Latin be spoken at the school was strictly enforced. Each week the schoolmaster appointed one of the students to be *lupus*, "the wolf." His job was to take down the name of every student who broke a school rule, including the rule forbidding the use of the German language. Every Saturday the list was given to the pastor, who administered the requisite punishment with a birch rod.[9]

The first class also learned Hebrew and Greek, with six hours per week of each. This is not unheard of in Latin schools, but it was by no means universal;

---

7 See WA 26:237–40; *LW* 40:315–20.

8 The count of hours is from Albrecht, "Bemerkungen," 629. It fits what is in the table, although it is sometimes difficult to know whether or not something should be considered instruction in Latin, as opposed to another subject.

9 Albrecht, "Bemerkungen," 623.

Melanchthon's visitation order of 1528 did not mention these languages, for instance. In Naumburg, this language instruction was the only explicit education the students received in the Bible, at least in the upper classes.

The catechism was not neglected in the curriculum. The six lower classes had catechism instruction on Wednesday and Saturday mornings, in German for the youngest students, then increasingly in Latin. A catechism examination was held Mondays and Fridays at Vespers during the summer. And one of the chief parts was recited with the cantor every day before the students were dismissed: the Ten Commandments on Monday, the Creed on Tuesday, the Lord's Prayer on Wednesday, Baptism on Thursday, the Sacrament of the Altar on Friday, and Luther's Morning Prayer and the following parts on Saturday.

The physical sciences did not occupy much instructional time, with only the first class having two hours per week of physics. Two hours of astronomy were also taught, but the instructional period was shared with Cicero.

Instruction in music occupied four hours per week in connection with arithmetic. This makes sense, for in medieval thinking music was a branch of arithmetic. Music actually gets short shrift in the Naumburg order; in many schools, instruction in music alone was allotted four to five hours per week.[10] But even in Naumburg, the three upper classes practiced Gregorian chant Wednesdays and Saturdays after Vespers, and the second class also practiced on the same days after the morning service. All the music was either theoretical or vocal; German schools did not instruct pupils in how to play musical instruments.

2 The Schoolboys' Role in the Latin Services

The boys spent much of their time in church during the week. The second, third, and fourth classes attended the early service and Vespers every school day (Monday through Saturday), for a total of twelve services per week. The first class had more instructional time and attended only eight services. The boys, by the way, did not merely sit in the pews and while away their time: the upper three classes, at least, served as the church's choir and sang the liturgy. That is why they rehearsed Gregorian chant twice per week.

10 Friedrich Sannemann (in *Die Musik als Unterrichtsgegenstand in den evangelischen Lateinschulen des 16. Jahrhunderts* [Berlin and Leipzig, 1904], 16–20) surveys the amount of music instruction in German schools during the sixteenth century. Johannes Rautenstrauch (in *Luther und die Pflege der kirchlichen Musik in Sachsen* [Leipzig, 1907], 64–74) provides a list of schools in Saxony during the sixteenth century and the number of hours of music instruction in each.

In many Lutheran cities, the early service during the week was Matins in Latin. In Naumburg, however, two types of services were done. One, on Mondays, Wednesdays, Fridays, and Saturdays, was a stripped-down Matins with parts in Latin and parts in German. The Benedictus was sung on Monday, the Athanasian Creed on Wednesday (since it was so long, half was sung one week and half the next), the Nicene Creed on Friday, and the *Te deum laudamus* on Saturday. There was no sermon. On Tuesdays and Thursdays there was a sermon, and the service was entirely in German.

Vespers was mostly in Latin, although the reading from an epistle of Paul was done in both Latin and German by two boys. After the reading, another boy recited a part of the catechism from memory; the six chief parts were done on the six weekdays. Then there were the Sunday services—Matins, mass, and Vespers—and the boys participated in all of those.

Fortunately, we have plenty of information on the content of the boys' choir activities. They sang the liturgy in either German or Latin and led the congregation in the singing of German hymns. In some churches the boys sang from music manuscripts (a few of these have survived), but many churches opted for a published collection of chants. At least a dozen such books intended for Lutheran use appeared between 1545 and 1627 (see the appendix "Printed Chant Collections for Lutheran Use").[11] Table 2, "Categories of Chant in the Chant Books," summarizes the contents of the books. It is immediately apparent that Ludecus 1589 and Magdeburg 1612–13 contain far more chants than the other books. They were both printed for use in a cathedral, where there was likely to have been more money available for printing multivolume chant collections and where professional singers who could manage a large repertoire of chant were more readily found. The other books were intended for use in parish churches, which generally lacked the financial resources available to cathedrals and where most of the singers were schoolboys. It is possible that additional chants were sung in parish churches as well, but that they were notated in manuscript rather than printed.

Not surprisingly, the most numerous chants are the brief antiphons, which have a multitude of uses, especially in the office. Next in number are the

---

11 Books surveyed for this study are marked with a plus (+). Nearly all the books on the list are from Germany, although there is one Scandinavian book—Niels Jesperssøn's *Gradual*—because its place of publication, Copenhagen, is close to Germany and because it is available in a reprint edition. Other Scandinavian sources are not listed, including the interesting *Graduale* of Guðbrandur Þorláksson, which appeared in thirteen editions between 1594 and 1739, all of which are in the National Library of Iceland (and most of which are digitized on the library's website).

responsories, and this requires some explanation. These chants follow the lessons in Matins and Vespers, the principal offices observed by Lutherans. (Matins is a combination of medieval Matins and Lauds, and Vespers is a combination of medieval Vespers and Compline.) In the Middle Ages, the offices were prayed mainly by professional clergy (and occasionally by exceptionally devout lay people). When Luther adapted Matins and Vespers for use in schools, he reduced the number of lessons by two-thirds because of his reasonable fear that schoolboys would not be able to sit through lengthy readings. The chant books, though, appear not to have reduced the number of responsories; and so even when there is only one appointed reading, the books may still provide three or four responsories. Presumably the cantor chose one from among them.

Other genres well represented are introits and hymns, with exactly a hundred each. Notable are the forty-three sequences. These chants, which follow the Alleluia of the mass, represent the continuation among Lutherans of a medieval genre that was all but eliminated in Catholic churches after the Council of Trent in the mid-sixteenth century. But Lutherans were not bound by the council's decisions, and they went right on singing the old sequences as long as Latin continued in use in Lutheran churches.

3 The Chant Books as Theology Textbooks

The Latin chants sung in Lutheran churches date, almost without exception, from before the Reformation. This raises the question of their doctrinal content. A large number of Lutheran church orders instruct that a "pure" introit, sequence, antiphon, hymn, or responsory be sung. The word "pure" refers here to Lutheran doctrinal purity: if a chant inherited from the medieval church contained questionable doctrine, either it was discarded or its text was revised. A leading reviser of texts was Hermann Bonnus, superintendent in Lübeck, and a few chant books adopted his revisions.[12] A somewhat cursory survey of the texts suggests that the chief concern in revising them was to eliminate any reference to praying to the saints, which was proscribed for Lutherans.

These chant books give us a fascinating picture of Lutheran teachings during the century after the Reformation. For example, the 1589 *Vesperale* of Matthäus Ludecus (for the Havelberg cathedral) contains an antiphon for the festival of

12 Hermann Bonnus, *Hymni et seqventiae, tam de tempore quam de Sanctis, cum suis Melodijs, sicut olim sunt cantata in Ecclesia Dei, & iam passim correcta* (Lübeck, 1559).

the Nativity of Mary (Example 10.1): *Gaude Maria virgo, cunctas haereses sola interemisti in universo mundo* ("Rejoice, O Virgin Mary; you only have killed all the heresies in the entire world"). The antiphon has a footnote that appeals to Urbanus Rhegius, Lutheran superintendent in the city of Celle and a leading apologist for the Lutheran cause, in justifying the perpetual virginity: "Mary only, says D. Urbanus Rhegius, has killed all heresies or denied heretics herself because in the act of parturition and following it she remained a virgin, even an instrument or the material cause, as it were, in which from her the Son of God assumed human nature without violating her virginity, to which miraculous and ineffable work only this virgin has been chosen by God." The next antiphon reads: *Post partum virgo inuiolata permansisti, Dei genetrix sit semper benedicta* ("After birth you remained an inviolate virgin; may the mother of God be ever blessed").

Today few Lutherans would acknowledge the perpetual virginity of Mary, but in the sixteenth century this teaching was apparently never questioned. The same chant texts are included in the *Psalmodia* of Lucas Lossius, the most widely used chant book in Lutheran churches.[13] In the *Psalmodia*, the two chants are combined into a single responsory for the Purification of Mary (Appendix: Example 10.2). A note in the left margin explains that the text is "against Nestorius, who taught that Christ was a man born of Mary alone, not of God." Another note, in the right margin, summarizes the responsory as "The inviolate and perpetual virginity of Mary, etc."

The marginal commentaries in Lossius's book are worth noting, because they interpret the chant texts according to evangelical teaching. Several chant books have such commentaries, and they demonstrate that a primary function of the liturgical chants was to instill correct doctrine in those who sang and heard them. In this way, the chant books were yet another textbook for the boys in the school.

13 The book was published in eight editions between 1552 and 1594 and was commended in several church orders, including the 1569 agenda for Pomerania (Sehling, 4:419–80), the 1573 church order for Oldenburg (Sehling, 7:2:1:986–1162), the 1575 church order for Lüneburg (Sehling, 6:1:650–90), the 1588 Vesper order for Lohr (Sehling, 11:699), and a semiofficial order for Rostock produced sometime between 1560 and 1576 (Sehling, 5:288–91). A full citation to Sehling is in the appendix "Printed Chant Collections for Lutheran Use."

4 Conclusion

In Naumburg, the choir of schoolboys sang at least one service in Latin every day of the week. Their role was not simply to sing music that might enhance the service; instead, they led the liturgy. What better way to encourage boys to learn the language than to have them use it every day in such an essential way? This was the case wherever Latin schools existed, and so the boys had ample opportunity to master the language and to internalize Christian doctrine in the process. And if singing the Christian faith into their hearts was not enough, the chant books also provided marginal explanations that interpreted the chants.

This was the way of life for Lutheran schoolboys for several generations. By the late seventeenth century, one occasionally heard complaints that such intensive study of Latin was unnecessary; but the Latin schools persisted, at least in the larger cities, well into the eighteenth century. Even in nineteenth-century America, the ability to converse in Latin was expected of German Lutheran pastors. Several years ago the *Concordia Historical Institute Quarterly* published the memoirs of a Missouri Synod pastor. He had attended Concordia Seminary in the 1880s and was asked to complete his studies a few months early in 1887 because a mission church was in urgent need of a pastor. Before he could graduate, however, he had to pass an examination conducted by the faculty and the vice president of the Lutheran Church's Missouri Synod. It was an oral exam, it lasted nearly four and a half hours, and it was conducted partly in Latin.[14]

This way of life is gone. What has been lost is not only the common knowledge of a language useful in theology nor even the "fine Latin songs" to which Luther referred, but also the use of chant to ingrain Christian doctrine. Lost, too, is the very idea that foreign-language instruction can be a means of Christian instruction. What is more, as choral singing of liturgical propers is no longer regarded as an essential part of the church's services, a vital incentive for learning them—the belief that having children leading the singing is essential to the conduct of the service—has also been lost.

---

14 Julius A. Friedrich, "*Vita Mea*: Biographical Data of My Life," *Concordia Historical Institute Quarterly* 76, no. 1 (Spring 2003): 10.

Appendices

TABLE 1 Class schedule for the Latin School in Naumburg, ca. 1537 (upper four classes)

First class (at times divided into upper and lower first)

		Monday	Tuesday	Wednesday	Thursday	Friday	Saturday
6:00 AM		ortho-graphy; etymology; syntax	ortho-graphy; etymology; syntax	Cicero; astronomy	grammar (Terence)	grammar (Terence)	Cicero; astronomy
7:00	Upper	church	church	church	church	church	church
	Lower	Virgil	church	Virgil	church	Virgil	Virgil
8:00		Terence	Terence	*examinat magister ludi scripta adiuvante infimo*	Terence	Terence	*lupus*
9:00		Hebrew (grammar)	Hebrew (grammar)	Hebrew (Psalms)	Hebrew (Genesis)	Hebrew (Genesis)	Hebrew (Psalms)
10:00–12:00		Break					
12:00 noon		arithmetic; music	arithmetic; music	Terence (comedies)	arithmetic; music	arithmetic; music	Terence (comedies)
1:00		Virgil; reading	Virgil; reading	*legit magister rationem conscribendorum versuum*	Virgil; reading	Virgil; reading	*legit magister rationem conscribendorum versuum*
2:00	Upper	dialectic	dialectic	Gregorian chant	rhetoric	rhetoric	Gregorian chant
	Lower	church	church		church	church	
3:00		Greek (Acts)	Greek (Acts)	Greek (Homer)	Greek (grammar)	Greek (grammar)	Greek (Homer)
4:00		physics	physics				

TABLE 1 Class schedule for the Latin School in Naumburg, ca. 1537 (upper four classes) (*cont.*)

Second class

	Monday	**Tuesday**	**Wednesday**	**Thursday**	**Friday**	**Saturday**
6:00 AM	grammar (Virgil)	grammar (Virgil)	writing	grammar (Virgil)	grammar (Virgil)	Colloquia Sacra
7:00	church; Latin grammar	church; Latin grammar	church; Gregorian chant	church; Latin grammar	church; Latin grammar	church; Gregorian chant
8:00	Terence	Terence	Cicero	Terence	Terence	*lupus*
9:00						
10:00–12:00	Break					
12:00 noon	arithmetic; music	arithmetic; music	Terence (comedies)	arithmetic; music	arithmetic; music	Terence (comedies)
1:00	Aesop's fables	Aesop's fables		orthography	orthography	
2:00	Vespers; Virgil	Vespers; Virgil	Vespers; Gregorian chant	Vespers; Virgil	Vespers; Virgil	Vespers; Gregorian chant

Third class

	Monday	**Tuesday**	**Wednesday**	**Thursday**	**Friday**	**Saturday**
6:00 AM	Aesop's fables	Aesop's fables	Colloquia Sacra; catechism	Aesop's fables	Aesop's fables	Colloquia sacra; catechism
7:00	church; Latin grammar	church; Latin grammar	writing	church; Latin grammar	church; Latin grammar	*lupus*
8:00	grammar (Virgil)	grammar (Virgil)		grammar (Virgil)	grammar (Virgil)	
9:00						
10:00–12:00	Break					
12:00 noon	arithmetic; music	arithmetic; music		arithmetic; music	arithmetic; music	

TABLE 1 Class schedule for the Latin School in Naumburg, ca. 1537 (upper four classes) (*cont.*)

	Monday	**Tuesday**	**Wednesday**	**Thursday**	**Friday**	**Saturday**
1:00	etymology; spelling	etymology; spelling		etymology; spelling	etymology; spelling	
2:00	Vespers; Virgil	Vespers; Virgil	Vespers; Gregorian chant	Vespers; Virgil	Vespers; Virgil	Vespers: Gregorian chant

Fourth class

	Monday	**Tuesday**	**Wednesday**	**Thursday**	**Friday**	**Saturday**
6:00 AM	Latin grammar	Latin grammar	Latin (Cato)	Latin grammar	Latin grammar	Latin (Cato)
7:00	church	church	church	church	church	church
8:00	Latin (Cato)	Latin (Cato)	catechism	Latin (Cato)	Latin (Cato)	catechism
9:00						
10:00–12:00	Break					
12:00 noon	arithmetic; music	arithmetic; music		arithmetic; music	arithmetic; music	
1:00	etymology; spelling	etymology; spelling		etymology; spelling	etymology; spelling	
2:00	Vespers; *Colloquia Hædionis*	Vespers; *Colloquia Hædionis*	Vespers	Vespers; *Colloquia Hædionis*	Vespers; *Colloquia Hædionis*	Vespers

TABLE 2 Categories of chant in the chant books

For full citations to the books, see the appendix "Printed Chant Collections for Lutheran Use."

	All sources	*Spangenberg 1545*	*Nürnberg responsoria 1548*	*Bonnus 1559*	*Lossius 1561*	*Nürnberg responsoria 1562*	*Keuchenthal 1573*	*Eler 1588*	*Ludecus 1589*	*Libellus 1605*	*Magdeburg 1612–13*
Alleluias	82	8			14		16	13	67		52
Antiphons	1320				208	8		261	466	192	1075
Collects	8								8		
Graduals	52	1		1	1		1		6		49
Hymns	100	3		35	42	5	6	21	65	28	45
Introits	100	17		4	55		65	47	76		119
Invitatories	63				9				40		47
Responsories	574	2	132		46	94	8	71	90	71	483
Sequences	43	8		24	30	6	19	9	30		21
Tracts	16	1		1			2	1	14	1	12
Holy Week chants	15								14	1	
Funeral chants	10				5	2	2	8		4	
Mass chants											
Kyrie		3			7		7	9	7		13
Gloria		3			4		4	5	5		7
Lesson tones		2							3		
Nicene Creed		1		2					1		
Prefaces		9			7		7	8	19		9
Sanctus		3			2		5	8	7		3
Agnus dei		3			1		6	8	6		3
Office chants											
Opening versicles									yes		
Venite					4				10	8	
Benedictus tones					yes				yes		
Magnificat tones					yes			yes	yes	yes	
Nunc dimittis tones					yes						
Psalm tones					yes			yes	yes	yes	
Te deum laudamus		1			2			1	2	1	1
Benedicamus					12			8	16	9	8
Miscellaneous chants	32	1	1	1	6	3		5	21	2	3

EXAMPLE 10.1 Two antiphons from Matthäus Ludecus, *Vesperale, et matvtinale* (Wittenberg, 1589), f. 245.

EXAMPLE 10.2 Responsory from Lucas Lossius, *Psalmodia hoc est cantica sacra veteris ecclesiae* (Wittenberg, 1561), ff. 196[b]–97[a].

Printed Chant Collections for Lutheran Use Arranged by Date of Publication

† published reprint available (details follow a dash)
* full text available online without charge at www.zvdd.de
** full text available elsewhere (access point follows a dash)
+ surveyed for this study

The books are arranged by the date of the earliest edition.

1545. Spangenberg, Johann. *Cantiones ecclesiasticae latinae / Kirchengesenge Deudtsch auff die Sontage vnnd furnemliche Feste durches gantze Jar.* The author was pastor in Nordhausen.
+ *Magdeburg: Michael Lotther, 1545. 2°: 2 vols. in 1: [3], clx, [2] f.; [3], cxcix, [45] f.
Mentioned in Oldenburg 1573 (Sehling 7:2:1:986–1162), Annaberg 1579.

1548. *Liber canticorvm, qvae vvlgo responsoria uocantur, secundum an|ni ordinem, Dominicis & Festis diebus hactenus seruatum.* Presumably for use in Nuremberg.
+ *Nürnberg: Johann VomBerg and Ulrich Neuber, [ca. 1548]. 8°: [168] f.
Nürnberg: Johann VomBerg and Ulrich Neuber, 1550. 8°: [167] f.

1550. *Responsoria, que annuatim in veteri Ecclesia de Tempore, Festis, et Sanctis cantari solent.*
*Nürnberg: Petreius, 1550. 8°: 152, [4] f. Presumably for use in Nuremberg.
*Nürnberg: Gabriel Hain, 1554. 8°: 150, [2] f.
Nürnberg: Gabriel Hain, 1557. 8°: 150, [2] f.
+ *Nürnberg: Valentin Neuber, 1562. 8°: 150, [2] f.
Nürnberg: Valentin Neuber, 1567. 8°: 150, [2] f.
A 1572 edition is mentioned in Hof 1592 (Sehling 11:405–77); no copy has been located.
*Nürnberg: Katharina Gerlach, 1576.
*Nürnberg: Fuhrmann, 1597.

1552. Lossius, Lucas. *Psalmodia hoc est cantica sacra veteris ecclesiae &c.* The author was conrector of the Gymnasium in Lüneburg.
Wittenberg: Georg Rhau, 1552. 2°: ? f. [cited in VD16: L 2827; not otherwise known]
Wittenberg: Johann Schwertelius, 1553. ?°: 360 f.
*Nürnberg: Gabriel Hayn, 1553. 2°: [4] f., CCCLVII [= 363], [1] p., [2] f.
+ † Wittenberg: Georg Rhau, 1561. 4°: [8], 360, [4] f.—Stuttgart: Cornetto-Verlag, 1996
**Wittenberg: Johann Schwertelius, 1569. 4°: 372 f.—(1) polona.pl; (2) www.manuscriptorium.com

*Wittenberg: Antonius Schön, 1579. 4°: [8], 398, [5] f.
Wittenberg: Anton Schöne, 1580. 4°: [8], 398, [5] f.
*Wittenberg: Zacharias Lehmann, 1594/95. 4°: [8], 398, [5] ff.
Mentioned in Pomerania 1569 (Sehling 4:419–80), Rostock [ca. 1560–76] (Sehling 5:288–91), Oldenburg 1573 (Sehling 7:2:1:986–1162), Lüneburg [1575] (Sehling 6:1:650–90), Lohr 1588 (Sehling 11:699); purchased in Braunschweig ca. 1600 (see Werner Greve, *"Musicam hab ich allezeit lieb gehabt ..."* [Braunschweig, 1985], 64).

1559. Bonnus, Hermann. *Hymni et seqventiae, tam de tempore quam de Sanctis, cum suis Melodijs, sicut olim sunt cantata in Ecclesia Dei, & iam passim correcta.* The author was superintendent in Lübeck.
+ **Lübeck: Georg Richolff d.J., 1559.—www.kb.se

1573. Jesperssøn, Niels. *Gradval: En allmindelig sangbog.* The author was bishop of Funen in Denmark.
† **Copenhagen: Laurentz Benedicht, 1573. [12], 460, [7] f.—Copenhagen: Dan Fog Musikforlag, 1986; ProQuest's *Early European Books* (online; subscription required)

1573. Keuchenthal, Johann. *KirchenGesenge Latinisch vnd Deudsch.* The author was pastor in St. Andreasberg (Harz).
+ *Wittenberg: Lorentz Schwenck, 1573. 2°: [4], 590[= 591], [10] f.

1588. Eler, Franz. *Cantica sacra, partim ex sacris literis desvmta, partim ab orthodoxis patribvs, et piis ecclesiae doctoribvs composita / Psalmi D. Martini Lvtheri & aliorum ejus seculi Psalmistarum, itidem Modis applicati.* The author was succentor of the Latin school of St. John in Hamburg.
+ † *Hamburg: Jacobus Wolff, 1588. 8°: [12] f., CCLXII p., [5] f., [1], LXXXVII p.—Hildesheim: Olms, 2002

1589. Ludecus, Matthäus. *Missale, hoc est cantica, preces, et lectiones sacrae, quae ad missam officium, ex pio primaevae ecclesiae instituto, in templis Christianorum, cantari usitate solent.* The author was dean of the Havelberg cathedral.
+ *Wittenberg, 1589. 2°: [3], 42[= 340], 72[= 73], [5] f.
1589. Ludecus, Matthäus. *Psalterium Davidis, prophetae ac regis, iuxta veterem translationem, una cum antiphonis et psalmorum tropis: in septem partis.*
+ *Wittenberg, 1589. 2°: [2], 129[= 128], [1] f.
1589. Ludecus, Matthäus. *Vesperale, et matvtinale: hoc est, hymni, et collectae, sive precationes ecclesiasticae, qvae in primis & secundis Vesperis, itemque Matutinis precibus, per totius anni circulum.*
+ † *[N.p., 1589]. 2°: [4], 42[= 342], 72, [1] f. — ed. A. Odenthal (Bonn: Nova & Vetera, 2007)

1592. ***Antiphonae et responsoria in vespertinis canenda.* Presumably for use in Riga. Riga: Mollinus, 1592. 8°: A—J.—staatsbibliothek-berlin.de

1605. *Libellvs Continens Antiphona, Responsoria, Hymnos, Versiculos, Benedicamus, Et Alia, Quæ In vespertinis precibus, per totius anni circulum, ad singulas Dominicas & Festa præcipua, in Ecclesia Curiensi decantantur.*
+ *Hof: Matthaei Pfeilschmidt, 1605. 8°: [12], 260, [6], 50 f.

1612. *Psalterium Davidis, prophetae et regis, juxta veterem translationem alicubi emendatam, cum canticis selectis veteris & novi testamenti, ad usum S. Metropolitanae Magdeburgensis ecclesiae.* For use at the Magdeburg cathedral.
+ *Magdeburg: Bezelius, 1612. 2°: 602, 58 p.—dbs.hab.de/katalog/?opac=wdb

1613. *Cantica sacra, quo ordine et melodiis, per totius anni curriculum, in matutinis et vespertinis, itemque intermediis precibus cantari solent, una cum lectionibus et precationibus in unum volumen congesta pro S. metropolitana.* For use at the Magdeburg cathedral.
+ *Magdeburg: Bezelius, 1613. 2°: [2] f., 1201 p., [12] f.

1627. *Libellus Continens Antiphona, Responsoria, Introitus, Sequent. Hymnos, Versicul., Et Officia Missae Germanicae.* Presumably for use in Nuremberg.
*Nürnberg: Sartorius, 1627. 8°: [1], 339 [i.e. 239], [4] f.

Antiphonae et responsoria in vespertinis canenda. Presumably for use in Riga.
*Riga: Mollinus, 1592. 8°: A—J.—staatsbibliothek-berlin.de

Bonnus, Hermann. *Hymni et seqventiae, tam de tempore quam de Sanctis, cum suis Melodijs, sicut olim sunt cantata in Ecclesia Dei, & iam passim correcta.* The author was superintendent in Lübeck.
+ **Lübeck: Georg Richolff d.J., 1559.—www.kb.se

Cantica sacra, quo ordine et melodiis, per totius anni curriculum, in matutinis et vespertinis, itemque intermediis precibus cantari solent, una cum lectionibus et precationibus in unum volumen congesta pro S. metropolitana. For use at the Magdeburg cathedral.
+ *Magdeburg: Bezelius, 1613. 2°: [2] f., 1201 p., [12] f.

Eler, Franz. *Cantica sacra, partim ex sacris literis desvmta, partim ab orthodoxis patribvs, et piis ecclesiae doctoribvs composita / Psalmi D. Martini Lvtheri & aliorum ejus seculi Psalmistarum, itidem Modis applicati.* The author was succentor of the Latin school of St. John in Hamburg.

+ † *Hamburg: Jacobus Wolff, 1588. 8°: [12] f., CCLXII p., [5] f., [1], LXXXVII p.—Hildesheim: Olms, 2002

Jesperssøn, Niels. *Gradval: En allmindelig sangbog*. The author was bishop of Funen in Denmark.
† **Copenhagen: Laurentz Benedicht, 1573. [12], 460, [7] f.—Copenhagen: Dan Fog Musikforlag, 1986; ProQuest's *Early European Books* (online; subscription required)

Keuchenthal, Johann. *KirchenGesenge Latinisch vnd Deudsch*. The author was pastor in St. Andreasberg (Harz).
+ *Wittenberg: Lorentz Schwenck, 1573. 2°: [4], 590[= 591], [10] f.

Libellvs Continens Antiphona, Responsoria, Hymnos, Versiculos, Benedicamus, Et Alia, Quœ In vespertinis precibus, per totius anni circulum, ad singulas Dominicas & Festa prœcipua, in Ecclesia Curiensi decantantur.
+ *Hof: Matthaei Pfeilschmidt, 1605. 8°: [12], 260, [6], 50 f.

Libellus Continens Antiphona, Responsoria, Introitus, Sequent. Hymnos, Versicul., Et Officia Missae Germanicae. Presumably for use in Nuremberg.
*Nürnberg: Sartorius, 1627. 8°: [1], 339 [i.e. 239], [4] f.

Liber canticorvm, qvae vvlgo responsoria uocantur, secundum an|ni ordinem, Dominicis & Festis diebus hactenus seruatum. Presumably for use in Nuremberg.
+ *Nürnberg: Johann VomBerg and Ulrich Neuber, [ca. 1548]. 8°: [168] f.
Nürnberg: Johann VomBerg and Ulrich Neuber, 1550. 8°: [167] f.

Lossius, Lucas. *Psalmodia hoc est cantica sacra veteris ecclesiae &c*. The author was conrector of the Gymnasium in Lüneburg.
Wittenberg: Georg Rhau, 1552. 2°: ? f. [cited in VD16: L 2827; not otherwise known]
Wittenberg: Johann Schwertelius, 1553. ?°: 360 f.
*Nürnberg: Gabriel Hayn, 1553. 2°: [4] f., CCCLVII [= 363], [1] p., [2] f.
+ † Wittenberg: Georg Rhau, 1561. 4°: [8], 360, [4] f.—Stuttgart: Cornetto-Verlag, 1996
**Wittenberg: Johann Schwertelius, 1569. 4°: 372 f.—(1) polona.pl; (2) www.manuscriptorium.com
*Wittenberg: Antonius Schön, 1579. 4°: [8], 398, [5] f.
Wittenberg: Anton Schöne, 1580. 4°: [8], 398, [5] f.
*Wittenberg: Zacharias Lehmann, 1594/95. 4°: [8], 398, [5] ff.
Mentioned in Pomerania 1569 (Sehling 4:419–80), Rostock [ca. 1560–76] (Sehling 5:288–91), Oldenburg 1573 (Sehling 7:2:1:986–1162), Lüneburg [1575] (Sehling 6:1:650–90), Lohr 1588 (Sehling 11:699); purchased in Braunschweig ca. 1600 (see Werner Greve, *"Musicam hab ich allezeit lieb gehabt ..."* [Braunschweig, 1985], 64).

Ludecus, Matthäus. *Missale, hoc est cantica, preces, et lectiones sacrae, quae ad missam officium, ex pio primaevae ecclesiae instituto, in templis Christianorum, cantari usitate solent.* The author was dean of the Havelberg cathedral.
+ *Wittenberg, 1589. 2°: [3], 42[= 340], 72[= 73], [5] f.

Ludecus, Matthäus. *Psalterium Davidis, prophetae ac regis, iuxta veterem translationem, una cum antiphonis et psalmorum tropis: in septem partis.*
+ *Wittenberg, 1589. 2°: [2], 129[= 128], [1] f.

Ludecus, Matthäus. *Vesperale, et matvtinale: hoc est, hymni, et collectae, sive precationes ecclesiasticae, qvae in primis & secundis Vesperis, itemque Matutinis precibus, per totius anni circulum.*
+ † *[N.p., 1589]. 2°: [4], 42[= 342], 72, [1] f.—ed. A. Odenthal (Bonn: Nova & Vetera, 2007)

Psalterium Davidis, prophetae et regis, juxta veterem translationem alicubi emendatam, cum canticis selectis veteris & novi testamenti, ad usum S. Metropolitanae Magdeburgensis ecclesiae. For use at the Magdeburg cathedral.
+ *Magdeburg: Bezelius, 1612. 2°: 602, 58 p.—dbs.hab.de/katalog/?opac=wdb

Responsoria, que annuatim in veteri Ecclesia de Tempore, Festis, et Sanctis cantari solent.
*Nürnberg: Petreius, 1550. 8°: 152, [4] f. Presumably for use in Nuremberg.
*Nürnberg: Gabriel Hain, 1554. 8°: 150, [2] f.
Nürnberg: Gabriel Hain, 1557. 8°: 150, [2] f.
+ *Nürnberg: Valentin Neuber, 1562. 8°: 150, [2] f.
Nürnberg: Valentin Neuber, 1567. 8°: 150, [2] f.
A 1572 edition is mentioned in Hof 1592 (Sehling 11:405–77); no copy has been located.
*Nürnberg: Katharina Gerlach, 1576.
*Nürnberg: Fuhrmann, 1597.

Spangenberg, Johann. *Cantiones ecclesiasticae latinae / Kirchengesenge Deudtsch auff die Sontage vnnd furnemliche Feste durches gantze Jar.* The author was pastor in Nordhausen.
+ *Magdeburg: Michael Lotther, 1545. 2°: 2 vols. in 1: [3], clx, [2] f.; [3], cxcix, [45] f.
Mentioned in Oldenburg 1573 (Sehling 7:2:1:986–1162), Annaberg 1579.

CHAPTER 11

"Exulting and Adorning in Exuberant Strains": Luther and Latin Polyphonic Music

Daniel Zager

In his *Formula Missae* of 1523 Martin Luther outlined and commented on the reformed Latin mass as he wished it to be observed in Wittenberg. Behind this bare historical fact is a significant fact that should not be taken lightly, namely, that Luther had no interest in jettisoning either the liturgy or the language of the medieval church, as he had come to know them. He valued continuity with the church's past, insofar as it was consonant with the Gospel. He could not have been more emphatic about this, writing in the *Formula Missae*:

> Imprimis itaque profitemur, non esse nec fuisse unquam in animo nostro, omnem cultum dei prorsus abolere, sed eum, qui in usu est, pessimis additamentis viciatum, repurgare et usum pium monstrare.[1]

> We therefore first assert: It is not now nor ever has been our intention to abolish the liturgical service of God completely, but rather to purify the one that is now in use from the wretched accretions which corrupt it and to point out an evangelical use.[2]

After outlining and discussing the various parts of the mass, Luther included, near the end of the *Formula Missae*, a call for vernacular hymns "which the people could sing during mass, immediately after the gradual and also after the Sanctus and Agnus Dei."[3] Luther wanted both: to retain the Latin mass *and* to employ vernacular hymns within the mass. Three years later, in 1526, he was even more explicit about continuing to use the Latin language. In the preface to his *Deutsche Messe*,[4] Luther's outline of the mass in the German language

1 WA 12:206.

2 *LW* 53:20.

3 *LW* 53:36. WA 12:218: … *quae populus sub missa cantaret, vel iuxta gradualia, item iuxta Sanctus et Agnus dei.*

4 *LW* 53:61–90.

 | DOI:10.1163/9789004206717_013

known as the *Gottesdienst* (Divine Service), he refers to the *Formula Missae* and his retention of the Latin mass:

> Denn ich ynn keynen weg wil die latinische sprache aus dem Gottis dienst lassen gar weg komen, denn es ist myr alles umb die jugent zu thun. Und wenn ichs vermöcht und die Kriechsche und Ebreische sprach were uns so gemeyn als die latinische und hette so viel feyner musica und gesangs, als die latinische hat, so solte man eynen sontag umb den andern yn allen vieren sprachen, Deutsch, Latinisch, Kriechisch, Ebreische messe halten, singen und lessen. Ich halte es gar nichts mit denen, die nur auff eyne sprache sich so gar geben und alle andere verachten.... und ist auch billich, das man die jugent ynn vielen sprachen ube, wer weys, wie Gott yhr mit der zeyt brauchen wird? dazu sind auch die schulen gestiffet.[5]

> For in no wise would I want to discontinue the service in the Latin language, because the young are my chief concern. And if I could bring it to pass, and Greek and Hebrew were as familiar to us as the Latin and had as many fine melodies and songs, we would hold mass, sing, and read on successive Sundays in all four languages, German, Latin, Greek, and Hebrew. I do not at all agree with those who cling to one language and despise all others.... It is also reasonable that the young should be trained in many languages; for who knows how God may use them in time to come? For this purpose our schools were founded.[6]

Thus, for Luther, retaining the Latin mass was important in part for education of the young, and for enriching their lives through continued use of the Latin language.

Luther's posture regarding languages for the mass finds parallels in his views on music: Latin chant is to be retained, *and* German hymns and psalm paraphrases are to be newly written; Latin polyphony (music composed of two or more independent parts) is to be retained, *and* polyphonic settings of German hymns are to be newly composed. Luther's view of music in the mass is inclusive: 1) in retaining the historic repertory of Latin chant as it had developed from the seventh century on, and 2) in continuing to cultivate Latin polyphony as it had developed during the fifteenth century in the hands of Franco-Flemish composers such as Guillaume Du Fay (1397–1474), Johannes Ockeghem (ca. 1410–97), and Josquin des Prez (1450/55–1521). Such

---

5 WA 19:74.
6 *LW* 53:63.

Latin polyphonic music would subsequently serve as models for composers like Luther's colleague Johann Walter (1496–1570); drawing on the musical language of Josquin and others, Walter would provide polyphonic settings of the newly developing repertory of German-language hymns (chorales).

In light of Luther's commitment to both Latin- and German-texted liturgy and music, let us now turn to Latin polyphonic music and its remarkable contrapuntal and stylistic development in the church of the fifteenth century. Indeed, the prominent fifteenth-century music theorist, writer, and composer Johannes Tinctoris (1430/35–1511) observed, in his 1477 *Liber de arte contrapuncti* (Book on the Art of Counterpoint), that "there is no composition written over forty years ago which is thought by the learned as worthy of performance."[7] While on its surface such a statement may seem audacious, even arrogant, the fifteenth century's music does in fact evidence by its midpoint a marked change in musical language. Notably, the previous layering of independent lines in late medieval polyphony gives way to a fresh musical language in which the various voice parts of the polyphonic texture become more homogeneous in character and more smoothly integrated one with the other. The later Latin polyphony is the kind that Luther knew and loved, and thus wished to retain. In composing it, Luther points back, on numerous occasions, to Josquin, the preeminent composer of the later fifteenth and early sixteenth centuries. As is recorded in *Table Talk* as having occurred sometime before December 14, 1531, Luther states that "God has preached the gospel through music, too, as may be seen in Josquin, all of whose compositions flow freely, gently, and cheerfully, and are not forced or cramped by rules like the song of the finch."[8] Yet another witness to Luther's view of Josquin is Luther's first biographer, Johann Mathesius (1504–65), who writes: "Sometimes during and after meals the doctor also sang, being a lutenist as well. I sang with him, and

7 Johannes Tinctoris, *The Art of Counterpoint* (*Liber de arte contrapuncti*), trans. and ed. Albert Seay, Musicological Studies and Documents 5 (Rome: American Institute of Musicology, 1961), 14. Johannis Tinctoris, *Opera Theoretica*, ed. Albert Seay, Corpus Scriptorum de Musica 22 (n.p.: American Institute of Musicology, 1975), II:12: *Neque quod satis admirari nequeo quippiam compositum nisi citra annos quadraginta extat quod auditu dignum ab eruditis existimetur.*

8 LW 54: 129–30; and Robin A. Leaver, *Luther's Liturgical Music: Principles and Implications* (Grand Rapids, Mich.: Eerdmans, 2007), 51, 368, note 199, where Leaver writes: "Theodore Tappert's translation ... makes Luther say that Josquin's compositions 'are like the song of the finch.' But Luther actually stated the opposite: Josquin's compositions are free in contrast to the song of the finch that always obeys the rules ... repetitious birdsong—beautiful but made up of unaltered repeated phrases." WA TR 2:11–12 (No. 1258): *Sic Deus praedicavit euangelium etiam per musicam, ut videtur in Josquin, des alles composition frolich, willig, milde heraus fleust, ist nitt zwungen und gnedigt per regulas, sicut des fincken gesang.*

he wove good remarks in between songs. 'Josquin,' he said, 'is the master of the notes—they had to do as he willed; the other choirmasters have to do as the notes will.'"[9] In 1537 Luther lamented "Alas, what fine musicians have died within the last ten years: Josquin [d. 1521], Pierre de la Rue [d. 1518], Finck [d. 1527], and many other excellent men."[10] A keen observer of the music of his time, and a man who loved music, Luther not only discerned the quality of Josquin's music but linked it to proclamation of the Gospel. Luther also corresponded with a well-known composer of the generation after Josquin, namely Ludwig Senfl (1489/91–1543), from whom Luther requested, in a letter dated October 4, 1530, a polyphonic setting of the chant antiphon "In pace in idipsum" (Psalm 4:8, "In peace I will both lie down and sleep").[11]

How did Luther know the music of Josquin? Did Luther at some point meet Senfl, thus explaining his very direct and cordial request of the composer? Such questions, to which we shall now turn, are concerned with Senfl's Latin polyphony, consideration of which will help to establish a basis for understanding Luther's love of Latin polyphony, which Luther expresses in no uncertain terms with great fervor and eloquence in his preface to Georg Rhau's *Symphoniae iucundae* of 1538, itself an anthology of Latin polyphony:

> Hic tandem gustare cum stupore licet (sed non comprehendere) absolutam et perfectam sapientiam Dei in opere suo mirabili Musicae, in quo genere hoc excellit, quod vna et eadem voce canitur suo tenore pergente, pluribus interim vocibus circum circa mirabiliter ludentibus, exultantibus et iucundissimis gestibus eandem ornantibus ...[12]

> ... it is possible to taste with wonder (yet not to comprehend) God's absolute and perfect wisdom in his wondrous works of music. Here it is most remarkable that one single voice continues to sing the tenor, while at the same time many other voices play around it, exulting and adorning it in exuberant strains....[13]

---

9 *Sixteenth-Century Biographies of Martin Luther*, ed. Christopher Boyd Brown, Luther's Works: Companion Volume (St. Louis: Concordia Publishing House, 2018), 454.

10 Walter E. Buszin, *Luther on Music*, Lutheran Society for Worship, Music and the Arts, Pamphlet Series, no. 3 (St. Paul, Minn.: North Central Publishing, 1958), 13 [reprinted from *Musical Quarterly* 1946]. Luther, WA TR 3:371 (No. 3516): *Ach, wie feine musici sindt in 10 jharen gestorben! Josquin, Petrus Loroe, Finck et multi alii excellentes.*

11 *LW* 49:427–29.

12 WA 50:372–73.

13 *LW* 53:324.

It is important to clarify here what the expression "one single voice continues to sing the tenor" connotes. A preexistent chant melody serving as the basis for a polyphonic setting was often placed in the tenor part—the part that quite literally "held" (*tenere*) the chant melody. Thus, "to sing the tenor," as the translator Ulrich Leupold has it, means to sing the preexistent chant melody, which may be referred to as the *cantus firmus* or the *cantus prius factus*.

Luther's familiarity with the magnificent and extensive Franco-Flemish repertory of fifteenth-century Latin sacred polyphony is in part indebted to the interest in ecclesiastical music of Frederick the Wise, Elector of Saxony from 1486 to his death in 1525. Frederick established his chapel of clergy and musicians—the *Hofkapelle*—in 1491, their responsibility being to furnish music for the daily mass and office liturgies wherever Frederick was "in residence," whether traveling, or in Wittenberg or Torgau, the latter being his primary place of residence.

In Wittenberg, Frederick's new Castle Church was dedicated on January 17, 1503, one year after he had established his new university in Wittenberg. Also known as the *Allerheiligenstiftskirche*, after the small *Allerheiligenkapelle*, or All Saints' chapel, which had previously occupied that site, the Castle Church had its own group of clergy and musicians responsible for an extensive daily round of mass and office liturgies, totaling, by one scholar's estimate, "over 1,000 [sung] Masses each year."[14] That pattern remained until late 1524 when, at Luther's urging, "all the masses except for the evangelical Sunday mass were discontinued."[15]

Latin polyphony for those liturgical observances was drawn from two groups of music manuscripts, those groups being distinguished one from the other by where they were copied. A total of nineteen manuscript sources of Latin polyphony used at the Castle Church have been preserved, all of which, save one, are now held by the university library in Jena; (the single exception resides in Weimar). The first group of eight manuscripts[16] was copied between approximately 1500 and 1520 at the Castle Church in Wittenberg for use at that establishment.[17] Those Wittenberg manuscripts preserve polyphony for both the Proper and Ordinary of the mass as well as music for Vespers. The second

14 Kathryn Ann Pohlmann Duffy, "The Jena Choirbooks: Music and Liturgy at the Castle Church in Wittenberg under Frederick the Wise, Elector of Saxony" (PhD diss., University of Chicago, 1995), 174.

15 Martin Brecht, *Martin Luther: Shaping and Defining the Reformation, 1521–1532*, trans. James L. Schaaf (Minneapolis: Fortress Press, 1994), 129.

16 Jena 30, 31, 32, 33, 34, 35, 36, and Weimar A.

17 Duffy, "The Jena Choirbooks," 2.

group, consisting of eleven manuscripts,[18] was copied between 1500 and 1525 in the famed scriptoria of Petrus Alamire (ca. 1470–1536) and his associates, located in present-day Belgium. Either these manuscripts were presented to Frederick as gifts by Margaret of Austria (or her father Holy Roman Emperor Maximilian I, r. 1493–1519) or were purchased by Frederick.[19] The Alamire manuscripts furnish predominantly music for the Ordinary of the mass as well as settings of the Magnificat. Ten of these eleven Alamire manuscripts were copied on parchment rather than paper, and exquisite miniature decorative artwork characterizes these sources, as is typical of manuscripts from that workshop. In contrast to these Alamire manuscripts, the eight manuscripts produced in Wittenberg were copied on paper rather than parchment and show very little in the way of artistic miniature illuminations. Both groups of these choirbooks testify to the fact that the first two decades of the century were a time of intensive effort to acquire Latin polyphony for use at Wittenberg's Castle Church.

Of these nineteen manuscripts used at the Castle Church, five include works attributed to Josquin and are primarily settings of the mass Ordinary. Of the Alamire manuscripts, Jena 3 includes five mass Ordinaries securely attributed to Josquin, with one more in Jena 7 and two in Jena 21. Of the manuscripts copied in Wittenberg, Jena 31 and 32 each preserve three mass Ordinaries by Josquin. From these sources alone it is clear that Luther had ample opportunity to hear the music of Josquin; indeed, in the mass Ordinaries preserved in these manuscripts, one finds some of Josquin's finest polyphony for the church.

While Luther certainly heard the music of Josquin sung at the Castle Church, it is likely that he personally knew Ludwig Senfl (b. ca. 1490), who, still a child, joined the court chapel of Emperor Maximilian I as a choirboy in 1498.[20] The previous year Heinrich Isaac (1450/55–1517) had been appointed court composer for Maximilian's chapel, which resided in Vienna when not accompanying Maximilian on his travels. When his voice changed (presumably between

---

18 Jena 2, 3, 4, 5, 7, 8, 9, 12, 20, 21, and 22.

19 For a recent detailed study of this group of eleven manuscripts see Hannah Hutchens Mowrey, "The Alamire Manuscripts of Frederick the Wise: Intersections of Music, Art, and Theology" (PhD diss., Eastman School of Music, University of Rochester, 2010). For descriptions of each manuscript see *The Treasury of Petrus Alamire: Music and Art in Flemish Court Manuscripts, 1500–1535*, ed. Herbert Kellman (Ghent: Ludion, 1999); the range of dates for these sources, 1500–1525, reflects the descriptions in this volume. Mowrey argues persuasively that the Alamire manuscripts were used at Frederick's Castle Church in Wittenberg rather than at his *Hofkapelle*; see pp. 362–77 of her dissertation.

20 Biographical details are drawn from http://senflonline.com, accessed June 12, 2016, and from Stefan Gasch and Sonja Tröster, *Grove Music Online*, "Senfl, Ludwig," accessed June 12, 2016, http://www.oxfordmusiconline.com/.

‿‿4 and 1507), Senfl went to the University of Vienna where he studied for three years. He then returned to Maximilian's chapel as a singer and copyist and became a student of composition under Isaac. When Isaac left the imperial chapel in 1515, it is possible that Senfl found additional opportunities as a composer there. At the death of Maximilian in 1519 the chapel was disbanded, and Senfl held no regular position until 1523, when he joined the Munich court chapel of Duke Wilhelm IV of Bavaria as a composer, remaining there for the rest of his life.

Senfl scholars Stefan Gasch and Sonya Tröster, currently working at the University of Vienna on a new edition of Senfl's works, suggest that Luther may have met Senfl at the Diet of Augsburg in 1518, though Martin Brecht, in his magisterial study of Luther, casts some doubt on that possibility, stating that the Diet had ended before the October 7 arrival of Luther in Augsburg for his meeting with Cardinal Cajetan, when Elector Frederick the Wise, for example, would have already left Augsburg (September 22).[21] Thus, it is possible that Maximilian and his chapel, including Senfl, may have departed Augsburg prior to Luther's arrival. Gasch and Tröster, however, maintain that Senfl traveled to the imperial Diet in Worms in 1521, though they offer no documentary evidence for that conclusion. If true, it would constitute another possible point of contact between the two men.

By the date of the 1530 Diet of Augsburg, Senfl was employed as a composer at the ducal court in Munich and would have attended the Augsburg meeting as a member of the chapel of Duke Wilhelm IV of Bavaria. Senfl's setting of Psalm 133, "Ecce quam bonum" ("Behold, how good and pleasant it is when brothers dwell in unity!") was sung at the beginning of the Diet.[22] Luther, unwelcome at the Diet, resided in Coburg, where he had arrived on April 24; he stayed there until October 4.[23] One of the first things Luther did on his arrival in Coburg was to have some of his favorite psalm verses painted on the walls of his rooms, verses that encouraged him during this particularly trying time: Psalm 118:17 ("I shall not die, but I shall live, and recount the deeds of the Lord"); and Psalm 1:6 ("For the Lord knows the way of the righteous, but the way of the wicked will perish").[24] He kept in touch with his colleagues who attended the Augsburg and Wittenberg meetings through written communications, as

21 Martin Brecht, *Martin Luther: His Road to Reformation, 1483–1521*, trans. James L. Schaaf (Minneapolis: Fortress Press, 1985), 250–51.

22 Leaver, *Luther's Liturgical Music*, 52.

23 Brecht, *Martin Luther: Shaping and Defining the Reformation*, 372, 407.

24 Brecht, *Martin Luther: Shaping and Defining the Reformation*, 372.

well as by receiving guests in his rooms at the Coburg castle. Brecht notes that "Although the place of Luther's stay was supposed to remain a secret, he was constantly receiving visitors."[25]

One of Luther's last letters from Coburg, dated October 4, 1530, was written to Senfl, and may well suggest that the two men had previously met. Interestingly, before making a specific request of Senfl, Luther takes the time to reflect on the nature and purpose of music:

> ... post theologiam esse nullam artem, quae musicae possit aequari, cum ipsa sola post theologiam id praestat, quod alioqui sola theologia praestat, scilicet quietem et animum laetum.... Hinc factum est ut prophetae nulla sic arte sint usi ut musica.... ut theologiam et musicam haberent coniunctissimas, veritatem psalmis et canticis dicentes.[26]

> ... except for theology there is no art that could be put on the same level with music, since except for theology, [music] alone produces what otherwise only theology can do, namely, a calm and joyful disposition.... This is the reason why the prophets did not make use of any art except music.... they held theology and music most tightly connected, and proclaimed truth through Psalms and songs.[27]

To "[hold] theology and music most tightly connected" is a recurring motif in Luther's thought, as is the premise that music is a means to "proclaim truth." Luther then makes a specific request of Senfl. Luther writes that he has always found delight in the chant antiphon "In pace in idipsum, dormiam et requiescam," Psalm 4:8 ("In peace I will both lie down and sleep").[28] Luther asks Senfl for a polyphonic setting of this text:

---

25 Brecht, *Martin Luther: Shaping and Defining the Reformation*, 376.

26 WA Br 5:639.

27 *LW* 49:428.

28 For a version of this chant melody in a contemporaneous source, see the 1519 *Passau Antiphonarium* (Vienna: Johannes Winterburger, 1519), fol. 36v, which is available digitally at VD16 as item number A 2946: http://www.gateway-bayern.de/index_vd16.html, and in a printed facsimile: *Antiphonale Pataviense (Wien 1519): Faksimile*, ed. Karlheinz Schlager, Das Erbe Deutscher Musik, Bd. 88 (Kassel: Bärenreiter, 1985). Liturgically this antiphon is designated in the Passau source for *Dominica quarta Quadragesima, ad Completorium* (Fourth Sunday in Lent, for the Office of Compline). A modern chant book, such as the *Liber Usualis*, designates this text for Matins of Holy Saturday and preserves a completely different chant melody, cf. *Liber Usualis*, 713.

> Ad te redeo et oro, si quod habes exemplar istius cantici: "In pace in id ipsum," mihi transcribi et mitti cures. Tenor enim iste a iuventute me delectavit, et nunc multo magis, postquam et verba intelligo.[29]

> I ask if you would have copied and sent to me, if you have it, a copy of that song: "In peace [I will both lie down and sleep]." For this tenor melody has delighted me from youth on, and does so even more now that I understand the words.[30]

Again, to clarify, "tenor melody," in this context, means that the preexistent Latin chant forming the basis of a newly composed polyphonic setting was most often placed in the tenor part of the polyphonic complex. Luther continues:

> Non enim vidi eam antiphonam vocibus pluribus compositam. Nolo autem te gravare componendi labore, sed praesumo te habere aliunde compositam. Spero sane, finem vitae meae instare, et mundus me odit nec ferre potest, ego rursus mundum mihi fastidio et detestor; tollat itaque animam meam pastor optimus et fidelis. Idcirco hanc antiphonam iam coepi cantillare et compositam cupio audire. Quod si non habes aut non nosti, mitto hic suis notis pictam, quam vel post mortem meam, si voles componere potes.[31]

> I have never seen this antiphon arranged for more voices [i.e., a polyphonic setting]. I do not wish, however, to impose on you the work of arranging; rather I assume that you have available an arrangement from some other source. Indeed, I hope that the end of my life is at hand; the world hates me and cannot bear me, and I, in turn, loathe and detest the world; therefore may the best and [most] faithful shepherd take my soul to him. And so I have already started to sing this antiphon and am eager to hear it arranged. In case you should not have or know it, I am enclosing it here with the notes; if you wish you can arrange it—perhaps after my death.[32]

---

29 WA Br 5:639.
30 *LW* 49:428.
31 WA Br 5:639.
32 *LW* 49:428–29.

This is an interesting excerpt from the letter, on several points. First, for a world-weary Luther this psalm-verse provides comfort, as it points him not merely to evening rest and sleep after the labors of a day, but more significantly to eternal rest for his soul. Second, it shows us just how deeply Luther loved the Latin chant of the church, how the melody of a single brief psalm antiphon could bring him much delight as a singer. Third, it shows us his musical background and training, which permitted him to notate the chant melody for Senfl's use. And finally it shows both how much Luther loved polyphony, with his desire that this single piece of chant form the basis of a larger polyphonic complex.

Mathesius offers additional insight on this episode, reporting in his 1566 biography of Luther that Senfl did, in fact, provide a polyphonic setting of "In pace in idipsum," and, in addition, a polyphonic setting of Psalm 118:17, "Non moriar, sed vivam."[33] That Senfl included this second motet is an interesting detail. As far as we know, Luther did not ask for a second polyphonic setting; so why did Senfl send him such a setting of "Non moriar"? One reasonable hypothesis is that Senfl visited Luther at Coburg castle (secretly, since Luther remained *persona non grata*) and saw that psalm verse painted on the wall of Luther's room. Senfl thus may have included the second polyphonic setting because he recognized how much that particular verse meant to Luther. Such a hypothetical visit to Luther at Coburg would account for the highly personal tone of Luther's October 4 letter to Senfl, on the assumption that the two had already met and become acquainted.

A four-part setting of "In pace in idipsum" is preserved in a set of manuscript partbooks from the mid-sixteenth century. That source, now held by the Zwickau Ratsschulbibliothek as Mus. Ms. 73, is known as the manuscript of Jodocus Schalreuter (born in Gera ca. 1487), who in his own hand identifies himself as the copyist and owner of the manuscript partbooks.[34] The polyphonic setting of "In pace in idipsum," however, is entered without composer attribution, without any reference to Senfl, though the same source includes thirteen polyphonic settings that are attributed by the copyist to Senfl. Accordingly, one might well wonder whether the setting of "In pace in idipsum," which the copyist declined to attribute to Senfl, is one that he wrote at Luther's request.

33 *Sixteenth-Century Biographies of Martin Luther*, 352–53; Leaver, *Luther's Liturgical Music*, 52, 369 note 204.

34 *Die Handschrift des Jodocus Schalreuter* (*Ratsschulbibliothek Zwickau Mus. Ms. 73*), ed. Martin Just and Bettina Schwemer, Das Erbe Deutscher Musik, Bd. 115–16 (Wiesbaden: Breitkopf & Härtel, 2004). Bd. 115a, vii.

Although Luther did not wish to impose on Senfl the work of composing a new polyphonic piece, Luther might have assumed that Senfl might have available "an arrangement from some other source" (*sed praesumo te habere aliunde compositam*). The editors of the 2004 edition of the Schalreuter manuscript are unwilling to ascribe the "In pace in idipsum" to Senfl without adding a question mark after Senfl's name.[35] While such problems of attribution are often difficult, in light of the compositions attributed to Senfl in this same source, the setting of "In pace in idipsum" appears sufficiently similar in terms of musical style and procedure to other Senfl compositions to inspire some confidence the 2004 edition's attribution. That said, it must be admitted that basing such an attribution on the "internal" evidence of the music itself is admittedly delicate, as Senfl's musical style and language is hardly unique compared to his contemporaries represented in this manuscript source.[36]

In the *prima pars* (mm. 1–49 of Kongsted's edition) of this polyphonic setting of "In pace in idipsum," nearly every note in the tenor part is taken from the chant, excepting only the flourish on the second pitch (mm. 9–11). It is useful to recall Luther's words from 1538 in praise of Latin polyphony: "Here it is most remarkable that one single voice continues to sing the tenor, while at the same time many other voices play around it, exulting and adorning it in exuberant strains." What Luther described in 1538 may be illustrated by this setting of "In pace in idipsum." The composer has taken a specific chant as the basis for his composition, preserving the pitches of the chant in the tenor, and, moreover, allowing the opening melodic profile of the chant to infuse the other three voice parts around the tenor (mm. 1–10). The chant melody that Luther so loved forms the basis of the polyphony, yet it is integrated with the other voice parts so that the whole composition sounds balanced, the preexistent chant melody not dominating the musical texture. While we might take that for granted, in terms of the characteristic overall sound of sixteenth-century Latin polyphony, we should not underestimate the compositional control that is at work here. Luther did not, as this comment recorded in *Table Talk* reveals:

35 Similarly, the Danish scholar Ole Kongsted adds a question mark after Senfl's name in his edition: *Motetter af Ludwig Senfl*, ed. Ole Kongsted, Capella Hafniensis Editions A. 1 (Copenhagen: The Royal Library, 2001), 12–17.

36 Without concordant sources attributing the composition to Senfl—a type of "external" evidence—it seems to me prudent to retain the question mark after Senfl's name. Bettina Schwemer goes a bit further: in her study *Mehrstimmige Responsorienvertonungen in deutschen Quellen des 15. und 16. Jahrhunderts*, Collectanea Musicologica 8 (Augsburg: Wißner, 1998), Bd. 2, 72, she indicates the authorship of this composition as "anonym."

> Da man etliche feine liebliche Moteten des Senfels sang, verwunderte sich D[oktor] M[artin] L[uther] und lobt sie sehr, und sprach: "Eine solche motete vermöcht ich nicht zu machen, wenn ich mich auch zureissen sollte, wie er denn auch wiederum nicht einen Psalm predigen konnte als ich."[37]
>
> After some fine and beautiful motets by Senfl had been sung, [Luther] was amazed, accorded them much praise, and said: "I would not be able to compose such a motet, even if I would tear myself to pieces in the attempt, just as he [Senfl] would not be able to preach a Psalm as I can."[38]

Unlike the setting of "In pace in idipsum" transmitted anonymously in the Schalreuter manuscript, there is no doubt about the four-part motet "Non moriar sed vivam" (Psalm 118:17), which is attributed to Senfl in manuscript sources in Berlin, Regensburg, and Zwickau.[39] The text of Psalm 118:17 is:

> Non moriar sed vivam, et narrabo opera domini.
>
> I shall not die but live, and tell the works of the Lord.[40]

Motets had no fixed functions within either mass or office liturgies; rather, they were employed with great flexibility for any given liturgical occasion, their use not being limited to where the specific texts might be appointed within those liturgies.[41] Moreover, as one can tell from Luther's *Table Talk*, motets were sung outside of liturgical occasions, as, for example, for recreational or devotional purposes by a group of associates or friends.

Senfl's motet "Non moriar sed vivam" is constructed economically by drawing on a small number of recurring musical ideas. The chant melody associated with this text is stated in its entirety twice: first in the soprano (or discant)

---

37 WA TR 1:490 (No. 968).

38 Leaver, *Luther's Liturgical Music*, 58–59, 371 n. 227; Buszin, *Luther on Music*, 7–8.

39 www.senflonline.com.

40 Luther tried his hand at setting this text. See Leaver, *Luther's Liturgical Music*, 58–60, and *Lutheran Choral Anthology: The 16th Century*, ed. Carl F. Schalk and William H. Braun (St. Louis: Concordia Publishing House, 2010), 165–69.

41 Anthony M. Cummings, "Toward an Interpretation of the Sixteenth-Century Motet," *Journal of the American Musicological Society* 34 (Spring 1981): 43–59; Cummings, "The Motet," in *European Music, 1520–1640*, ed. James Haar (Woodbridge, UK: The Boydell Press, 2006), 130–56; David Crook, "The Exegetical Motet," *Journal of the American Musicological Society* 68 (Summer 2015): 255–316.

voice (mm. 9–24) and later in the tenor voice (mm. 46–62).[42] Senfl uses the first phrase of this chant melody in the opening measures, where alto, tenor, and bass successively preview the preexistent chant melody about to be sung in its entirety by the soprano voice. As this chant melody sounds forth in slower note values, Senfl employs quicker figures on the word *vivam*, thereby adding forward momentum to the polyphonic complex. A new and distinctive musical idea appears with the second textual phrase: *et narrabo opera*. This musical idea at times uses only two pitches, the pitch repetition providing an essentially rhythmic idea that contrasts with the opening melodic gesture derived from the preexistent chant.[43]

In summary, Luther desired to retain the Latin mass, even as he took the lead in creating a repertory of vernacular hymns and a vernacular form of the mass. Retaining the Latin mass meant that the young, especially, would still have the benefit of using the Latin language. Moreover, in terms of music, Latin chant and Latin polyphony—each a remarkable heritage of the Western church, would also be retained, insofar as individual chant texts and motet texts were consonant with the Gospel. Significantly, Luther knew the music of Josquin, and came to know Ludwig Senfl sufficiently well to request a specific Latin polyphonic setting from him. And central to the topic of Latin polyphony is Luther's own love for this music and his sense of wonder at such music—a sense of wonder that reminds us not to take for granted the inherent beauty and the consistent compositional craftsmanship of those repertories from the fifteenth and sixteenth centuries.

A final question to pose here is simply this: To what extent did Latin polyphony continue to be used in Lutheranism *after* Luther's death in 1546? Luther's bilingual model for liturgy found a parallel in terms of musical composition and performance throughout the sixteenth and seventeenth centuries and well into the eighteenth century, which is to say that the German chorale in all of its musical manifestations coexisted with the continuing use of Latin chant and polyphony in the Lutheran church.

Johann Walter, Luther's most immediate musical colleague, is best known for his 1524 published polyphonic settings of German chorales—a landmark collection in the sense that it was the first in what would become a flood of

42 For the chant melody see Leaver, *Luther's Liturgical Music*, 53, 59. Measure numbers refer to Kongsted's edition (see note 28 above).

43 For a compact disc recording of "Non moriar sed vivam" see *Ludwig Senfl (1486–1542): Komponist der Reformation*, Ensemble Officium, Wilfried Rombach, Christophorus CHR 77226.

vocal and instrumental elaborations of chorale melodies.[44] But Walter also composed much Latin polyphony, including a five-part setting of "Non moriar sed vivam."[45]

Georg Rhau (1488–1548), a composer and music theorist who served briefly (1518–20) in Leipzig as cantor at the St. Thomas School (a Latin school)—a position that some two centuries later would be held by Johann Sebastian Bach—returned to his hometown of Wittenberg in 1523, where he became a leading printer and publisher for the emerging church, editing and printing eleven volumes of Latin polyphony, as well as music theoretical and pedagogical works written in Latin. Illustrative of his published anthologies is his 1538 *Symphoniae iucundae* (with a preface by Luther), which contained fifty-two Latin motets.[46]

The great Lutheran cantor, composer, and music theorist Michael Praetorius (1571–1621) had a direct link to the Luther circle in Wittenberg since his father was a colleague of Johann Walter. Praetorius was one of the most prolific of all Lutheran composers, both with respect to the German chorale—where he most often provided multiple settings of a given chorale—but also with respect to Latin polyphony. In 1611, for example, he published separate collections of his own Latin polyphony: mass movements (predominantly but not exclusively for the Ordinary), Latin hymns for the church year, and Magnificat settings.[47]

A final example illustrating the continuing use of Latin polyphony in the Lutheran sphere is the extensive anthology of Latin motets compiled by Erhard Bodenschatz (1576–1636), Lutheran cantor, pastor, composer, and music editor. His *Florilegium portense*, a Latin motet anthology in two parts, was published between 1603 and 1621. The first part, published in 1603 and subsequently enlarged in 1618, included 115 Latin motets by 48 German composers, including Bodenschatz himself. In the second volume of 1621, Italian composers predominate. These two volumes enjoyed continuous use in schools and

---

44 A facsimile was published as Johann Walter, *Das geistliche Gesangbüchlein "Chorgesangbuch,"* Documenta Musicologica, Erste Reihe: Druckschriften-Faksimiles 33 (Kassel: Bärenreiter, 1979).

45 For Walter's setting of "Non moriar sed vivam" see Johann Walter, *Geistliches Gesangbüchlein, Wittenberg 1551, zweiter Teil: Cantiones Latinae*, Sämtliche Werke (Kassel: Bärenreiter; St. Louis: Concordia Publishing House, 1953), vol. 2, 168–70.

46 Georg Rhau, *Symphoniae jucundae, 1538*, ed. Hans Albrecht, Musikdrucke aus den Jahren 1538 bis 1545 in praktischen Neuausgabe (Kassel: Bärenreiter; St. Louis: Concordia Publishing House, 1959), vol. 3.

47 See Michael Praetorius, *Gesamtausgabe der Musikalischen Werke*, ed. Friedrich Blume (Wolfenbüttel: Georg Kallmeyer, 1928–40); for his Latin polyphony see particularly volumes 11–14.

churches in the German-speaking lands, specifically in cities and towns having Latin schools.

Bach, for example, used these volumes during his years in Leipzig (1723–50). His appointment was as cantor of the aforementioned St. Thomas school and director of music in Leipzig, responsible to the Town Council. As Director of Music he was responsible for all of the music at four Leipzig churches, not only the two so-called principal churches, St. Thomas and St. Nicholas, but also St. Peter's and the so-called New Church, which was opened in 1699 to alleviate overcrowding at the two principal churches. Thus, Bach, with the help of student assistants, prepared and supervised four choirs for these four churches on a weekly basis. In a document from August 1730, written by Bach and directed to the Leipzig town council, he describes the graded choir program at the St. Thomas school and how he allocated his approximately fifty-five students among the four churches for Sunday morning music. He wrote: "St. Peter's receives the residue, namely, those who do not understand music and can only just barely sing a chorale."[48] He added, "In the 3 churches, namely, St. Thomas's, St. Nicholas's, and the New Church, the pupils must all be musical."[49] A Latin motet was a standard part of the Sunday morning music at all three of those churches.

This motet repertory consisted not of the elaborate motets composed by Bach himself, but rather older and simpler Latin motets of the type found in the Bodenschatz anthologies. In 1729 the St. Thomas school records show a payment of twelve thaler to Bach for a *Florilegium portense* "which the pupils need in the churches."[50] Just as Luther would not jettison the Latin language, the Latin mass with its chant, or Latin polyphony, opting instead for liturgical and musical continuity with the rich traditions of the Western church, so also Lutheran worship in eighteenth-century Leipzig, among other cities, continued to draw on Latin polyphony in the form of a motet placed at the very beginning of the Divine Service.[51]

While the Calvinist reform movement in Switzerland and France took a cautious approach to music in the church, limiting it to unaccompanied unison singing of metrical psalms, Luther recognized and loved the musical heritage of the Western church and advocated for the continuing use of Latin chant and

---

48 *The New Bach Reader: A Life of Johann Sebastian Bach in Letters and Documents*, rev. and enl. Christoph Wolff (New York: W.W. Norton, 1998), 146.

49 *The New Bach Reader*, 146.

50 Andrew Parrott, *The Essential Bach Choir* (Woodbridge, UK: The Boydell Press, 2000), 21–22.

51 See the *New Bach Reader*, 113, for Bach's own outline for the "Order of the Divine Service in Leipzig."

Latin polyphony. This openness to the best sacred music traditions of his time effectively set a precedent for music in Lutheran worship. While it is not the case that Latin polyphony found a permanent place in Lutheran liturgies, such polyphony from the late fifteenth through the early seventeenth centuries was invariably well-crafted music from well-trained composers working in the traditions of Western art music, and it is those factors that constitute this precedent. Those polyphonic musical repertories established high standards of quality—not necessarily complexity, but *quality*—that ultimately manifested itself in musical genres as diverse as motets, baroque vocal concertos, cantatas, and anthems, among others. Just as Luther recognized the rich musical traditions of the Western church, so he also discerned the very best composers of his time. That commitment to continuity with the church's traditions and to quality in newly composed music set a course for Lutheran church music, a course that has provided—and continues to provide—extensive and rich repertories of sacred music for use in the church today and in the future.

CHAPTER 12

Tradition and the Individual Talent: Some Verse-Paraphrases of Psalm 1

E.J. Hutchinson

1 Introduction

For a period of about one hundred and twenty years, from around 1500 to 1620, a new genre of poetry flourished in Europe, the genre of poetic psalm-paraphrases in classical Latin meters, and then just as quickly disappeared.[1] The popularity of this genre cut across confessional boundaries, thriving among Roman Catholics, Lutherans, and the Reformed, both on the Continent and in the British Isles.[2] There were at least one hundred authors of such poems,[3] whether they versified only selections of the Psalter (e.g., the penitential psalms) or the whole of it, and, to judge from the multiple printings and editions of many of these collections, there existed also a large reading public.[4]

1 For speculation on why this is so, see Johannes A. Gaertner, "Latin Verse Translations of the Psalms: 1500–1620," *Harvard Theological Review* 49 (1956): 271–305. For verse-paraphrases of other books of the Bible from roughly the same period, see W. Leonard Grant, "Neo-Latin Verse-Translations of the Bible," *Harvard Theological Review* 52 (1959): 205–11. For the liturgical contexts of Latin in the sixteenth century, see Ann Moss, "Latin Liturgical Hymns of the Reformation Crisis (1520–1568)," *Humanistica Lovaniensia* 40 (1991): 73–111.

2 Though Ian D. McFarlane, *Buchanan* (London: Duckworth, 1981), 248, notes the importance of evangelical influences in particular on the genre.

3 Gaertner, "Latin Verse Translations," 293–300, catalogues close to one hundred instances, but also states, 277, that he "believes he has tabulated *at least half* of all the writers that published significant Psalm translations in Holland, Switzerland, England, Germany, France and possibly Italy between 1500 and 1620" (emphasis mine), so the actual number of paraphrases, either of the whole Psalter or of parts of it, will be significantly higher.

4 Buchanan's paraphrases, for example, found almost instant use as a school text, for they were put to that purpose as early as *c.*1570 in Glasgow: see McFarlane, *Buchanan*, 260–61. Roger P.H. Green, "George Buchanan, Arthur Johnston, and William Laud," *Scottish Literary Review* 2 (2010): 5, remarks that Buchanan's paraphrases went through nearly one hundred editions in the four hundred years that elapsed after their initial publication. For the polyphonic musical settings of Buchanan's Psalms 1–41 by the French Huguenot composer Jean Servin, see James Porter, "The Geneva Connection: Jean Servin's settings of the Latin Psalm Paraphrases of George Buchanan," *Acta Musicologica* 81 (2009): 229–54.

 | DOI:10.1163/9789004206717_014

Of these myriad authors, three of the most popular were the German Helius Eobanus Hessus (1488–1540),[5] the Scot George Buchanan (1506–82),[6] and the Frenchman Theodore Beza (1519–1605). Hessus's *Psalterium Davidis carmine redditum*, in which Melanchthon claimed to have found "remedy and relief for my miseries in the midst of most bitter anxieties"[7] and which Luther said he "has read, reads, and will always read with the highest pleasure,"[8] appeared first in Marburg in 1537 and subsequently saw more than fifty printings;[9] Buchanan's *Psalmorum Davidis paraphrasis poetica*, begun while Buchanan was imprisoned by the Inquisition in a Portuguese monastery, was first published in 1565 or 1566, in Geneva or Paris;[10] and the *Psalmorum Davidis et aliorum Prophetarum libri quinque* of Beza, whom Sir Philip Sidney in *The Defence of Poesy* called a "famous preacher and teacher,"[11] was published in Geneva in 1579.[12] All three versified the entire Psalter. In addition, Buchanan and Beza

5 For a brief account of Hessus's background and life, see Harry Vredeveld, "Eobanus Hessus," in *German Writers of the Renaissance and Reformation, 1280–1580*, ed. James Hardin and Max Reinhart (Detroit: Gale Research, 1997), 97–110, as well as Harry Vredeveld, *The Poetic Works of Helius Eobanus Hessus*, vols. 1–2 (Tempe, AZ: Arizona Center for Medieval and Renaissance Studies, 2004, 2008) and vols. 3–4 (Leiden: Brill, 2012, 2016).

6 McFarlane, *Buchanan*, 247, notes that there are "over a hundred editions of the paraphrases on their own or with certain other texts by Buchanan."

7 Philip Melanchthon, *Epistolae* 7.1596, in CR 3:393.

8 Martin Luther, *Epistola* 3167, in WA Br 8: 107. Both letters, written on 1 August 1537, were used as front-matter for editions of Hessus's paraphrase.

9 Harry Vredeveld, "Hessus, Eobanus," in *The Oxford Encyclopedia of the Reformation*, ed. Hans J. Hillerbrand, (Oxford: Oxford University Press, 1996), 2:238.

10 Cf. McFarlane, *Buchanan*, 254–55. The "first definitive version to have [Buchanan's] blessing, however, did not appear until 1571": see Roger P.H. Green, "Davidic Psalm and Horatian Ode: Five Poems of George Buchanan," *Renaissance Studies* 14 (2000): 93; on the textual history of the paraphrases, more broadly, see Roger P.H. Green, "The Text of George Buchanan's *Psalm Paraphrases*," *The Bibliotheck* 13 (1986): 3–29. An earlier version of the poem was printed in Henricus Stephanus, ed., *Davidis psalmi aliquot Latino carmine expressi a quatuor illustribus poetis: quos quatuor regiones, Gallia, Italia, Germania, Scotia, genuerunt* (n.p.: Henricus Stephanus, 1556), sigs. Aiii–iv, which is followed by the paraphrase of Hessus and which differs slightly from later versions (which in turn differ from each other in some small respects). I cite the text as given in Roger P.H. Green, ed., George Buchanan, *Poetic Paraphrase of the Psalms of David* (Geneva: Librairie Droz, 2011), 102–4.

11 Cited in Anne Lake Prescott, "English Writers and Beza's Latin Epigrams: The Uses and Abuses of Poetry," *Studies in the Renaissance* 21 (1974): 95. Sidney in the same passage praises Buchanan's "so piercing wits."

12 An earlier, and slightly different, version of Beza's Psalm 1 was published already in the 1560s with paraphrases by Buchanan, though there seems to be a discrepancy as to when precisely. McFarlane, *Buchanan*, 256, appears to link the inclusion of some of Beza's paraphrases to the first dated edition (which is not the *editio princeps*) of Buchanan's

were close personal associates. These literary productions of Hessus, Buchanan, and Beza doubtless had an important devotional impetus and justification. But the piety of the exercise was not exclusive of what Roger Green refers to as "scholarly competitiveness" among paraphrasts of the psalms.[13] Some indications that the authors treated here were emulating both classical predecessors as well as each other will be examined below.[14]

As a preliminary assessment, therefore, of the characteristics of their methods of verse-paraphrase, particularly in terms of their literary and theological relationship to their source-text, the Bible, to the ancient poets whom they emulate, and to one another, this chapter compares certain features of their respective versions of Psalm 1 while using the Vulgate translation as a base text.

There are at least two aspects of the last sentence that need accounting for. First, why the Vulgate? It is of course true that there were other Latin versions of the Bible available, in addition to vernacular translations. Buchanan, for instance, was influenced by the Zürich Latin Bible of 1543,[15] and he also knew Hebrew,[16] as did Beza. Yet the Vulgate was still the most familiar Latin version

---

psalm-paraphrases in 1566, published by Henricus and Robertus Stephanus, while Green, *Poetic Paraphrase*, 26, remarks that they are present in the *editio princeps*, also published by Henricus and Robertus Stephanus but with no date or place of publication on the title page (cf. the discussion in McFarlane, *Buchanan*, 255–57, and Green, *Poetic Paraphrase*, 26–28). I have been able to consult the latter edition, and can verify that the Beza paraphrases are included, and that this fact is acknowledged on the title page. They also appear in a 1566 edition by Josiah Rihel published in Strasbourg. In this chapter, I cite the text of Buchanan as given in Green, *Poetic Paraphrase*, 102–4, and the text of Beza as found in the complete edition of his psalm-paraphrases of 1579: Theodore Beza, *Psalmorum Davidis et aliorum prophetarum libri quinque, argumentis et Latina paraphrasi illustrati, ac etiam vario carminum genere Latine expressi* (Geneva: n.p., 1579). There is another complete edition of Beza's Psalter (also published in Geneva in the same year, with the same artwork surrounding the title page, and again with no publisher named) that lacks the *argumenta*, prose *paraphrasis*, and prose *interpretatio* that are found in the edition I cite.

13 Green, "Davidic Psalm," 91.

14 Elwira Buszewicz, in an essay detailing the profound influence of Buchanan's poetry, which was exercised as far afield as Poland, notes that the original 1556 collection already had an agonistic aspect. See Elwira Buszewicz, "Poetry and the *Respublica Literarum* in the Sixteenth Century. The Communication of Ideas: George Buchanan and Jan Kochanowski," *Renaissance and Reformation* 36 (2013): 55.

15 See Roger P.H. Green, "Horace's Odes in the Psalm Paraphrases of Buchanan," in *Acta Conventus Neo-Latini Guelpherbytani: Proceedings of the Sixth International Congress of Neo-Latin Studies*, ed. Stella P. Revard, F. Rädle, and M.A. di Cesare (Binghamton, NY: Center for Medieval and Early Renaissance Studies, 1988), 72.

16 For Buchanan's interest in Hebrew studies, and probable influences upon him, see McFarlane, *Buchanan*, 34–37, 249.

of the Bible and its influence was enormous from its long use.[17] It is therefore serviceable as a point of departure for determining degrees of poetic license and innovation.[18]

Secondly, why Psalm 1? John Calvin, a contemporary of the three authors under discussion here, wrote at the beginning of his commentary on the Psalms,

> He who collected the Psalms into one volume, whether Ezra or some other person, appears to have placed this Psalm at the beginning, by way of preface, in which he inculcates upon all the godly the duty of meditating upon the law of God. The sum and substance of the whole is, that they are blessed who apply their hearts to the pursuit of heavenly wisdom; whereas the profane despisers of God, although for a time they may reckon themselves happy, shall at length have a most miserable end.[19]

Psalm 1, then, is programmatic for the book of Psalms, and I shall assume as well that its versification is therefore programmatic for versifications of the Psalter.[20]

My treatment is organized in three sections. First, I shall discuss the meter employed by each author for the first psalm, and the possible reasons for that choice. Second, I shall examine their practices of *amplificatio* through an analysis of each author's treatment of the simile in verse 3. Finally, I shall note some uses of classical allusion in order to see what they might tell us about each author's technique and mode of interacting with early modern Europe's ancient Roman inheritance.

---

17 Cf. Roger P.H. Green, "Classical Voices in Buchanan's Hexameter Psalm Paraphrases," *Renaissance Studies* 18 (2004): 59. In the first dated edition (the second edition overall) of Buchanan's paraphrases (1566), the *incipits* of the Vulgate were included with the versifications (see McFarlane, *Buchanan*, 257). Green, "Davidic Psalm," 93, notes that "[t]he Vulgate is quite clearly [Buchanan's] base text." Roger P.H. Green, "Poetic Psalm Paraphrases: Two Versions of Psalm 1 Compared," in *Acta Conventus Neo-Latini Budapestinensis: Proceedings of the Thirteenth International Congress of Neo-Latin Studies*, ed. Rhoda Schnur (Tempe, AZ: Arizona Center for Medieval and Renaissance Studies, 2010), 265–66, likewise uses the Vulgate as a basis for comparison.

18 The Vulgate version of Psalm 1 is cited in the edition of Robert Weber: *Biblia sacra iuxta vulgatam versionem*, vol. 1 (Stuttgart: Deutsche Bibelgesellschaft, 1985).

19 John Calvin, *Commentary on the Book of Psalms*, trans. James Anderson (Edinburgh: Calvin Translation Society, 1845), 1:1.

20 For Buchanan in particular, cf. Green, "Classical Voices," 87, though we think it programmatic for different, but not incompatible, reasons.

2 Meter

Hessus's first psalm is written in elegiac couplets. This is not remarkable, however, for he transposed all one hundred and fifty psalms into elegiac couplets, a meter that Buchanan uses on only three occasions.[21] At the time, exclusive use of elegiac couplets was common practice: Francois Bonade and Johann Spangeberg did the same in their versifications of the entire Psalter, and Nicolas Bourbon and Philip Melanchthon had used the meter for individual psalms, as Green has pointed out.[22] Hessus's use of this meter for every psalm obviously means that we cannot attach any particular significance to its employment in this instance.

George Buchanan, on the other hand, wrote his first psalm in dactylic hexameters. As Green has remarked elsewhere, this meter "was not at all common in poetic paraphrases of the Psalms," a fact that, he says, "may even have commended its use here to announce a set that is conspicuously inclusive in metrical terms."[23] That is to say, the hexameter would have been a sign of innovation. Buchanan, who used a total of twenty-nine different meters in his collection,[24] also employed hexameters for Psalms 18, 45, 78, 85, 89, 104, 107, 132, and 135. Though one might suspect that its use is furthermore intended to recall heroic poetry, Green asserts that "there is no obvious thematic or generic link with

---

21 See Green, "Classical Voices," 56. Buchanan uses elegiac couplets in 88, 114, and 137. After Buchanan's metrical innovation, his later rival Arthur Johnston would return (with the exception of Psalm 119) to the use of elegiac couplets. See Roger P.H. Green, "On Not Being Buchanan: Arthur Johnston's *Magnum Opus*," in *Acta Conventus Neo-Latini Upsaliensis*, ed. Astrid Steiner-Weber (Leiden: Brill, 2012), 444; Arthur Johnston, *Psalmorum Davidis paraphrasis poetica et canticorum evangelicorum* (Aberdeen: Raban, 1637).

22 Green, "Horace's Odes," in *Acta Conventus Neo-Latini Guelpherbytani: Proceedings of the Sixth International Congress of Neo-Latin Studies*, ed. Stella P. Revard, F. Rädle, and M.A. di Cesare (Binghamton, NY: Center for Medieval and Early Renaissance Studies, 1988), 71–72.

23 Green, *Poetic Paraphrase*, 522. Green, "Classical Voices," 87, had previously suggested that Buchanan originally may have intended the inclusion of the hexameter to distinguish himself from the metrical eccentricity of Jean Gagnay, who avoided the "commoner metres." I give my own hypothesis for the use of the hexameter above.

24 See Green, *Poetic Paraphrase*, 627–28. As he remarks elsewhere, "[m]etrical inventiveness, but within the bounds set by Horace and the later writers Ausonius and Prudentius, is Buchanan's forte" ("Davidic Psalm," 92). For a sensitive reading of the three psalms paraphrased in elegiac couplets (88, 114, and 137), see John Wall, "The Latin Elegiacs of George Buchanan (1506–1582)," in *Bards and Makars: Scottish Language and Literature: Medieval and Renaissance*, ed. Adam J. Aitken, Matthew P. McDiarmid, and Derick S. Thomson (Glasgow: University of Glasgow Press, 1977), 184–93.

epic."[25] This latter claim is more dubious: for what, precisely, would the generic message, as it were, have been for the poem's audience when it encountered an opening poem in dactylic hexameters? If we posit a learned audience educated in the humanistic fashion, it seems inevitable that, when its members read a hexameter poem about a heroic and blessed individual completing a successful journey—*felix ille animi, quem non de tramite recto*—[26] they would have thought of the great classical epics, and especially of Virgil's *Aeneid*; for still in the Renaissance "the hexameter was known as the 'metrum heroicum' or 'heroum.'"[27] In addition, the hexameter, in traditional terms, was the meter not only of heroic epic but also of didactic poetry: compare Lucretius's *De rerum natura*, for example, or Virgil's *Georgics*, not to mention Hesiod's *Works and Days*. The didactic and heroic elements of hexameter poetry had already been combined and used to paraphrase biblical material hundreds of years before by poets such as Sedulius (fifth century) and Arator (sixth century), both of whom wrote Latin biblical epic. Finally, the dactylic hexameter was the normal meter employed in Roman satire, the purpose of which was (often, at least) moral instruction, as one finds in, for example, Horace's *Sermones*.[28] Given the strength of these customary associations of the dactylic hexameter, it is plausible to suggest, even if it cannot be demonstrated with certainty, that Buchanan's use of it in his opening poem would have been evocative for his audience of the broad Latin hexameter tradition in its general outlines, and that Buchanan would have known it to be so. If that is the case, the signal Buchanan sends his readers with this first poem is that they are about to encounter highly wrought poetry on a grand scale, classical in manner and didactic in its pious and moral intent.

Beza does something different again from both Hessus and Buchanan with respect to meter: he uses couplets made up of iambic trimeters followed by iambic dimeters (i.e., iambic couplets), a meter used frequently by Buchanan

---

25 Green, "Classical Voices," 56, notes that the iambic couplet is the commonest meter in Buchanan's paraphrases. Thus, even if it is true, as Green, "Davidic Psalm," 94–95, states, that it is "usual" that "one cannot be certain why he chooses a particular metre," more confidence is warranted in this case; cf. n. 18.

26 The opening line of Buchanan's paraphrase of Psalm 1. It is possible that Buchanan avoids the Vulgate's *beati* here (to which Beza will later revert; see below) because in classical Latin the word often means "prosperous" instead of "happy": see Green, "Davidic Psalm," 105. In any case, his use of *felix* echoes the opening of Hessus's poem.

27 Green, "Classical Voices," 57.

28 This use in moralizing satire is not surprising, given that the hexameter was the normal meter for didactic poetry in general.

as well[29] but only rarely by classical poets; this is perhaps evidence for Buchanan's influence on Beza,[30] though without further evidence such a claim would be bare conjecture. More significantly (and regardless of Buchanan's possible influence here), the meter, precisely because of its infrequent use among the ancients, unmistakably marks Beza's main classical model: rather than conjuring the ghost of classical heroic or didactic poetry, Beza instead recalls Horace's first ten *Epodes*, which are all written with this iambic combination. At first glance, this may seem an odd choice, for iambic poetry traditionally was associated with invective and abuse, though it could also be used for purposes of public instruction and exhortation, a function which brings it into some relation with the first psalm. But as I shall argue below, there is an even more significant reason for Beza's use of it here, a reason that is discerned through allusions to ancient and contemporary poets in the opening of the poem.

3 *Amplificatio*

Now let us turn to an examination of our authors' expansions of the biblical model, for which the handling of the simile in verse 3 will serve as a representative example. In that simile, the righteous man is likened to a flourishing tree. As the Vulgate has it:

> *et erit tamquam* lignum quod plantatum est secus decursus aquarum, quod fructum suum dabit in tempore suo, et folium eius non defluet; et omnia quaecumque faciet presperabuntur.

Or, in the Authorized Version:

> *And he shall be like* a tree planted by the rivers of water, that bringeth forth his fruit in his season; his leaf also shall not wither; and whatsoever he doeth shall prosper.

29 Psalms 3, 6, 10, 21, 22, 27, 34, 38, 39, 41, 44, 48, 53, 62, 74, 76, 79, 87, 92, 110, 112, 115, 120, 127, 133, 134, 139, and 141. See Green, *Poetic Paraphrase*, 627, as well as Roger P.H. Green, "George Buchanan's Psalm Paraphrases: Matters of Metre," in *Acta Conventus Neo-Latini Sanctandreani: Proceedings of the Fifth International Congress of Neo-Latin Studies*, ed. Ian D. MacFarlane (Binghamton, NY: Center for Medieval and Renaissance Studies, 1986), 51–60.

30 Buchanan had already used the meter three times in Stephanus's 1556 collection.

A consultation of the texts of the poems of Hessus, Buchanan, and Beza in the appendix immediately reveals that each of the three uses a construction to make the comparison that differs both from the Vulgate *and* from the other two poets. Hessus uses the adjective *assimilis* (9) followed by the dative, Buchanan *velut* (7) followed by the nominative, and Beza *qualis* (11) followed by the nominative. In terms of the number of words used to paraphrase this simile, moreover, all three authors show an increase over their model as the simile is classicized.[31] For both Buchanan and Beza, there is a 26 percent increase in length in comparison with the Vulgate rendering; for Hessus, the amplification is a startling 100 percent.

In addition to changing the manner of introduction and doubling the length of the simile in his source-text, Hessus makes several changes to individual words and the conceptualization of the simile as well. First, whereas the original psalm refers simply to a tree, *lignum*, planted by streams of water, Hessus speaks of a palm tree, *palmae* (9), that is teeming or pregnant (*gravidae*, 9) in its branches and that stands by a lake (*lacus*, 10) swelling with waves.[32] The lexicographical choice of *palma* presumably has symbolic value, since the palm traditionally is a symbol of victory in contests, including poetic contests,[33] though I would suggest that that is not its primary referent here. The primary referent is rather a Christian one: for Christians in particular the palm is a symbol of the victory of Christ and, through him, of Christians over death[34]—a significant christological addition in the opening poem of the collection. This tree, like the man about whom the psalm speaks, is obedient to the commands (*iussa*, 10)[35] it has received that promote its flourishing. Again, rather than simply "bringing forth fruits in season," the tree performs its "duty" (*munera*, 12), a humanization and moralization of the tree itself, whereas in the psalm there is, we might say, an "arborization" of man. Nature, now to a certain degree personified, serves as a doublet of man in his duty and obedience to God. Whereas

31 Cf. Green, "Classical Voices," 86.

32 *lacus* is a poetic plural. The change from "river" to "lake" is curious, and it is possible that Hessus is using *lacus* in its comparatively rare (alleged) poetic signification as "river" (cf. LS, s.v. *lacus* II, though it is not at all clear that the word means "river" in the two passages from Vergil, *A*. 8.66 and 74, cited there as proof).

33 Cf. Ausonius *Epistulae* 18.5.

34 Cf. the use of palms as a symbol of Christ's victory on Palm Sunday: *Oxford Dictionary of the Christian Church*, ed. F.L. Cross and E.A. Livingstone, 3rd ed. (Oxford, UK: Oxford University Press, 1997), s.v. "Palm Sunday." The palm is also an important biblical image, from its use as a decorative motif in Solomon's Temple (1 Kings 6) and palace (1 Kings 7), to its use in the Triumphal Entry (John 12:13) and in the scourging of Christ (Matt. 26.67), and, finally, in the worship of the redeemed heavenly multitude (Rev. 7:9).

35 Here a participle modifying the relative pronoun *quae* whose antecedent is *palmae*.

the psalm leaves the human analogue of the fruit borne by the tree latent in the comparison, Hessus makes it explicit with an added parallelism in lines 13–14: just as the tree (*illius*, 14) does not lose its leaves, so the just man (*huic*, 13) does not lose his rewards (*honores*, 13). In the last two lines of his version of the simile (15–16) Hessus returns to the tree. He maintains the Vulgate's *quaecumque* to refer to the tree's fruit, but again heightens the effect of the tree's production: it now yields the "best" fruit (*optima*, 15), it is lavish (*prodiga*, 15) with produce that is "true" (*veris*, 15)[36]—another term with moral resonance, particularly in Scripture—and it will always have desirable wealth (*opes*, 16).

Changes are even more drastic, in terms of content if not of length, when we turn to Buchanan's version. To refer to the tree itself, Buchanan forgoes the Vulgate's unclassical *lignum* and bypasses Hessus's *palma*, and instead calls the tree an *arbor*, a word Virgil uses frequently in the *Eclogues* and *Georgics*. In one respect, Buchanan hews more closely to the biblical archetype by referring to the tree as "planted," which Hessus did not do, though Buchanan does not use the Vulgate's *plantatum est*, instead substituting *consita est* (7). For Buchanan, though, the tree is not just "along" the stream, but at the very "edge of the bank" (*margine ... ripae*, 7). Why this change to *margine consita ripae* (7)? In part, perhaps, because of the biblical resonances of the image of "sowing" (e.g., Matt. 13:1–9). But in addition, Buchanan is probably alluding ornamentally to Ovid, *Heroides* 5.27, where this phrase is found, as Green notes,[37] but with the order of the first two words reversed. The point is not that one must choose between these two explanations; the point is rather that one ought to choose both, for this is poetry that is both biblical and classical and that keeps both traditions constantly before our eyes. Here an Ovidian turn of phrase adorns a biblical image.[38]

Beyond these superficial matters, however, Buchanan makes some still more striking changes to the psalm. First, he introduces in classicizing fashion the idea of seasonal extremes of weather that are unable to shake the tree's fruit: neither the Dog-Star of summer (*Sirius*, 8) nor the storms of winter (*hiems*, 9) can harm the tree. There is a Virgilian parallel here that will be discussed below. Through heat and the chill of winter, Buchanan says, the tree remains lavish in its issue. The word he uses is *prodiga* (9), the same one Hessus had employed, and Buchanan, who was familiar with Hessus, does this perhaps

36 Taking *veris* as from the adjective *verus* rather than as the genitive singular of the noun *ver* ("spring"). The ambiguity may be intentional.

37 Green, *Poetic Paraphrase*, 522.

38 A fuller discussion of allusive practice is found in the following section.

under his influence. But Buchanan then adds an entirely new element:[39] this produce makes the farmer happy (*beat agricolam*, 10); Buchanan's farmer introduces a human perspective entirely lacking in both the Bible and Hessus. This farmer clarifies Buchanan's interpretation of the image in verse 3 as specifically "georgic." The tree does not allure the master to no purpose with flattering hope (*blanda dominum spe lactat inanem*, 11)—in other words, the tree is not hypocritical; one might recall the humanization of the tree in Hessus discussed above. The image is psychologized from a human point of view in terms of the farmer's cultivation of nature, but the true nature of the plant's growth that pleases the farmer also directs the reader's attention upwards for who but the Lord (cf. *dominum*, 11) is the tender of the just man?[40]

What do we find when we turn to Beza's treatment of this simile? Beza rephrases the whole verse in a *qualis* ... *talis* construction and inverts the order of the source-text, placing the tree first and the man only at the end of the simile. In his treatment of particulars Beza shows the influence of both Hessus and Buchanan. He uses the word *arbos* (13) for "tree," as Buchanan does, and also borrows his phrasing for the placement of the tree from him: it is *ripae margine* (11). Like Hessus, he personifies nature, such that the tree is happy (*laeta*, 11),[41] and (oddly) *superbiens*.[42] In a possible reminiscence of Hessus, Beza writes that the branches are *graves* (14) (cf. Hessus's *gravidae*, 9). From Buchanan, Beza retains the introduction of the farmer or husbandman, but without the additional resonance of God as cultivator or reference to human hypocrisy; and rather than an *agricola*, he is now a *colonus* (13). Beza also retains Buchanan's idea, grafted onto the biblical text, of the tree's ability to withstand winter's cold—indeed, it "smashes" it (*et vim rigentis dura frangens frigoris*, 15)—as well as Hessus's verb *virere* (16), to describe the tree's flourishing, and his term *honores* (16); but this last he transfers from the man's fruit in Hessus's poem to the tree's fruit in his own. These "honors" are maintained in opposition to external violence (*vim*, 15), just as they are in Hessus (*vis*, 13).

39 Also remarked by Green, *Poetic Paraphrase*, 522.

40 Green notes the introduction of the idea of hypocrisy, prominent in the Psalms, but does not make connection between the *dominus* and the Lord.

41 Buchanan uses the adjective as well (9), though there it describes the tree's fruit rather than the tree itself.

42 Here the participle presumably means no more than "splendid," with, perhaps, the additional idea of "tall" (i.e., with head held high). But it is difficult to escape the conclusion that its use in association with the righteous man in Psalm 1 is clumsy, given that the primary meaning of *superbire* is "to be haughty/proud," a vice that is everywhere condemned in the Psalter.

I have examined the three treatments of the simile of verse 3 as a case study to show the paraphrastic procedures of each poet and to illustrate some of the possible relations between them. All three expand on the biblical base text; all three show some humanization of nature (or "naturization" of man), a common enough feature of classical poetry, with Buchanan as perhaps the most adventurous. As we turn now to their relations to earlier poets, Hessus and Beza come into their own in terms of innovation by superimposing new layers of complexity onto the psalm through allusion.

4 Classical Allusion

I propose in this section to treat one instance of allusion each from Hessus and Buchanan, and to examine at greater length a virtuosic triple allusion in Beza's poem.

Hessus opens his programmatic first line of his programmatic first psalm with a pointed and contrastive allusion to Virgil. Whereas the Vulgate describes the happy man simply as *beatus vir*, Hessus exclaims: *felix, o nimium felix!* In so doing, he recalls Virgil's *Aeneid* 4.657: *felix, heu nimium felix*. Who speaks these words? No one, of course, but *infelix Dido*. They come as part of her final remarks before committing suicide after she has been abandoned by Aeneas and are the apodosis of a contrafactual condition: "I would be happy—oh, excessively happy!—if only the Trojan ships had never touched our shores."[43] Upon speaking these words, she presses her face into the couch and prepares to die.

Hessus's appropriation of the words, on the other hand, brings them squarely into the realm of the indicative: "Happy—oh, exceedingly happy!—is he who, not looking upon the impious deeds of the wicked, has not wished to follow any of them" (1–2).[44] The seemingly small substitution of *o* for Virgil's *heu*, moreover, serves as an index of the different emotional register the words carry in Hessus's poem. *Facta ... impia* (1–2) is yet a further allusion to *Aeneid* 4, for in 4.596 Dido says of herself, *infelix Dido, nunc te facta impia tangunt?*[45] Aeneas, who is supposed to be pious or loyal (*pius*),[46] has done wicked or impious deeds to her. Hessus's man, on the other hand, does not even look at such deeds, let alone commit them, and thus he is happy (*felix*, 1) where Dido is

43 *felix, heu nimium felix, si litora tantum/numquam Dardaniae tetigissent nostra carinae.*

44 *felix, o nimium felix, qui facta malorum/impia conspiciens, noluit ulla sequi.*

45 "Unhappy Dido, do impious deeds now touch you?"

46 See *A.* 1.220 and *passim.*

unhappy (*infelix*). Where Dido presses her face into the couch before dying, Hessus's man does *not* ascend the pernicious seat of the wicked, and therefore lives. Happiness for Dido exists as a possibility only to be denied, for it "exists" only in the realm of the unreal and the contrafactual—and, thus, not at all—whereas for the man of God happiness, or blessedness, is both real and factual, and it is accompanied by life rather than death.

Virgilian allusion is likewise prominent in Buchanan's poem. In his adding to the biblical text remarks about the heat of summer and the cold of winter as things that do not destroy the good tree's fruit (*quam non violento* ***Sirius*** *aestu / **exurit,** non **torret** hiems*, 8–9),[47] Buchanan alludes to at least one, and possibly two, Virgilian passages that speak of the *Sirius*, the Dog-Star. The first, *A.* 3.141–42, Green notes but does not discuss:[48] *tum sterilis* ***exurere Sirius*** *agros, / arebant herbae et victum seges aegra negabat.*[49] These lines occur when Aeneas and his Trojan followers have gone to Crete, mistakenly believing that this is where they are to make their home in obedience to the will of the gods. Aeneas tries to act the part of a king and gives out laws (*iura ... dabam*, 137), but to no success: plague strikes their trees (*arboribus*, 139) and crops. There is no fruit, only death; all is sterile. How different the man of Psalm 1, who truly knows and understands God's will and Law: the tree to which he is compared is not troubled by the heat of the Dog-Star and, far from being dessicated by adverse weather, bears its fruit at the proper time.

The other possible reference in lines 8–9 is to *Georgics* 4.425–27: *iam rapidus* ***torrens*** *sitientis* ***Sirius*** *Indos / ardebat caelo et medium sol igneus orbem / hauserat....*[50] The passage comes from the middle of the Aristaeus-Proteus-Orpheus epyllion (4.315–558). The lines quoted describe, in particular, the heat of Proteus's environment at midday. Though Proteus is a seer with insight into the divine, the overwhelming thrust of the whole sequence of the epyllion is one of loss. This of course contrasts in general terms with Buchanan's first psalm, but beyond that I can find no particular significance to the allusion (if that in fact is what it is). Even an ornamental allusion, however, such as this may be, has the effect of importing the Virgilian georgic and bucolic worlds

47 "... which neither the Dog-Star burns with violent heat nor the cold of winter dries up."

48 Green, *Poetic Paraphrase*, 522.

49 "Then the sterile Dog-Star was burning the fields, the grass was parched and sick crops were denying food." Contrast Green, "Classical Voices," 85, where he claims that "there is no detectable allusion to epic or any other kind of hexameter writing."

50 "Now the consuming Dog-Star, scorching, was burning the thirsty Indians and the fiery sun had swallowed up half his orbit." I borrow "consuming" from Richard F. Thomas's translation of *rapidus* in Richard F. Thomas, ed., *Virgil: Georgics* (Cambridge: Cambridge University Press, 1988), 2:222.

into the world of the Psalms, as noted above also in the case of *beat agricolam*, and thus of casting over the poem, and by extension the Scriptures as a whole, a classical and Virgilian shade.

Perhaps the most interesting instance of allusion in these three poems is the "window reference," to use Richard Thomas's term,[51] at the opening of Beza's poem. Beza's markedly different metrical choice for Psalm 1 was remarked upon above, and to fill the first iamb Beza uses the word *beatus* (∪ — ∪) to describe the happy or blessed man rather than *felix* (— —), though the latter would have been metrically permissible as well. It is well known that Beza was very interested in Hebrew studies, and at first glance it may appear that he simply thought, along with Jerome in the Vulgate, that *beatus*[52] was a better rendering of the Hebrew word,[53] for this is the same term Beza uses in his prose *interpretatio* and freer *periphrasis* of Psalm 1, though he does not hesitate to depart from Jerome in other instances. But this appearance would be deceiving.

51 Richard F. Thomas, "Virgil's *Georgics* and the Art of Reference," *Harvard Studies in Classical Philology* 90 (1986): 188–89, 197 n. 61.

52 Jerome uses *beatus* in both the *iuxta Septuaginta* and the *iuxta Hebraicum* versions of the Psalter.

53 For instance, Allan Menzies claimed over a hundred years ago that a chief difference between "Reformers" and "Humanists" in versifying the Psalms was one of faithfulness to the original, with "Beza's Psalms being based on the Hebrew," in contrast to the greater freedom taken by "Humanists" who relied on the Vulgate (from his essay in *George Buchanan: A Memorial*, p. 136). This analysis, especially playing "Reformers" against "Humanists" in this way, leaves much to be desired. Contrast, e.g., Robert D. Linder, "Calvinism and Humanism: The First Generation," *Church History* 44 (1975): 167–81 (which treats Calvin, Beza, and Pierre Viret); Kirk Summers, "Theodore Beza's Classical Library and Christian Humanism," *Archiv für Reformationsgeschichte* 82 (1991): 193–207; Kirk Summers, ed., *A View from the Palatine: The* Iuvenilia *of Thédore de Bèze* (Tempe, AZ: Arizona Center for Medieval and Renaissance Studies, 2002); Kirk Summers, *Morality after Calvin: Theodore Beza's Christian Censor and Reformed Ethics* (New York: Oxford University Press, 2017); E.J. Hutchinson, "Written Monuments: Beza's *Icones* as Testament to and Program for Reformist Humanism," in *Beyond Calvin: Essays on the Diversity of the Reformed Tradition*, ed. W. Bradford Littlejohn and Jonathan Tomes (Lincoln, NE: Davenant Press, 2017); Scott M. Manetsch, "Psalms before Sonnetts: Theodore Beza and the *Studia Humanitatis*," in *Continuity and Change: The Harvest of Late Medieval and Reformation History*, ed. Robert J. Bast and Andrew C. Gow (Leiden: Brill, 2000), 400–416; Jens Zimmermann, ed., *Re-Envisioning Christian Humanism: Education and the Restoration of Humanity* (Oxford: Oxford University Press, 2017); Carl P.E. Springer, *Cicero in Heaven: The Roman Rhetor and Luther's Reformation* (Leiden: Brill, 2018). Gaertner, "Latin Verse Translsations," 289, is little impressed with his Hebrew in his remarks on Beza's versification of Psalm 70: "Beza's hold on the original seems to be the most tenuous" (289) of all the paraphrasts whose translation of this psalm he examines (in addition to Beza, Ganeius, Buchanan, Toscanus).

It is more probable that the word, together with the iambic meter itself, is meant to refer to Paulinus of Nola's (ca. 354–431) *Carm.* 7, a late antique poetic paraphrase of Psalm 1 written in iambic trimeters between 389 and 394.[54] For Beza re-uses not just the first word of that poem, but the first three words, along with the fifth word:

> *beatus ille qui* nec incedit malos
> *vitae* magistros appetens ...
> BEZA, 1–2

> "Happy that man who does not walk in search
> of evil teachers of life ..."

> *beatus ille qui* procul *vitam* suam
> ab inpiorum segregarit coetibus ...
> PAULINUS OF NOLA, 1–2

> "Happy that man who has separated his life
> far off from the gatherings of the wicked ..."

By pointing readers back to Paulinus of Nola in this way, Beza connects himself with the ancient church and the period in which elegant Latin translations of parts of the Bible were first being attempted. As a good humanist, he shows that his pedigree is long and distinguished.

But there is more to say. Paulinus's own opening had been an allusion to the opening words of Horace's second *Epode*, written in iambic couplets: ***beatus ille qui** procul negotiis*. In that poem, Horace calls "happy" or "blessed" the man who lives the rustic, simple life in contrast to the hurried and harried life of city folk. Paulinus's allusion to the poem, then, will have been a correction as he recasts the theme of happiness in the moral and religious terms of the first psalm. Beza presumably means for us to envision himself participating in this same correction, especially because, where Paulinus's poem raises the expectation in its first line that it will be in the same meter as Horace's poem only to disappoint that expectation in the second line, Beza returns to the meter used by Horace: alternating iambic trimeters and dimeters. Thus Beza goes back through Paulinus to restore the poem's original form while modifying its content, with the result that we may see it as a "correction" of both Paulinus, who

54 I follow Dennis Trout, *Paulinus of Nola* (Berkeley, CA: University of California Press, 1999), 290, on the dating of *Carmen* 7.

altered Horace's content *and* his form—the latter perhaps unnecessarily, Beza seems to say—and Horace, whose literary form was admissible, but whose content was not. Beza, in other words, keeps the "baby" of Horatian form while discarding the "bathwater" of his false notion of happiness.

In fact, the situation is even more complex than my discussion has indicated. For Beza does not simply refer to Horace via Paulinus of Nola; he refers to both Horace and Paulinus of Nola via another Latin verse-paraphrase of the first psalm written shortly before his own and included with an early edition of paraphrases featuring Buchanan and Hessus, among others. One of them is the Italian humanist Marcantonio Flaminio (ca. 1498–1550)—a Roman Catholic, but one who was heavily influenced by the Protestant Reformation.[55] Flaminio's Psalm 1 is, like Beza's and like Horace's second *Epode*, written in alternating iambic trimeters and dimeters. The first words? ***Beatus ille qui nec*** *audit impios*....[56] Beza's own opening, then, is in reality a double "window reference," as it looks through Flaminio to Paulinus and through Paulinus, in turn, to Horace, subsuming Roman Catholic, late Roman Christian, and Roman pagan poetry into Beza's own Protestant poetics at the programmatic outset of his psalm collection—just the sort of erudite display that one expects in humanist Neo-Latin poetry and that demands further investigation.

5 Conclusion

This essay has only scratched the surface of the richness of these poems. There is much more that could be said about any one of these three verse-psalms in any of the three subject-areas here treated, let alone about the technique of each writer considered more broadly. But I would like to conclude with a programmatic statement of my own. What we see here are not bloodless specimens of school-exercises but works of poetic art and theological interpretation in their own right, composed by authors who were simultaneously rigorously humanistic and deeply pious. It is past time for more of this material to receive the attention from classicists and scholars of the Renaissance and Reformation that it so manifestly deserves.

55 Flaminio in turn influenced the Protestants—not only Beza, as his allusion shows, but also Buchanan, on whom see McFarlane, *Buchanan*, 248.

56 *Davidis psalmi aliquot*, 8, where it follows directly after the paraphrases of Psalm 1 by Buchanan and Hessus. Flaminio also uses the opening *beatus ille qui* in *Carm.* 6 of his *Carmina sacra*, written in repeated iambic dimeters. See Marcantonio Flaminio, *Carminum libri VIII* (Padua: Josephus Cominus, 1727), 245–66.

Appendix: The Vulgate and Three Versifications of Psalm 1

The Vulgate	**Hessus (Elegaic Couplets)**
(1) Beatus vir qui non abiit in consilio impiorum et in via peccatorum non stetit et in cathedra pestilentiae non sedit	Felix o nimium felix, qui facta malorum impia conspiciens, noluit ulla sequi. Cui via displicuit pro veris falsa sequentum, perditus incautum ne graderetur iter: (4) qui neque conscendit damnosae fulcra cathedrae, quam derisorum turba maligna tenet,
(2) sed in lege Domini voluntas eius et in lege eius meditabitur die ac nocte	huius erit Domini lex infinita voluptas, quam labi ex animo, tempora nulla sinent.
(3) et erit tamquam lignum quod plantatum est secus decursus aquarum quod fructum suum dabit in tempore suo et folium eius non defluet et omnia quaecumque faciet prosperabuntur	Hic erit assimilis gravidae sua brachia palmae, quae stat ad undantes iussa virere lacus. (10) Quae feret opportuna suos in tempore fructus, et sua quae debet munera ferre, feret. Huic non ulla suos vis perturbarit honores, nec folia a ventis illius ulla cadent. (14) Haec quaecumque dabit, dabit optima, prodiga veris foetibus, optandas semper habebit opes.
(4) non sic impii non sic: sed tamquam pulvis quem proicit ventus a facie terrae:	Tam bona non capiet, non impius ista videbit praemia, non tales talia dona decent. Sed velut a terra paleae sparguntur inanes, quas quocunque volet quaelibet aura rapit. (20) Impius instabiles sic evanescit in auras, et nullum poterit certus habere locum.
(5) ideo non resurgent impii in iudicio neque peccatores in consilio iustorum	Ergo salutiferae nec stabit in ordine turbae, cum iusto reprobus nec sociandus erit.
(6) quoniam novit Dominus viam iustorum et iter impiorum peribit	Novit enim Dominus iustos, et vota piorum, (25) quorum avida iustas percipit aure preces. Sed cadet, et poenas dabit impius omnis, et horum omne quod instituent dissolvetur opus.
Total number of words: 95	Total number of words: 181 (190.5% of the length of the Vulg.)

Buchanan (dactylic hexameters)	**Beza (iambic couplets)**
Felix ille animi, quem non de tramite recto impia sacrilegae flexit contagio turbae: non iter erroris tenuis, sessorve cathedrae pestiferae, facilem dedit irrisoribus aurem:	Beatus ille qui nec incedit malos vitae magistros appetens, nec improborum in omne praecipitem scelus ingressus insistit viam. Nec execrandis mixtus irrisoribus, (5) profanus assidet comes:
sed vitae rimatur iter melioris, et alta (5) mente dei leges noctesque diesque revolvit.	summi sed usque verba sancta numinis omni anteponit gaudio: et illa secum sorte contentus sua, noctes diesque cogitat. (10)
ille, velut riguae quae margine consita ripae est arbor, erit, quam non violento Sirius aestu exurit, non torret hiems, sed prodiga laeto proventu beat agricolam: nec flore caduco (10) arridens, blanda dominum spe lactat inanem.	Qualis virentis laeta ripae margine densis superbiens comis, arbos colono grata ramos porrigit ponderibus annuis graves, et vim rigentis dura frangens frigoris, (15) honore constanti viret: talis vir ille, quicquid aggreditur, boni securus exitus facit.
non ita divini gens nescia foederis, exlex, contemptrixque poli: subito sed turbine rapti pulveris instar erunt, volucri quem concita gyro aura levis torquet vacuo ludibria caelo. (15)	Non sic scelesti: gluma sed ut inutilis iactata venti turbine, (20)
ergo ubi veridicus iudex in nube serena, dicere ius veniet, scelerisque coarguet orbem, non coram impietas maestos attollere vultus, nec misera audebit iustae se adiungere turbae. (19)	non iam supremi ferre vultum iudicis, nec verba poterunt aspera: nec in bonorum mixta coetu innoxio, scelesta consistet cohors. (24)
Nam pater aethereus iustorum et fraude carentum novit iter, sensumque tenet: curvosque sequuta impietas fraudum anfractus scelerata peribit.	Nanque ut bonorum facta Numen approbat, sic funditus perdit malos.
Total number of words: 141 (148.4% of the length of the Vulg.)	Total number of words: 116 (122.1% of the length of the Vulg.)

CHAPTER 13

Imitate the Lutherans: Catholic Solutions to Liturgical Problems in Late Eighteenth-Century Vienna

Jane Schatkin Hettrick

The Lutheran Church became legal in Austrian territory on 13 October 1781, when Holy Roman Emperor Joseph II (1741–90) issued a *Toleranzedikt* (Edict of Tolerance), which granted to Protestants and Greek Orthodox Christians the right to practice their religion openly.[1] With their newly gained religious freedom, Lutherans in Vienna quickly organized a congregation and raised funds to acquire a building. Still, the Catholic Church remained culturally dominant. How is it, then, that we find Lutheran chorales in the music of Catholic composers of the time?

To answer this question, we must look at the state of Catholic liturgy and music in that period. Evidence suggests that there were problems. Of course, the existence of problems in church music was not new. In particular, concerns about theatricality in church music come up already in ancient history. St. Jerome talked about it. With manifest disdain for supposed theatrical practices, he urged the singer of psalmody in church not to "anoint his throat and lips with sweet ointment, as theatrical actors do, to produce theatrical melodies and songs in Church."[2] The early Greek church father St. John Chrysostom (ca. 347–407) scolded his listeners in a sermon, calling them "destroyers of church music." He likened their music to that of harlots: "You sing: Lord have mercy, but you do it in a way that must nullify all mercy. You cry: Lord save us, but your whole demeanor cries out the contrary. To what end this mindless shrieking wherewith nothing but the long duration and the power of breath may be discerned? You do it like loose women who let their seductive songs be heard on public streets and like those who ply their trade with their voice on the stage. And you dare to mingle this idolatrous nonsense with the angelic

1 This document is preserved in the *Haus-, Hof-, und Staatsarchiv* (Karton 33) in Vienna.

2 Robert F. Hayburn, *Papal Legislation on Sacred Music, 95 A.D. to 1977 A.D.* (Collegeville, MN: The Liturgical Press, 1979; reprint: Harrison, NY: Roman Catholic Books, n.d.), 98.

 | DOI:10.1163/9789004206717_015

hymn of praise?"[3] Such criticisms continued for centuries. The Council of Trent (1545–63) tried to purge sacred music of impurity and suppress the intrusion of secular elements, although in the end it made only a brief and general statement: "Truly, they shall ban from the churches all kinds of music, whether by the organ or singing, in which anything lascivious or impure is mingled."[4]

Disputes over music in the church, especially music perceived as theatrical, never really died out, and several documents issued by the church in the mid-eighteenth century reflect ongoing controversy. The most important of these was the encyclical *Annus qui*, promulgated by Pope Benedict XIV in 1749. This pope finds many faults with contemporary church music, and theatricality comes up again and again. For example: music must be "executed in such a way as not to appear profane, worldly, or theatrical." Music must show "a certain difference between ecclesiastical chant and theatrical melodies ... the use of theatrical and profane chant must not be tolerated in churches." Church music must have "a character altogether different from that of the theatrical musical concerts."[5] He foresees a slippery slope that begins with theatricality and ends in "grave sins and scandals." Already two years before *Annus qui*, the first Caecilian Society had been organized in Austria. In 1747, with the patronage of Dowager Empress Maria Amalia (1701–56), the Cäcilian Bruderschaft[6] was formed to address the problem of secular elements in sacred music.[7] Given

3 Quoted in Hieronymus Joseph Colloredo, "Hirtenbrief auf die am 1ten Herbstm. dieses 1782ten Jahrs, nach zurückgelegten zwölften Jahrhundert, eintretende Jubelfeyer Salzburgs," *Der aufgeklärte Reformkatholizismus in Österreich*, ed. Peter Hersche (Bern: Verlag Herbert Lang, 1976), 77. (Unless otherwise noted, all translations are my own.)

4 *Ab ecclesiis vero musicas eas ubi sive organo sive cantu lascivum aut impurum aliquid misceatur ... arceant.* In: *"Decretum de observandis et vitandis in celebration Missae," Concilium Tridentinum—Canones et Decreta (Altera Lectio).* Available online: https://libguides.stthomas.edu/c.php?g=88946&p=572345. See Craig A. Monson, "The Council of Trent Revisited," *Journal of the American Musicological Society* 55, no. 1 (Spring 2002): 11.

5 Hayburn, *Papal Legislation*, 95–96, 101.

6 *Bruderschaft* (brotherhood) is a "pious religious union affiliated with the church." Numerous *Bruderschaften* (up to 234) were active in eighteenth-century Vienna until 1783 when Joseph II abolished them all. These fraternal organizations contributed greatly to worship practices and related musical forms in the city. They sponsored liturgies such as the litany, Miserere, and Vespers; most importantly, they provided for members' funeral arrangements, Requiem, and memorial masses. Two *Bruderschaften* were devoted to music: St. Nicolai and St. Cecilia. For an excellent study see Geraldine M. Rohling, "Exequial and Votive Practices of the Viennese *Bruderschaften*: A Study of Music and Liturgical Piety" (Ph.D. diss., Catholic University, 1996).

7 Paul Weber, "Josef Gabriel Rheinberger and the Reform of Catholic Church Music, Part I," *The American Organist* 48, no. 10 (Oct. 2014): 49.

this level of argumentation, it is not surprising that debates about church music heated up in Vienna around the time of Mozart (in the 1780s).

Music was a prominent feature in Viennese Catholic worship around 1781. There were at least fifty churches in greater Vienna, and every church had music—by today's standards, a lot of music. Moreover, Catholic worship went beyond Sunday to include daily mass, as well as many Holy Days, other liturgies, and para-liturgical devotional services. Music was performed by choirs, soloists, and instruments. British music historian Charles Burney visited Vienna in 1772 and attested to the popularity of musical services there: "There is scarce a church or convent in Vienna that has not every morning its mass in music: that is, a great portion of the service of the day, set in parts, and performed with voices, accompanied by at least three or four violins, a tenor and base [sic], besides the organ."[8]

One outspoken critic of church music was the author of an anonymous pamphlet *Ueber die Kirchenmusik in Wien* (About Church Music in Vienna), published in Vienna in 1781.[9] Under this plain title, the author harshly satirizes perceived abuses in church music. In his view, the church has been turned into a concert hall. He too sees a downward path towards "grave sins and scandals." He paints a vivid picture: Worshippers in Vienna were being entertained by strains from an opera, masquerading only thinly as sacred music. The piece would have been culled from an opera in the current repertoire; people would already have heard it. Despite the sacred text, listeners would recognize it for what it was—a theater piece with secular words. Other voices raised the same complaint. Travel writer Friedrich Christoph Nicolai (1733–1811) noted in 1781: "Nowadays, operatic music also forces its way into churches everywhere. In Vienna too, I found it all too prevalent. During many a credo or benedictus, I really did not know whether I was hearing some piece of music from an Italian opera buffa."[10] The book *Bildergalerie katholische Misbräuche* (Picture Gallery of Catholic Abuses, 1784) ridicules sardonically all things Catholic, and it attacks specifically music in Chapter 6, "Ueber die Kirchenmusik, und Cäciliavesper." The author condemns both the music and its performers: "Thus

8 Charles Burney, *The Present State of Music in Germany, the Netherlands, and United Provinces* (London, 1775; reprint, New York: Broude Brothers, 1969), 226–27.

9 A copy of this pamphlet is preserved in the *Österreichische Nationalbibliothek, Musiksammlung* in Vienna, shelf number 396.051-A.M. For an annotated English translation see Jane Schatkin Hettrick, "Colorful Comments on Church Music in Vienna around 1780," *The American Organist* 34, no. 5 (May 2000): 77–81.

10 Friedrich Christoph Nicolai, *Beschreibung einer Reise durch Deutschland und die Schweiz, im Jahre 1781, nebst Bemerkungen über Gelehrsamkeit, Industrie, Religion und Sitte* (Berlin: Nicolai, 1783–96), 4:544–45.

first a trio from a minuet, then a trunk of a symphony, gradually fragments of a waltz, and finally half and entire opera arias have crept unnoticed into the church style.… The prima donna, who sang to us in the theater about love and lust, now desires by a soothing *Stabat Mater* to atone for her own and our sins."[11]

To be sure, musical recycling was an accepted practice of the day. It enabled busy composers to get extra mileage out of their own or others' works. Karl Ditters von Dittersdorf (1739–99) reports with approval in his autobiography how a colleague "altered the [secular] words for the songs and the choruses, without changing a single note of my score and made them suitable for the church."[12]

The state, possibly affected by Vatican directives and itself attempting to absolutize religious thought, also sought to correct and control the practice of church music. In the 1750s in Vienna the imperial government published several decrees (*Hofreskripte*) intended to curb perceived excesses in church music. We can trace the ongoing concern about theatricality through a series of such decrees issued during the following sixty years or more. As late as 1806 a decree bans the performance of music that sounds more as if it was written for the theater than for the church.[13]

In 1783 Emperor Joseph put out a new *Gottesdienstordnung* (Order of Worship). With this document he had two goals: to impose the Enlightenment ideal of simplicity on music and liturgy in the church and to cut the costs of musical performance. To accomplish these purposes, the new "Order of Worship" greatly reduced the number of services and severely restricted the amount of music used in them.[14] Instrumental music was hard hit. Many church musicians lost their jobs and complained bitterly about the massive changes; a lot of the clergy did not like it either.

A zealous spokesman for the emperor's reform program was Archbishop Hieronymus Colloredo, remembered today as the autocratic employer of both Leopold and Wolfgang Amadeus Mozart in Salzburg. In 1782 Colloredo penned a lengthy pastoral letter to all clergymen under his aegis, in which he

---

11 Joseph Richter, *Bildergalerie katholischer Misbräuche: Von Obermayr: Mit Kupfern und anpassenden Vignetten* (Frankfurt und Leipzig: 1784); ed. Dr. Otto Maußer (Munich: Janus Verlag, 1913), 32. Joseph Richter (1749–1813), often under a pen name, wrote numerous pamphlets and books satirizing aspects of Viennese life and culture.

12 Karl Ditters von Dittersdorf, *Lebensbeschreibung* (Leipzig: Breitkopf & Härtel, 1801), tr. A.D. Coleridge, *The Autobiography of Karl Ditters von Dittersdorf* (London: Bentley, 1896; reprint, New York: Da Capo Press, 1970), 149.

13 Ernst Tittel, *Österreichische Kirchenmusik: Werden, Wachsen, Wirken* (Vienna: Verlag Herder, 1961), 179.

14 Reinhard G. Pauly, "The Reforms of Church Music under Joseph II," *The Musical Quarterly* 43 (July 1957): 376–77.

articulated his views on the current state of music in the church.[15] He found fault with elaborate church music, by which he meant the standard orchestral mass. He speaks repeatedly about "abuses" and strengthens his argument with support from the church fathers, for example, the fifth-century saint Isidore of Pelusium (d. 449/50), who condemned "sumptuous church music, because it turns the heart to lustful feelings; one goes there for pleasure, just as you attend a performance of theater music."[16]

So what did the authorities decide to do about these problems? It seems that both the Emperor and the Archbishop came to the same solution: imitate the Lutherans! As mentioned above, the Lutheran Church became legal in Austrian areas in 1781; with it came hymn-singing. Two years later, the first official Lutheran hymnal in Austria was published: *Christliches Gesangbuch zum Gebrauche der Gemeinen der Augsburgischen Confessionsverwandten in den k. k. Erblanden* (1783, Georg Philipp Wucherer).[17] Significantly, Emperor Joseph's "Order of Worship" contained a provision for "Normalgesang," that is, vernacular hymns to be sung by the congregation.[18] Archbishop Colloredo in his pastoral letter vigorously promoted the singing of vernacular hymns as a remedy for the abuses: "Next to the Bible, good church hymns in the mother tongue are one of the most excellent means of making public worship edifying and conducive to the awakening of religious feelings."[19] He goes on to illustrate at length the theological superiority of good hymns to existing musical practice: "The difference is between true devotion and insincere irreverence (*Andächteley*), between heartfelt religion and thoughtless participation in empty rites or meaningless mummery, between true piety and religious play-acting or deceptive hypocrisy."[20] The Archbishop also presents biblical evidence for the value of hymn-singing, again quoting Isidore: "As much as the apostles [tried to] forbid all indecent prattle from our worship gatherings, and to show as models a holy modesty and seriousness, nevertheless, they very wisely permitted that everyone regardless of class, age, and sex, may sing along."[21]

---

15 Colloredo, "Hirtenbrief," 45.
16 Colloredo, "Hirtenbrief," 78.
17 See Jane Schatkin Hettrick, "A Lutheran Hymnal of the Enlightenment," in *More than Luther: The Reformation and the Rise of Pluralism in Europe*, ed. Karla Boersma and J. Selderhuis (Göttingen: Vanderhoeck & Ruprecht, 2019). This hymnal is preserved in the Österreichische Nationalbibliothek, accessible online: http://data.onb.ac.at/ABO/%2BZ184529805.
18 Pauly, "Reforms," 375.
19 Colloredo, "Hirtenbrief," 74.
20 Colloredo, "Hirtenbrief," 90.
21 Colloredo, "Hirtenbrief," 78.

Actually, Lutheran hymns had been around Catholic territories for a long time. Seeing the power of hymnody, the Counter-Reformation tried to introduce congregational singing and adopted (or adapted) Lutheran hymns for the purpose. The largest and most widely distributed hymnal of the Counter Reformation was *Geistliche Lieder und Psalmen*, compiled and published in 1567 by priest Johann Leisentrit (1527–86).[22] Among its 250 hymns we find a number of Lutheran hymns, including six of Luther, probably borrowed from the Babst Hymnal of 1545.[23]

***Hymns by Martin Luther in* Geistliche Lieder und Psalmen**[24]
Ach Gott vom Himmel, sieh darein
Bei deiner Kirch erhalt uns Herr
Christum wir sollen loben schon
Komm, Gott Schöpfer, Heiliger Geist
Mensch, willst du leben seliglich
Verleih uns Frieden gnädiglich

In 1574 Andreas Gigler, a Catholic priest in Graz (Steiermark, Austria), assembled a hymnal entitled *Gesang-Postill*, containing hymn texts for every Sunday and other feasts of the liturgical year.[25] The foreword to the volume explains that he composed these hymns "for the sake of the common and unlearned man and the youth, that they can praise God, and practice spiritual songs with suitable material."[26] In an appendix (*Noten Anhang*) Gigler also provided music for singing the hymns. Ten of the melodies he composed himself, and ten he describes as "old, previously familiar" melodies. They are presented in four-part

22 Richard Wetzel and Erika Heitmeyer, *Johann Leisentrit's* Geistliche Lieder und Psalmen, 1567: *Hymnody of the Counter-Reformation in Germany* (Madison and Teaneck: Fairleigh Dickinson University Press, co-published with The Rowman & Littlefield Publishing Group, 2013). The reader should be aware that this annotated translation contains numerous serious errors; see my review in *The American Organist* 49, no. 6 (June 2015): 70–73.

23 Valentin Babst, *Geystliche Lieder. Mit einer newen vorrhede D. Mart. Luth.* Facsimile reprint: *Das Babstsche Gesangbuch von 1545*, ed. Konrad Ameln, Documenta musicologica, series 1, no. 38 (Kassel: Bärenreiter, 1988).

24 Because spelling of German hymns varies among the sources cited, all titles of German hymns are given in modern spelling here.

25 *Gesang-Postill Das ist: Evangelia auff alle und jede Sontag und fürnemste Feste durchs gantze Jar / in Gesang verfast / vor oder nach der Predig zu singen / Sampt einem Christlichen Gebet.* See Hans Joachim Moser, "Johannes de Cleve als Setzer von zehn Lutherischen Melodien," *Tijdschrift van de Vereniging voor Nederlandse Muziekgeschiedenis* 16, no. 16 (1946): 31–35.

26 Moser, "de Cleve," 33.

settings composed by Johannes de Cleve (ca. 1529–82);[27] all place the *cantus firmus* (hymn melody) in the tenor part, rather than according to the newer style, in which the melody appears in the highest part or soprano. Significantly, all the "old previously familiar" melodies are core Lutheran hymns.[28]

***Lutheran hymns in Gigler,* Gesang-Postill (*1574*)**
(* = hymn texts by Martin Luther)
*Ach Gott vom Himmel, sieh darein
*Aus tiefer Not
*Aus tiefer Not (Strassburg, 1525)
Es ist das Heil uns kommen her (Speratus, 1524)
*Es spricht der Unweisen Mund wohl
Herr, wer wird wohn'n in deiner Hütt (Hans Sachs, 1526)
*Nun freut euch, lieben Christen gmein
*Nun freut euch, liebe Christen gmein (Klugsches Gesangbuch, 1535)
*Wär Gott nicht mit uns diese Zeit
*Wo Gott der Herr nicht bei uns hält

To varying degrees, Lutheran hymns continued to appear in Catholic hymnals through the seventeenth century. Certain Catholic hymnals adopted Lutheran hymns for the specific purpose of luring converts to Lutheranism back into the Catholic fold, "so that after their return they would not have to renounce their trusted hymnody." This is illustrated by the *Rheinfelsisches Gesangbuch* (1666), which contained four hymns of Luther, with the texts adjusted according to Catholic doctrine.[29] A Catholic hymnal published in Leipzig in 1724[30] contains at least 24 hymns identifiable as Lutheran. As Robin A. Leaver has shown,

---

27 Johannes de Cleve was a Netherlandish Kapellmeister in the Habsburg court of Erzherzog Carl in Graz.

28 Since the present article was completed, the article by Franz Karl Praßl, "Luther in Graz, oder: Die *Gesang Postill* des Andreas Gigler (1569/1574), ein fast vergessenes hymnologisches Kleinod," was published in *Hymnody and Hymnology in Times of Transformation, Part II: Proceedings of the 29th Biennial IAH Conference, in Logumkloster DK 2017*, IAH Bulletin No. 46 (2018), ed. Martin J.M. Hoondert (Tilburg, 2019), 35–49. The author discusses the *Gesang Postill*, gives examples of de Cleve's settings, and provides the historical context in which a Catholic priest created a hymnal prominently featuring Lutheran hymns.

29 Christiane Schäfer, "Die Lieder Martin Luthers in der deutschsprachigen katholischen Gesangbuchrezeption," *Internationale Arbeitsgemeinschaft für Hymnologie Bulletin* 45 (2017): 85–86.

30 *Catholisches Gesang-Buch zum Gebrauch der Römisch-Catholischen Gemeinde in Leipzig*, first edition 1715.

however, certain of these hymns derived from pre-Reformation folk hymns and thus from a common heritage.[31] Others already existed from translations made in the Reformation period, again, with "Catholicized" wordings. A shift of attitude towards Lutheran hymnody in Catholic hymnals occurs later in the eighteenth century. We see this clearly in two editions of the *Catholisch-Paderbornisches Gesangbuch*,[32] which began as an attempt to be ecumenical, in the spirit of the Enlightenment. The first edition (1765) contained 80 hymns by Lutheran authors, including three of Paul Gerhardt. Five years later, a second edition (1770) eliminated almost all of these.[33] It must be pointed out, however, that vernacular hymn singing was common in various types of Catholic worship apart from the mass (e.g., in the Hours, benedictions, funeral rites, novenas, and in-house devotions); in these settings the practice of singing Lutheran hymns may never have been abandoned.

When Emperor Joseph II and Archbishop Colloredo called for hymn singing in the Church, they were surely aware not only of congregational singing in general, but probably also of specific Lutheran hymns. Some of these great melodies had already made their way into the public sphere and even into the world of secular music. Less than a decade after Emperor Joseph's "Order of Worship," we find the tune associated with Martin Luther's hymn text "Ach Gott vom Himmel sieh darein" (1524) adapted and used prominently in Mozart's last opera *Die Zauberflöte* (1791).

> W.A. Mozart, *Die Zauberflöte*, KV 620 (Vienna, 1791)
> Act II, scene 28, libretto text: Two men in armor
> (Chorale melody: *Ach Gott, vom Himmel sieh darein*)
> Text by librettist Emanuel Schikaneder
>
> Der, welcher wandert, diese Straße voll Beschwerden,
> Wird rein durch Feuer, Wasser, Luft und Erden;
> Wenn er des Todes Schrecken überwinden kann,
> Schwingt er sich aus der Erde himmelan.
> Erleuchtet wird er dann imstande sein,
> Sich den Mysterien der Isis ganz zu weihn.

---

31 Robin A. Leaver, "A Catholic Hymnal for Use in Lutheran Leipzig: *Catholisches Gesang-Buch* (Leipzig 1724)," in *Bach and the Counterpoint of Religion*, ed. Robin A. Leaver (Urbana: University of Illinois Press, 2018), 47.

32 *GOTT, und der allerseeligsten Gottes-Gebährerin, und Jungfrauen MARIAE gewidmetes, Neues, verbessert- und vermehrtes Catholisch Paderbornisches Gesang-Buch* (Paderborn, 1765).

33 Schäfer, "Die Lieder," 87.

He who travels this road full of troubles,
Becomes pure by fire, water, air, and earth;
If he can overcome the terrors of death,
He will ascend from the earth up towards heaven.
Enlightened, he will then be able
To devote himself wholly to the mysteries of Isis.

This piece occurs at "the drama's decisive turning point."[34] It is sung in octaves by two men in black armor, the melody also doubled by woodwinds and trombone, while strings play a strict fugue in the background. Mozart's music paints a bare and somber scene. It is beyond the scope of this article to analyze the Enlightenment philosophy embedded in the opera text. Emanuel Schikaneder's fairy-tale libretto incorporates aspects of the sacred mysteries of ancient Egypt and symbolism used in Freemasonry, which was popular at the time.[35] Significantly, this secular text conveys something of the message of Luther's hymn-paraphrase of Psalm 12. Stanza 5 (derived from verse 6 of the psalm) speaks of God's word being like silver purified by fire seven times and the Word of God being proved [verified, tested] by the cross—images recast by Schikaneder in eighteenth-century terms.[36] Possibly this dramatist, singer, dancer, and theater manager had gained some biblical knowledge from his Jesuit high-school education, and remembered Psalm 12 when he wrote the libretto of *Die Zauberflöte.*

Where did Mozart, who was Catholic, find this chorale melody? Probably in the music textbook, *Die Kunst des reinen Satzes in der Musik* (The Art of Strict Musical Composition), published in the 1770s, by Johann Philipp Kirnberger.[37] The teaching method in this book uses chorale tunes to illustrate different

34 Hermann Abert, *W.A. Mozart*, tr. Stewart Spencer, ed. Cliff Eisen (New Haven and London: Yale University Press, 2007), 1290.

35 In 1784 Mozart joined the lodge "Zur Wohltätigkeit," which later was folded into the lodge "Zur neugekrönten Hoffnung." For more on Mozart, Freemasonry, and his Catholicism, see Nicholas Till, *Mozart and the Enlightenment: Truth, Virtue and Beauty in Mozart's Operas* (New York and London: W.W. Norton & Company, 1992).

36 Stanza 5 of Luther's hymn reads: *Das Silber, durchs Feur siebenmal bewährt, wird lauter funden; am Gotteswort man warten soll desgleichen alle Stunden; es will durch Kreuz bewähret sein, da wird sein Kraft erkannt und Schein und leucht stark in die Lande.* See *Kirchen-Gesangbuch für Evangelisch-Lutherische Gemeinden ungeänderter Augsburgischer Confession* (St. Louis, Missouri: Concordia Publishing House, 1892).

37 Johann Philipp Kirnberger, *The Art of Strict Musical Composition*, tr. David Beach and Jurgen Thym (New Haven and London: Yale University Press, 1982). Kirnberger (1721–83), a pupil of Bach, was a composer, theorist, and respected author of theoretical treatises; he served as a violinist in the court of Frederick the Great.

aspects and types of composition. Thus, Catholic musicians who learned counterpoint or composition with Kirnberger's textbook became intimately familiar with Lutheran chorales. Interestingly, the author used the chorale "Ach Gott vom Himmel sieh darein" in fourteen examples,[38] while most of the other chorales appear only once, while a few occur two or three times.[39] Kirnberger's repeated choice of this unusual (hypo-phrygian) melody may reflect its original status. Joseph Herl dubbed it "the battle hymn of the Reformation," citing its ubiquitous use as a protest song in early Lutheranism.[40]

Even before Emperor Joseph and Archbishop Colloredo introduced the new "Order of Worship," the Catholic authorities were looking to promote vernacular hymn-singing by the congregation, and several German-language hymnals were already in use.[41] Empress Maria Theresia (1717–80) sponsored the production of a hymnal for use by her subjects. Published in Vienna around 1774, it is entitled *Katholisches Gesangbuch, auf allerhöchsten Befehl Ihrer k. k. apost. Majestät Marien Theresiens zum Druck befördert.*[42] It contains 87 German texts, including hymns for the seasons, sections of the mass, special feasts and saints' days, and several Marian hymns.[43] In addition there are hymns for the sections of the Requiem Mass, and finally, a German Te Deum. Forty-eight melodies appear as a separate section, and a melody is assigned to each hymn. Unlike hymnals of the Counter Reformation (and the seventeenth century), this volume contains no Lutheran hymns—even with reworked text. The total absence of Lutheran hymnody may reflect the intense Catholicism of the Habsburg monarchs even this late. For centuries, Austrian piety (*pietas austriaca*), stemming from the divine right of kings, rested on the veneration of the Holy Eucharist, the adoration of the cross, and especially, the

---

38 For example, in one instance he demonstrates how the melody is used in three four-part settings, in which it serves as the *cantus firmus* successively in the soprano, alto, and tenor parts (Kirnberger, *Art*, 176–81).

39 Kirnberger uses 27 other chorale tunes in his examples.

40 Joseph Herl, *Worship Wars in Early Lutheranism: Choir, Congregation, and Three Centuries of Conflict* (Oxford and New York: Oxford University Press: 2004), 90.

41 Tittel, *Österreichische Kirchenmusik*, 183; see also Franz Karl Praßl, "Kirchengesangbuch," in *Oesterreichisches Musiklexikon*, ed. Rudolf Flotzinger (Vienna: Verlag der Österreicher Akadamie der Wissenschaft, 2003).

42 A complete copy is preserved in the special collections division of the library of Wellesley College. I am grateful to Associate Curator Mariana S. Oller for making this volume available to me.

43 About half of these hymns were written by ex-Jesuit Johann Michael Kosmas Denis (1729–1800). His own hymnal *Geistliche Lieder zum Gebrauche der hohen Metropolitankirche bey St. Stephan in Wien und des ganzen wienerischen Erzbistums* was published in 1774.

Immaculate Conception of the Blessed Virgin Mary. Habsburg rulers long supported the Immaculate Conception (though the church did not recognize it as official dogma until 1854), and the House of Habsburg relied on the power of Mary Immaculate to intercede on behalf of imperial causes as well as for Catholic intentions.[44] This all-embracing Austrian piety did not end with the Enlightenment. For one thing, the longstanding authority of the Jesuits, despite the official abolition of the order from 1783 to 1814, remained a dominant influence.[45] But the quality of the hymns produced did not really help their cause. It would be fair to say that the material in this collection—both texts and music—does not match the power and quality of the old Lutheran hymns. To my knowledge, only one hymn (text and music) from the Maria Theresia hymnal made its way into modern (Lutheran) hymnals: the German version of the Latin Te Deum, "Grosser Gott, wir loben dich."[46]

Austrian historian Ernst Tittel describes Catholic hymn texts of this period as lacking simplicity, depth, feeling, and originality, with an avoidance of poetic expression. They fail to stress faith and belief and rarely contain words like *Gnade*, *Opfer*, and even *Liebe*. Instead they tend to express a practical Christianity, aiming to edify, preach, and teach. In giving advice, they could descend into the trivial, as in this stanza:

> Ergab ich mich dem Saufen?
> Beherrschte mich das Frass?
> Und hielt ich beim verkaufen
> Das festgesetzte Maass?
>
> Was I given to drunkenness?
> Did gluttony rule my life?
> When selling, did I keep
> To the correct measure?[47]

---

44 Anna Coreth, *Pietas Austriaca*, tr. William D. Bowman and Anna Maria Leitgeb (West Lafayette, Indiana: Purdue University Press, 2004), 46–47, 64–65.

45 David Wyn Jones, *Music in Vienna: 1700, 1800, 1900* (Woodbridge U.K.: The Boydell Press, 2016), 83.

46 The author of this hymn was J.M.K. Denis (see note 43 above); it has twelve stanzas. Under the English title "Holy God, We Praise Thy Name," it is found with shorter texts in *The Lutheran Hymnal* (no. 250) and *Lutheran Service Book* (no. 940). See *The Lutheran Hymnal* (Saint Louis, Missouri: Concordia Publishing House, 1941) and *Lutheran Service Book* (Saint Louis: Concordia Publishing House, 2006).

47 Quoted in Pauly, "Reforms," 375.

Some even featured coarse expressions, such as *Ich Sündenschwein* (sinful pig) or *Ich Sündenlümmel* (sinful lout). The music fared no better. Most Catholic hymn tunes produced in the eighteenth century are extremely regular in rhythm and form. According to Tittel, they are typically weak, insipid, and trifling. Some hymnal compilers rejected the older hymns specifically on musical grounds. The preface to the 1741 hymnal *Tochter Zion* states that older hymn melodies must be "made more graceful" or "more happy."[48]

Despite all efforts by the authorities, Catholic congregations often did not accept the new practice of hymn-singing. People missed the musical liturgy, and music lovers avoided churches that offered only hymn-singing accompanied by the organ. In Salzburg territory, "congregations passively resisted the introduction of German hymns by not singing them, and worshippers in parishes near the border attended services in Bavarian churches, where instruments were still allowed."[49] Some complained that hymn-singing disturbed their private prayers.[50] Thus, evidence suggests that efforts to get Catholic congregations to sing hymns did not succeed.[51] On the other hand, this opinion was not unanimous. Contradiction of these reports comes from Johann Pezzl (1756–1823), whose humorous observations of the current culture in Vienna were published in his book *Skizze von Wien* (Sketch of Vienna, 1780s). In Chapter 91, "Kirchen," he notes the disorder prevalent in Catholic worship and reports on a number of changes in liturgical practice that he considers to be improvements. On music he writes: "popular German hymns have been introduced to replace the profane yodeling [*Geludle*][52] that often transforms a chorus from an opera buffa into a Sanctus, which is so sweetly screeched down [*heruntergekräht*] during the most sacred religious actions."[53]

Pezzl does not elaborate here or give examples. Therefore, the question remains: "what popular German hymns?" Given the above-mentioned negative

---

48 Tittel, *Österreichische Kirchenmusik*, 180.

49 Cliff Eisen, "Salzburg under Church Rule," in: *The Classical Era*, ed. Neal Zaslaw (Englewood Cliffs, NJ: Prentice Hall, 1989), 180.

50 Hans Hollerweger, *Die Reform des Gottesdienstes zur Zeit des Josephinismus in Österreich* (Regensburg: Verlag Friedrich Pustet, 1976), 472.

51 Correspondingly, Lutheran records of the time show a similar pattern: that is, congregations often rejected new hymnals. See Hettrick, "A Lutheran Hymnal" (see note 17 above).

52 Noun made from the verb *ludern*, which, according to Grimm, *Deutsches Wörterbuch*, may equal *leiern* (grind an organ) or *dudeln* (play the bagpipes); in Austrian usage it often meant yodeling. Also possibly related is *Luder*, which denotes one who is a "jerk." In any event, here it intended to be derogatory or sarcastic.

53 Johann Pezzl, *Skizze von Wien: Ein Kultur- und Sittenbild aus der josefinischen Zeit*, ed. Gustav Gugitz and Anton Schlossar (Graz: Lehkam Verlag, 1923), 281; Pezzl's comments on "Churches" are summarized in H.C. Robbins Landon, *Mozart and Vienna* (New York: Schirmer Books, 1991), 161.

reactions of congregations to the new directions, probably not those from official Catholic hymnals. Is it possible that Pezzl's phrase referred to Lutheran hymns being sung in Catholic worship?[54] As we have seen, the Habsburg monarchs of the later eighteenth century generally rejected things Lutheran in official Catholic hymnals. In spite of this restriction, however, Lutheran chorale melodies apparently did make their way into (formal) Catholic worship, at least indirectly. That is, Catholic musicians wrote organ chorale preludes on Lutheran hymn tunes. So they knew those tunes and were inspired to write musical settings of them. One leading figure who composed Lutheran chorale preludes was Johann Albrechtsberger (1736–1809). Highly regarded as a theorist and teacher of counterpoint, he was a sought-after instructor of numerous pupils, most notably Beethoven. He spent most of his working life in Vienna, where he served in key musical posts in the two most important ecclesiastical institutions in that city: organist in the imperial chapel (1772–93), and Kapellmeister of St. Stephan's Cathedral (1793–1809).

Albrechtsberger's settings of Lutheran chorale preludes include the following pieces:

Ach, was soll ich Sünder machen
Christ ist erstanden
Erhalt uns, Herr, bei deinem Wort
Jesu, meines Lebens Leben
Komm heiliger Geist mit deiner Gnad
O wie selig seid ihr doch, ihr Frommen
Erwünschter Brunnquell aller Freuden

A musician holding these high posts was in a position to influence repertoire and mold musical taste. At the same time, he may also have responded to an awareness by Catholic worshippers of Lutheran hymns and hymn singing. Given that Albrechtsberger composed organ chorale preludes, and since he was an organist, it is reasonable to assume that he played his own settings of Lutheran chorales in religious services where he presided over the music. Thus Lutheran chorales probably would have been heard during mass in the two highest ecclesiastical institutions in Vienna: the imperial chapel and the cathedral. More research will be needed to determine to what extent music based on Lutheran hymns was performed in Catholic churches during this period (ca. 1780–1810).

---

54 As mentioned above, vernacular (including Lutheran) hymn-singing may have continued uninterrupted in lesser liturgies (i.e., non-Mass) or private worship settings.

There are several areas to be explored. First, it will be important to establish a wider repertoire, that is, to document the existence of Lutheran chorale preludes by other Catholic composers working in Catholic churches. This could be a challenging task, because much of the sacred music of possible composers remains unexamined in archives, awaiting study and editing. We would have to look at the works of organists and Kapellmeister who served in the numerous other Catholic churches in Vienna.[55] Further complicating the issue is that by training and tradition organists often improvised music and did not necessarily write down what they played. Of course, improvised music is forever lost. We know, for example, that J.S. Bach was widely known and admired as a master-improviser.[56] Finally, it will be instructive to know whether the use of Lutheran-based organ chorale preludes continued or expanded in nineteenth-century Catholic practice. Looking at the two institutions considered above, we find that Simon Sechter (1788–1867), who served as court organist in the imperial chapel from 1824 to his death in 1867, wrote numerous organ settings of Lutheran chorales. Moreover, many of his chorale preludes were published during his lifetime.[57] Publication of these works is significant in two ways: it indicates that there was a demand for such pieces and it probably corroborates their use in Catholic liturgical music in the nineteenth century. It is likely that Sechter played his own chorale preludes during the liturgies he accompanied in the imperial chapel during his 43 years of service there.

In conclusion, we can say two things. First, the general example of hymn singing by the Lutherans definitely influenced the development of Catholic liturgical practice in late eighteenth-century Vienna and environs. Church and state authorities made every effort to introduce hymn-singing in congregations, if only with limited success. Second, and perhaps more significant, in spite of official rejection, Catholic composers were attracted to Lutheran hymns and wrote organ pieces using them. Thus, Lutheran hymns found their way into Catholic sacred music by various unofficial means.

55 These would include the *Augustinerkirche, Franziskanerkirche, Jesuitenkirche, Karlskirche, Maria am Gestade, Michaelerkirche, Minoritenkirche*, and the *Piaristenkirche*, among many others.

56 His obituary notes: "how new, how expressive, how beautiful were the ideas that occurred to him when improvising! How consummately he brought them out!" Peter Williams, *Bach: A Musical Biography* (Cambridge: Cambridge University Press, 2016), 619. It also recounts that he "performed extempore the chorale *An Wasserflüssen Babylon* at great length (for almost a half-hour) and in different ways." *The Bach Reader: A Life of Johann Sebastian Bach in Letters and Documents*, ed. Hans T. David and Arthur Mendel (New York: W.W. Norton & Company, 1945), 219.

57 Sechter's chorale preludes were published in Vienna by Anton Diabelli (Diabelli & Comp) and Cranz in Hamburg. Today most are out of print.

PART 3

Lutheran Readings of Philosophy and Poetry

CHAPTER 14

Melanchthon, Luther, and Indexing the Classics

William P. Weaver

Not many theologians or Bible scholars today would aspire to merely indexing Scripture. Academic theologians typically have their sights set on loftier triumphs. This is true also of academics who do not take divinity for their subject matter. In classical studies, the indexing of a scholarly edition is often farmed out to a graduate student. It is not the stuff of scholarly ambition, not great material to put forward to a tenure committee, and hardly the thing to inspire the next generation of scholars. But during the Reformation in Wittenberg, a modest "indexing" of Scripture and the classics alike drew numerous students to lectures by the young Professor of Greek, Philip Melanchthon (1497–1560). And it drew the commendation of Martin Luther. In 1522 Luther praised Melanchthon's teaching of Scripture, describing it as an "index" and as an alternative to commentary.[1] Luther might have said the same thing about Melanchthon's roughly contemporary lectures on Virgil's *Georgics*, which were recorded by students and preserved in printed editions of the poem beginning in 1530.[2] Like the notes on Scripture, the notes on the *Georgics* combat entrenched forms of academic discourse such as commentary and attempt a new kind of instruction.[3] More spare than even the economical notes on

1 WA 10II:310. See below for the text and discussion.

2 They were edited in *CR* 19:349–58. The editor omits catchphrases, or words simply carried from the text into the margins. Longer notes on the *Georgics*, copied from Melanchthon's later lectures and printed in 1544, are not considered here. See *CR* 19:359–434. For a description of the Virgil notes, see Craig Kallendorf, "Virgil in the Renaissance Classroom: From Toscanella's *Osservationi* [...] *supra l'opere di Virgilio* to the *Exercitationes rhetoricae*," in *The Classics in the Medieval and Renaissance Classroom: The Role of Ancient Texts in the Arts Curriculum as Revealed by Surviving Manuscripts and Early Printed Books*, ed. J.F. Ruys, J.O. Ward, and M. Heyworth (Turnhout: Brepols, 2013), 309–28. Since the writing of this article, Kallendorf has expanded his study of Melanchthon's Virgil annotations. See *Printing Virgil: The Transformation of the Classics in the Renaissance* (Leiden: Brill, 2020).

3 Melanchthon's commentaries on Scripture have been the subject of extensive study. See, for instance, Timothy J. Wengert, *Philip Melanchthon's* Annotationes in Johannem *in Relation to its Predecessors and Contemporaries* (Geneva: Droz, 1987); *Human freedom, Christian righteousness: Philip Melanchthon's exegetical dispute with Erasmus of Rotterdam* (Oxford: Oxford University Press, 1998); and essays in the collection *Philip Melanchthon (1497–1560) and the Commentary*, ed. Timothy J. Wengert and Patrick M. Graham (Sheffield: Sheffield Academic Press, 1997). Melanchthon's reading of the classics is underrepresented in these

 | DOI:10.1163/9789004206717_016

Scripture, they cannot be mistaken for a commentary, and arranged a little differently, they might even be called an "index" as we use the term today.

Motivated by reforms in the liberal arts, especially rhetoric and logic, and animated in no small way by Luther's doctrine of Scripture, Melanchthon was applying a new way of reading texts as if they were speech: pointing out (hence "indexing") and labeling different speech genres in the text for the sake of some further operation (for example translating, paraphrasing, teaching or preaching). It is the purpose of this essay to describe the quality and appeal of Melanchthon's method of teaching the classics, illustrated by his annotations on Virgil's *Georgics*, and to situate the method in the context of Renaissance humanism and Luther's theology.

I begin with Luther's praise of Melanchthon's lectures on Paul's letters and his characterization of his colleague's notes as an "index," which turns out to be a very illuminating way of looking at this method of reading and teaching. Luther applied the label in a polemical fashion, juxtaposing his colleague's modest approach to Scripture with the vain and prideful approaches of a sweeping range of misguided theologians, from an Alexandrian scholar of the third century to a Dominican friar of the thirteenth. I wish to show that Luther favored an index over a commentary based on his high view of the word of God and his dim view of what he called "human learning." His praise of Melanchthon stems from two principles of his theology. First, God speaks through a word that is real, concrete, and audible. This implies the value of historical, philological study of languages and literatures, and it is an important point of convergence of Renaissance humanism and Reformation theology. Second, and crucially, God's word does not need human help. This would seem to contradict the implication of the first principle, but we can reconcile the two views by getting perspective on Melanchthon's notes. Melanchthon's modest, rhetorical-dialectical reading of texts (whether classics or Scripture) supports a Christian learning that does not supplement but amplifies Scripture and makes it more audible. In the words of Timothy Wengert, writing about Melanchthon's *Annotations on Romans* (published in 1522), "he produced a commentary that to contemporary readers, who were also steeped in humanism's rhetorical techniques, would have sounded like the Apostle Paul's own

---

studies. Scholarship on his annotations on pagan authors is relatively scarce. Helpful starting points are Stefan Rhein, "Melanchthon and Greek Literature," in Wengert and Graham, *Melanchthon and the Commentary*, 149–70, and Peter Mack, "Melanchthon's Commentaries on Latin Literature," in *Melanchthon und Europa II: Westeuropa*, ed. Günter Frank and Kees Meerhoff (Stuttgart: Thorbecke, 2002), 29–52.

voice commenting from the first century on the sixteenth century's most critical theological debates."[4]

Turning to Melanchthon, I describe his early career in Wittenberg and characterize his lectures in the context of the liberal arts. The liberal arts curriculum of schools and universities is a vital context for understanding approaches to the classics by Luther and his Wittenberg colleagues, and the place of ancient poetry in the training of pastors and theologians. Because of reforms within the liberal arts, Melanchthon was attempting novel approaches to reading texts, and his approach is fruitfully viewed as an anti-commentary, an alternative that showcases the text and not the annotator's learning. Melanchthon's notes on Virgil's *Georgics* illustrate the fruits of such an approach. They represent a modest, learned attempt to characterize the poem as speech and as persuasive argument.

That approach bore more fruit over the course of the sixteenth century, in different contexts and for different purposes. In the third part of this chapter, I turn to three Renaissance uses of the *Georgics* annotations, including one actual index of Virgil's poems, which in a sense realizes the index that Luther saw reflected in Melanchthon's annotations.[5] Although only one of the three uses qualifies as an index, all three are productively viewed as humanist attempts to leave the commentary behind and develop new forms of scholarship.

1 In Praise of the Index

However differently he might have viewed diplomacy and handled emergent political situations, however differently constituted from his colleague, Luther was warm in his admiration and candid in his praise of Melanchthon. His hyperbolic praise of Melanchthon's outline of theology, the *Loci Communes* (1521), is well known.[6] That work grew out of Melanchthon's lectures on Paul's letter to the Romans, and it was written at the time of his lectures on the letters

4 Timothy Wengert, "Philip Melanchthon's 1522 Annotations on Romans and the Lutheran Origins of Rhetorical Criticism," in *Biblical Interpretation in the Reformation: Essays Presented to David Steinmetz in Honor of his Sixtieth Birthday*, ed. R.A. Muller and J.L. Thompson (Grand Rapids: Eerdmans, 1996), 118–40, quotation from p. 118.

5 The branch of the history of scholarship dealing with technologies of organizing, labeling, and finding textual information is illustrated by Ann Blair, *Too Much to Know: Managing Scholarly Information before the Modern Age* (New Haven: Yale University Press, 2011).

6 In the dispute with Erasmus over the freedom of the will, Luther described the *Loci Communes* as "an unanswerable little book which in my judgment deserves not only to be immortalized but even canonized." *Luther and Erasmus: Free Will and Salvation*, ed. E. Gordon Rupp and Philip S. Watson (Philadelphia: Westminster John Knox, 1969), 102.

to the Corinthians, while Luther was hiding in the Wartburg and translating the New Testament into German.[7] After he returned to Wittenberg in March 1522, Luther published student notes from Melanchthon's lectures on Romans and 1 and 2 Corinthians. Luther wrote an admiring preface, which also served as an apology for publishing the notes against Melanchthon's wishes. Among other things, he characterized the notes as an index not a commentary. He wrote,

> Scripture alone, you say, must be read without commentary. This is well spoken regarding Jerome, Origen, Thomas and their ilk. For they wrote commentaries, in which they imparted more of their own [doctrine] than Pauline or Christian [doctrine]. No one would call your annotations a commentary but instead an index for reading Scripture and recognizing Christ, something which no commentary has yet accomplished.[8]

Luther places his colleague in opposition to a wide range of scholars, from the Alexandrian scholar Origen, famous for his allegorical interpretation of Scripture, to the Western father Jerome, translator and interpreter of the Vulgate, to a whole unspecified group of scholastic theologians characterized by the Dominican Thomas Aquinas, who was in fact a representative of only one school of medieval theology. By characterizing his colleague in opposition to a wide range of scholarship, Luther draws on some of Melanchthon's own rhetoric of the *Loci Communes*, which has a strong polemical tone and aims among other things to take down human presumption.

In fact, as Timothy Wengert has shown, Melanchthon did avail himself of tradition, especially patristic exegesis, and his Romans annotations show some acquaintance with medieval commentary.[9] Wengert nonetheless defends the novelty and significance of Melanchthon's exegetical method, arguing that his use of tradition was complex and regulated by a principle he shared with Luther: "Opposed to the simplicity of Scriptural truth are human traditions

7 For the circumstances of the writing of the *Loci Communes*, see William P. Weaver, "A More Excellent Way: Philip Melanchthon's Corinthians Lectures of 1521–1522," *Renaissance and Reformation/Renaissance et Réforme* 37 (2014): 31–63.

8 WA 10II:310. In the same letter, Luther confesses his "theft" of the letters.

9 Wengert, *Philip Melanchthon's* Annotationes in Johannem, 57–119. For Luther's reading of Scripture, see Robert Kolb, *Martin Luther: Confessor of the Faith* (Oxford: Oxford University Press, 2009), 42–71; Robert Kolb, *Martin Luther and the Enduring Word of God: The Wittenberg School and Its Scripture-Centered Proclamation* (Grand Rapids: Baker, 2016), esp. 98–131, 239–73.

and carnal reason."[10] Like Luther, Melanchthon was seeking alternative academic discourses based in the literal or historical meaning of Scripture.[11]

Luther's lumping together of allegorists like Origen and Jerome with scholastic theologians like Thomas Aquinas reflects the broader context of his critique. He places Melanchthon's annotations on Scripture not in a battle of the letter vs. the spirit or the literal vs. the spiritual sense, but in a battle of divine wisdom against human wisdom. As early as the Heidelberg Disputation (1518), Luther was criticizing contemporary academic theology as a "theology of glory," seeking to reveal by its own lights the hidden things of God and neglecting the revealed truth of God in Christ the incarnate word.[12] More generally, drawing on Paul's antithesis of human and divine wisdom in 1 Corinthians, he criticized academic theology as "human learning" or simply "philosophy," a godless teaching that opposed itself to the Spirit. In Luther's view, much academic theology was opposed to the Spirit in its pride, self-sufficiency, and its hoarding of knowledge. By seeking its own, academic theology obscured the truth of Scripture.

Luther's broad antithesis of human and divine learning is illustrated by his response to a critique by Jerome Emser of Leipzig (1478–1527) in 1521.[13] Emser had attacked Luther's appeals to Scripture in the *Open Letter to the German Nobility of the German Nation, concerning Reform of the Christian Estate* (1520) as simplistic and literalistic, and argued for the need for spiritual (i.e. allegorical) interpretation of such statements as Peter's exhortation "you are a royal priesthood" (1 Pet. 2:9). In his lengthy and animated response, Luther certainly does get into the nitty-gritty of Scriptural interpretation, its literal and allegorical meanings, but he also more generally characterizes Emser's appeal to the spiritual sense and spiritual masters in broad terms as *human* learning: "He thinks he has hit the mark and need not look at clear Scripture because he has human teaching. He would also like me to follow him, to let Scripture go and take up human teaching."[14] Luther's assault on human teaching in

10 Kolb, *Wittenberg School*, 93.

11 Iain Provan has recently made an eloquent and spirited defense of Reformation hermeneutics in *The Reformation and the Right Reading of Scripture* (Waco: Baylor University Press, 2017).

12 For the theology of glory and the theology of the cross, see Kolb, *Confessor of the Faith*, 55–59.

13 "An Answer to the Hyper-Christian, Hyper-Spiritual, and Hyper-Learned Book by Goat Emser in Leipzig—Including Some Thoughts on His Companion the Fool Murner (1521)," in WA 7:621–88, *LW* 39:175–203. For the "Answer" in the context of Luther's understanding of law and gospel, see Reinhard Schwarz, *Martin Luther Lehrer der christlichen Religion* (Tübingen: Mohr Siebeck, 2015), 39–42.

14 *LW* 39:175; WA 7:647.

this book is caustic, and he even calls for burning human teaching and canon law,[15] probably thinking back to a bonfire at the Elster Gate in Wittenberg in December 1520, when Melanchthon gathered a group of students to burn, among other writings, a copy of canon law and the Papal Bull "Exsurge Domine." In Luther's view, the battle between God's word and human teaching is a perennial battle, represented in Scripture itself: "Is there any greater labor on the part of all prophets than that of fighting against human teaching and keeping only God's word in a people?"[16]

Such a view might not seem to leave a lot of room for scholarship or learning, and thus may well make us wonder: what is the university for, and what learning ought pastors to seek? Granted, we ought to keep in mind the ironic tone of the letter and the ironic quality of Luther's description of Emser and his masters' learning. In fact he didn't think their learning worth the name. But even allowing for this irony, what kind of learning does Luther oppose to prevailing forms? He appeals in the same response to the teaching of grammar, and his high valuation of grammar learning is generally known.[17] Grammar was one of the seven liberal arts, specifically one of the three verbal arts called the *trivium* or three-fold way: grammar, logic, and rhetoric.[18] Luther assumes that any learned reader of Scripture will bring grammatical lore with him, learned as early as elementary school.[19] In the course of his argument, he discusses the meaning of Greek, Latin, and Hebrew terms. None of this is extraordinary. What is distinctive is Luther's characterization of Scripture as speech, and it is in this context that we should understand his appeals to grammar (and his implicit appeals to logic and rhetoric). Scripture speaks and preaches, so that when he says he brings nothing but Scripture, Luther means that he is bringing certain proclamations, namely commandments and promises. As Robert Kolb and others have described Luther's understanding of Scripture, the written word of God is active, doing things through its proclamations.[20] It is not primarily a set of signs or propositions awaiting interpretation or illumination.

---

15 *LW* 39:187; WA 7:658.

16 *LW* 39:194, WA 7:664.

17 He appeals to grammar categories in key parts of his debate with Erasmus over human will. See Brian Cummings, *The Literary Culture of the Reformation: Grammar and Grace* (Oxford: Oxford University Press, 2002), 159–75.

18 The liberal arts numbered seven and were conventionally divided into the verbal arts or *trivium* (the threefold way of grammar, logic, and rhetoric), and the numeric arts or *quadrivium* (the fourfold way of arithmetic, geometry, astronomy, and music). These subjects supplied an outline for training young persons (predominantly though not exclusively men) for cultured literacy and moral maturity.

19 *LW* 39:180; WA 7:651.

20 Kolb, *Martin Luther and the Enduring Word of God*, 35–74.

Luther's high view of grammar as a needful study to perceive and proclaim the *spoken* word is evident in his objection to the term "literal" or "written meaning":

> Thus "written meaning" (*schrifftlich synn*) is not a good term, because Paul interprets "the letter" (*buchstaben*) quite differently than they do. Those who call it "grammatical, historical meaning" do better. It would be appropriate to call it the "meaning of the tongue or of speech" (*der tzungen oder sprachen synn*) as St. Paul does in 1 Corinthians 14[:2–19], because, according to the sound of the tongue or speech, it is understood in this way by everyone.[21]

Believing comes through hearing, and hearing is of a concrete, historical language. It is not (and here I am drawing on Renaissance humanist polemics) through Aristotelian terms or other artificial languages, terminologies special to a cadre of professional theologians, that believing comes. This commonsense view of language and persuasion implies the necessity for a grammatical study of language. From this perspective, even the elementary study of figures of speech and other idiomatic expressions takes on a new importance.

It is in the context of this polemic against human learning and this understanding of the Word of God as commandments and promises proclaimed in a human tongue or language that we can appreciate what so impressed Luther in student notes taken down in Melanchthon's classroom. I have written elsewhere on Melanchthon's lectures on 1 and 2 Corinthians, the subject of Luther's praise cited above.[22] Here I wish to expand and complement that study by considering Melanchthon's lectures on a pagan poem, Virgil's *Georgics*. How did reading the *Georgics* complement the reading of Scripture?

2 The *Georgics* Annotations in the Context of Melanchthon's Early Career in Wittenberg

In his early years at Wittenberg, in well-attended lectures in both the arts faculty and, after defending his *Baccalaureus biblicus* theses in September 1519, the theology faculty, Philip Melanchthon developed a modest, rhetorical-dialectical method of teaching ancient texts that supported the new kind of

21 *LW* 39:181; WA 7:652. I have slightly modified the *LW* translation to emphasize Luther's comparison of a *written meaning* and a *spoken word*.

22 Weaver, "A More Excellent Way," 31–63.

Biblical learning that Luther was promoting. As Professor of Greek, he was responsible for giving students literacy in the New Testament in its original language, but he saw his task more broadly, as training students in a kind of humane literary judgment that was analogous with moral judgment. This required fluency in the best of what the Greeks wrote in many genres (and in different dialects).[23] In his inaugural lecture in August 1518, Melanchthon announced his first lectures for the Winter Semester 1518/1519: Homer (presumably the *Iliad*) and the Epistle to Titus. From the outset, he declared the complementarity of ancient and Biblical learning.[24]

He also took to task contemporary modes of philosophy and theology, implicitly criticizing not just the standard theology text of the era, the *Sentences* of Peter the Lombard, but also the method in which it was learned—through commentary.[25] Commentaries on the *Sentences* had accumulated over the centuries since it was written in the twelfth century, because a commentary on the *Sentences* was a step on the way to the Doctor of Theology degree. Melanchthon never wrote a comment on the *Sentences*, making the *Baccalaureus biblicus* his highest theological degree. Like Luther, he was seeking to shake up settled forms of academic learning from the date of his arrival in Wittenberg.

His critique of the commentary in theological study is reflected in his attempts to simplify the study of the liberal arts, especially the study of logic or "dialectic," his preferred label, which stems from a Greek word meaning "to converse."[26] Melanchthon had read a 1515 edition of *On Dialectical Invention*, Rudolf Agricola's novel and influential mash-up of rhetoric and dialectic, and it greatly influenced his view of literary texts and their place in a liberal arts education.[27] While Agricola's and Melanchthon's reform of dialectic lies

23 In 1518 Melanchthon published a Greek grammar that he wrote while teaching as an MA in Tübingen. The book introduces the already demanding study of Greek through a comparison of the dialects, and dialectical variants are recorded throughout the work. See *CR* 20:3–147, omitting the tables that appear in later editions of the Greek grammar. See also Paul Botley, *Learning Greek in Western Europe, 1396–1529* (Philadelphia: American Philosophical Society, 2010), 45–47.

24 *CR* 11:15–25.

25 *CR* 11:21.

26 For a synthetic study of Melanchthon's view of liberal arts education, see Volkhard Wels, *Triviale Künste: Die humanistische Reform der grammatischen, dialektischen und rhetorischen Ausbilding an der Wende zum 16. Jahrhundert* (Berlin: Weidler, 2000).

27 A liberal arts education was a constant in the West from the late antique to the early modern period, though different periods and places refined or revised the basic outline, recalibrating the arts to serve present needs or priorities. Such a recalibration happened on a large scale beginning in Italy in the fifteenth century and moved north of the Alps

outside the boundaries of this study, one important quality of *On Dialectical Invention* must be noted.[28] Agricola not only quoted liberally from ancient literature to illustrate the canons of dialectic, he quoted or construed literary text as if it were speech obeying many of the rules of usage governing speech. The upshot of this was a new kind of learned discourse, nourished by the utterances of the past, intelligible to a literate public, and governed by rules of common sense, occasion, and usage. Such a basic reframing of the aim and context of dialectic, in line with the language philosophy of Lorenzo Valla and other humanists, animated Melanchthon's teachings reflected in numerous textbooks on rhetoric and dialectic. It arguably underlies his bold attempt in 1521 to write a new outline of theology, the *Loci Communes* or "Common Topics or Outline of Theological Subjects."[29]

Speech, not abstract ideas or canons, was to be the basic framework in which the liberal arts grammar, logic, and rhetoric would be taught in Wittenberg, and that had a great impact on teaching ancient texts. Though theological writing, diplomacy, and eventually intra-Lutheran controversy occupied increasing amounts of his time, Melanchthon taught numerous Greek and Latin authors throughout his more than four-decade career.[30] Lecture notes were avidly sought out and in some cases published in unauthorized editions. Such was the case with notes published in editions of Virgil's poems beginning in 1530. Because the *Georgics* notes have a rich reception in the following decades, I will focus on these. The *Georgics* annotations are viewed productively as an anti-commentary, and the three "uses" that I will consider in the final section position themselves as rivals to commentaries, as alternative ways to read a text.

The most striking thing about Melanchthon's 1530 notes on the *Georgics* is their brevity.[31] They first and typically thereafter appeared in the margins of diminutive octavo editions of Virgil's works, a word or two every ten or twenty

---

by the end of the century. Historians have described this late medieval or Renaissance transition from scholastic to humanist learning in terms of the verbal arts of the *trivium*. See Wels, *Triviale Künste*, and Ann Moss, *Renaissance Truth and the Latin Language Turn* (Oxford: Oxford University Press, 2003), esp. 157–80.

28 For Agricola's work in the context of humanist reforms, see Peter Mack, *Renaissance Argument: Valla and Agricola in the Traditions of Rhetoric and Dialectic* (Leiden: Brill, 1993), 135–67.

29 The full title of the 1521 work is *Loci Communes seu Hypotyposes Rerum Theologicarum*.

30 See Rhein, "Melanchthon and Greek Literature," and Mack, "Melanchthon's Commentaries on Latin Literature."

31 *CR* 19:349–58. See above, note 2.

lines.[32] Only the occasional note could be called "interpretive" in the general meaning of the word. Most (about half) describe the topic or contents of the text. The next most frequent kind of note (about one in three) indicates the rhetorical strategy of the text, typically a genre or figure of speech. *Propositio*, *adhortatio* (exhortation), and *excursus* represent some of the genres, *hypotyposis* (vivid description), *epiphonema* (concluding point), and *collatio* (comparison) some of the figures of speech. The notes thus appear rather like a marginal table of contents, parceling up the text into units of discourse defined by their rhetorical strategy or subject matter, or by both (as in a number of notes that indicate the "description" of one thing or another).[33]

This extremely economical form of note-taking arose in part from the Reformation controversy over Scriptural authority, a battle in which Melanchthon played a strong supporting role in the 1520s. As early as 1519, when he began lecturing on Scripture, Melanchthon began using rhetoric and dialectic to construct an alternative to scholastic methods of commentary. He long demurred to write a commentary, and his refusal to publish even his lecture notes reflects his antipathy to conventional forms of learning and study.

He found an alternative in some doctrines of rhetoric. In his 1521 lectures on rhetoric (published with his reluctant blessing), Melanchthon described a key use of the figures of speech: "For when the teacher of rhetoric will merely point out the kinds of ornament, numerous [examples] will present themselves at once in the reading of learned writings. From these [examples] you will be able to make judgments even without instruction from the teachers of rhetoric."[34] The Virgil *scholia* are consistent with this call for the teacher's restraint, and the student's own discovery and judgment of a work—it is not the teacher's job to resolve a discourse on behalf of the student, nor should we

32 I have consulted *Virgilius, Philippi Melanchthonis Scholiis, ut brevissimis ita doctissimis, ubique exactissime adnotatus* (Cologne: Johann Gymnich, 1533). LW1533.2 in Craig Kallendorf, *A Bibliography of the Early Printed Editions of Virgil 1469–1850* (New Castle, DE: Oak Knoll Press, 2012). Hereafter cited as Kallendorf, *Bibliography*. In this and subsequent footnotes, entries in Kallendorf's *Bibliography* contain "LW" or "LG" followed by numbers. "LW" in these citations does not refer to *Luther's Works*, but his own system of categorizing editions of Virgil's works.

33 Some numbers help put the notes in perspective. The *Georgics* contains 2,188 lines and a total of 14,185 words. Melanchthon's *scholia* are limited to 585 words: a fractional amount in comparison with the text. The 4th century grammarian Servius, by comparison, wrote an influential commentary of 53,472 words on the *Georgics*, about four times the length of the poem.

34 My translation from the *Institutiones rhetoricae*, in Philipp Melanchthon, *Principal Writings on Rhetoric*, ed. William P. Weaver, Stefan Strohm, and Volkhard Wels, vol. 2, bk. 2, of *Opera omnia: Opera philosophica* (Berlin, 2017), 234.

look to Melanchthon's marginal notes to do so. The notes are instead *exemplary*, showing the kind of observation that might lead to a more complete analysis or judgment of a work.

It was perhaps inevitable that the meager marginal notes on the *Georgics* would be supplemented and/or augmented.[35] As early as 1533, Melanchthon's notes were supplemented in print by the notes of Christoph Hegendorff, the Leipzig humanist who more famously annotated Desiderius Erasmus's *De copia*. Hegendorff's notes are labeled in different editions as *nova scholia, notae, doctae et perbreves annotationes*, or *annotatiunculae*.[36] Probably written independently of Melanchthon's notes, and first added to them by an editor, Hegendorff's notes make a perfect complement, extending the "exemplary" and "partial" work of the Wittenberg humanist. Hegendorff's additions resemble Melanchthon's in their brevity and in their primary attention to the rhetorical artifice of the text. It is the copious discourse, verbal and mental, of the *Georgics* that is on display in these notes.

In 1539 appeared yet more *scholia* and a full-blown commentary on the *Georgics*, both of which draw on the combined notes of Melanchthon and Hegendorff. The *scholia* or brief annotations were by a Venetian humanist named Nicola Rossi, called Nicolaus Erythraeus, about whom I have been able to find scant information. He is most famous as an indexer of Virgil's works, and his verbal index (a type of concordance) was standard for over a century.[37]

Erythraeus's notes, published in the margins of a 1539 octavo edition of Virgil's works, incorporate verbatim many of Melanchthon's and Hegendorff's notes. But Erythraeus is far from servile. His scholia extend even further the rhetorical observations of Melanchthon and Hegendorff.[38] Furthermore, he

35 The early print history of the Virgil notes illustrates the partial and provisional quality of the notes. In my research, I have made a preliminary investigation of the dozens of early editions of Virgil that include Melanchthon's marginal notes; my study has been limited to the *Georgics* notes.

36 See *CR* 19:285–97. The earliest edition I have been able to consult is *Vergilivs Philippi Melanthonis Scholiis doctissimis illustratus* (Mainz: Georg Wagner, 1556). Kallendorf, *Bibliography*, LW1556.3.

37 Mario Emilio Cosenza, *Biographical and Bibliographical Dictionary of the Italian Humanists and the World of Classical Scholarship in Italy, 1300–1800* (Boston: G.K. Hall, 1962–67), 2:1313 and 5:661. In a dedication of the Virgil *Scholia* to Francesco Contarini, Erythraeus indicates that he studied civil law in Pavia before returned to Venice. Nicolaus Erythraeus, *P. Vergilii Maronis Bucolica, Georgica, & Aeneis* (Venice: Giovanni Antonio Nicolini da Sabbio, 1538–39), sig. a2r. Kallendorf, *Bibliography*, LW1538–1539.1.

38 Printed separately as the "Observations of Erythraeus" in a 1587 edition of his index, *P. Vergilii Maronis Bucolicon, Georgicon, & Aeneidos vocum omnium, ac sylvae rerum index* (Venice: Damiano Zenaro, 1587), sigs. 241a–271b. Kallendorf, *Bibliography*, LW1587.3.

cross-references the figures of speech in the marginal notes. This constitutes (in my view) a "use," and I will have more to say about Erythraeus's notes and index.

3 Three Uses of Melanchthon's Index

In the third and final section of this chapter, I will consider three works as "uses" of the rhetorical gloss of Melanchthon and Hegendorff. Each of these works counts as a "use" because it moves beyond interpretation into a kind of production or action. These "uses" do not aim at the production of meaning, whether the meaning of the text itself or the received wisdom of the commentaries. They are productive, rather, of intellectual habits or dispositions. The text (the *Georgics*) is more than an occasion for these projects, but it is not the ultimate "thing," either. The "thing" in question is the use or practice being exercised.

The first use is found in the marginal notes of Nicolaus Erythraeus discussed earlier. In a striking contribution to the rhetorical gloss, Erythraeus cross-references the notes of the entire Virgilian corpus, cross-referencing especially the genres, topics, and figures of speech indicated in the notes. In other words, he makes a literal index of Melanchthon's figurative index. This use of the marginal notes makes explicit something implicit in Melanchthon's and Hegendorff's additions: the figures and genres are to be understood, recognized, and compared not in isolation but in comparison with other parts of the work (or corpus).

The cross-referenced marginal notes participate in a much larger project that helps illustrate their "use" in Erythraeus's edition. For Erythraeus had undertaken an extremely ambitious, if not foolhardy, project. In a dedication of the annotated Virgil to his friend, he writes that he had intended to compile an index of the "best" Greek and Latin writers.[39] But urged on by his friend's entreaties (here compiled in an artful *prosopopoeia* or "impersonation"), he revised his plan to index *all* Greek and Latin writers![40] Why this extremely ambitious undertaking? Erythraeus describes its utility and purpose:

> If [students] will go through these indexes (let no one cavil at the word) with something of the investigator's skill, then they might arrive at a compendium of eloquence no less than if they had perused our

39 *P. Vergilii Maronis Bucolica, Georgica, & Aeneis* (LW1538–1539.1), sig. a2r.

40 Erythraeus, *Vergilii vocum index*, sig. a2v.

> commentaries, even when these have been digested with the utmost skill for finding, and written most precisely.[41]

There it is again, Luther's antithesis of the index and the commentary: here the index serving as a proxy, and even a replacement, for a commentary that might or might not be completed. Erythraeus presents the *Index* as a tool that will facilitate his own work as well as the eloquence of the studious.[42] The index places the burden of discovery and judgment on the reader, facilitating the study of eloquence through a mediated encounter with authors. To be clear about what kind of index this is, it is a *verbal* index (like a concordance). In the index, Erythraeus indexes words, phrases, and even genres of speech. This range of reference makes his ambitious undertaking appear all the more Herculean.

The cross-referenced marginal notes are not technically part of the *Index* (which is an index of the text, not of the marginal notes, after all), but they do complement it in an important way. The cross-references create a fascinating interface with the text, mapped out (so to speak) not by its subject matter but by its verbal art. Extending the strictly verbal units indexed in the *Index* itself, they expand the mental and verbal context in which a reader is invited to see (or hear) an utterance, and they supply numerous points of unexpected, nonlinear resonance within the text.

In the same year that Erythraeus published his edition of Virgil, the physician, university instructor, and polymath Jodocus Willich published a lengthy, learned commentary on the *Georgics*.[43] Although not the primary object of the commentary, rhetoric contributes a basic lens through which to read the poem and understand its composition, and Willich rehearses several of the rhetorical observations of Melanchthon and Hegendorff. If the technical vocabulary of rhetoric is dwarfed by the massive learning in this commentary, rhetoric nonetheless represents a basic means by which Willich approaches and describes the poem. One of the innovative things that Willich does in the commentary is to subdivide the four books of the poem into parts, and he uses rhetoric to describe these parts (*narratio*, *egressio*, etc.).

---

41 Erythraeus, *Vergilii vocum index*, sigs. a2v–a3r.

42 "That having written these down, we might employ them for the completion of our task, and that the studious, meanwhile, might have their desire (as you call it) alleviated while our own books are maturing." Erythraeus, *Vergilii vocum index*, sig. a2v. He later refers to one of his books, "On the Instruction of the Perfect Poet," sig. a4v.

43 Jodocus Willich, *Georgicorum libri quatuor Pub. Virgilij Maronis commentarijs doctissimis illustrati* (Basel: Bartholomaeus Westheimer, 1539). Kallendorf, *Bibliography*, LG1539.1.

In 1551 Willich published a work called the *Dialysis* (or "resolution") *of the Four Books of Virgil's Georgics*.[44] It is the second use and forms an interesting contrast with Willich's own commentary. If that commentary incorporated humanist note-taking practice into a more conventional form, the *Dialysis* is explicitly experimental, perhaps even "disruptive," in its form. Willich had described the project in a work entitled *On Method* and published the year before:

> If you were to begin with the definition [of the *Georgics*] gathered from the four types of agriculture (there are just so many books), and then you join to each its circumstances according to its tradition and precept, from which (circumstances) are born the causes, elements, differences, and finally the very precepts (of each type of agriculture); then assuredly by this method you would grasp the art more correctly, and having grasped it would teach it more rightly, than has been achieved to date by countless commentaries.[45]

Going further than Erythraeus's comparison between his indexes and commentaries, Willich describes an adversarial relationship between his "method" and commentaries.[46] This is especially interesting in light of the lengthy commentary that he had published hardly a decade before! But he has retained from that commentary something for which I think he was deeply indebted to Melanchthon and the art of rhetoric more generally: a sense of the *Georgics* as an organic whole.

In the *Dialysis of the Four Books of the Georgics*, Willich attempts just what he suggested in *De Methodo*: to exhaustively define the four types of agriculture (farming, viticulture and arboriculture, animal husbandry, and beekeeping) by proceeding through a topical analysis of the four books of the *Georgics*. The *Dialysis* is both analytic, using the topics of invention (circumstances,

---

44 Jodocus Willich, *Dialysis quatuor librorum in Georgicis Virgilii* (Frankfurt an der Oder: Johann Eichorn, 1551). Kallendorf, *Bibliography*, LG1551.1. It was printed with Willich's *Signorum Prognosticorum de Tempestatibus Aeris Physica Explicatio*.

45 Jodocus Willich, *De methodo omnium artium et disciplinarum informanda opusculum* (Frankfurt: Johann Eichorn, 1550), sigs. D3v–D4r.

46 The "method" spoken of here is one of six methods discussed in the treatise *De methodo*. Citing Galen as his primary authority, Willich runs through three procedures by which the arts and sciences can be described: analytically, synthetically, and by definition. The third method, called *dialysis* or *exegesis ex horou*, or simply "definitional," begins with a complete definition of an art and proceeds to break the definition into its parts, and those parts into their parts, ad infinitum. The remaining three methods treated in *De Methodo* relate to complex arguments—i.e., syllogisms.

causes, parts, differences, etc.) to break the *Georgics* into meaningful parts, and elaborative, using the topics of invention to fill out and complete the picture of farming that Virgil describes in each part.[47]

The *Dialysis* could never be mistaken for a commentary. It is rather an attempt, as described above, to reduce both the *Georgics* and the art of agriculture to a speculum (a survey) in which the student can grasp the art (both theory and practice) in its entirety and in its parts. And the method is drawn from works on dialectic and rhetoric by Agricola, Erasmus, Melanchthon, and perhaps Petrus Ramus, whose works had begun to be disseminated in Germany in the 1540s. The 1551 edition even included a fold-out diagram of the whole work in outline—not a ramification, in my opinion, but a reification of the "one page" mused by Willich in his Galenic *De Methodo*. In that treatise he wrote, "This method contributes to strengthening memory, placing before the eyes a compendious summa as if on a single page."[48]

My third and last example of a use of the "rhetoricized Virgil" is a prose paraphrase of the *Georgics*.[49] In the only surviving edition of the work, printed in London in 1591, the Latin prose paraphrase (*Paraphrasis*) is attributed to Nicholas Grimald (1519–62), English poet who contributed 40 poems to *Tottel's Miscellany* (a pioneering printed collection of English lyric).[50] The title page is very specific in its attribution. It states that Grimald wrote the *Paraphrase* in Oxford in the second year of Edward the Sixth's reign. Edward was crowned on February 20, 1547, and Grimald gave lectures at Christ Church beginning in 1547, so the attribution does at least correlate with some data of the poet's life.

Whoever wrote it (its authorship is not critical to my argument), the *Paraphrase* clearly has an academic audience and use in view. It suffers greatly by comparison with the *Georgics*! But it cannot be faulted for that, and what it does it does very well. For it was not meant as a work of rivalry or imitation, but clarification. In the liberties of prose, it freely paraphrases the four books of the *Georgics*, explaining references and allusions (geographical, historical, mythical), elaborating brief or obscure passages, clarifying ambiguities, resolving figures of speech or exaggerating them in order to draw attention to Virgil's rhetorical artifice, supplying a number of synonyms, and amplifying the purple passages, especially descriptions or similes. These were all duties

47 And there is yet another object in view—to supply teachers with a method of definition that could be used to unfold any art or science, and many a learned text.

48 Willich, *De methodo*, sig C6r.

49 The phrase is found in Kallendorf, "Virgil in the Renaissance Classroom."

50 Nicolas Grimald, *Nicolai Grimoaldi viri doctiss. in P.V. Maronis quatuor libros Georgicorum in oratione soluta paraphrasis* (London: George Bishop and Ralph Newbery, 1591). Kallendorf, *Bibliography*, LG1591.1.

of the schoolmaster as directed by Erasmus and numerous other humanist authorities.[51]

Apart from the notice on the title page, the *Paraphrase* was published without any indication of its purpose or context. But in my research I have stumbled upon a major source for the *Paraphrase*: the above-mentioned commentary on the *Georgics* by Jodocus Willich. After the *Georgics*, Willich's commentary is probably the most important source for the *Paraphrasis*. I have not combed through the 569-page commentary to discover the full extent of Grimald's debt to Willich, but I can speak to his indebtedness to the structure and scheme of Willich's commentary. In the first place, Willich's interesting scheme of subdividing the books of the *Georgics* is taken over by Grimald—in fact, this subdivision is basic to Grimald's construction of the prose paraphrase as a series of orations (or "narrations"). For instance, Grimald follows Willich exactly in describing book 1 as a *narratio* with five parts, and his segmentation of book 1 closely corresponds to Willich's five "parts."[52] Conceptually, Grimald takes over from Willich's commentary a sense of the poem as an integral whole. At many points in his paraphrase, he introduces transitions that look to this integrity.[53] Similarly at many points he addresses Maecenas, the dedicatee of Virgil's poem.[54] This repeated address to Maecenas has the effect of keeping the poem's audience ever in mind. These are just some of the ways in which the *Paraphrasis* makes transparent its rhetorical interpretation of the poem. In the 1591 London edition, there are marginal notes that bear some resemblance to the topical and rhetorical notes of Melanchthon's "brief scholia."

The *Paraphrasis* functions like a digest of Willich's *Commentary* but takes an entirely different form. By taking the form of a paraphrase, it disguises the written genre of the commentary in a spoken form (it appears ready-made for reading aloud in the classroom). And if there is manifestly no rivalry with Virgil's *Georgics* in the *Paraphrasis*, I do believe there is a hidden rivalry with the *Commentary*. Grimald takes a distinctively humanist form and uses it to perform the most essential duties of the commentary. And this may be the main point of rivalry: where the discrete, fragmented form of the commentary has the disruptive effect of breaking the poem into seemingly unrelated segments,

---

51 For instance, Erasmus enumerates several of these duties in "On the Method of Study" (*De Ratione Studii*). See *Collected Works of Erasmus* (Toronto, 1974–) 24:682–91.

52 See headnote to the text of the first part of the "narration" in Grimald, *Paraphrasis*, fol. 4a, and subsequent headnotes, fols. 7a, 8b, 11a, 17a. Cf. Willich, *Georgicorum Libri Quatuor Pub. Virgilij Maronis Commentarijs doctissimis illustrati*, 68, 69, 97, 110, 121, 174.

53 See, for instance, Grimald, *Paraphrasis*, fols. 9b (where there is the marginal note *Transitus*), 25a (marginal note *Transitio*), 34b, 35a (*Hactenus* ...). 50b, and passim.

54 For example, Grimald, *Paraphrasis*, fols. 27b, 30b.

the interpretive paraphrase preserves, and even restores, a presumed unity and discursive continuity of the poem.

This is a common aim of the three uses of Melanchthon's "index" considered in this chapter: to discover and preserve the continuity and the organic wholeness of the four books of the *Georgics*. I conclude with an observation and a suggestion. First, I put forth an observation or simply a reiteration of something already well established by scholars of Renaissance rhetoric: the art of rhetoric supplied humanist educators with a vital apparatus not only for transforming conventional forms of learning, especially those inherited from late scholastic logic, but also for exploring and experimenting with new forms of teaching. Second, I offer a suggestion or hypothesis that needs further research: the Reformation in Germany, with its controversial and revolutionary construal of Scriptural authority, made this use of rhetoric all the more urgent and promoted innovative and even aggressive transformations of the classical tradition.

CHAPTER 15

An Intended Reformulation: Of Brad Gregory, Duns Scotus, and Early Modern Metaphysics

Jack D. Kilcrease

1 Introduction

In his work *The Unintended Reformation* (2012), the Reformation historian Brad Gregory argues at length that the Reformation accidentally created a pluralistic, secular Western society that by the early twenty-first century has become hostile to Christianity.[1] Gregory makes this argument through a series of shorter studies on specific topics in the development of Western culture from the early Modern period down to the present which he weaves into a single grand narrative of devolution. Because of the length and complexity of Gregory's work, we cannot engage all of his arguments. Rather, we will primarily focus on his description of late medieval and early Modern metaphysics, and their interrelationship with the theological development of Roman Catholic and Reformation theology.

It will be our central contention that in describing the development of metaphysics throughout this period Gregory does not take all the historical data into account and imputes to the Protestant Reformers (and their heirs in Protestant Scholasticism) metaphysical positions that they did not hold. Contrary to many of Gregory's claims, a great body of evidence demonstrates that whatever disagreements the Magisterial Reformers and their heirs had with the late medieval Western church, their metaphysical views largely stood in continuity with medieval models, most particularly those found in Thomism. This Protestant appropriation of medieval models relates to two areas: the acceptance of the analogy of being and the use of Aristotelianism as an ancillary philosophy.

1 Brad Gregory, *The Unintended Reformation: How a Religious Revolution Secularized Society* (Cambridge, MA: Belknap Press, 2012).

 | DOI:10.1163/9789004206717_017

2 *Analogia Entis*: What Is at Stake?

In the first chapter of *The Unintended Reformation*, Gregory examines what he regards as the degeneration of philosophical ontology in the centuries following the Reformation. The questions of ontology and of epistemology are very important to Gregory[2] because he operates with the Thomistic conception of theology as a universal and speculative science (in the Aristotelian sense)[3] that discerns the relationship of God to all things and all things to God.[4] Since theology forms a universal matrix to which all knowledge must be related as a science, it is essentially civilization forming. It is a comprehensive knowledge that specifies proper *theoria* and *praxis*, thereby giving a proper shape to civilization. Within this matrix, ontology is foundational insofar as it forms a comprehensive description of the relationship between being and becoming, and likewise the true and proper *telos* of all things.

According to Gregory, prior to John Duns Scotus in the fourteenth century most Western Christian theologians followed something quite closely approximating the idea of the analogy of being, i.e., the idea that God is, properly speaking, being itself and its transcendental properties (wisdom, goodness, etc.), whereas creatures are analogically or derivatively beings.[5] Aquinas

---

2 Gregory, *Unintended Reformation*, 364.

3 See discussion in the following: Heinrich Fries, *Fundamental Theology*, trans. Robert Daly (Washington, D.C.: Catholic University of America Press, 1996), 132–34; Nicholas Healy, *Thomas Aquinas: Theologian of the Christian Life* (Burlington, VT: Ashgate Publishing, 2003), 34–36; Bruce Marshall, "Quod Scit Una Uetula: Aquinas on the Nature of Theology," in Rik Van Nieuwenhove and Joseph Wawrykow, eds., *The Theology of Thomas Aquinas* (Notre Dame: University of Notre Dame Press, 2010), 1–35; Jean-Pierre Torrell, *Saint Thomas Aquinas: Spiritual Master* (Washington, D.C.: Catholic University of America Press, 1996), 2:7–9, 17–18; Rudi te Velde, *Aquinas on God: The 'Divine Science' of the Summa Theologiae* (Burlington, VT: Ashgate, 2006), 23–28.

4 "All things are dwelt on by this science [theology], yet held in their relationship to God"; Thomas Aquinas, *Summa Theologiae*, 1a, q. 1, art. 7; *Summa Theologiae*, Black Friars Edition (New York and London: McGraw-Hill, 1964–), 1:27. From this citation forward, the *Summa* will be cited as "ST," whereas the page citation from the Black Friar's edition will be cited as "BF." Similarly, Yves Congar summarizes St. Thomas's position in several works: "By this intellectual effort *sacra doctrina* will reproduce, as far as it can, God's science, that is to say, the order according to which God, in His wisdom, links all things together, each according to its degree of intelligibility and being, and finally brings all things to Himself." Yves Congar, *A History of Theology*, trans. Hunter Guthrie (Garden City, NY: Doubleday, 1968), 95.

5 See the following select biography on the doctrine of the analogy of being: James Francis Anderson, *Reflections on the Analogy of Being* (The Hague: Martinus Nijhoff, 1967); Lawrence Dewan, *Form and Being: Studies in Thomistic Metaphysics* (Washington, D.C.: Catholic University of America Press, 2006), 81–96; George Peter Klubertanz, *Saint Thomas Aquinas*

followed suit and made it the foundation for his understanding of theology. The goal of the scheme of the analogy of being was to give a description of the transcendence of God, while at the same time accounting for the possibility of critically realistic propositional statements concerning him.

According to Aquinas's theory of analogy, God can be known through his positive attributes (*via positiva*). We can indeed call God "good" and "wise" without dragging him down to the level of "goodness" and "wisdom" that one finds in created beings. Insofar as these qualities apply to the divine, they are predicated in a true, proper, and exemplary sense, whereas with regard to creatures these qualities are predicated in a derivative sense. God is being itself, and not a being among beings, as were the gods of Greek mythology.[6]

This description of the analogy of being is what we might call a minimal "thin-description" that could probably be agreed upon by theologians of many different Western theological traditions. As we will see, even Protestant theologians found this thin-description[7] of analogy as an essential component when

---

on Analogy: A Textual Analysis and Systematic Synthesis (Chicago: Loyola University Press, 1960); Steven A. Long, *Analogia Entis: On the Analogy of Being, Metaphysics, and the Act of Faith* (Notre Dame: University of Notre Dame Press, 2011); Ralph McInerny, *Aquinas and Analogy* (Washington, D.C.: Catholic University of America Press, 1998); Ralph McInerny, *The Logic of Analogy: An Interpretation of St Thomas* (The Hague: Martinus Nijhoff, 1971); Bernard Montagnes and Andrew Tallon, *The Doctrine of the Analogy of Being According to Thomas Aquinas* (Milwaukee: Marquette University Press, 2004); John Mortensen, *Understanding St. Thomas on Analogy* (CreateSpace Independent Publishing, 2010); Barry Pearlman, *A Certain Faith: Analogy of Being and the Affirmation of Belief* (Lanham, MD: University Press of America, 2011); Gerald B. Phelan, *St. Thomas and Analogy* (Milwaukee: Marquette University Press, 1941); Erich Przywara, *Analogia Entis: Metaphysics: Original Structure and Universal Rhythm*, trans. John Betz and David Bentley Hart (Grand Rapids: Wm. B. Eerdmans, 2013); Victor M. Salas, *The Analogy of Being According to Thomas Aquinas: Its Twofold Character and Judgmental Method* (Saint Louis: Saint Louis University Press, 2008); Michael De Temple, *Univocity and Analogy of Being in the Latin Metaphysics of Avicenna* (Washington, D.C.: Catholic University of America, 1974); Thomas Joseph White, S.J., *The Analogy of Being: Invention of the Antichrist or Wisdom of God?* (Grand Rapids: Wm. B. Eerdmans, 2010); John Wippel, *The Metaphysical Thought of Thomas Aquinas: From Finite Being to Uncreated Being* (Washington, D.C.: The Catholic University of America Press, 2000), 65–94.

6 See Aquinas on analogy in: ST 1a, q. 13, art. 5; BF 3:61–67. Also see Cross's summary of Aquinas's position in: Richard Cross, "Duns Scotus and Suarez at the Origins of Modernity" in *Deconstructing Radical Orthodoxy: Post-Modern Theology, Rhetoric, and Truth*, ed. Wayne Hankey and Douglas Hedley (Burlington, VT: Ashgate Publishing, 2005), 88–89.

7 I use the terms "thick" and "thin" description here somewhat more loosely than Geertz's technical usage. By "thin-description" we mean that it gives the basic conceptual components of the meaning of analogy in the historic Christian tradition. This would be different than a "thick-description" that would give not only the basic conceptual element of the concept of analogy, but also show its significance as a kind of theological scaffolding for a whole series of theological commitments that Roman Catholics do not share with other theological

discussing the relationship between creatures and their creator, as well as the epistemology of revelation. Indeed, coming out of the same stream of Western Christian tradition, the Protestants of the early Modern period had very few other available models than the ones bequeathed to them by the medieval church.

Nonetheless, for the Thomistic tradition (of which Gregory is quite clearly a proponent), the analogy of being has a much more profound significance. Beyond the thin-description offered above, there is within the Thomistic tradition what one might call a "thick-description" of the analogy of the being. Within Aquinas's theology, such a thick-description is a key to understanding the relationship between faith and reason, as well as the unity between all knowledge. According to this theological outlook, creaturely reason partially mirrors divine rationality in that all creatures have an inherent likeness to, and their true end in, their creator. God himself is the exemplary cause of all created being, and therefore knowledge of God is the highest and most perfect fulfillment of all epistemic projects. Human reason, therefore, when augmented by divine grace and illuminated by the light of revelation, is competent to "think-into" (so to speak) both revelation and created order[8] and see the analogical unity and coherence of the doctrines of the faith with all other forms of knowledge.[9] Theology synthesizes all human epistemic projects in

---

traditions. This is similar to Geertz's anthropological use of the term, wherein a "thin-description" refers to the act of anthropologists simply documenting a particular cultural practice or series of cultural practices. A "thick-description" would be a description of these practices according to their wider significance in the culture. See Clifford Geertz, "Thick Description: Toward an Interpretive Theory of Culture," in *The Interpretation of Cultures: Selected Essays* (New York: Basic Books, 1973), 3–30.

8 Yves Congar writes regarding Thomas's position: "The scientific quality of sacred doctrine consists then in the fact that starting with the truths of faith taken as principles we can, by reasoning, establish other truth which will appear certain through the certitude of the first." Congar, *History*, 95. Also see comments regarding the role of deduction in Congar, *History*, 97–98.

9 Yves Congar writes regarding Thomas's position: "When certain less known truth are made manifest to the human intellect by their connection with better known truths, that he [Aquinas] says, is science. God has a perfect scientific knowledge of all things, for He sees the foundation of effects in their causes, of properties in their essences and finally of all things in Himself, of Whom they are a participation. By grace, faith in us is a divine knowing, a definite communication of God's knowledge. But this communication is imperfect and the human spirit naturally desires a fuller grasp of the objects revealed. This grasp can be sought either by supernatural activity in the vital manner and tending to imitate the mode of apprehension of God Himself, or by a properly intellectual activity which follows our human mode and is, on the whole, the work of theology." Congar, *History*, 93. See similar observations in Montague Brown, *The Romance of Reason: An Adventure in the Thought of Thomas Aquinas* (Petersham, Mass: St. Bede's Publications, 1991), 29. Also look at Ulrich Leinsle's summary

the light of revelation. The thick-description of analogy thereby makes theology the queen of the sciences within Thomistic thought.[10]

This is the reason why Gregory repeatedly describes the analogical view of reality as "sacramental."[11] By this designation he seems to be thinking in terms of the Roman Catholic sacramental theory,[12] based in Augustine's Neo-Platonically inspired distinction between *signum* and *res*.[13] For Augustine, there is a distinction between the visible sign (*signum*) of the sacrament and the invisible grace that is being communicated (*res*). For Augustine (as for subsequent Roman Catholic theology), in seeing the outward sign, one is prompted to ascend intellectually above the merely visible reality of the sacrament and to perceive the intelligible reality of grace that underpins it.

Therefore, when Gregory applies the term "sacramental" to the ontological and epistemological project of Catholic theology, his meaning is clear. What he implicitly proposes is that the analogy of being allows one to see past the visible disunity of the various arts and sciences. Through the power of graced reason and the light of revelation, it is therefore possible to understand all things in their proper reality as being related to God, who is, after all, their true end (*telos*).[14] Within this scheme, the infallible authority of the Church plays a significant role in that it expounds and guarantees the content of revelation that will serve as the synthetic key to bring to light the unity of all knowledge. Therefore, rejection of this thick-description of the analogy of being is utterly destructive of the very notion of theology and the unity of knowledge as defined by Thomism.

---

of the scientific character of theology in Ulrich Leinsle, *Introduction to Scholastic Theology*, trans. Michael Miller (Washington, D.C.: The Catholic University of America Press, 2010), 167–71.

10 See the helpful summary of Thomas's and Medieval theology's self-conception and its attending problems in Bernard Lonergan, *Insight: A Study of Human Understanding* (Toronto: University of Toronto Press, 1958), 1:743–44.

11 Gregory, *Unintended Reformation*, 32, 53. This language here is reminiscent of another recent work to argue this particular narrative of western theology and philosophy. See Hans Boersma, *Heavenly Participation: The Weaving of the Sacramental Tapestry* (Grand Rapids: Wm. B. Eerdmans, 2011).

12 The current Catholic Catechism defines sacraments in this way: "The sacraments are efficacious signs of grace, instituted by Christ and entrusted to the Church, by which divine life is dispensed to us; the visible rites by which the sacraments are celebrated signify and make present the graces proper to each sacrament. They bear fruit in those who receive them with the required dispositions." *Catechism of the Catholic Church* (Rome: Libereia Enditrice Vaticana, 1994), 1131.

13 See the masterful discussion in Philip Cary, *Outward Signs: The Powerlessness of External Things in Augustine's Thought* (New York: Oxford University Press, 2008), 155–252.

14 See: ST 1a, q. 1, art. 7; BF 1:27.

Likewise, for Gregory, the Magisterial Reformers' doctrine of *Sola Scriptura* removes the unchallenged authority of the content of revelation. It therefore divides persons into factions based on their differing opinions regarding what the content of revelation is.[15] Since through the Reformation's scriptural principle, the content of theology has now become challengeable like all other forms of human knowledge (i.e., it is possible that someone might have misread the Bible), it cannot hold a privileged position as the unchanging norm and anchor of all other forms of human rationality. Lacking an unchallengeable content, theology becomes marginalized from its position as the queen of the sciences (something Gregory laments in the final chapter).[16] As a result, the unity of knowledge is found in other disciplines (such as science and math within the Modernist paradigm) or denied entirely (as in Postmodernism). Hence, the analogical unity of all knowledge and its civilization-forming potential are utterly destroyed if theological dissent is allowed.

3 The Role of Scotus in Gregory's Narrative

The primary object of Gregory's polemics in the first chapter of *The Unintended Reformation* is not Martin Luther, but the Franciscan theologian, Scotus.[17] According to Gregory, Scotus destroyed the intellectual synthesis of medieval theology as it had culminated in Thomas Aquinas with the doctrine of the "univocity of being," whereby he claimed that "being" and other attributes could be predicated of God and creatures in a univocal manner ("God is good" in the

15 Gregory, *Unintended Reformation*, 86–96.

16 Gregory, *Unintended Reformation*, 298–364.

17 See the following select biography on Scotus: Egbert P. Bos, ed., *John Duns Scotus: Renewal of Philosophy* (Amsterdam: Rodiopi, 1998); Richard Cross, *Duns Scotus* (New York: Oxford University Press, 1999); Richard Cross, *Duns Scotus on God* (Burlington, VT: Ashgate, 2005); William A. Frank and Allan Bernard Wolter, *Duns Scotus, Metaphysician* (West Lafayette, IN: Purdue University Press, 1995); Alex Hall, *Thomas Aquinas and John Duns Scotus: Natural Theology in the High Middle Ages* (London: Continuum, 2007); Ludger Honnefelder, Rega Wood, and Mechthild Dreyer, eds., *John Duns Scotus: Metaphysics and Ethics* (Leiden: Brill, 1996); Mary Beth Ingham, *Scotus for Dunces: An Introduction to the Subtle Doctor* (St. Bonaventure, NY: The Franciscan Institute, 2012); Mary Beth Ingham and Mechthild Dreyer, *The Philosophical Vision of John Duns Scotus: An Introduction* (Washington, D.C.: The Catholic University of America Press, 2007); Antonie Vos Jaczn, *Johannes Duns Scotus* (Leiden: Groen & Zoon, 1994); Cyril L. Shircel, *The Univocity of the Concept of Being in the Philosophy of John Duns Scotus* (Washington, D.C.: The Catholic University of America Press, 1942); Thomas Williams, ed., *The Cambridge Companion to Duns Scotus* (Cambridge, UK: Cambridge University Press, 2003).

same sense as "creatures are good").[18] Gregory regards this way of looking at God and creatures to be disastrous, because it made God a being among beings and a cause among causes: "By predicating being of God and creatures univocally, Scotus brought both within the same conceptual framework."[19] God and creatures were now subordinated to a common conceptual category of being that encompassed them both. For the first time, Scotus had created what the philosopher Martin Heidegger called "onto-theology."[20] By "onto-theology" Heidegger means the idea that God is only a being among other beings, rather than the ground of being itself. In the modern period, it is often charged that the concept of God as a being among beings made God seem mythological and absurd to the educated, thereby leading to the rise of atheism.

Ultimately, such a move opened Christian theism to what Gregory views as the facile criticisms of secular modernity. Echoing a similar argument in the work of Hans Urs von Balthasar,[21] Gregory claims God could be picked apart by the omni-competent human reason.[22] Differing claims about what constituted human reason then led to conflict in philosophical theology, thereby marginalizing theology even more as a form of academic discourse and giving rise to scientism and secularism.[23]

In describing Gregory's interpretation of the course of theology and philosophy in the late Middle Ages, it is important to pause for a moment and examine from whence he is drawing this particular narrative. Although Gregory explicitly cites the work of Amos Funkenstein,[24] in footnote 26 of the first chapter he mentions in passing the work of John Milbank and the Radical Orthodox theologians.[25] When Milbank and his group claim that Scotus destroyed

18 Gregory, *Unintended Reformation*, 36–37.

19 Gregory, *Unintended Reformation*, 37.

20 See Martin Heidegger, "The Onto-theo-logical Constitution of Metaphysics," in *Identity and Difference*, trans. Joan Stambaugh (New York: Harper and Row, 1969), 42–74. Also see: Jean-Luc Marion, *God without Being*, trans. Thomas Carlton (Chicago: University of Chicago Press, 1991) and Merold Westphal, *Overcoming Onto-theology: Toward a Postmodern Christian Faith* (New York: Fordham University Press, 2001).

21 Hans Urs von Balthasar, *The Glory of the Lord: A Theological Aesthetics* (San Francisco: Ignatius, 1982–91), 5:28–29.

22 Gregory, *Unintended Reformation*, 48–50.

23 Gregory, *Unintended Reformation*, 50–51.

24 Amos Funkenstein, *Theology and the Scientific Imagination from the Middle Ages to the Seventeenth Century* (Princeton: Princeton University Press, 1986).

25 Gregory, *Unintended Reformation*, 400–401. Radical Orthodoxy holds that modern secularity is not a reality that theology must conform to but is simply an alternative metanarrative among other metanarratives. In fact, instead of being post-theological, modern and postmodern thought is simply a series of covert anti-theologies. See the following examples of John Milbank's work: John Milbank, *Being Reconciled: Ontology and Pardon*

Western Christianity and gave rise to secularism (in particular, in the form of secular social theory), they draw on earlier narratives constructed by late nineteenth and early twentieth century Roman Catholics.[26]

As the Reformation historian Steven Ozment has pointed out, this narrative of a fall from the purity of Thomistic analogy to Scotus and Nominalist univocity (and from there, on to nihilism) has many detractors and was in fact largely popularized by the work of the highly influential philosophical historian of the Middle Ages, Étienne Gilson.[27] Richard Muller[28] has also pointed to the work of the Catholic Reformation scholar Joseph Lortz.[29] Wherever we trace the ultimate source of this common Catholic narrative, all point in one direction: Aquinas's theology (particularly his use of analogy) was the highest point of Christian theology. Scotus, by introducing univocity laid the path

---

(London: Routledge, 2003); *Beyond Secular Order: The Representation of Being and the Representation of People* (Malden, MA: Wiley-Blackwell, 2013); *The Future of Love: Essays in Political Theology* (London: SCM Press, 2009); *The Religious Dimension in the Thought of Giambattista Vico, 1668–1744: The Early Metaphysics* (Lewiston, NY: Edwin Mellen Press, 1991); *The Suspended Middle: Henri de Lubac and the Debate Concerning the Supernatural* (Grand Rapids: Wm. B. Eerdmans, 2005); *Theology and Social Theory: Beyond Secular Reason* (Malden, MA: Blackwell Publishers, 2008); *The Word Made Strange: Theology, Language, Culture* (Malden, MA: Wiley-Blackwell, 1997). Among the Radical Orthodox Theologians, see the works of the Catherine Pickstock, e.g. *After Writing: On the Liturgical Cosummation of Philosophy* (Malden, MA: Wiley-Blackwell, 1998). Also, cf. the writings of Graham Ward, e.g., *Barth, Derrida and the Language of Theology* (Cambridge, UK: Cambridge University Press, 1995); *Christ and Culture* (Malden, MA: Wiley-Blackwell, 2008); *Cities of God* (London: Routledge, 2000); *Cultural Transformation and Religious Practice* (Cambridge, UK: Cambridge University Press, 2005); *The Politics of Discipleship: Becoming Postmaterial Citizens* (London: SCM Press, 2009); *Theology and Contemporary Critical Theory* (New York: St. Martin's Press, 2000); *True Religion* (Malden, MA: Wiley-Blackwell, 2002).

26 See Milbank, *Theology and Social Theory*, 14–15.

27 See Steven Ozment, *The Age of Reform, 1250–1550: An Intellectual and Religious History of Late Medieval and Reformation Europe* (New Haven: Yale University Press, 1981), 9. Ozment refers to two books in particular: Étienne Gilson, *History of Christian Philosophy in the Middle Ages* (New York: Random House, 1955) and his *Reason and Revelation in the Middle Ages* (New York: Charles Scribner, 1963).

28 See Richard Muller, "Not Scotist: Understandings of Being, Univocity, and Analogy in Early Modern Reformed Thought," *Reformation & Renaissance Review* 14, no. 2 (2012): 128–29.

29 See Joseph Lortz, *Die Reformation in Deutschland*, 2 vols. (Freiburg in Breisgau: Herder Verlag, 1949). Regarding Lortz's claim that Luther did not actually know the work of the *via Antiqua* in general and Aquinas in particular, see its refutation in the groundbreaking works: Denis Janz, *Luther and Late Medieval Thomism: A Study in Theological Anthropology* (Waterloo, Ontario: Wilfried Laurier Press, 1983) and his *Luther on Thomas Aquinas: The Angelic Doctor in the Thought of the Reformer* (Wiesbaden: Franz Steiner Verlag, 1989).

for Nominalism, the Reformation, and later for the theological/philosophical maladies of secular modernity.

As noted, this narrative is by no means universally accepted. Indeed, its prevalence is the reason why Heiko Oberman sought to rehabilitate late medieval thought (notably the *schola Augustiniana moderna* and Nominalism), which he believed had been unfairly denigrated. Hence Oberman titled his work on the subject *The Harvest of Medieval Theology*[30] since he wished to emphasize that the thought of the later Middle Ages was not a falling away from the glorious summit of Thomism, but in many respects a fulfillment of its trajectory.

Accordingly, it is ultimately not difficult to ascertain why this view would appeal to modern Roman Catholics as well as to many Anglo-Catholics. It may be suggested that since, after the Reformation,[31] Roman Catholics eventually came to view Thomas Aquinas as the "Teacher of the Church," the developments that came after him (i.e., Scotists, Nominalists, and Reformers) were viewed (in the vein of Gilson) as a falling away from perfection. In the early twentieth century, this basic paradigm for understanding the flow of philosophical/theological history was likely hardened by the Neo-Thomistic revival and the subsequent Modernist crisis.[32] All this of course does not make the Gregory/Milbank/Gilson/Lortz narrative about late medieval and early Modern thought false per se. It merely suggests that there is a good reason why this narrative has had such an appeal for Roman Catholic theologians and historians, irrespective of the evidence.

What is perhaps more problematic about Gregory's narrative is that its starting point is what many perceive as a fundamental misreading of Scotus's theology. Richard Cross, who is one of the most highly regarded Scotist scholars in the Anglophone world[33] has convincingly argued that John Milbank and the Radical Orthodox (and by proxy, Gregory) have essentially misinterpreted Scotus on the issue of univocity of being.

In his article "Duns Scotus, Suárez, and the Origins of Modernity," Cross demonstrates that in asserting that one could predicate "being" of God and

30 Heiko Oberman, *The Harvest of Medieval Theology: Gabriel Biel and Late Medieval Nominalism* (Grand Rapids: Baker Academic, 2001).

31 See brief discussion of Thomas's status in the Catholic Church in Hans Küng, *Great Christian Thinkers: Paul, Origen, Augustine, Aquinas, Luther, Schleiermacher, Barth* (London: Continuum, 1994), 114. For Thomas's standing in the modern Catholic Church see Leo XIII, *Aeterni Patris: On the Restoration of Christian Philosophy* (Boston: St. Paul Editions, date unknown).

32 Marvin O'Connell, *Critics on Trial: An Introduction to the Catholic Modernist Crisis* (Washington, D.C.: Catholic University of America Press, 1994).

33 See comment in: Daniel Horan, *Postmodernity and Univocity: A Critical Account of Radical Orthodoxy and John Duns Scotus* (Minneapolis: Fortress Press, 2014), 97–98.

creatures univocally, the Subtle Doctor (Scotus) was not in fact engaging in Heideggerian "onto-theology." Rather, what Scotus proposed was that "being" as a predicate was merely a label that signified that an entity existed. Hence, insofar as both God and creatures existed, "being" could be predicated of them both equally.[34] This does not put creatures and God on the same ontic level (as Gregory and many other charge), because what Scotus was merely claiming was that saying that something "is" tells us nothing about an entity's metaphysical status.[35] Hence, the univocity of being that Scotus spoke of was only one of predication (i.e., it was purely linguistic), and not one of an ontological property shared by God and his creatures in an absolutely identical fashion.[36]

Seen from this perspective, it could be argued that the historic Thomistic criticism of Scotus's univocity (embodied in Gregory and Milbank's critiques) is merely a matter of reading the premises of one's own position into the thought of one's opponent. That is to say, if being is a transcendental property (as Thomism has historically claimed[37]) then univocal predication of it between God and creatures would indeed make God a being among beings. Nevertheless, if being is merely a label, qualified by "created" or "uncreated" (as Cross interprets Scotus), then this critique would appear to miss the mark.

Beyond this dichotomy, Cross shows significant continuities between the positions of Aquinas and Scotus. He demonstrates through extensive citations from Scotus's work *Ordinatio*, that on an ontological (rather than linguistic) level, God for the Subtle Doctor is in a very real sense "being" and "goodness" itself and creatures possess these realities only by participation.[38] Therefore, according to Cross's reading of the data, there is in truth little difference between Scotus and Thomas in the realm of ontology. The difference primarily lies within the realm of linguistic theory.[39] As Cross writes: "The difference is

---

34 Cross, "Duns Scotus, Suárez," 90–91. Although Scotus discusses the univocity of being in several of his works, his most expansive discussion can be found in his commentary on Peter Lombard's *Sentences* titled *Ordinatio*. See his basic definition and discussion of univocity in: John Duns Scotus, *Ordinatio* 1.3, in *Omnia Opera* (Civitas Vaticana: Typis Polyglottis Vaticanis, 1950–2013), 3:16–20.

35 Cross, "Duns Scotus, Suárez," 90–91.

36 Cross, "Duns Scotus, Suárez," 92.

37 See W. Norris Clark, *The One and the Many: A Contemporary Thomistic Metaphysics* (South Bend, IN: University of Notre Dame Press, 2016), 25–91.

38 Cross, "Duns Scotus, Suárez," 92.

39 Cross, "Duns Scotus, Suárez," 92. Robert Sweetman actually goes so far as to state that from a certain perspective Scotus could be viewed as a legitimate continuer of Aquinas. See Robert Sweetman, "Univocity, Analogy and the Mystery of Being According to John Duns Scotus" in *Introducing Radical Orthodoxy: Mapping a Post-Secular Theology*, ed. James K.A. Smith (Grand Rapids: Baker Academic, 2005), 83–85.

that Scotus does not build the notion of imitation into his univocity theory [as Aquinas did], which remains in itself a merely semantic theory."[40]

This of course raises the question as to why Scotus would reject analogical predication in favor of a univocal mode of predication. According to Cross, Scotus claimed that certainty of deductions can only be achieved with univocal, rather than analogical signifiers.[41] This is an important issue for Scotus because, much like Aquinas, he believed that theologians should be able to engage divine revelation using the tools of logic.[42] In the mind of the Subtle Doctor, analogical terms are intrinsically uncertain terms, and therefore would not yield certain and rational conclusions if used in syllogisms. Ultimately, if the words that we apply to God are similar, yet infinitely different from the way that they are applied to creatures (analogical predication),[43] then the question arises as to whether these terms are being used equivocally: is not the logical implication of the "infinite difference" that the signifier bears no real resemblance to the signified at all? For this reason, Scotus asserts that without univocal terms, no meaningful thought about God would be possible and the rational character of theology would be almost completely compromised.[44] In all this, it should also be borne in mind that Scotus is reacting less to Aquinas's work and more to that of Henry of Ghent, who claimed that predication of the same terms when applied to God and creatures was not merely analogical, but equivocal.[45] It should also be noted Cross's interpretation of Scotus has recently also been corroborated by both Thomas Williams and Daniel Huran.[46]

Cross's well-documented alternative reading of Scotus raises a number of issues with Gregory's interpretation. First, in light of the extent of Cross's scholarship on Scotus, and his extensive documentation of his position directly from Scotus's works (something largely missing from Gregory's book), it is deeply puzzling that Gregory feels little need to engage Cross. Second, it should be granted that Gregory could claim that he is not dealing with what Scotus taught per se, but with how Scotus was received and appropriated by his

40 Cross, "Duns Scotus, Suárez," 92.

41 Cross, "Duns Scotus, Suárez," 93–94.

42 Cross, "Duns Scotus, Suárez," 93–94.

43 The Fourth Lateran Council's famous description of *analogia entis*. See Heinrich Denzinger, *The Sources of Catholic Dogma*, trans. Roy Deferrari (St. Louis: Herder, 1957), 171.

44 Cross, "Duns Scotus, Suárez," 93.

45 Ulrich Leinsle makes roughly the same points as Cross. See Leinsle, *Scholastic Theology*, 213–14. Also see Robert Sweetman's similar although distinct points on the relationship in Sweetman, "Duns Scotus," 78–82.

46 See Daniel Horan, *Postmodernity and Univocity*, 157–88; Thomas Williams, "The Doctrine of Univocity Is True and Salutary," *Modern Theology* 21, no. 4 (2005): 575–85.

interpreters in the later Middle Ages and early Modern period. Nevertheless, in *The Unintended Reformation* he makes no distinction between Scotus's reception and actual teaching. Moreover, he makes no effort to demonstrate with historical data the extent of Scotus's influence, or the nature of his reception. Finally, as we will demonstrate, there is evidence that Scotus and his doctrine of the univocity of being were interpreted in the early Modern period in a manner similar to Gregory's interpretation. Nevertheless, Scotus's position was rejected for precisely this reason.

4 The Univocity of Being and the Reformation[47]

Irrespective of the origins of the onto-theological tendencies of modern thought, there is, contrary to Gregory's claim, little or no evidence that the Protestant Reformers or the later Protestant Scholastics had much to do with the creation or promotion of these trends.

First, in the later Middle Ages and the early Modern period, there were numerous schools of thought, most of which did not directly stand in the tradition of Scotus or his metaphysical views.[48] Moreover, because of the variety of metaphysical options available in the late Middle Ages, the Protestant Reformers who had philosophical and theological training[49] hailed from a number of different philosophical and theological traditions: Martin Luther: Augustinian and Nominalist;[50] Ulrich Zwingli: Thomist and Scotist;[51] Nicholas

---

47 See similar arguments and discussion in this section in: Jack Kilcrease, "Johann Gerhard's Reception of Thomas Aquinas's *Analogia Entis*," in *Aquinas among the Protestants*, ed. Manfred Svensson and David VanDrunen (Oxford: Wiley-Blackwell, 2018), 118–21.

48 Alister McGrath, *The Intellectual Origins of the Reformation* (Malden, MA: Blackwell Publishers, 2004), 18–28, 67–116.

49 I do not mention Calvin or Melanchthon on this list because they were primarily humanists. The sources of Calvin's thought are a hotly debated. See: Richard Muller, *The Unaccommodated Calvin: Studies in the Foundations of a Theological Tradition* (Oxford: Oxford University Press, 2001). Below, we will engage in a more extensive discussion of Melanchthon's use of neo-Aristotelianism.

50 Paul Althaus, *The Theology of Martin Luther*, trans. Robert Schultz (Philadelphia: Fortress Press, 1966), 16–19, 31–33, 51–53, 64–71, 123–25, 387–90; B.A. Gerrish, *Grace and Reason: A Study in the Theology of Luther* (Eugene, OR: Wipf & Stock Publishers, 2005); Bernhard Lohse, *Martin Luther's Theology: Its Historical and Systematic Development*, trans. and ed. Roy A. Harrisville (Minneapolis: Fortress Press, 1999), 196–207.

51 August Baur, *Zwinglis Theologie: Ihr Werden und Ihr System* (Zurich: Georg Olms Verlag, 1983–4), 1:19–26; G.R. Potter, *Zwingli* (Cambridge, UK: Cambridge University Press, 1976), 18–19, 111, 150; W.P. Stephens, *The Theology of Huldrych Zwingli* (Oxford: Clarendon Press, 1986), 6, 23–25, 222–23.

von Amsdorf: Scotist;[52] Martin Bucer: Thomist;[53] Peter Martyr Vermigli: Thomist;[54] Andreas Karlstadt: Thomist.[55] Hence, contrary to what some might imply, the Reformers are not somehow heirs to Scotism simply because they were chronologically later than the Subtle Doctor.

In light of such inherent diversity of theological perspectives, a number of things should be observed. First, among the Reformers, there appears to have been little direct correlation between their confessional commitment and their philosophical school. From this it follows that attributing the emergence of certain Reformation doctrines to specific metaphysical commitments is highly problematic. Second, although this list is by no means exhaustive, among this sample of the major Reformers, few were Scotists or even Ockhamists. Indeed, many were strongly influenced by the Thomistic tradition. In light of such influence, it would be difficult to impute an overwhelming influence of Scotistic univocity to the major architects of key Reformation theological concepts.

Moreover, one would be hard pressed to find many lengthy discussions of the question of univocity and analogy in the works of the Magisterial Reformers. As we will see, Gregory is unable to cite any passages in the Reformers that affirm the univocity of being. The focus of the Reformers' writings is generally on the subject of soteriology and its practical effects on the reform of the Church. To the extent that they engaged metaphysical question, their writings predictably follow pre-Reformation medieval models from various schools.[56] In this, they are not always completely consistent. Luther, in spite of his Ockhamist background, even appears to have indirectly affirmed the analogy of being in his treatment of God's positive attributes in the *Heidelberg Disputation* of 1518.[57]

Turning to the later Protestant Scholastics, Richard Muller has recently surveyed a significant number of Reformed Protestant authors of the era on the

52 Martin Brecht, *Martin Luther: His Road to Reformation*, 1483–1521 (Philadelphia: Fortress Press, 1985), 167–68; Robert Kolb, *Nicholas von Amsdorf: Champion of Luther's Reformation* (St. Louis: Concordia Publishing House, 2019), 12.

53 Martin Greschat, *Martin Bucer: A Reformer and His Times* (Louisville: Westminster/ John Knox Press, 2004), 22.

54 Luca Baschera, "Zwischen Philosophie und Theologie: Aspekte der Aristoteles-Auslegung Peter Martyr Vermiglis," in *Konfession, Migration und Elitenbildung: Studien zur Theologenausbildung des 16. Jahrhunderts*, eds. Herman Selderhuis and Markus Wriedt, (Leiden: Brill, 2007), 85–97; J.C. McClelland, "Calvinism Perfecting Thomism: Peter Marytr Vermigli's Question," *Scottish Journal of Theology* 31, no. 6 (1978): 571–78.

55 Euan Cameron, *The European Reformation* (Oxford: Oxford University Press, 2012), 121.

56 See discussion in: Richard Muller, *Post-Reformation Dogmatics: The Rise and Development of Reformed Orthodoxy, ca. 1520 to ca. 1725* (Grand Rapids: Baker Academic, 2003), 1:1:270–310, 1:360–405.

57 See comments in WA 1:363; *LW* 31:55.

issue of analogy and univocity. He documents that most of these theologians accept the analogy of being, as well as the stock criticisms of the Thomistic tradition of the univocity of being.[58] This means that they largely interpret Scotus's concept of the univocity of being in the same manner that Gregory does, and therefore reject it on the same grounds. Ultimately, Muller demonstrates that with some very few exceptions, there is no evidence that early modern Reformed theology was based on an assumption of the univocity of being, or in any way promoted the concept. He writes: "The large number of Reformed denials of univocity of being calls into question both the positive and the negative readings of the Reformation as foundationally Scotist in its philosophical directions."[59] Muller further concludes:

> Against the negative approach of Radical Orthodoxy and [Brad] Gregory, we offer a significantly firmer verdict. Whatever one concludes concerning the implications of the univocity of being, the claim that the concept invested itself in Protestant theology cannot be sustained, nor indeed that early modern Protestant thought evidenced a "shift" away from a "metaphysics of participation." In short, their claim that the absorption of the concept of the univocity of being into early modern Protestantism accounts for the perceived problems of twentieth and twenty-first century secular culture is seen to be a sorry imposture.[60]

By no means is Muller alone in his conclusions about the Reformed Scholastic tradition's acceptance of an essentially Thomistic account of ontology. In the 1970s, John Patrick Donnelly famously showed an enormous Thomistic influence on Reformed Scholastic metaphysics, going so far as to dub the phenomenon "Calvinist Thomism."[61]

On the Lutheran side of Protestant Scholasticism, one finds a very similar situation. During and after the Hoffmann Controversy (1598–1601), which centered on the compatibility of faith and philosophy,[62] Jakob Martini of the University of Wittenberg developed an elaborate analogical account of human

58 See the aforementioned Muller, "Not Scotist," 127–50.

59 Muller, "Not Scotist," 146.

60 Muller, "Not Scotist," 146.

61 John Patrick Donnelly, "Calvinist Thomism," *Viator: Medieval and Renaissance Studies* 7 (1976): 441–55.

62 Georg Christian Bernhard Pünjer, *History of the Christian Philosophy of Religion from the Reformation to Kant*, trans. W. Hastie (Edinburgh: T & T Clark, 1887), 178–90; Joar Haga, *Was there a Lutheran Metaphysics?: The Interpretation of the Communicatio Idiomatum in Early Modern Lutheranism* (Göttingen: Vandenhoek & Ruprecht, 2012), 196–202, 213.

conceptual language about God.[63] Like Aquinas, Martini sees analogy of being as based on an analogy of attribution, rather than proportion.[64] In many respects, this mirrored Martini's Thomistic account of faith and reason (reason as a first stage of knowledge about God, fulfilled and transcended by revelation) that he pressed against Daniel Hoffmann and his insistence that statements of philosophy and theology could contradict one another. In the aftermath of the controversy, Lutheran theologians by and large sided with Martini against Hoffmann on the question of faith and reason, and also widely accepted his view of analogy. Consequently, the theologians of what Robert Preus refers to as the "Silver Age"[65] of Lutheran Scholasticism (that is, the period immediately following the Thirty Years War, notably the time of Abraham Calov and Johannes Andreas Quenstedt) adopted an analogical concept of Scripture's language about God.[66]

One exception to the consensus of Lutheran Scholastic Orthodoxy on the issue of the analogy of being can be found in the highly influential Johann Gerhard (1582–1637).[67] Nevertheless, Gerhard does not argue in favor of the univocity of being, but rather rejects both analogy and univocity. God is infinite and eternal and therefore utterly different from his creation and, consequently, analogy is not a genuine possibility.[68] At this point, Gerhard actually goes so far as to quote the Eastern Church Father John of Damascus, an advocate of views influenced by Pseudo-Dionysius (God is "essence beyond essence"). Gerhard argues that God is utterly different from his creatures because "… there is no proportion between the infinite and the finite." In other words, to say that there is a similarity between God and his creatures within an infinite dissimilarity makes all language dependent on a perceived similarity between God and his creatures impossible. Infinite dissimilarity will ultimately trump whatever similarity one can find between human and divine wisdom, power, or goodness. God is absolutely unique and therefore all predicates are uniquely attributed to him without analogy. In using the example of how "spirit" is normally predicated of angels and God he writes: "Therefore this [the predicate of

63 See Jakob Martini, *Partitiones & Quaestiones Metaphysicae* (Wittenberg, 1615), 636. Also see discussion in Robert Preus, *The Theology of Post-Reformation Lutheranism*, (St. Louis: Concordia Publishing House, 1970–72), 2:39–40.

64 Preus, *Post-Reformation Lutheranism*, 2:40.

65 Preus, *Post-Reformation Lutheranism*, 1:45–46.

66 Preus, *Post-Reformation Lutheranism*, 2:41–43.

67 See similar and larger discussion in: Kilcrease, "Johann Gerhard," 120–23.

68 Johann Gerhard, *On the Nature of God and On the Most Holy Mystery of the Trinity*, trans. Richard Dinda (St. Louis: Concordia Publishing House, 2007), 93.

"spirit"] is predicated of God not only [as one who is] excellent but [as one who is] completely unique."[69]

At this point, many advocates of analogy might suggest that Gerhard is being unfair both to Aquinas and the Thomistic tradition. First, it should be observed that in his treatment of the divine being in the *Summa*, Aquinas shares with Gerhard and the Eastern Fathers apophatism.[70] Nonetheless, for Aquinas this fact does not rule out analogy. As we saw earlier, even if God is infinitely different and therefore incomprehensible in relationship to his creatures, creation still remains an expression of his will and transcendental attributes. Consequently, it is only logical to think that it bears some analogical resemblance to God. From this it could be argued that Gerhard is not genuinely grappling with Aquinas's position.

Second, although Gerhard directly quotes Thomas, he seems to assume a concept of analogy greatly at odds with how contemporary scholars interpret the Angelic Doctor's (Aquinas') version of the doctrine. Gerhard interprets analogy in terms of Cajetan's analogy of proportion. Analogy of proportion refers to the idea that analogy is established by the fact that God is infinitely what the creature is finitely. Hence there is a similarity or analogy between God and creatures based on their proportion of being. Within Gerhard's historical context, this makes a great deal of sense, in that Cajetan's was a popular interpretation of Aquinas in the early Modern period.[71]

Gerhard's own solution to the problem of the language of attribution is in many ways rather novel. He invokes Augustine's distinction between "knowing" and "comprehending,"[72] although he mainly cites a number of Eastern Fathers in support of this conceptual distinction. God and his attributes are knowable from the words the Bible applies to him. That being said, although we can know that these words truthfully apply to God, we cannot fully comprehend how they apply to him due to the infinite chasm between creator and creature. Nevertheless, we can know their meaning well enough from how Scripture uses them so as to be able to speak about God in an intelligent way in our doctrinal formulations.[73] Ultimately, all this suggests that although Gerhard rejected the analogy of being, he did so only because he misunderstood it as promoting a form of onto-theology.

---

69 Gerhard, *On God and the Trinity*, 93.

70 ST 1a, q. 12, art. 1–13; BF 3:2–45.

71 Placher, *The Domestication of Transcendence: How Modern Thinking about God Went Wrong* (Louisville: Westminster John Knox, 1996), 71–74.

72 Gerhard, *On God and the Trinity*, 95. See discussion in Gerard O'Daly, *Augustine's Philosophy of Mind* (Berkley: University of California Press, 1987), 213–16.

73 Gerhard, *On God and the Trinity*, 94–95. See discussion in Preus, 2:47.

In light of what we have observed, Gregory has very few grounds for claiming that the Reformers or their heirs were promoters of Scotist univocity. Indeed, Gregory makes very little effort to support his contention that the Reformers were promoters of the univocity of being with direct citations from their works. Rather, more often than not he simply asserts that they were.

Gregory's only attempt to connect the Reformers directly to the doctrine of univocity is in a very brief and strained argument about the origins of Zwinglian Eucharistic theology. According to Gregory, Zwingli's rejection of the real presence was based on the univocity of being:

> Whether it was explicitly recognized by its protagonists or not, the denial that Jesus could be *really* present in the Eucharist—which is particularly clear, for example, in Zwingli's spatial dichotomizing of Jesus's divine and human natures, and the claim that "he sits at the right hand of the Father, has left the world, is no longer among us"—is the logical corollary of metaphysical univocity. A "spiritual" *presence* that is contrasted with a real presence presupposes an either-or dichotomy between a crypto-spatial God and the natural world that precludes divine immanence in its desire to preserve divine transcendence.[74]

Gregory's statement is problematic for a number of reasons. First, he does not give sufficient documentation for interpreting Zwingli's motivations as being rooted in a belief in metaphysical univocity. Indeed, although Gregory contends that Zwingli's view of the Eucharist implies an understanding of God in spatial terms, all he actually succeeds in showing is Zwingli's attempt to uphold the historic Christian claim that Christ as God is omnipresent and as man is circumscribed. Omnipresence, as Gregory is certainly aware, does not mean spatial extension.

Second, as is well documented, in Zwingli's Eucharistic theology, his major concern was not in interpreting God's reality in spatial terms, but rather in defending Christ's humanity. He affirmed that if Christ's body was real (as the Chalcedonian formula claimed), then it must follow the laws of circumscription like other bodies. The alternative would be a revival of Eutychianism.[75] For many, this will of course be seen as a highly flawed understanding of the

74 Gregory, *Unintended Reformation*, 42–43.

75 See in particular the following writings by Zwingli: Ulrich Zwingli, "A Friendly Exegesis, That is, Exposition of the Eucharist," in *Huldrych Zwingli: Writings*, trans E.J. Furcha and H. Wayne Pipkin (Allison Park, PA: Pickwick Publications, 1984), 2: 251–55, 2:301–3, 314–15, 337–38. Also see the following discussions in W.P. Stephans, *Huldrych Zwingli* (New York: St. Martin's Press, 1977), 100; W.P. Stephans, *The Theology of Huldrych Zwingli* (Oxford:

communicatio idiomatum. That being said, it has little to do with the univocity of being.

Third, many medieval theologians questioned the real presence of Christ in the Eucharist long before Zwingli. This raises the question: If rejection of the real presence necessarily implies an acceptance of the univocity of being, then why did Ratramnus, Gottschalk,[76] and Berengar[77] also do so when they lacked Scotus as an intellectual resource? Perhaps Gregory would contend that the rejection of the real presence does not necessarily suggest an acceptance of the univocity of being, but Zwingli's particular arguments against the real presence of Christ do. Nevertheless, Gregory makes very little effort to demonstrate that Zwingli's objections to the real presence were fundamentally different from these earlier figures, or that these objections were in some special way based on the univocity of being.

Finally, Gregory ignores Luther's championing of the real presence against Zwingli,[78] as well as Calvin's attempt to create a mediating position in the form of what John Nevin in his classic study of the subject correctly called "the mystical presence."[79] Therefore, even if Zwingli really were deeply influenced by the notion of the univocity of being in his Eucharistic theology, there is little evidence that any of the other Reformers were. Since these other Reformers' positions became the basis of the major confessional traditions of the Protestant world[80] and Zwingli's was not, any alleged Zwinglian/Scotist connection sinks into the mire of irrelevance for much of early Modern Protestantism and its

---

Clarendon Press, 1986), 243–44; and W.P. Stephans, *Zwingli: An Introduction to His Thought* (Oxford: Clarendon Press, 1992), 100–103.

76 See discussion in Celia Chazelle, "The Eucharist in Early Medieval Europe," in *A Companion to the Eucharist in the Middle Ages*, ed. Ian Levy, Gary Macy, and Kristen Van Ausdall (Leiden: Brill, 2012), 205–50.

77 See A.J. Macdonald, *Berengar and the Reform of Sacramental Doctrine* (London: Longmans, Green, 1930).

78 See the masterful (if slightly outdated) analysis of Herman Sasse, *This Is My Body: Luther's Contention for the Real Presence in the Sacrament of the Altar* (Eugene, OR: Wipf & Stock, 2001).

79 John Nevin, *The Mystical Presence: A Vindication of the Reformed or Calvinistic Doctrine of the Holy Eucharist* (Eugene, OR: Wipf & Stock Publishers, 2000).

80 Both the Consensus Tigurinus and the other Reformed confessions bear the mark of Calvin more than Zwingli. See Jan Rohls, *The Reformed Confessions: Theology from Zurich to Barmen* (Louisville: Westminster/John Knox, 1998), 219–36. Likewise, the Formula of Concord reflects Luther's own sacramental views. See discussion in James Nestingen, Robert Kolb, and Charles Arand, *The Lutheran Confessions: History and Theology of the Book of Concord* (Minneapolis: Fortress Press, 2012), 227–54. Also see Timothy Wengert, *A Formula for Parish Practice: Using the Formula of Concord in Congregations* (Grand Rapids: Wm. B. Eerdmans, 2006), 125–36.

effects on Western metaphysics. If most forms of the Magisterial Reformation rejected a Eucharistic theology supposedly based on the univocity of being, how can the Reformation have been a major conduit for the promotion of onto-theology? For these reasons, Gregory's argument simply does not add up.

5 The Reformation and Aristotelianism

Beyond Gregory's contention that the Reformation promoted the univocity of being, he also argues that the Reformers helped give rise to modern Naturalism and Scientism by their rejection of Aristotelianism. According to Gregory, because Protestants attacked Aristotle, the Catholic Church was forced to double down on his philosophy at the Council of Trent and in the Baroque Scholasticism that emerged from the Counter-Reformation.[81]

Gregory argues that as a result of its continuing commitment to Aristotle the Roman Catholic Church was made to appear regressive and anti-scientific when the Scientific Revolution of the seventeenth century finally overturned the authority of the Philosopher. Because of its initial resistance to the Scientific Revolution, secular intellectuals were driven away from the Church of Rome. This not only had the negative effect of separating Catholicism from the high intellectual culture of the West, but it impeded the integration of the new scientific discoveries with existing Church dogma.[82]

Gregory appears to be making a generalization about the Reformation and Protestantism based on the attitude of the young Luther. We observed something similar in reading univocity into Zwingli's doctrine of the Eucharist and then imputing his supposed onto-theological tendencies to the whole of the Magisterial Reformation. In the *Heidelberg Disputation* (1518) and his *Disputation against Scholastic Theology* (1518), Luther did indeed attack Aristotle, along with the Scholastic theology that he had inspired.[83] Luther believed that the Philosopher's ethical theories were particularly pernicious when applied to the divine-human relationship.[84] Although this dislike of Aristotle in soteriological matters was generally shared by the other Reformers, the young Luther had a negative opinion of him on virtually all subjects.[85]

81 Gregory, *Unintended Reformation*, 45–46.
82 Gregory, *Unintended Reformation*, 45–46.
83 See Theodor Dieter, *Der junge Luther und Aristoteles: Eine historisch-systematische Untersuchung zum Verhältnis von Theologie und Philosophie* (Berlin: Walter De Gruyter, 2001).
84 WA 1: 221–28; *LW* 31:9–15.
85 WA 1:355; *LW* 31:41–42. Also see WA 6: 457–58; *LW* 44:200–201.

Nevertheless, Luther's negative opinion of Aristotle was by no means universally shared with other early Modern Protestants. For example, the young Melanchthon aspired to edit a critical edition of Aristotle's works from the original Greek sources.[86] Despite some initial resistance from Luther,[87] Melanchthon successfully made Aristotle the cornerstone of instruction at Wittenberg after the 1530s.[88] He defended this decision in his *Oratio de Aristotle* (1544).[89] Melanchthon and his colleagues edited a series of compendiums of the works of Aristotle that served as an important basis of education in Germany throughout the seventeenth century.[90] As a result of Melanchthon's influence, Lutherans of the sixteenth and seventeenth centuries generally conducted their theological debates using the terminology of Aristotelian metaphysics.[91] The Lutheran Formula of Concord is replete with Aristotelian terminology, particularly in the sections on Original Sin.[92]

Protestant Scholasticism of the seventeenth century (of both the Lutheran and Reformed varieties) used a wide variety of ontological and philosophical resources,[93] but most prominently they relied on Aristotelianism as their basic framework of operation.[94] Hence, Gregory's claim of an almost wholesale Protestant rejection of Aristotle is false. Likewise, his explanation that the Council of Trent and Baroque Catholicism continued their commitment to

86 Ozment, *Age of Reform*, 311.

87 Ozment, *Age of Reform*, 310. Also see: Wilhelm Link, *Das Ringen um die Freiheit der Theologie von der Philosophie* (Munich: C. Kaiser, 1955).

88 See for example the case of Melanchthon in the following: Nicole Kuropka, "Melanchthon and Aristotle," in *Philip Melanchthon: Theologian in Classroom, Confession, and Controversy*, ed. Irene Dingel, Robert Kolb, Nicole Kuropka, Timothy Wengert (Göttingen: Vandenhöck & Ruprecht, 2012), 19–28; Sachiko Kusukawa, *The Transformation of Natural Philosophy: The Case of Philip Melanchthon* (Cambridge, UK: Cambridge University Press, 2006).

89 Philipp Melanchthon, "Oratio de Aristotele," in *Melanchthons Werke*, ed. R. Stupperich (Gütersloh: Verlagshaus Gerd Mohn, 1951–55), 3:122–34.

90 Jaroslav Pelikan, *From Luther to Kierkegaard: A Study in Historical Theology* (St. Louis: Concordia Publishing House, 1963), 51.

91 See discussion of the effects of neo-Aristotelianism in: Peter Petersen, *Geschichte der aristotelischen Philosophie im protestantischen Deutschland* (Leipzig: F. Meiner, 1921); Walter Sparn, *Wiederkehr der Metaphysik: Die Ontologische Frage in der Lutherischen Theologie des frühen 17. Jahrhunderts* (Stuttgart: Calwer, 1976); Max Wundt, *Die deutsche Schulmetaphysik des 17. Jahrhunderts* (Tübingen: J.C.B. Mohr, 1939).

92 Eric Gritsch and Robert Jenson, *Lutheranism: The Theological Movement and Its Confessional Writings* (Philadelphia: Fortress Press, 1976), 60–61.

93 Muller, *Post-Reformation Dogmatics*, 1:371–82.

94 Muller, *Post-Reformation Dogmatics*, 1:371–82. Also see the appropriation of Aristotelianism in various Lutheran scholastic authors in Preus, 1:77–79, 1:115–16, 1:130–32, 1:159–60, 1:195–96, 1:202–3, 1:238–39.

Aristotelianism purely as a reaction to Protestantism must also be judged to be false.

Another narrative regarding the role of Aristotelianism that Gregory promotes echoes that of the contemporary Roman Catholic philosopher Alasdair MacIntyre.[95] MacIntyre has asserted that Aristotelian virtue ethics (as promoted by Aquinas and the medieval Church) were definitively rejected by the Reformation. Both Gregory and MacIntye claim that because the Reformers' believed in the total fallenness of human nature they assumed that training in virtue was impossible.[96] Part of the problem with the position of Gregory and MacIntyre is that they seem to rest on a generalization about the Reformation based on the young Luther's negative remarks about the role of virtues in the divine-human relationship. As some have shown, Luther did not reject the concept of virtue entirely, but rather limited Aristotle's ethical ideas to a role in promoting civil order and righteousness.[97]

Moreover, Gregory's and MacIntyre's claims about Luther and the other Magisterial Reformers' views of fallen human agency do not take into consideration a series of important distinctions they made. First, Luther believed that regarding the divine-human relationship ("things above us"), human beings were incapacitated in their ability to establish or promote their relationship with God. In the relationship with other human beings ("things below us"), humans can make moral and rational choices. While these external deeds do not in any way establish or promote a good relationship with God, they do make for good citizenship.[98]

This distinction also feeds into another distinction that Luther makes between "two kinds of righteousness." Humans have a "passive righteousness" wherein through faith they inertly receive God's justifying judgment for the sake of Christ and are therefore seen as just by God (*coram Deo*). Since humans are morally impotent in their relationship with him, they can only receive righteousness before God (*coram Deo*) passively. In the sphere of freedom and rational agency ("that which is below us"), humans can actively perform

---

95 See Alasdair MacIntyre, *A Short History of Ethics: A History of Moral Philosophy from the Homeric Age to the Twentieth Century* (London: Routledge, 1998), 118, 122; Alasdair MacIntyre, *After Virtue: A Study in Moral Theory* (South Bend, IN: University of Notre Dame Press, 2007), 53.

96 Gregory, *Unintended Reformation*, 206–8.

97 See discussion in: Ivar Asheim, "Lutherische Tugendethik," *Neue Zeitschrift für Systematische Theologie und Religionsphilosophie* 40, no. 3 (1998): 242–50.

98 WA 18:634–39; *LW* 33:64–70. See good discussion in Gerhard Forde, *The Captivation of the Will: Luther vs. Erasmus on Freedom and Bondage* (Grand Rapids: Wm. B. Eerdmans, 2005), 47–59.

righteousness and can possess an "active righteousness."[99] This likewise means that they can be trained to pursue certain behaviors that are more virtuous than others. Although we cannot go into detail here, Calvin and the young Melanchthon shared this same essential ethical/anthropological outlook as Luther.[100]

Hence, there is a fundamental category confusion in this critique of Gregory and MacIntyre. Essentially, these authors have made the mistake of applying what Luther and many of the other Reformers say about the inner person (and his or her relationship to God) to the external person and its capacity to engage in specific moral decisions within the kingdom of the world.

Beyond these difficulties, there is the additional problem of the overwhelming evidence that both the Lutheran and Reformed traditions taught and promoted Aristotelian virtue ethics. Within the Lutheran tradition, Philip Melanchthon believed that along with the Ten Commandments, Aristotle's ethics were a good guide to civil righteousness. For this reason, he promoted Aristotelian virtue ethics through his commentaries on Aristotle's *Politics* and his *Nicomachean Ethics*.[101] As noted, Melanchthon's works on Aristotle were extremely influential in Germany.

Similarly, in the Scandinavian context, one can point to the influential work of Niels Hemmingsen, a Danish student of Melanchthon.[102] In his *On the Law of Nature*, Hemmingsen devotes an entire chapter to expounding the cardinal virtues (prudence, justice, courage, and temperance).[103] Hemmingsen affirms that the promotion and development of the cardinal virtues are absolutely necessary for a healthy civil order.[104]

Parallel to these developments in the Lutheran tradition, the Reformed theologian Peter Martyr Vermigli also wrote a lengthy commentary on the

99 See: WA 2:144–52; *LW* 31:297–306. Robert Kolb, "Luther on the Two Kinds of Righteousness; Reflections on His Two-dimensional Definition of Humanity at the Heart of His Theology," *Lutheran Quarterly* 13, no. 4 (1999): 449–66.

100 John Calvin, *The Bondage and Liberation of the Will: A Defense of the Orthodox Doctrine of Human Choice against Pighius*, trans. G.I. Davies (Grand Rapids: Baker Academic, 2002), 29; Philip Melanchthon, "Loci Communes: 1521," in *Melanchthon and Bucer*, ed. Wilhelm Pauck (Philadelphia: The Westminster Press, 1959), 26–27.

101 Kuropka, "Melanchthon and Aristotle," 26–27. Gregory mentions Melanchthon's positive assessment of Aristotle's ethics, but gives it little weight.

102 Eric Lund, "Baltic and Nordic Lutheranism," in *Lutheran Ecclesiastical Culture: 1550–1665*, ed. Robert Kolb (Leiden: Brill, 2008), 419.

103 Niels Hemmingsen, *On the Law of Nature: A Demonstrative Method*, trans. E.J. Hutchinson (Grand Rapids: CLP Academic, 2018), 103–64.

104 Hemmingsen, *Law of Nature*, 103–5.

Nicomachean Ethics.[105] As Sabastian Rehnman demonstrates, Vermigli distinguishes between "acquired" and "infused" virtues in a manner almost identical to Thomas Aquinas.[106] The cardinal virtues of which Aristotle spoke are the acquired virtues. Human beings are capable of developing these virtues within themselves through right practice. They are useful for civil righteousness, although not for righteousness before God.[107] For righteousness before him, one must possess those virtues communicated by grace that Paul speaks of in 1 Corinthians 13:13: faith, hope, and love. These virtues cannot be developed by humans but are received through God's grace.[108] The only major difference between Vermigli and Aquinas here appears to be that Vermigli (in the manner of the Reformers) views faith as primarily trust in the gospel, rather than the ability to believe supernaturally revealed truths with full credulity (as Aquinas taught).

Although we do not have the space for an exhaustive examination of all the evidence for the Protestant use of virtue ethics, it is clear, at a minimum, from the examples of Melanchthon, Vermigli and Hemmingsen, that the picture is far more complex than Gregory makes it out to be. That is to say, what we have very clearly established is that some influential figures of the first and second generations of the Reformation accepted and promoted virtue ethics. In his treatment of Vermigli, Rehnmann goes a step further, firmly stating that:

> ... Vermigli is not alone among confessional Protestants to take this position. For the same argument could be developed from Philip Melanchthon, Lambert Daneau, Andreas Hyperius, Rudolph Goclenius, Bartholomeus Keckermann, Franco Burgersdijk, Christoph Lüthard, William Pemble, Antonius Waleus, Peter van Mastricht and other.[109]

With such a large number of Reformation era theologians and Protestant Scholastics who accepted and promoted Aristotelian virtue ethics, it is difficult not to conclude that the picture Gregory is offering is false.

---

105 Pietro Martire Vermigli, *In primum, secundum et initium tertii libri Ethicorum Aristotelis ad Nicomachum commentarius*, ed. Guilio Santerenziano, Luca Baschera and Christopher Moser (Leiden: Brill, 2011).

106 Sabastian Rehnman, "Virtue and Grace," *Studies in Christian Ethics* 25, no. 4 (2012): 481–88.

107 Rehnman, "Virtue and Grace," 483–85.

108 Rehnman, "Virtue and Grace," 476–83.

109 Rehnman, "Virtue and Grace," 488.

6 Conclusion

It should be clear from this short survey that Gregory's claims frequently lack evidence. Indeed, in many cases, a significant amount of positive evidence exists against them. Many contemporary scholars agree that Scotus did not teach the univocity of being in the manner that Gregory and others have claimed he did. If Gregory disagrees with their interpretation, he should at a very minimum have mounted an argument why contemporary scholarship on the subject is wrong. What seems even clearer is that to the extent that the Subtle Doctor was understood during the early Modern period in a manner similar to that of Gregory, he was rejected almost universally by Protestant theologians.

With regard to Aristotelianism, Protestants like their Catholic contemporaries used Aristotle as an ancillary philosophy, albeit it in ways modified by their commitment to key Reformation principles. This is particularly the case with regard to Aristotle's virtue ethics, which a significant number of Protestant theologians and ethicists held to be essential for civil righteousness. Taken together, these facts significantly challenge the picture of Reformation theology and its relationship to medieval philosophical heritage painted by Gregory and others.

CHAPTER 16

Ad normam veritatis christianae: Correcting Aristotle in Protestant Commentaries on the *Nicomachean Ethics*

Manfred Svensson

1 Introduction[1]

Two competing prejudices have plagued the study of Protestant Aristotelianism. One is the narrative that describes the Reformation as a complete break with the Aristotelian tradition (if not with the classical heritage as a whole).[2] This view competes with its portrayal as a derailed return to Aristotelian method, ultimately leading to a Protestant scholasticism that loses its connection with the living faith of the church.[3] The student of Protestant Aristotelianism thus has to confront two incompatible objections: the subject of his study does not exist, and—if it exists—it is dull and perhaps even damaging to the faith. The first of these objections is of course easier to reject, and it has been debunked numerous times. Even a cursory glance at the titles that Protestants were publishing throughout the sixteenth and seventeenth century reveals that the suggestion of a break with the tradition is untenable. Correcting the impression of a sterile and endless repetition of already surpassed theses is a more demanding, but also more rewarding task.

Such a task can be undertaken in several ways. One can show, for instance, that commenting on Aristotle's *corpus* has regularly been a place not for tedious repetition, but for fertile discussion and for the advancement of new positions. This is a well-known phenomenon in medieval intellectual life, and it undoubtedly continued to be the case in the early modern Aristotelian tradition, as Protestants struggled with tensions within the Western philosophical

---

1 Research for this article was possible thanks to the funding of Fondecyt Project nr. 1170628. "De Felipe Melanchthon a Johannes Eisenhart: La distinción entre lo justo legal y lo justo natural en los tempranos comentarios protestantes a *Ética a Nicómaco* V, 7 1134b18–35a5."

2 The latest version of this narrative is Brad S. Gregory, *The Unintended Reformation. How a Religious Revolution Secularized Society* (Cambridge, Mass.: The Belknap Press of Harvard University Press, 2012).

3 Herman Bavinck, *Reformed Dogmatics*. Volume 1: *Prolegomena* (Grand Rapids: Baker Academic, 2003), 143.

 | DOI:10.1163/9789004206717_018

tradition. Aristotle's critique of the Platonic idea of the good in *Nicomachean Ethics* I, 6, for example, regularly confronts later commentators not with a single Aristotelian thesis, but with the need to adjudicate between the two Greek philosophers.[4] Another approach, the one taken here, focuses on the degree to which the commentators were conscious of tensions between Aristotle's text and their own Christian faith. Searching for commentators that engage this challenge leads us to particularly dynamic commentaries. Once we get minimally acquainted with such works, any suggestion of acritical reception of Aristotle among the Christians is easily laid to rest.

This chapter will focus on the most conspicuous cases of such Protestant correction of Aristotle. But how common was this approach to Aristotle's text? The correction of Aristotle is sometimes supposed to be a late achievement, a disposition peculiar to figures like the Socinian Johann Crell, who published a commentary with the eloquent title *Ethica Aristotelica, ad sacrarum litterarum normam emendata*.[5] Socinians claimed to be recovering the ethical core of Christianity amidst the confessional disputes that engulfed Christendom. Socinianism is, furthermore, often associated with the idea that Christ had brought new laws; and if a new law is a Christian distinctive, only those who are conscious of this distinctive feature will be able to successfully contrast Aristotelian and Christian ethics. But the reader of Crell's commentary seeks in vain for the promised emendation. His work is simply a standard exposition (with some systematic reordering) of Aristotle's text.[6] As this chapter will show, orthodox Protestant commentators in fact have a much more distinguished career as correctors of Aristotle than Socinians like Crell.

In the first section, I will offer some remarks on the correction of Aristotle in pre-Reformation traditions, tracing its presence from the late-Ancient world to the sixteenth century. Next, I will focus on five Protestant commentators in which different degrees and forms of correction of Aristotle can be found. Four of these commentators belong to the Reformed tradition: Omer Talon, Peter Martyr Vermigli, Rudolph Goclenius, and Antonius Walaeus; the fifth is the Lutheran Johannes Trygophorus. There are all types of differences in the way these authors approach Aristotle, but the differences can hardly be traced to their confessional allegiances. As I will show, their works rather remind us

4 Alfonso Herreros, "A Case Study of the Reception of Aristotle in Early Protestantism: The Platonic Idea of the Good in the Commentaries on the Nicomachean Ethics," *Renaissance & Reformation* 43, no. 3 (2020): 41–69.

5 *Ethica Aristotelica, ad sacrarum literarum normam emendata*. Selenoburgi [Lüneburg]: Sumptibus Asteriorum, 1650. Further editions in 1656, 1663, and 1681.

6 Mark Edwards, *Aristotle and Early Christian Thought* (London and New York: Routledge, 2019), 78.

of the degree to which Protestant Aristotelianism fits within the longer and varied tradition of Christian Aristotelianism.

2 Correcting Aristotle: Pre-Reformation Traditions

A blunt and rather myopic history of Aristotle's Christian reception sometimes suggests the following steps. First comes the early Church, which had no special interest in Aristotle (an educated Christian was simply a Platonic Christian). Next comes the Western recovery of Aristotle's works in the thirteenth century. Here they "baptized" Aristotle, the specificity of Christian thought was gradually lost, and Aristotle came to stand above Scripture. Finally, the sixteenth-century Reformation led the Church back to the sources. Augustine again prevailed over Aristotle (in some territories, at least), though for a time the aberration of Protestant Aristotelianism persisted. Even Reformation scholars who are well-informed about this aspect of sixteenth-century thought often echo parts of this narrative. Thus Joseph C. McLelland writes that Vermigli "steers the fine line between the Scylla of the Scholastics, who made theology conform to Aristotle, and the Charybdis of contemporaries like Melanchthon and Hyperius, who concentrated so much on theology that they help us understand Aristotle but little."[7] This appreciation for the unique nature of Vermigli's commentary is justified. But though a Scylla and a Charybdis in the adoption of Aristotle surely exist, they lie far away from the points McLelland suggests (if anything, Vermigli's commentary is more theological than Hyperius'). The portrayal of Aristotle's reception in Christianity sketched above is indeed not only exaggerated (that much should be obvious); it is a completely misleading depiction of all its phases.

Before turning to the Protestant reception of Aristotle, I will briefly consider some of these previous stages. Protestant Aristotelianism, as we will see, can to a large degree be considered as a faithful continuation of the previous critical reception Christians made of Aristotle. A recent monograph by Mark Edwards covers the beginnings of that reception during the first six centuries of our era. While he does not deny that some form of Platonism was indeed the prevailing philosophy among the Christians, its precise form is relevant for the subsequent reception of Aristotle. The rise of Neoplatonism in the fourth century, he argues, reduced the distance between the schools of Plato and

7 Joseph C. McLelland, "Introduction," in *Commentary on Aristotle's Nicomachean Ethics* (Kirksville, MO.: Truman State University Press, 2006), xiv.

Aristotle. In the process, some distinctively Aristotelian concepts—those of *ousia* and *dynamis*—turned out to become the most important parts of the Neoplatonism adopted by the Christians.[8] In a then not-too-distant future were the translations of Aristotelian texts by Christians like Marius Victorinus and later Boethius, while between them Philoponus was the first Christian to write commentaries on Aristotle's works. As told by Edwards, Philoponus's story shows how some acquaintance with Aristotle's works gradually became common among educated and orthodox Christians. It is a story that, however, barely includes the *Ethics*. The reason for this absence is not peculiar to the Christian reception, since this work was hardly the object of any commentary among the ancient pagan commentators either.

The exception to that late-ancient rule is Aspasius (second century), whose partial commentary would later be included in a Byzantine collection of commentaries. During the twelfth century, the circle around the princess Anna Komnene—above all Eustratius and Michael of Ephesus—produced this first medieval commentary on the *Ethics*. Scholars that have studied these commentaries, written around 130 years before the first Latin commentaries on the work,[9] agree on the juxtaposition of Christian and Greek themes as one of their key features. In the words of the editor of the joint commentary, H.P.F. Mercken, "Eustratius interprets the work from his own theological-philosophical point of view, which is that of a Christian." As he further explains, this Christian outlook "is cast in a philosophical mould," one that is best described as a "Christian Neoplatonism."[10] One can safely say that there is a broad agreement around this point.[11] In these commentaries this Christian interpretation is not itself the object of explicit discussion, as it will be in the sixteenth century. But the role they played for a continued Christian reception is fundamental. These commentaries were not only translated into Latin during the thirteenth-century reception of Aristotle's thought: they stood at the very center of that

8 Mark Edwards, *Aristotle and Early Christian Thought*, 78.

9 H.P.F. Mercken, "The Greek Commentators on Aristotle's Ethics," in *Aristotle Transformed: The Ancient Commentators and Their Influence*, ed. Sorabji, Richard (London: Gerald Duckworth, 1990), 407–44.

10 Mercken, "The Greek Commentators," 416–19; here 416.

11 On these commentaries see Charles Barber and David Jenkins, eds., *Medieval Greek Commentaries on the Nicomachean Ethics* (Leiden: Brill, 2009); The point is more emphatically raised with regard to Eustratius than Michael of Ephesus. So, for instance, Mercken, "The Greek Commentators," 436: "Michael is obviously not interested in relating Aristotle to the dogma of the Church or to the Christian way of life." The difference between the two Byzantine commentators is arguably more one of degrees. But in any case, Eustratius is certainly more important for the Protestant commentators.

reception, since their translator was the same Robert Grosseteste who translated the *Ethics* itself into Latin. In rendering the *Nicomachean Ethics* and the commentaries as a single project, Grosseteste sought to transmit a specific reading of Aristotle to the West.[12] And to a large degree he succeeded: in medieval commentaries on the *Ethics* the label "the Commentator" refers not to Averroes, but to Eustratius. As the work of Bonaventure shows, this is the case not only in commentaries on Aristotle.[13] In the spirit of this "commentator," the great systems of the thirteenth century all offer some form of this Christian appropriation of Aristotle.[14]

We can leave the Middle Ages behind after briefly considering how the landscape changed after the condemnation of 1277. The condemnation of "radical" Aristotelianism reminds us that such an Aristotelianism of course existed. Its description as "radical," though it often was simply Aristotelian, reminds us to what a significant degree the main currents of medieval Aristotelianism were themselves shaped by the previous Christian reception. But if tensions between the Aristotelian and Augustinian tradition had until this point been managed in ways leading to some kind of synthesis, more open conflict became common after the condemnation. A century later, the Augustinian Hugolino of Orvieto complained about philosophy's prevalence over theology, presenting the Aristotelian understanding of happiness as a central example of this unwarranted subjugation of theology to philosophy. Such were the questions—the fears of naturalism and immanentism—being raised on the eve of the Reformation: around 1514, Martin Luther himself read the commentary on Lombard's *Sentences* in which Orvieto's critique was formulated.[15]

---

12 This point has been argued by José Antonio Poblete, "El papel de la traducción latina de Roberto Grosseteste en la transmisión medieval del pasaje aristotélico sobre lo justo natural (Ethica Nicomachea 1134b18–35a5)," Diss. Universidad de los Andes, Santiago de Chile, 2019.

13 See *Collationes in Hexaemeron* VI, 4.

14 The Christian corrections of Aristotle within these commentaries have hence been the cause for debate about the theological or philosophical nature of these works, and about the degree to which they contain an author's—and specifically Aquinas'—own views. Christopher Kaczor, "Reading Aquinas's Commentary on Aristotle's Nicomachean Ethics: A Reply to Mark D. Jordan," in *Theology Needs Philosophy: Acting against Reason Is Contrary to the Nature of God*, ed. Matthew L. Lamb (Washington, D.C.: Catholic University of America Press, 2016), 279–92. The position defended here by Kaczor could well be applied to the Protestant commentaries as well.

15 Adolar Zumkeller, "Die Augustinertheologen Simon Fidati von Cascia und Hugolin von Orvieto und Martin Luthers Kritik an Aristoteles," *Archiv für Reformationsgeschichte* 54 (1963): 15–37.

3 Protestant Corrections of Aristotle

I turn now to the Protestant reception of Aristotle during the sixteenth and seventeenth centuries. I should stress that here I focus exclusively on commentaries on Aristotle's *Ethics*, not on the wider presence of Aristotle in early Protestant moral reflection. Protestant treatises of moral philosophy and theology that are shaped by fundamental Aristotelian assumptions can be counted in the hundreds. In fact, even the number of preserved commentaries is large enough to make one pause. Elsewhere I have discussed forty-six such works by a roughly similar number of Lutheran and Reformed authors, evenly distributed along the sixteenth and seventeenth centuries.[16] But we are only beginning to explore this commentary tradition and the nature of its Aristotelianism. These commentaries vary significantly in their character. Some are mainly expositive, some are philologically richer than others, some were written by extremely competent philosophers, and some were written for predominantly pedagogical reasons. Most of these approaches rarely led their authors to make the correction of Aristotle a significant aspect of their work. But for some it was a defining purpose.

Before addressing some cases in which such a correction did take place, it is important to mention the role played by the prologues to these commentaries. Such prologues are no new feature, but medieval prologues—as, for instance, Aquinas's prologue to his commentary—often served for a simple description of the field of enquiry, its object, and method. Starting with Melanchthon, Protestant commentaries tend to make the relationship between moral philosophy and the Christian gospel their explicit object of reflection (the main instrument for that reflection being the law/gospel distinction).[17] Such considerations do not in themselves constitute corrections of Aristotle. They do, however, put Aristotle in his place, so to speak. However enthusiastic a commentary might turn out to be, the first word was one of acknowledgment of limits: philosophy alone would leave us lame-handed.[18] These prologues can

16 Manfred Svensson, "Aristotelian Practical Philosophy from Melanchthon to Eisenhart: Protestant Commentaries on the Nicomachean Ethics 1529–1682," *Reformation and Renaissance Review* 21:3 (2019): 218–38.

17 Though it remains an important feature during the next century as well, in the sixteenth century these prologues are nearly a universal feature of the Protestant commentaries.

18 Samuel Heiland, *Ethica ad Nicomachum libri decem ..., breviter et perspicue per quaestiones expositi* (Tubingae: Georg Gruppenbach, 1579), Praef.: *sine ea [Theologia] omnem Philosophiam plane mancam et inanem esse.* This is evidently Melanchthonian language. See CR 16:364: *philosophica sunt manca.*

serve as a first indication of the freedom with which commentators approached the text.

3.1 *Omer Talon (1510–62)*

Such freedom was first claimed by Omer Talon (or Audomarus Talaeus), a close associate of Petrus Ramus whose commentary I want to consider first. Talon's confessional allegiance is less clear than that of the authors to be discussed next: he moved in Huguenot circles, but Ramus himself converted only the year of Talon's death. In any case, his orientation is decisively reform-minded. His commentary deals with book I alone, and it is dedicated to the Cardinal of Lorrain (as all of Ramus's works were). Recent scholarship has stressed that the opposition between Ramism and Aristotelianism is much more nuanced than claimed in previous decades: Ramists did not necessarily break with the general principles of Aristotle's philosophy, though they pleaded for pedagogical simplifications that implied the rejection of Aristotelian exposition and commentary as the dominant ways of teaching.[19] An inspection of Ramist or semi-Ramist commentaries on the *Ethics* (the few that were produced under that logic) confirms this view.[20] But Talon must then be singled out as a significant exception. The prologue to his commentary opens with a declaration of "philosophical liberty," through which he affirms that he will distinguish truth from falsehood in Aristotle. But this *philosophica libertas* is actually a Christian freedom: as a pagan philosopher, he writes, Aristotle was ignorant both about the origin and the end (*principium et extremum*) of human life. As a consequence of this ignorance, Talon continues, Aristotle wanders in circles. Talon grants that some Aristotelian teachings—like his views on the difference between action and production, or on the unity of ethics and politics—are right.[21] Christians and philosophers furthermore agree on the fact that the question of happiness is the supreme question.[22] But as soon as Aristotle descends to particulars, Talon affirms that he errs as much as anyone (*tam procul aberrat ab eo quod inquirit, quam qui maxime*).[23]

---

19 Howard Hotson, *Commonplace Learning: Ramism and Its German Ramifications 1543–1630* (Oxford: Oxford University Press, 2007).

20 For illustration of both the Ramist and semi-Ramist approach see Henricus Gutberleth, *Ethicae liber unus* (Herborn: ex officina Christophori Corvini, 1612); and Wilhelm Scribonius, *Ethica ex Aristotele et aliis summis philosophis repetita* (Francofurti: Johann Wechel, 1589).

21 Omer Talon, *In primum Aristotelis ethicum librum explicatio* (Paris: Mathieu David, 1550), 7 and 10–11.

22 Talon, *Explicatio*, 9.

23 Talon, *Explicatio*, 9.

Talon's criticism relates above all to Aristotle's view of happiness. But it should be pointed out that it extends to many other aspects as well, even to the way Aristotle treats his predecessors, which Talon describes as disparaging.[24] But let us focus on the problem of inner-worldly happiness. In Talon's words, Aristotle's conception of such a happiness not only fails in the fact that it ignores its other-worldly continuation; it thereby despises God and takes him out of our present lives as well (*Deum contemnit, irridet, de medio rerum tollit*).[25] True happiness, then, can only be found in the vision of God, "as the theologians say."[26] Though there is no small amount of verbal abuse of Aristotle throughout the commentary, Talon claims that his chief rival is not the Stagirite, who would obviously have adopted a Christian notion of happiness had he lived in our times. The contest is with those Christians who read the pagan philosopher as if his words were inspired (one can find this critique in other commentaries of the period as well, but it is a critique that tends never to identify its target explicitly.)[27] In any case, it is interesting to note that for all this explicitly Christian rejection of the Aristotelian view, the pagan tradition is much more vividly present in Talon's commentary than the Christian one. Plato, Cicero, Horace, Livy, and Quintilian are opposed to a Christian tradition that is nominally represented by Augustine alone. This feature of the commentary is particularly visible when Talon discusses chapter six of Aristotle's first book. Talon's point is that not only Christians, but Aristotelians themselves condemn Aristotle for his rejection of Plato's idea of the good, and he lists Themistius, Simplicius, and Eustratius as Aristotelians that exemplify this claim.[28] But framing the issue in these terms, Talon actually puts Eustratius, the first Christian (and Neoplatonist) commentator on the *Ethics*, on the pagan side.

If we compare Talon with the other commentators I will discuss below, his should perhaps be counted as a rejection rather than as a correction of Aristotle. In terms of its substance, it reminds us rather of late-medieval Augustinians like Orvieto, who rejected Aristotle on the same account as Talon. But there is something unique to Talon: rejections of Aristotle are not unusual, but I know of no case in which such outright rejection uses a commentary on Aristotle himself as its vehicle.

---

24 Talon, *Explicatio*, 18.
25 Talon, *Explicatio*, 33.
26 Talon, *Explicatio*, 33.
27 Talon, *Explicatio*, 10.
28 Talon, *Explicatio*, 32–33.

3.2 *Peter Martyr Vermigli (1499–1562)*

Let us turn to Vermigli, who offers a strikingly different approach to Aristotle's text. Though it only reaches into book III, this has rightly been acclaimed as one of the more distinguished Protestant commentaries on the *Ethics*.[29] At the beginning of the work, Vermigli explains the way in which he will proceed. He will dissect a passage, explain its scope and proposition, he will comment on terms that may require exegesis, he will expose eventual doubts, and "discuss those passages that agree or disagree with scripture."[30] Vermigli sticks in a fairly close way to this program, and raises this question of concordance at the end of almost every chapter.[31] Once he puts the question in terms of agreement or conflict "with religion;"[32] otherwise, it is framed in the more Protestant terms of agreement or conflict with Scripture. Though I will stick to this aspect of his commentary, I must emphasize that this is only one dimension of the book, detailed commentary constituting the bulk of the work.[33]

How should Vermigli's reply to the question of agreement be characterized? Three different accents are present throughout the commentary. First, a spirit of general agreement is affirmed, though this concord can have both the mild form of a coincidence and a stronger form in which Aristotle and distinctively Christian teachings mutually reinforce each other; second, he presents observations about Aristotle's limits; third, some corrections of specific teachings of Aristotle are discussed. Let me briefly go through instances of these. The general agreement of Aristotle's *Ethics* with Scripture is clearly asserted from

---

29 Laudatory references to his commentary can be found among several other commentators. See, for instance, Hubert van Giffen, *In decem libros Aristotelis ad Nicomachum* (Francofurti: Impensis Lazari Zetzneri, 1608), 4; and Samuel Rachelius, *Aristotelis ethicorum ad Nicomachum libri decem, cum Dionysii Lambini versione Latina a Matthia Bergio interpolata* (Helmstedt: Typis et sumptibus Henning Muller, 1660), 140. Had the commentary been completed by Vermigli with as substantive commentary for the later books as he dedicated to the first three, it would have competed with Wolfgang Heider's as the longest of the Protestant commentaries.

30 I quote the English translation Peter Martyr Vermigli, *Commentary on Aristotle's Nicomachean Ethics* (Kirksville, MO.: Truman State University Press, 2015), 13; the translation is based on the first edition. Petrus Martyr Vermigli, *In primum, secundum et initium tertii libri Ethicorum ad Nicomachum ... Commentarius doctissimus* (Tiguri: Apud Christophorum Froschoverum, 1563). There is also a 1582 edition with minor variations, and the the 1598 edition by Goclenius that will be discussed below.

31 Chapter's I, 6 and 7 are somewhat exceptional in this regard, and I, 8 discusses this concordance already at the beginning of the chapter.

32 Vermigli, *Commentary*, 58.

33 For a thorough discussion of the work and its theologico-philosophical context see Luca Baschera, *Tugend und Rechtfertigung: Peter Martyr Vermiglis Kommentar zur Nikomachischen Ethik im Spannungsfeld von Philosophie und Theologie* (Zürich: TVZ, 2008).

the beginning. Philosophical ethics, writes Vermigli, conflicts with piety as much as the nautical or military arts might do.[34] Sometimes the concordance regards rather trivial points. Vermigli writes, for instance, that Christ's teaching regarding the wide road to perdition coincides with Aristotle's condemnation of the vulgar pleasures of the masses.[35] But often the claim to agreement rests on more substantive ground. Thus, Aristotle's initial observations about every art, method, and action aiming at some good, for instance, are put into the theological context of the goodness of creation.[36] As I mentioned, there are also stronger versions of this concordance. This same orientation of human action to a hierarchical web of ends leads Vermigli not only to a discussion of the supremacy of faith, hope, and love, but to a discussion of the relation between the two tables of the law. Luther's repetition of the goal of the first table before each precept of the second table is thus turned into an illustration of the Aristotelian view of a hierarchy of goods governing all human action.[37] This, and not Luther's critique of Aristotle, is in fact the only mention of the German reformer in this commentary.

What, then, about Aristotle's insufficiency? Let us first consider it in the light of Vermigli's commentary on book I, chapter 3, where Aristotle mentions the diversity and uncertainty of right actions, concluding that they seem to be based on convention and not on nature. Vermigli is of course aware that this is not Aristotle's settled opinion. "Aristotle does not say that it *was* so; he said that it seems to be so."[38] But though he acknowledges that Aristotle has quite a subtle view on these matters, and one with which Vermigli largely agrees, his commentary on this paragraph clearly affirms that Aristotle binds morality too strongly to convention. We must remember that Vermigli's commentary did not reach book V, chapter 7, where Aristotle offers a more detailed account of the relation between conventional and natural justice.[39] Had he commented on that chapter, it is likely that Vermigli would have taken exception to Aristotle's views in terms similar to those he uses when commenting on book I. Vermigli is namely adamant on the centrality of divine law for our

34 Vermigli, *Commentary*, 15.

35 Vermigli, *Commentary*, 109.

36 Vermigli, *Commentary*, 26.

37 Vermigli, *Commentary*, 36 (the translation does not include Luther in the Index of subjects).

38 Vermigli, *Commentary*, 52.

39 For the reception of that passage among other Protestant commentators see my "The Aristotelian Conception of Natural Law and its Reception in Early Protestant Commentaries on the *Nicomachean Ethics*," forthcoming in *Perichoresis. The Theological Journal of Emanuel University*.

understanding of the human good. "If anyone investigates the question more deeply, he will understand that the whole of nature depends on this kind of law," he writes.[40] He affirms that, acting as a philosopher, he will say nothing more about that divine law in this place. After a few lines, he introduces the distinction between ceremonial, civil, and moral law, asserting that change can only be admitted for the former two. If we consider that in book V Aristotle presents not only conventional, but also natural justice as subject to change, it seems safe to assume that Vermigli's correction would have been even firmer had he commented on that passage.[41]

Let us consider another, more typical, example of Aristotle's limitations. Commenting on the first chapter of the *Ethics*, Vermigli writes that "Aristotle does not mention faith, hope, and charity, nor even grace or the inspiration of the Holy Spirit."[42] This is a simple matter of fact, "because he had no knowledge of them."[43] But knowledge of Aristotle's limits of course does affect the way in which his text will be rendered. Leonardo Bruni translated *t'agathon* as "the supreme good." Following Cardinal Bessarion and Argyropoulos, Vermigli affirms that such a translation is made under the assumption of Aristotle's acquaintance with a more robustly Christian view of God. A sober assessment of Aristotle's limits, by contrast, leads us to translate it as "the good itself."[44] As these discussions show, not all of Aristotle's deficiencies are of the same kind. Some of Vermigli's claims imply that the Stagirite must be corrected, others that his views must be brought to completion with truths he could not have known. In different places of the commentary, a single topic can in fact fall under any of those descriptions. Towards the end of the commentary on book I, for instance, Vermigli rejects Aristotle's inclusion of virtue in the definition of happiness, since "happiness rests in reconciliation with God through Christ."[45] Here Aristotle's ignorance about salvific history seems to jeopardize his definition of virtue. But the same point is made in far milder terms elsewhere. Commenting on chapter two of the same book, Vermigli writes that

40 Vermigli, *Commentary*, 55.

41 Interestingly, here Vermigli instead weighs in against contemporary Christians who see divorce and polygamy as acceptable changes to moral norms. Vermigli, *Commentary*, 59; The position rejected by Vermigli can be found in Andreas Hyperius, *In Aristotelis Ethica Nicomachica annotationes haud inutiles* (Basileae: ex officina Oporiniana, 1586), 251 (first edition in Vermigli's lifetime, 1553). Given these remarks, it will come as no surprise that Vermigli stresses the existence of some exceptionless moral rules more than Aristotle. See Vermigli, *Commentary*, 248 and 377.

42 Vermigli, *Commentary*, 27.

43 Vermigli, *Commentary*, 27.

44 Vermigli, *Commentary*, 20–21.

45 Vermigli, *Commentary*, 283.

"the difference between us and pagan philosophers is that they suggest the ultimate end should be achieved by one's own virtue and zeal, whereas we say on the basis of divine scripture that the supreme good cannot be obtained unless we are assisted by the spirit and grace of Christ."[46] Here Vermigli does not suggest that Aristotle's failure ruins his definition of virtue or of the ultimate end. There is no doubt about Aristotle's limits in this front, but Vermigli can refer to these shortcomings both in correcting and in more harmonizing terms.[47]

But there are observations on Aristotle's text that can only be adequately described as corrections. The most prominent example of such a correction is Vermigli's discussion of the audience of moral education. Aristotle famously excludes young people from such reflection, since only those with adequate experience can profit from these lectures. Twice in his commentary Vermigli addresses this restriction, arguing for the broadest possible audience since "no one must be prevented from hearing the word of God."[48] This is a quite peculiar form of correction: Vermigli is rejecting Aristotle's pessimistic view of the benefits of moral philosophy for the unexperienced, but he does so basically because he is treating Aristotle's *Ethics* and Christian preaching according to the same standard. This argument is, moreover, the occasion for one of the few references to contemporary events in the commentary: the example of Edward VI, a young man equipped with ever possible virtue, serves Vermigli as the perfect counterexample to Aristotle's position.[49] Vermigli of course agrees that not everybody will profit from teaching; but since we have no external identifiers for those who sin against the Holy Spirit, they cannot be excluded in advance.[50]

The persistence with which Vermigli raises questions about Aristotle's agreement with Christianity—of which I have only discussed some—is unique in the history of Aristotelian commentary. But however far he pushes the discussion, he stands on the shoulders of a previous tradition of commentary, and especially of the collection of Byzantine commentaries, which went through a second wave of influence during the sixteenth century.[51] Vermigli engages

46 Vermigli, *Commentary*, 41; see also 78.

47 For another instance of harmonization around the same difficulty see Vermigli, *Commentary*, 197.

48 Vermigli, *Commentary*, 70–71.

49 Vermigli, *Commentary*, 63.

50 Vermigli, *Commentary*, 71.

51 In 1541 the commentary was the object of a new translation by Bernardus Felicianus, based on the new Greek text of the Aldine edition. On that influential translation see David A. Lines, "Giovanni Bernardo Feliciano and the Edition of 'Eustratius,'" in Eustratius, Aspasius, Michael Ephesius et al.: *Aristotelis Stagiritae Moralia Nicomachia*, Übersetzt von Johannes Bernardus Felicianus; (Paris 1543; reprint, Stuttgart/Bad-Cannstatt:

Eustratius's commentary frequently but with much independence.[52] I will bring this discussion of Vermigli to a close by noting one instance in which Vermigli believes to be correcting Eustratius, but actually thereby rejects Aristotle. As we have seen, Eustratius offers an interpretation of the *Ethics* that can adequately be described as that of a Neoplatonic Christian. The ethical life is thus portrayed in terms of an upward journey, with purgative virtues following the political ones, and with the end being a life of contemplation in solitude. Christian hermits thus represent the highest point of this path.[53] After reporting this reading by Eustratius, which above all emphasizes that man's political nature does not oblige us all to an active life, Vermigli writes that "I do not at all subscribe to his views."[54] Vermigli's contention is that one should not be exclusively devoted to any of those ways of life in an exclusive way, that both philosophy and the scriptures aim at a mixed life. One Christian interpretation of Aristotle is thus corrected by another one, as Vermigli' civic republicanism collides with Eustratius's Neoplatonism. In the process, both reject Aristotle's actual teaching about two good but competing ways of life.

3.3 *Rudolph Goclenius (1547–1628)*

Talon's commentary was published in 1550, Vermigli's posthumously in 1563. If Vermigli played a significant role in the history of Protestant theology, the same must be said about the place of Rudolph Goclenius in philosophy.[55] From the late 1580s until the turn of the century, Goclenius wrote several disputations on particular books of the *Nicomachean Ethics*, though no full commentary of his own. In 1592 he published a first more systematic approach, the *Exercitationes Ethicae*, a work in which he eclectically draws from

frommann-holzboog, 2006), v–xviii Vermigli, however, seems to have worked directly with the Greek text.

52 In the sixteenth century, Vermigli was accused of merely repeating Eustratius's opinions, e.g., by his former colleague (and proto-Socinian) Simon Simonius. Simon Simonius, *Commentariorum in ethica Aristotelis ad Nicomachum liber primus* (Geneva: Apud Ionnem Crispinum, 1567), Ep. dedic.; This is hardly a fair assessment of Vermigli's relation to Eustratius. Beyond the case I discuss here, one can find divergences from Eustratius's readings in Vermigli, *Commentary*, 24, 49, and 167.

53 This aspect of Eustratius's commentary is accurately described by Mercken, "The Greek Commentators," 416–17.

54 Vermigli, *Commentary*, 178.

55 Guido Giglioni, "What's Wrong with Doing History of Renaissance Philosophy? Rudolph Goclenius and the Canon of Early Modern Philosophy," in *Early Modern Philosophy and the Renaissance Legacy*, ed. Cecilia Muratori and Gianni Paganini (Dordrecht: Springer, 2016), 21–39.

different classical philosophical traditions to discuss the main topics of moral philosophy.[56] In 1598 he finally turned to the genus of the commentary, but as publisher of Hyperius's and Vermigli's commentaries as a single work, with a few glosses of his own. Unlike the previous Protestant commentators, here the project of a contrast with Scripture is for the first time present in the title of the work: *Meditationes ethicae sive Aristotelis Ethicorum Nikomacheion perspicua ac perquam erudita, cum moribus sacris, id est, in sacra pagina descriptis, collata explicatio.* Here I will only briefly consider his introduction to this "supercommentary."

Goclenius's reflections show us to what degree authors working within the Reformed tradition were aware of the critical nature of their appropriation of Aristotle. As we have seen, this critical Christian appropriation is part of the medieval heritage of early Protestant thought, but it was not directly reflected upon by the medieval commentators in the way it begins to be here. Goclenius's praise for Vermigli in this introduction is, indeed, especially strong for having offered more than a mere exposition of Aristotle. He describes Vermigli's work as encompassing exposition, disputation, but also contrast with the sacred scriptures, "so that here we can see agreement (*convenientia*) in some places, and discrepancy (*discrepantia*) in others."[57] In Goclenius's view, Vermigli is consciously seeking a third way between those who oppose Aristotle's view and Christianity too sharply, and those who offer too easy an harmonization. Perhaps the most interesting feature of this work is Goclenius's list of Aristotelian teachings that can be subjected to such nuanced evaluation. This is not a summary of Vermigli's views, which are for the reader to find out. Goclenius simply picks out some that are particularly significant to himself.

First, he writes that Aristotle's conception of happiness has been corrected by his Christian commentators, ordering the temporal happiness of civil life to our eternal good promised in the Scriptures (an Augustinian vocabulary of *sempiternitatis fruitio* is used in the consideration of this highest good). Second, Goclenius describes the Aristotelian understanding of voluntary action. But contrary to common expectations, this is not a point in which Goclenius believes that substantive correction is necessary. Goclenius

56 This work has recently been translated into German. Rudolph Goclenius, *Übungen zur Ethik/Exercitationes Ethicae*, trans. Hans Günter Zekl (Würzburg: Königshausen & Neuman, 2010).

57 Rudolph Goclenius, Petrus Martyr Vermigli, and Andreas Hyperius, *Meditationes ethicae sive Aristotelis ethicorum Nikomacheion perspicua ac perquam erudita, cum moribus sacris, id est, in sacra pagina descriptis, collata explicatio* (Lich: Nikolaus Erben, 1598), Praef. 2 There is a second dedicatory preface; the discussion I report here belong to the first "*Ad philosophiae studiosos praefatio.*"

is especially concerned with the fact that we are rightly corrected for those actions which flow from the vices for whose origin we ourselves are responsible. Pointing to chapter 7 of the *Letter to the Romans*, Goclenius finds that on this point Aristotle perfectly agrees with Christian theology. That there is dissension (*dissidium*) between our affections and our reason, that we often act against better knowledge, is thus presented as a teaching that is shared by philosophy and Christianity. Third, Goclenius briefly mentions that Aristotle and Paul agree in the rejection of a utilitarian approach to ethics. When book VI of the *Ethics* calls for a deliberation regarding good and licit means, he sees it as congruous with Paul's warning against doing evil so that good may come.[58] Finally, Goclenius again turns to corrections, though not to one we typically expect post-Reformation scholars to be discussing. As he points out, Aristotle describes the celestial bodies as more preeminent than men. But man, he writes, "surpasses the world (*mundo longe antecellit*), since he is an intelligent nature created in God's image."[59] Once we are aware that man's mortality is caused by sin and not by nature, the reasons for preferring the celestial bodies disappear. As this observation shows, the discussion is not restricted to the way in which Christianity and Aristotle agree or not in the approach to particular moral teachings; some attention is also paid to the way in which different accounts of man's place in the cosmos will affect our moral vision.

3.4 *Antonius Walaeus (1573–1639)*

While Goclenius is aware that one can err on the side of harmonization and on the side of opposition, he does not seem to consider Vermigli an exception for his balanced achievement. When he introduces the correction of Aristotle's view of happiness, for instance, he obviously has a tradition of Christian commentary in mind. The best commentators, he tells us, have interpreted and perfected (*aequiores interpretantur ac perficiunt*) the Aristotelian understanding of happiness.[60] Walaeus agrees with Goclenius in bringing the contrast with Christian truth into focus already in the title of his work: *Compendium ethicae aristotelicae ad normam veritatis christianae revocatum*, published in 1620, in the aftermath of the Synod of Dort.[61] But he is less persuaded than Goclenius that the commentary tradition has been thus balanced. In the first

58 Goclenius, Vermigli, and Hyperius, 3.

59 The disputed teaching is in NE VI, 7. Goclenius wrongly attributes it to book VII. Goclenius, Vermigli, and Hyperius, *Meditationes ethicae*, 3.

60 Goclenius, Vermigli, and Hyperius, *Meditationes ethicae*, 2.

61 For this context see Henri A. Krop, "Philosophy and the Synod of Dordt: Aristotelianism, Humanism, and the Case Against Arminianism," in *Revisiting the Synod of Dort (1618–1619)*, ed. Aza Goudriaan and Fred van Lieburg (Leiden: Brill, 2010), 52–63.

pages, he laments that Christian readers have not exercised their liberty to criticize Aristotle more firmly.[62]

Just like Goclenius, he is consciously commenting on the *Ethics* within a Protestant tradition of commentary. He explicitly points to Melanchthon and Danaeus, though slightly distancing himself from their work.[63] They took a few things (*paucula tantum*) from Aristotle, he writes, but they also transferred much from the Holy Scriptures into their commentaries, in a way that makes them rather unhelpful for the understanding of Aristotle (a judgment that is coincident with the words of McLelland quoted above). But if this is the problem he believes his predecessors have fallen into, how should we understand the program announced in the title of his work? In Walaeus's view, many have made Aristotle speak against his own mind in order to make him compatible with Christianity.[64] So the problem is not that Christians have become prey of an Averroist or naturalist interpretation of Aristotle, but rather the other way around. Some may consider this to be less problematic, but Walaeus points to a significant risk involved in too strong (and implicit) identification of Aristotle and Christianity: once students grow up and tensions become visible, the presumption of an absolute harmony will incline them to adjust Christianity to Aristotle.[65]

The exposition of Aristotle is hence intertwined with presentations of the *sententia vera et Christiana* on various problems.[66] But Walaeus's procedure is rarely to simply point out Aristotelian shortcomings and to offer a Christian doctrine that must be accepted in its place without further deliberation. Consider the discussion of the unity of the virtues. This is a teaching that he describes as disputed among the ancients and the moderns.[67] But after reporting the Scotist denial of the doctrine, Walaeus describes the Aristotelian position as both more truthful and more widely received (*verior et receptior*):

62 Antonius Walaeus, *Compendium ethicae aristotelicae ad normam veritatis christianae revocatum* (Lugduni Batavorum: Impensis Asingae Elhardi, 1625), 6. The work was reprinted more than ten times, here I quote from the first enlarged edition.

63 Several shortcomings of Aristotle that Walaeus points out are, however, the same noted by his predecessors. The precepts of the first table were better understood by Pythagoreans and Platonists; important virtues linked to the second table, like mercy and obedience, are omitted by Aristotle. Aristotle offers a correct description and analysis of virtues, Walaeus goes on, but he omits God as the main cause of these. Walaeus, *Compendium ethicae*, 83–84; Vermigli stresses the same point in Vermigli, *Commentary*, 296.

64 Walaeus, *Compendium ethicae*, 7.

65 Walaeus, *Compendium ethicae*, 5.

66 Walaeus, *Compendium ethicae*, 124 and 130. After announcing the *sententia Christiana* in p. 130, Walaeus immediately moves to the reasons on its behalf.

67 Walaeus, *Compendium ethicae*, 96.

There is no true justice where there is no true prudence, and so on.[68] And here Christianity comes not to correct, but to support the Aristotelian position. He who loves God cannot hate his neighbor, he who says that he has faith must have works.[69] If there are any corrections here, it is an Aristotelian and Christian correction of the pagan Stoic and of the Christian Scotist positions. The Stoics are namely singled out for adding to the unity of virtues the false teaching of the parity of the vices, while the Scotists are the only rivals of the teaching of the virtues' inseparability that Walaeus identifies.[70] Though concerned with preserving the language of Scripture, with clarifying some important omissions, and with showing adequate balances, the *sententia vera et Christiana* for which Walaeus pleads is seldom the substitution of an Aristotelian doctrine for a Christian one, and it is not a "point-by-point revision of Aristotle."[71] He is rather a speaker for a Christian Aristotelianism that wants to remain conscious about its distance from Aristotle.

3.5 *Johannes Trygophorus (1580–1626)*

I close with Johannes Trygophorus. His commentary on the *Nicomachean Ethics* was published a few years before Walaeus', but it reflects the nature of Protestant seventeenth-century commentaries much more closely. While Walaeus refers almost exclusively to Plato, the Stoics, and the tradition of *theologi*, Trygophorus's range of references goes from Parmenides to Plato, from Averroes to Piccolomini. Organized as a substantive series of disputations on each book of the *Ethics*, the subtitle of the *Concertationes Ethicae* announces that he will explore Aristotle's work *una cum applicatione ad ethicam Christianam*. Instead of a correction, then, we have an application. But introducing his first disputation, he speaks of a comparison between both views instead of an application (*cum collatione quadam ad ethicam Christianam*).[72] These two, application and comparison, need not be opposed; considering their simultaneous presence, we should perhaps speak more simply of a Christian appropriation of Aristotle.

If we look at these disputations, we can see that the relation between philosophical and Christian ethics is treated in two successive steps: first comes the discussion of the main topics of a given book, then a series of "ethicotheological

68 Walaeus, *Compendium ethicae*, 98.

69 Walaeus, *Compendium ethicae*, 99, referring to 1 John 3 and James 2.

70 Walaeus, *Compendium ethicae*, 96 and 101–2.

71 Contra Donald Sinnema, "The Discipline of Ethics in Early Reformed Orthodoxy," *Calvin Theological Journal* 28 (1993): 20.

72 Johannes Trygophorus, *Concertationes ethicae ex Aristotelis X. libris Nicomachiis, una cum applicatione ad ethicam Christianam* (Gryphiswaldiae: Ferber, 1606), 1.

theses" follows. Working through the first book, for instance, Trygophorus first discusses the limited nature of philosophical ethics, with simple distinctions like the one between complete and incomplete virtues, stressing that one kind of good, the divine and spiritual one, does not abolish the human and moral one.[73] So the standard disputation or commentary already comes from a distinctively Christian outlook. In the ethicotheological disputation that follows, we have a more general discussion of Christianity and ethics, and some ideas and discussions that are unique to Trygophorus. Philosophical ethics, he for instance claims, has only a distant concern for individual human beings, while these are the central preoccupation of Christian ethics. Echoing Aristotle's discussion about whether it is the same to be a good man and a good citizen, he further writes that there can be a good citizen who is not a good man, and a good citizen and good man who is not a Christian; but not the other way around.[74] Whatever discussion of Christianity the disputations on the successive books of the *Ethics* may lead him to develop, they all close with this kind of *disputationes ethicotheologicae*.

These disputations not only raise questions that are often absent from previous commentaries. They also have a peculiar relation to the Christian intellectual tradition. While Trygophorus's commentary includes pagan, Muslim, and various Christian thinkers in its initial discussion of each book, the partners in this dialogue change when we arrive at the ethicotheological section. Luther, who is absent from nearly all Protestant commentaries on the *Ethics*, makes an appearance here. It is not Luther as critic of Aristotle, however, but Luther of the *Commentary on Genesis*, with his insistence on the place for human virtues in relation to earthly matters.[75] Beyond this mention of Luther, the prevailing voice in these sections is that of Augustine,[76] followed in a remarkably close way by twelfth-century authors like Lombard and Bernard.[77] The Christian "application" of Aristotelian ethics, in other words, implies not only an adjustment of some key concepts, but a mediation through Patristic and medieval spiritual literature.

73 Trygophorus, *Concertationes ethicae*, 19.
74 Trygophorus, *Concertationes ethicae*, theses 3 and 4 in 22.
75 Trygophorus, *Concertationes ethicae*, 20.
76 Trygophorus, *Concertationes ethicae*, 20, 64, 86. This sometimes involves some quite remote anti-Pelagian writings.
77 See, for instance, Trygophorus, *Concertationes ethicae*, 64–68.

4 Conclusions

To conclude, I would like to stress a few facts that in my view emerge clearly from a perusal of these commentaries. In the book summarized above, Edwards closes his description of the ancient Christian reception of Aristotle writing about his apparent defeat "by a coalition of Platonism and Bibliolatry" in the sixteenth century.[78] But if Augustinian concerns were central to the Reformation, neither Platonism nor Bibliolatry are its main expressions. Sober correction within commentaries on Aristotle—whose work continued to be the fundamental textual instrument for moral education—were indeed a most significant venue.

Protestant commentators of Aristotle who embarked in the correction of some of his views, did so working within a longer Christian tradition of such correction. They sometimes intensified these corrections; but when they did, it was drawing from that same tradition. Assaults on other authors for blindly following Aristotle are present, but they only have a strong version in Talon. When Vermigli accuses someone of Christianizing Aristotle too rashly (in a way that even affects the translation), it is Bruni and not the medieval scholastics who is the object of the reproach. Though justification by faith is frequently present in the discussions of Vermigli and Trygophorus, there is no suggestion in these commentaries that we should expect different types of moral philosophy among Protestants and Roman Catholics.

Though a fruitful tension between the Augustinian and the Aristotelian tradition is part of this story throughout, the exact way in which each commentator appeals to Augustine against Aristotle varies significantly. Only in Talon do we find an either/or; but, on the other hand, Talon is the only one of these commentators who has no clearly defined confessional allegiance and who includes no single discussion of Christian Scripture in his commentary. In different forms and degrees, Vermigli, Walaeus, and Trygophorus rather exemplify an integration of traditions. Finally, it is worth stressing that though these corrections are presented as Christian corrections, and are mostly carried out by theologians, they imply as much argumentative work as the exposition of Aristotle.

78 Edwards, *Aristotle and Early Christian Thought*, 195.

CHAPTER 17

Influence and Inspiration: Archias and Staupitz as Didactic Models for Cicero and Luther

John G. Nordling

Every great scholar, every great statesman, every great philosopher has had a teacher or teachers who had a major impact on his or her development. In this chapter I shall apply the perspectives of influence and inspiration to two persons whose works matter and whose courage and vision made a difference in the course of history: Marcus Tullius Cicero (106–43 BC) and Martin Luther (AD 1483–1546). Luther read the orations of Cicero as a schoolboy in his own development as a Latinist and someone skilled in both rhetoric and philosophy.[1] Cicero, too, had teachers who got the best out of him, and thus helped him to develop into Rome's greatest orator.[2] Of course, we should not think that Archias for Cicero or Staupitz for Luther were the *only* teachers to whom the two were exposed, nor were they necessarily the best teachers; in Cicero's case, Scaevola would had greater immediate impact on Cicero's legal knowledge and Molon may have had greater influence on Cicero in terms of rhetorical delivery. Yet Archias played the primary, formative role in shaping the young Cicero as Staupitz did Luther. Thus, the relationships explored here establish the fact that a pedant's influence can inspire the growth, maturation, and (sometimes)

---

1 For Luther's early training as a Latinist see Roland H. Bainton, *Here I Stand: a Life of Martin Luther* (Nashville: Abingdon Press, 1950), 18; E.G. Schwiebert, *Luther and His Times: the Reformation from a New Perspective* (St. Louis: Concordia, 1950), 110–17; and Martin Brecht, *Martin Luther.* Vol 1: *His Road to Reformation, 1483–1521* (trans. James L. Schaff; Philadelphia: Fortress Press, 1985), 12–15. For Luther's maturation as a Latinist, and his appreciation of Cicero in particular, see "'The Real German Cicero'," in Carl P.E. Springer, *Cicero in Heaven: The Roman Rhetor and Luther's Reformation* (Leiden and Boston: Brill, 2018), 55–100. In his writings Luther referred to Cicero (or quoted from his works) more than 300 times. See Carl P.E. Springer, "Martin's Martial: Reconsidering Luther's Relationship with the Classics," *International Journal of the Classical Tradition* 14, no. 1/2 (Summer 2007): 31–32.

2 By contrast with Cicero, Julius Caesar was accorded the status "second best" orator at Rome—an assessment shared by several of the ancients who evaluated the Roman orators. See, e.g., Quintilian 10.1.114; Plutarch *Caes.* 3.2; Tacitus *Dialog.* 25.3. For modern proponents of Caesar's "second best" status see Nordling, "Indirect Discourse," 26 n. 46.

 | DOI:10.1163/9789004206717_019

spectacular fruitfulness of a later student. My own was Gottfried G. Krodel, Martin Luther Professor of Reformation History at Valparaiso University.[3]

1 Archias and Cicero

Cicero's speech on behalf of his former teacher known as the *Pro Archia Poeta* has garnered the attention of many readers for its stalwart defense of liberal learning. I myself admire the speech in no small part because the oration is not simply on behalf of any poet, but the one who had been Cicero's early teacher from boyhood—so in a sense Cicero was repaying a debt. Moreover, the speech, like few specimens drawn from classical literature, in celebrating the liberal arts extols the value of art and eloquence for its own sake. For example, Cicero avers that these studies (*haec studia*)—i.e. literary pursuits—are meant:

> ... adolescentiam acuunt, senectutem oblectant, secundas res ornant, adversis perfugium ac solacium praebent, delectant domi, non impediunt foris, pernoctant nobiscum, peregrinantur, rusticantur.
>
> *Arch.* 16

> ... sharpen one's adolescence, please one's old age, adorn favorable circumstances, provide refuge and solace amid adversities, delight one at home, do not hamper one abroad, pass the night with us, travel with us, live in the country with us.[4]

At the beginning of the speech Cicero reveals how indebted to Archias he was in becoming Rome's greatest orator. With apparent sincerity the orator

3 See my tribute to him in John G. Nordling, *Philemon*. Concordia Commentary Series (St. Louis: Concordia, 2004): xiv. Dr. Krodel had been forced to belong to the Hitler Youth as a young boy in Germany during World War II. I personally have a high regard for him as a Luther scholar and in this chapter I have availed myself of his translations of important letters Luther wrote to Staupitz. See Gottfried G. Krodel, ed. and trans., *Letters I*. Vol. 48 in *Luther's Works* (Philadelphia: Fortress Press, 1963); idem, ed. and trans., *Letters II*. Vol. 49 in *Luther's Works* (Philadelphia: Fortress Press, 1972).

4 Unless otherwise noted, the translations of the Latin texts cited in this chapter are my own. I would like to thank Benjamin Mayes and Roland Ziegler, my colleagues at Concordia Theological Seminary, Fort Wayne, IN, for their help with Luther's German. I would also like to thank Rev. Roger Peters, assistant to the director of library and information services at the seminary for his considerable help in locating materials in the Wayne and Barbara Kroemer Library.

maintains that if ever he had been of service to anyone—"succoring some and saving others [*ceteris opitulari et alios servare*]"—this was because his own voice in earlier life had been "formed" by Archias's "encouragement and precepts [*vox, huius hortatu praeceptisque conformata*]" (*Arch.* 1).[5] This is high tribute, considering that Archias's influence upon Cicero's earlier life and upbringing are not often acknowledged;[6] we know that Cicero's father moved both the future orator and brother Quintus from Arpinum to a house in Rome on the Esquiline Hill where the two boys attended lectures by Epicureans and Academics; moreover, a blind Stoic named Diodotus lived in the house with the family.[7] Like many contemporaries, Cicero was drawn to ancient philosophy as a solace and translated several Greek tracts into Latin in the last few years of his life.[8] Yet well before his post-exile philosophical period Cicero was thoroughly conversant in the two leading schools of ancient philosophy at the time, Epicureanism and Stoicism, and he himself dabbled eclectically in both to enhance his rhetorical craft.

When Cicero was a young man, some of the most dominant orators of the age were holding forth in the forum: Quintus Hortensius Hortalus, the legate Publius Sulpicius Rufus, the tribune Quintus Varius "Hybrida," Gnaeus Papirius Carbo, and Gnaeus Pomponius—all of whom "all but lived on the rostra [*hi quidem habitabant in rostris*]," as Cicero quips (*Brut.* 305).[9] Such oratorical activity transpired at the height of the Social War (91–88 BC), and the chaotic legislation these eloquent speakers promulgated left a huge impression upon the developing orator (Cicero donned the toga of manhood in about 93 or 92 BC).[10] Nor was he content merely to listen to speeches delivered from the

---

5 I have used the Latin text of N.H. Watts, trans., *The Speeches* Pro Archia poeta, Post reditum in senatu, Post reditum ad Quirites, De domo sua, De haruspicum responsis, Pro Plancio, LCL (Cambridge, MA: Harvard University Press; London: William Heinemann, Ltd., 1955), 6–41.

6 See the pithy comments in Aubrey Gwynn, *Roman Education from Cicero to Quintilian* (Oxford: Oxford University Press, 1926; reprint, New York: Teachers College Press, 1966), 69; E.S. Gruen, *The Last Generation of the Roman Republic* (Berkeley, Los Angeles, London: University of California Press, 1974), 267; S.F. Bonner, *Education in Ancient Rome* (Berkeley and Los Angeles: University of California Press, 1977), 76–77.

7 Despite his disability Diodotus was a skilled musician and gave lectures in geometry. Cicero *Tusc.* 5.39, 113. In Bonner, *Education in Ancient Rome*, 77 n. 19.

8 E.g., *Consolatio* (45 BC); *De natura deorum* (45); *De divinatione* (44); *De fato* (44). Cicero was himself murdered by the forces of Mark Antony on 7 December 43.

9 I cite the Latin edition of the *Brutus* by G.L. Hendrickson and H.M. Hubbell, trans., *Cicero: Brutus, Orator*, LCL (Cambridge, MA: Harvard University Press; London, UK: William Heinemann, Ltd., 1952), 18–293.

10 Gwynn, *Roman Education*, 64.

rostra: he himself wrote and declaimed daily "with unflagging interest [*acerrimo studio*]" (*Brut.* 305). Suffice it to say that Cicero was subjected to a Roman gentleman's education from earliest life to young manhood: rhetorical studies in boyhood, as we have seen; the study of civil law, philosophy, dialectic, the delivering of declamations in later youth (*Brut.* 306); then a study tour—first to Athens in about 79 BC and Rhodes somewhat later (*Brut.* 315–16). By this time Cicero was gradually coming into prominence in the Roman law courts (81–79 BC). In his adolescence, however, the orator was given to an excessive wordiness, lack of focus, and a resulting over-exertion of his voice and lungs that severely curtailed his effectiveness as an advocate (*Brut.* 313–14). Hence, the culmination of his studies was private lessons with Apollonius Molon in Rhodes, someone with whom he had studied previously in Rome (*Brut.* 307, 312). Molon made it his task, Cicero says,

> ... si modo id consequi potuit, ut nimis redundantis nos et supra fluentis iuvenili quadam dicendi impunitate et licentia reprimeret et quasi extra ripas diffluentis coerceret. Ita recepi me biennio post non modo exercitatior sed prope mutatus. Nam et contentio nimia vocis resederat et quasi deferverat oratio lateribusque vires et corpori mediocris habitus accesserat.
>
> *Brut.* 316

> ... to repress us if possible from a certain youthful impunity and license of excessive redundancy and excessive fluency, and to check it so to speak from flowing beyond the banks. Thus, I betook myself home two years later not only better trained but nearly transformed. For the excessive exertion of my voice had settled down, my language had, as it were, ceased boiling, strength had been added to my lungs, and a moderate bearing characterized my body.

It is tempting to suppose that this tortured text is a throwback to the type of breathy oratorical performance Cicero used to offer before his private studies with Molon would have made a difference. The style of Cicero's literary output did not remain entirely uniform—so, for example, his earlier orations (e.g., *Pro Roscio Amerino* [80 BC]) show tendencies of Asianism.[11] However, the orator's

11 Thus, John Hedley Simon and Dirk Obbink, "Tullius Cicero, Marcus," *OCD*, 1560. Of the two styles, "Asianism" and "Atticism," the former was considered more florid and bombastic than the latter—and Cicero was criticized as an "Asian" by what he represents in

youthful exuberance was later tempered by increasing maturity and changes in oratorical fashion. It seems quite possible that by 46 BC (the year *Brutus* appeared) Cicero thought back to the type of Latinity he produced as a young, relatively inexperienced orator, and let fly in the older, pre-Molonic manner. Generally, however, Cicero's prose seems less pretentious—and so, more accessible to a modern mind. The orations are "consistent in their rhythmical regularity, their smooth and balanced sentence-construction, and their careful choice of vocabulary and idiom."[12]

This survey suggests that Cicero was beholden to a raft of former teachers and mentors, the full number of whom cannot be dealt with here—and that Archias, though an early influence in Cicero's maturation as an orator, perhaps was not as important to Cicero's full development as Molon had been. Nevertheless, Cicero gladly presented the case of his earlier Greek teacher, even preparing a rich and thoughtful oration on his behalf—something he did not do, so far as we know, for others engaged in educational pursuits.

Archias found himself in need of Cicero's help in no small part simply because the poet was largely a victim of his times. Cicero undertook his defense of Archias's impugned citizenship in 62 BC when the orator was at the height of his prestige, having successfully baffled Catiline's conspiracy in the preceding year. In the way that he handled that pivotal event, Cicero had given his opponents an opportunity to turn what he regarded as an act of heroism against himself, for Cicero had the conspirators executed without trial. The signal aim of the opposition, led by Publius Clodius Pulcher, was to bring down Cicero—and with him, the whole fabric of the senatorial order of which he was the avowed protector.[13] During a series of eastern campaigns against Mithridates VI of Pontus, Archias had been enlisted by one Lucius Licinius Lucullus to record in glorious poetry the latter's military exploits.[14] Moreover, the entire Luculli family, according to Cicero, had welcomed Archias to their home in Rome after the young Lucullus had donned the toga of manhood (in

---

the *Brutus* and the *Orator*, both written in 46. See Michael Winterbottom, "Asianism and Atticism," OCD, 191.

12 Simon and Obbink, "Cicero," 1560.

13 Watts, "Introduction," in *The Speeches*, 3. Also, "Pompey had not shown sufficient appreciation of Cicero's greatness in saving his country from Catiline" (H.H. Scullard, "The Political Career of a *Novus Homo*," in T.A. Dorey, ed., *Cicero* [London: Routledge & Kegan Paul, 1964], 13).

14 "Again, my client has treated in its entirety the great and difficult theme of the war with Mithridates, pursuing all its diverse operations by land and sea, and his work sheds luster not only on the gallant and renowned Lucius Lucullus [*L. Lucullum, fortissimum et clarissimum virum*], but also upon the fame of the Roman people" (*Arch.* 21).

about 102 BC). That same family affectionately offered shelter to the poet in his declining years (*Arch.* 5).[15]

Lucius Lucullus returned to Rome in 64, igniting hope in the senatorial party that he might protect them against the encroachments of the Pompeians.[16] Thus the attack on Archias really was an attack on Lucullus—and, given his commitments to the senatorial party, an attack on Cicero himself. Archias was simply caught in the cross-hairs.[17] The prosecutor was a certain Gratius, otherwise unknown;[18] Cicero's opponents demanded documentary evidence that Archias had been enrolled as a citizen at Heraclea—evidence which, unfortunately, had been destroyed in the burning of the record-office during the Social War (*Arch.* 8).[19] But why should Gratius (or anyone else) insist upon documentary evidence—which could no longer be produced—while shutting one's ears to the testimony of living men: representatives of Heraclea who had come to Rome for the express purpose of presenting their city's official evidence of Archias's enrollment (*Arch.* 8), and of Marcus Lucullus (brother of Lucius)[20] who was ready to state "not what he thinks but what he knows [*qui* [*dicit*] *se non opinari, sed scire*], not that he heard but that he saw [*non audisse, sed vidisse*], not that he merely was present at the event but that he was the agent of it [*non interfuisse, sed egisse*]" (*Arch.* 8). According to Cicero anybody who was somebody—and several who were not—were on intimate terms with Archias; these included Metellus, the hero of Numidia,[21] and his

15 For the date see Bonner, *Education in Ancient Rome*, 76.

16 Watts, "Introduction," 3.

17 "The gentle and aged poet was harmless—and no political figure" (Gruen, *The Last Generation of the Roman Republic*, 267).

18 The name appears twice in the vocative case (*Grati* = "O Gratius") in *Arch.* 8 and 12.

19 In addition to Heraclea, "other cities" apparently possessed Archias's name on their rolls (Rhegium, Locri, Neapolis, and Tarentum are listed in *Arch.* 10) but Archias had not availed himself of the presence of his name on these lists "because he had always desired to belong to Heraclea [*quod semper se Heracliensem esse voluit*]" (*Arch.* 10).

20 The Luculli brothers, Lucius and Marcus, were consuls at Rome in the years 74 and 73 BC, respectively. As members of the *gens Licinia* the Luculli brothers were the source of Archias's *gentilicium*, Licinius. So Dan Hanchey, "Typically Unique: Shared Strategies in Cicero's *Pro Archia* and *Pro Balbo*," *Classical Journal* 108, no. 2 (2012/2013): 163–64.

21 In 109 and 108 BC Metellus had charge of the war against Jugurtha, winning a triumph and the title Numidicus. So Charles E. Bennet, *Cicero's Selected Orations* (Boston, New York, Chicago: Allyn and Bacon, 1904), 238.

son, Q. Metellus Pius;[22] Marcus Aemilius;[23] Q. Catulus, both father and son;[24] L. Crassus;[25] the Luculli, of course;[26] M. Livius Drusus;[27] the Octavii;[28] Cato;[29] and "the whole family of the Hortensii"[30] (*Arch.* 6). So honorable a position did Archias hold, continues Cicero,

> ... adficiebatur summo honore, quod eum non solum colebant qui aliquid percipere aut audire studebant, verum etiam si qui forte simulabant.
> *Arch.* 6

> ... he was greatly honored because not only those who were desirous of perceiving and hearing anything [he wrote] were cultivating him, but even if there were some [tagalongs] who were feigning such desire.

And so Cicero builds the case for his erstwhile Greek professor, plank by bombastic plank. The *Pro Archia* is a short, relatively unpretentious oration, so far as Cicero's orations go; but, as often happens in other Ciceronian extravaganzas of this type, the sentences used to express his boundless esteem for Archias frequently run away with themselves and so make translation of these overextended periods a real chore. We see in this oration, however, plenty of evidence that former students in ancient times came to the spirited defense of—and so honored—a respected, if beleaguered, professor. In his way Archias inspired

---

22 Q. Metellus Pius received the surname Pius for having secured the recall of his father, the elder Metellus, from exile. See Bennett, *Cicero's Selected Orations*, 238.

23 Marcus Aemilius Scaurus, consul in 115 and 107 BC, a leading orator of the day and long the leader of the Senate. So Bennett, *Cicero's Selcted Orations*, 238.

24 The father was Marius's colleague. The son was consul in 78 BC. So Bennett, *Cicero's Selected Orations*, 239.

25 Lucius Crassus was a famous orator who died in 91 BC. See Bennett, *Cicero's Selected Orations*, 239.

26 The Luculli were celebrated family, the two most conspicuous members of which—as we have seen—were Lucius and Marcus.

27 Marcus Livius Drusus was the aristocrat who, in 91 BC, broke away from his party and urged the granting of citizenship to the Italian *socii*. So Bennett, *Cicero's Selected Orations*, 239.

28 Distinguished members of this family were Gnaeus Octavius, consul with Cinna in 87 BC, and son Lucius, consul in 75 BC. Bennett, *Cicero's Selected Orations*, 239.

29 Probably the father of Cato Uticensis, the contemporary of Cicero. Bennett, *Cicero's Selected Orations*, 239.

30 The orator Q. Hortensius, the most eminent member of the family, figured in the debate on Pompey's appointment. His father was consul in 97 BC. Bennett, *Cicero's Selected Orations*, 239.

Cicero to give his all for his former teacher, a point by no means difficult to substantiate—and appreciate—still today.

2 Staupitz's Influence upon Luther

The story of Staupitz's influence upon Luther is long and complicated. Here I shall focus upon Staupitz's early relationship with Luther as a mentor, his initial support of Luther as a colleague, and, more briefly, on how the two parted company.

Johannes von Staupitz (d. 28 December 1524) was born in the town of Motterwitz in Saxony sometime during the decade of the 1460s.[31] Unlike Luther, Staupitz was descended from nobility and grew up as the friend and companion of Frederick the Wise (1463–1525), the duke and elector of Ernestine Saxony, who would protect Luther. Staupitz became Vicar-general of the Observant Order of the Friar Hermits of St. Augustine in Saxony-Thuringia in May 1503, and wrote a new constitution for the order, the title of which seems revealing for what must have been his overall intent: *The Constitutions of the Order of Hermits of Saint Augustine, Prepared under Apostolic Privilege for the Reformation of Germany* [*pro Reformatione Alemanie*].[32] By "reformation" Staupitz apparently desired to strengthen the position of the Observant Augustinians in Germany over against that of the Conventuals, the specifics of which cannot be entered into here;[33] however, given Staupitz's evangelical

31 For some standard treatments on Staupitz in English, see David Curtis Steinmetz, *Misericordia Dei: The Theology of Johannes von Staupitz in its Late Medieval Setting* (Leiden: E.J. Brill, 1968); idem, *Luther and Staupitz: An Essay in the Intellectual Origins of the Protestant Reformation* (Duke Monographs in Medieval and Renaissance Studies 4; Durham, NC: Duke University Press, 1980); Lothar Graf zu Dohna, "Staupitz and Luther: Continuity and Breakthrough at the Beginning of the Reformation," in Heiko A. Oberman and Frank A. James, III, eds., *VIA AUGUSTINI: Augustine in the Later Middle Ages, Renaissance and Reformation. Essays in Honor of Damasus Trapp, O.S.A.* (Leiden, New York, Kobenhavn, Köln: E.J. Brill, 1991), 116–129; Franz Posset, *The Front-Runner of the Catholic Reformation: The Life and Works of Johann von Staupitz* (Aldershot, UK: Ashgate, 2003); Judith Rossall, "The Cost of Supporting Luther: The Role of Johann von Staupitz in the Early Reformation." *Lutheran Forum* 53, no. 4 (2019): 16–22.

32 The full Latin title is in Steinmetz, *Misericordia Dei*, 6. I have followed the translation provided in Rossall, "The Cost of Supporting Luther," 16.

33 See Heinrich Boehmer, *Martin Luther: Road to Reformation* (trans. by John W. Doberstein and Theodore G. Tappert; Cleveland and New York: World Publishing, 1965), 58–81; Steinmetz, *Misericordia Dei*, 6–10; Richard D. Balge, "Martin Luther, Augustinian," in Edward C. Fredrich, Siegbert W. Becker, David P. Kuske, eds., *Luther Lives: Essays in Commemoration of the 500th Anniversary of Martin Luther's Birth* (Milwaukee, WI:

insights and influence upon Luther, it seems possible that the busy administrator and churchman intended "reformation" to possess something of the meaning it would possess later as Luther's teachings spread throughout Germany and beyond.[34] In 1502 Staupitz established the Augustinian monastery at Wittenberg which obviously was to be connected to the university.[35] In 1503 Staupitz became provost of the newly founded university at Wittenberg, and in that capacity possessed considerable influence over the teaching, preaching, and learning that went on in Saxony, and over Luther personally.

It is unclear when Luther met Staupitz for the first time.[36] Luther had been appointed by Staupitz to fill the Augustinian chair in moral philosophy in 1508,[37] but it is unclear whether the two men were even friends at this time.[38] Nevertheless, their eventual relationship has been noted and commented upon by many. Steinmetz summarizes thus:

> They did not meet in the classroom or library, but in the chapel, the refectory, and the confessional. Luther met Staupitz as youth meets middle age, as a penitent meets his confessor, as a friar meets his superior, as the grandson of peasants meets a cultured Saxon nobleman, as a recent Master of Arts meets a learned Doctor of Divinity. Even before they met, Luther owed Staupitz obedience and respect, both as the vicar general of his order and as a doctor of the Church. While their first encounter blossomed into friendship, Luther was always quite specific in locating the crucial moments of that relationship in the confessional or in pastoral conversation relating to the confessional. Luther did not listen to a course of theological lectures by Staupitz or participate with him in a

---

Northwestern Publishing House, 1983), 8; Brecht, *Martin Luther: Road*, 54–55; zu Dohna, "Staupitz and Luther," 118–22; Posset, *Front-Runner of the Catholic Reformation*, 7–31.

34 See Posset (*Front-Runner of the Catholic Reformation*, 27) for the meaning which "reformation" had by many forward-thinking friars at the turn of the fifteenth to the sixteenth century: "Everyone wanted reform, or professed to want reform. How to reform and what to reform was not so clear" (Owen Chadwick, *The Reformation* [Baltimore: Penguin Books, 1964], 12).

35 Brecht, *Martin Luther: Road*, 121.

36 Possibly 1506, when Staupitz would have been visiting the friary at Erfurt in his capacity as Vicar-general, and where Luther would have been a novice of about 23 years old. So Brecht, *Martin Luther: Road*, 70–71, 86; Rossall, "The Cost of Supporting Luther," 17.

37 Steinmetz, *Misericoria Dei*, 9.

38 Staupitz's travels to the Augustinian communities over which he was in charge might have kept him from the University of Wittenberg during Luther's early years there. See Alfred T. Jorgensen, *Martin Luther: Reformer of the Church* (Minneapolis: Augsburg Publishing House, 1953), 70–71; Boehmer, *Martin Luther*, 53; Steinmetz, *Misericordia Dei*, 9.

> seminar on a biblical subject. Most of what Staupitz said to Luther that really mattered was protected by the seal of the confessional. If Luther had not revealed what took place in those conversations, we should never have heard about them at all.[39]

Thus, for example, Luther would comment in later years that, had it not been for Staupitz, he would certainly have been "swallowed up and left in hell."[40] Staupitz had a way of getting Luther to come to terms with real sins, not peccadillos:

> Christ is the forgiver of real sins, like murdering one's parents [*die Aeltern ermorden*], engaging in public blasphemy [*offentlich lästern*], despising God [*Gott verachten*], breaking one's marriage [*die Ehe brechen*], etc.... You must keep a register wherein downright sins stand if Christ shall help you; you must not mess around with such worthless works and make-believe sins [*mit solchem Humpelwerk und Puppensünden*], and make an offense out of every fart [*aus einem jglichen Bombart*]!
>
> WA TR 6:106–7, no. 6669

The worst thing a pastor-confessor can do with an earnest penitent is nurse along vapid neuroses, shield one from honest confrontation with the fact that an unwillingness to take God's mercy to heart can have perilous and eternal consequences.[41] When Luther was at a corpus Christi procession, he was filled with such dread of the sacrament that sweat broke out and he was convinced that he would die;[42] later at confession, when Luther cried out to Staupitz about the experience, the astute confessor exclaimed, "Dear me [*Ei*], your thoughts are not Christ [*Euer Gedanken sind nicht Christus*]!" Luther

---

39 Steinmetz, *Luther and Staupitz*, 30–81.

40 So Gordon Rupp, *Luther's Progress to the Diet of Worms* (London: S.C.M. Limited, 1951; reprinted by Harper and Row, Publishers, 1964), 31 n. 3, on the basis of WA 58.1, pgs. 27ff. A better source for this reflection is the letter Luther wrote to Graf Albrecht von Mansfeld on 23 February 1542: "And in case Doctor Staupitz, or rather God through Dr. Staupitz, had not rescued me, I would long have drowned (in sea of confusion) and been in hell [*so were ich darinn ersossen undt langst in der helle*]" (WA 9 no. 3716, pg. 627, lines 24–25). The English translation is in Schwiebert, *Luther and His Times*, 777 n. 68. For some additional engagement with the passage see Bainton, *Here I Stand*, 53; Jorgensen, *Martin Luther*, 71.

41 Steinmetz, *Luther and Staupitz*, 32.

42 In Otto Scheel, ed., *Dokumente zu Luthers Entwicklung* (second edition; Tübingen: Verlag von J.C.B Mohr [Paul Siebeck], 1929), no. 201. The date may have been 7 June 1515. So Scheel, *Dokumente*, 79 n. 1.

concludes the reminiscence with the observation that he took Staupitz's word *mit Freuden* ("with joy"), and that it was for him *sehr tröstlich* ("very comforting"). On another occasion, when Luther poured out to Staupitz "how horrendous and terrifying were his cogitations [*quam horrendas et terrificas cogitationes*]," the confessor pointed out that God would use the *tentatio* to shape Luther as a servant "for the accomplishment of great things [*ad res magnas gerendas*]" (Scheel, *Dokumente*, no. 138; written at Coberg in 1530, possibly in July).[43]

I could go on, as others have—more adept than I at exploring Luther's inner demons;[44] what should be emphasized here, however, is how central Staupitz was to Luther's maturation as a Christian and finding himself. Before leaving this early period of Luther's life, I should mention that it was solely due to Staupitz's influence that the eventual reformer prepared himself for preaching and to become a Doctor of Theology.[45] When the younger man pleaded that this new venture would surely be the death of him, Staupitz quipped that Luther would have plenty to do in heaven: "Do you not know that our Lord hath many great things to accomplish? There he needs many wise and clever people too who can counsel him. If you die you'll have to be his counselor!" (WA TR 2:379, no. 2255a, lines 15–17).[46] Luther perceived in this quip a kind of prophecy that would be carried out four years later when he began "to wage war on" (*belligerari*) the pope and all his affairs (WA TR 2:379, no. 2255a, lines 17–19).[47] Staupitz also arranged things so that the elector Frederick generously picked up the tab for the cost of Luther's doctoral degree.[48] It seems that Staupitz may

---

43 Other letters wherein Staupitz urged on Luther the usefulness of his temptations are Scheel, *Dokumente*, nos. 207, 210. See Steinmetz, *Luther and Staupitz*, 32 n. 116.

44 E.g., Bainton, *Here I Stand*, 53–60; Schwiebert, *Luther and His Times*, 169–74; Jorgensen, *Martin Luther*, 71–72; Rupp, *Luther's Progress*, 26–35; Boehmer, *Martin Luther*, 92–109; Balge, "Martin Luther, Augustinian," 8.

45 About which see Bainton, *Here I Stand*, 59–60; Schwiebert, *Luther and His Times*, 193–94; Jorgensen, *Martin Luther*, 76; Rupp, *Luther's Progress*, 24; Boehmer, *Martin Luther*, 83; Brecht, *Martin Luther: Road*, 125; Marilyn J. Harran, "Luther as Professor," in Marilyn J. Harran, ed., *Luther and Learning: The Wittenberg University Luther Symposium* (London and Toronto: Associated University Presses, 1985): 29–30.

46 Schwiebert's translation (*Luther and His Times*, 194) seems more like a paraphrase—possibly because he weighs more evidence in accounting for Luther's hesitancy and Staupitz's reply, each version putting the matter slightly differently. In addition to this letter see also WA TR 3:187–88 (no. 3143b); and WA TR 4:13 (no. 3924). The references are in Schwiebert, *Luther and His Times*, 780 n. 123.

47 For further evidence of this "prophecy" see Luther's statement that "this prophetic voice was fulfilled toward me [*haec vatidica vox in me impleta est*]" (WA TR 4:13.35 [no. 3924]).

48 Schwiebert, *Luther and His Times*, 194; Boehmer, *Martin Luther*, 84.

have viewed Luther as his own eventual replacement at the university from a quite early time period.[49]

As Luther grew in stature, Staupitz trusted him the more. There is much that could be stated regarding Staupitz's initial support of Luther as a colleague. The Augustinians were a preaching order, and Luther possessed a flair for preaching;[50] so in 1511 he was appointed official preacher for the Black Cloister, and in 1514 began to preach in the Town Church several times per week.[51] In 1512 Staupitz withdrew from the university, appointing Luther as a professor of Theology in his place.[52] In 1515 Staupitz selected Luther as district vicar responsible for the oversight of ten or eleven convents in Meissen and Thuringia: "How he found time to lecture at all is a mystery."[53] In early 1518, scant months after Luther's *Ninety-Five Theses* had rocked Europe (31 October 1517), Staupitz found himself under pressure to deal with "the Luther problem."[54] An opportunity to do so presented itself at the chapter meeting of the German Augustinians that began in Heidelberg on 25 April 1518, by all accounts a raucous affair.[55] However, far from ordering Luther to keep silent, Staupitz invited Luther to write up some theses and chair the disputation: "Father Martin

49 Bainton, *Here I Stand*, 60; Schwiebert, *Luther and His Times*, 294; Jorgensen, *Martin Luther*, 76; Rupp, *Luther's Progress*, 20–21; Steinmetz, *Luther and Staupitz*, 9; Harran, "Luther as Professor," 29–30.

50 See e.g. Boehmer, *Martin Luther*, 156. For the eventual role that preaching would play at Wittenberg during the Reformation and beyond see Bainton, *Here I Stand*, 348–55.

51 These details are in Schwiebert, *Luther and His Times*, 282; and Brecht, *Martin Luther: Road*, 150–55. Luther entered the Black Cloister of the Augustinian Hermits at Erfurt on 17 July 1505, at age 21, after the terrible thunderstorm that wrung from him the prayer to St. Anne and vow to become a monk. The black garb of the Augustinian Hermits gave the cloister its name. See "Luther, Martin," in Erwin L. Lueker, ed., *Lutheran Cyclopedia* (St. Louis: Concordia, 1975): 483.

52 Brecht, *Martin Luther: Road*, 96. For several members of the theology faculty at Wittenberg in 1512 see Brecht, *Martin Luther: Road*, 120. Luther had occupied a position in the Master of Arts faculty since 1508/09.

53 Schwiebert, *Luther and His Times*, 282. On Luther's busyness during this time see Harran, "Luther as Professor," 30.

54 The *Ninety-Five Theses* had reached Rome by early 1518. Pope Leo X then wrote to Gabriel della Volta, prior general of the Augustinian Order, beseeching him to "take care of the problem of Martin Luther." See Rupp, *Luther's Progress*, 55; Henry Ansgar Kelly, "Luther at Augsburg, 1518: New Light on Papal Strategies," *Journal of Ecclesiastical History* 70 no. 4 (2019): 806; Rossall, "The Cost of Supporting Luther," 17.

55 "The debate was lively and there was some opposition, but when the junior Heidelberg divine shouted angrily, 'If the peasants heard that, they would stone you!' his voice was drowned in general laughter. But it was among the younger men that Luther made his conquests that day." So Rupp, *Luther's Progress*, 56. Also Bainton, *Here I Stand*, 86–87; Schwiebert, *Luther and His Times*, 328; Brecht, *Martin Luther: Road*, 215.

Luther, master of sacred Theology, will preside" (WA 1:353, 3).[56] The other side was not amused. On 25 August 1518 della Volta took the drastic step of writing Gerard Hecker, provincial of the rival Augustinian Conventuals, to "imprison, bind, and detain" Luther.[57] Since the same letter mentions that "all those under us" should help Hecker in this task, it seems likely that there is a reference here to Staupitz—and anyone else who would not fall into line.[58] Luther's trial was held at Augsburg in October 1518 before the papal nuncio, Cardinal Cajetan.[59] Staupitz was there too, at great risk to himself, and when asked to use his influence on Luther, the Vicar-general replied that he was no match for Luther "in knowledge of Scripture and in talents [*in sacris literis & ingenio*]" (WA Br 1, no. 99, lines 44–45);[60] therefore, the cardinal would have to persuade Luther himself (*ut ipsemet persuaderet*, WA Br 1, no. 99, line 46). But as the two were at loggerheads, that solution was impossible. Staupitz beat a hasty retreat from Augsburg without paying farewell respects to the nuncio, and Luther bolted in the middle of the night several days later—alarmed by a rumor that his opponent possessed a mandate to put both Luther and Staupitz in prison.[61] It was during this tense time that Staupitz released Luther from his monastic vow, thus liberating him from obedience to the order. Probably this was for Luther's safety—and to avoid the possibility of bringing further disrepute upon the order.

---

56 The opponents of Luther hoped to silence him at the meeting, but Staupitz was determined to give him a fair hearing. In twenty-eight theses Luther opposed William of Occam's *theologia crucis* with his own *theologia crucis*, and the philosophy of Aristotle with the theology of St. Paul. So "Heidelberg Disputation," in Lueker, *Lutheran Cyclopedia*, 368.

57 "Therefore we command you under pain of losing all your promotions, dignities and offices, when you receive this letter, to proceed to capture the said Brother Martin Luther, have him bound in chains, fetters and handcuffs [*in vinculis compedibus et manicis ferreis*], and detained under strict guard in prison [*sub arta custodia detineri*] at the instance of our Supreme Lord Leo X" (*Zeitschrift für Kirchengeschichte* 2 [1878]: 477, as translated in Preserved Smith, ed., *Luther's Correspondence and Other Contemporary Letters*, Vol. 1 [Philadelphia: The Lutheran Publication Society, 1913], 107).

58 So Rossall, "The Cost of Supporting Luther," 18.

59 For the proper chronology see Kelly, "Luther at Augsburg, 1518," 814.

60 As trans. in Krodel, *Letters I*, 86. Dated 14 October 1518.

61 "Having endured the same silence on the fifth day, at last, due to the counsel of friends, especially since he [Cajetan] had bandied it about [*iactasset*] that he had a mandate to incarcerate both me and the vicar [*sese habere mandatum, ut et me et vicarium incarceraret*]..., I withdrew [*recessi*], having supposed that I had endured an obedience that was sufficiently dangerous [*sat periculosam obedientiam me praestitisse arbitratus*]" (WA 2, page 17, lines 31–36). See also Schwiebert, *Luther and His Times*, 353–54; Brecht, *Martin Luther: Road*, 257–58; Kelly, "Luther at Augsburg, 1518," 814.

Amid such happenings, it is difficult to avoid the impression that Staupitz unqualifiedly supported Luther as a colleague in a great many matters—ready even to die for the latter, should circumstances warrant. Staupitz joined Luther in attacking the notion that only those who had papal permission could examine the Scriptures;[62] the Vicar-general supposed, with Luther, however, that Christ commands this search from any as might follow him (see e.g. John 5:39; Rom 15:4; 16:25–27)—so to restrict the study of the Scriptures to the pope and his counselors was plainly too narrow.[63] At any rate, Staupitz concluded the letter with the invitation for Luther to leave Wittenberg "so that we may live and die together [*ut simul vivamus moriamurque*]" (WA Br 1, no. 119, line 10).[64] There is some dispute about the date of this letter. Smith supposed Staupitz wrote it from Salzburg on 14 September 1518, one of the days associated with the celebration of the Holy Cross.[65] However, the editors of WA Br 1 point out (pg. 265) that Staupitz "scarcely" (*kaum*) could have been in Salzburg on that date and argue, on the basis of much external evidence (pp. 264–67), for an early to mid-December date. The matter cannot be decided here—but note how the letter concludes:

> Datum Saltzburgae, die Exaltationis sanctissimae crucis, anno M.D. XVIII. Frater tuus Iohannes Staupitius D.
>
> WA Br 1, no. 119, lines 12–14

> Dated at Salzburg, on the day of the exaltation of the most holy cross, in the year 1518. Your brother John Staupitz, D[octor].[66]

62 Staupitz to Luther: "Unless I mistake, the opinion prevails that no one should examine the Scripture without leave of the Pope in order to find for himself, which Christ certainly commands us to do [*ad inveniendum se quod utique Christus ut fieret iussit*]" (WA Br 1, no. 119, Salzburg, as translated in Smith, *Luther's Correspondence*, 1:113).

63 Rossall, "The Cost of Supporting Luther," 18.

64 Regarding which see Bainton, *Here I Stand*, 100; Boehmer, *Martin Luther*, 229; Brecht, *Martin Luther: Road*, 251; Rossall, "The Cost of Supporting Luther," 18.

65 This could be supported by Staupitz's assertion, "with so great hatred was Christ once crucified [*olim in tanto odio fuisset crucifixus Christus*], and to-day I see nothing waiting for you but the cross [*et quid hodie praeter crucem te maneat non video quicquam*]" (WA Br 1, no. 119, lines 4–5, as translated in Smith, *Luther's Correspondence*, 1:113). Brecht concurs with this possibility (*Martin Luther: Road*, 515 n. 61), as does Posset (*Front-Runner of the Catholic Reformation*, 235).

66 In addition to Good Friday there was on 3 May another festival of the cross called the "Invention of the Cross," celebrating the discovery of the cross by St. Helena, Constantine's mother. This was always a "secondary celebration," however, so suppressed by the Roman Catholic Church in AD 1960. Thus Philip H. Pfatteicher, *Festivals and Commemorations: Handbook to the Calendar in Lutheran Book of Worship* (Minneapolis: Augsburg

Suffice it to say that battle lines had been clearly drawn by at least the autumn of 1518, nearly a year after the *Ninety-Five Theses* appeared. At a meeting of the German Augustinians in Eisleben on 28 August 1520 Staupitz voluntarily stepped down from his office as Vicar-general of the order, was permitted to join the Benedictines (26 April 1521, Rome), and consecrated abbot of the Benedictine monastery at Salzburg (St. Peter's Abbey) on 15 August 1521.[67] Luther, meanwhile, possessed little direct knowledge of these developments—only a rumor that the "dear Father Staupitz" was now a man of the court who "stays with the 'idol' of Salzburg [*audio ... eum idoli Salzburgensis aulicum esse*]" (WA Br 2, no 446, line 35, dated 18 December 1521, from the Wartburg, as trans. in Krodel, *Letters I*, 359)—referring to Matthew Lang (AD 1468–1540), archbishop of Salzburg, and known to be "a bitter opponent of the Reformation."[68] Luther was greatly put out that his former confessor had become an abbot,[69] that he had put himself into the hands of "that monster, your Cardinal [*monstro illi famoso, Cardinali tuo*],"[70] and that he feared for Staupitz's soul:

> It will be a wonder if you do not fall into danger of denying Christ [*mirum, si non Christum negare pericliteris*]. Therefore it is our earnest hope and prayer that you may be given back to us and be released from the prison

Publishing House, 1980), 354. The Festival of the Exaltation of the Holy Cross, first clearly mentioned by Pope Sergius (687–701), recalls the display of the true cross at Jerusalem in 629 by the emperor Heraclius after recovery from the Persians who had captured it at the destruction of the church of the Holy Sepulchre in 614. So Pfatteicher, *Festivals and Commenmorations*, 353. Though it is difficult to determine how long 14 September has been associated with Holy Cross Day, this reference to the date in Staupitz's letter could suggest that the association had been established at least by the early sixteenth-century.

67 Steinmetz, *Misericordia Dei*, 14. The decision could have been brewing for some time. Posset supposes (*Front-Runner of the Catholic Reformation*, 264) that Staupitz may have had plans as early as 1518 to accept a position at Salzburg.

68 So Smith, *Luther's Correspondence*, 1:113 n. 1. About Archbishop Lang's hostility to the Reformation see further Krodel, *Letters I*, 99 n. 14; Martin Brecht, *Martin Luther*. Vol. 2, *Shaping and Defining the Reformation, 1521–1532* (trans. James L. Schaff; Minneapolis: Fortress Press, 1985), 97; and Posset, *Front-Runner of the Catholic Reformation*, 278 n. 86.

69 "... in my ignorance I cannot see how it can be God's will that you should become an abbot [*ut abbas fieres*], nor do I think this advisable [*neque mihi consultum videtur*]" (WA Br 2, no. 512, lines 7–8, dated 27 June 1522, from Wittenberg; trans. in Krodel, *Letters II*, 11); "I also have to say that it is true that it would have been more agreeable to me had you not become an abbot [*sed hoc etiam verum esse fatear ... te non esse factum Abbatem*]" (WA Br 3, no. 659, lines 8–9, dated 17 September 1523, from Wittenberg; trans. in Krodel, *Letters II*, 48). See Steinmetz, *Misericordia Dei*, 14 nn. 4–5.

70 Archbishop Lang again. WA Br 3, no. 659, line 12. See references in Preserved Smith, ed., *Luther's Correspondence and Other Contemporary Letters*, Vol 2 (Philadelphia: The Lutheran Publication Society, 1918), 202 n. 3.

> of that tyrant [*ex istius tyrannidis carcere*];[71] we hope that you are of the same mind. There is no way in which I, who have known you before, can reconcile these two contradictory things, namely, that you are the same man that you were, if you have made up your mind to stay there; or if you are the same man, [that] you do not try to leave. But we will think the best of you and hope the best for you, and hold to the latter alternative with good hope, though it is somewhat dashed by your long silence [... *spe bona, licet diuturno tuo silentio satis fortituer pulsata*].[72]

And he wrote this after acknowledging that it was through Staupitz that "the light of the gospel first began to shine out of the darkness in my heart [... *primum coepit euangelii lux de tenebris splendescere in cordibus nostris*]" (WA Br 3, no. 659, lines 7–8, as trans. in Smith, *Luther's Correspondence*, 2:202).[73] Luther himself would later say of Staupitz that "he had begun this doctrine [*Staupitz hat die doctrinam angefangen*]" (WA TR 1:255, no. 526, dated Spring 1533).[74]

Some six months later (1 April 1524) Staupitz finally wrote back to Luther from Salzburg, his last letter to the reformer (WA Br 3, no. 726).[75] He claimed that his faith in Christ and in the gospel were as constant as ever, even if he was in need of prayer that Christ "might help my unbelief [*Christus adiuvet incredulitatem meam*]" (line 7; cf. Mk 9:24 Vulg), and that he might "abhor human things, and [not] love the church lukewarmly [*detesterque humana, et ecclesiam*

71 Still another reference to Archbishop Lang. See notes 68 and 70, above.

72 WA Br 3, no. 659, lines 14–21, as trans. in Smith, *Luther's Correspondence*, 2:203. By "long silence" Luther apparently refers to that period of time that had extended from 27 June 1522 (when he had written WA Br 2, no. 512 [see note 69, above]) until 17 September 1523 (when he wrote WA Br, no. 659 [see note 69, above]).

73 There is an allusion here to 2 Cor 4:6 with its statement that light had "shone out of darkness [*de tenebris lucem splendescere*]," which "shone in our hearts [*qui inluxit in cordibus nostris*] to the illumination of the knowledge of the clarity of God, in the face of Christ Jesus" (Vulg). See the the editor's comment in WA Br 3, pg. 156 n. 2. Paul in turn had alluded to Gen 1:3. 2 Pet 1:19 also seems quite similar.

74 "It is really strange that this clear statement of Luther is not generally taken seriously in Luther scholarship" (zu Dohna, "Staupitz and Luther," 120). Likewise, see Luther's testimony (dated February or March, 1532) that from Erasmus he had received "nothing [*nihil*]," but "I got everything from Dr. Staupitz; he gave me the *occasionem* (motivation)" (WA TR 1:80 [no. 173], as trans. in zu Dohna, "Staupitz and Luther," 120).

75 The translation in Smith, *Luther's Correspondence*, 2:225–227, is essential and shall be relied upon below. The Latin text also appears as letter 22 in Theodore Kolde, *Die deutsche Austiner-Congregation und Johann von Staupitz. Ein Beitrag zur Ordens- und Reformationsgeschichte nach meistens ungedruckten Quellen* (Gotha: Friedrich Andreas Perthes, 1879), 446–47. About the letter see also Bainton, *Here I Stand*, 256; Steinmetz, *Misericordia Dei*, 15; Brecht, *Martin Luther: Shaping*, 97; zu Dohna, "Staupitz and Luther," 120; Rossall, "The Cost of Supporting Luther," 22.

tepide amplectar]" (lines 7–8).[76] Likewise, his love for Luther was "most constant [*constantissimus*]," exceeding—like Jonathon's love for David—even man's love for women (lines 8–9; cf. 2 Sam 1:26 Vulg). Paraphrasing what obviously seems a tortuous text, perhaps written under duress, we see that Staupitz faults Luther for condemning mere externals, finding fault with the monk's cowl, and not realizing that abuses creep into all things human. Luther should "remember the little ones" (cf. Mk 9:42) and "not disturb fearful consciences" (line 20):

> We owe you much, Martin, for having led us from the husks of swine [cf. Lk 15:16] back to the pastures of life [cf. Jn 10:9] and words of salvation. The Lord give you increase [cf. 1 Cor 3:6–7] as far as the Gospel is served thereby. This we see to be the case, and many tell us of it, howbeit I see the Gospel message abused unto the liberty of the flesh [cf. Gal 5:13]. But the wind bloweth where it listeth [cf. Jn 3:8]; we owe you thanks for planting and watering [cf. 1 Cor 3:6–8], saving the glory of God, to Whom alone we attribute the power of making sons of God [Jn 1:12]. I have written enough; I wish that I could talk to you even one hour and open the secrets of the heart [*utinam vel unica hora liceret tibi colloqui et aperire secreta cordis*].
>
> WA Br 3, no. 726, lines 22–30, as trans. in Smith, *Luther's Correspondence*, 2:226[77]

Within days of having dispatched this letter to Luther, Staupitz informed Father Chilian in Salzburg that he was in poor health and living under the supervision of a physician.[78] He became physically weaker thereafter and would die on 28 December 1524, buried at St. Peter's in Salzburg.[79] In 1559 Staupitz's works

76 The Latin is unclear. The editors offer several possibilities in WA Br 3, pg. 264 n. 4.

77 For the many scriptural allusions contained herein cf. WA Br 3, pg. 264 nn. 10–16. Posset refers to Staupitz as a "biblical scholar" (*Front-Runner of the Catholic Reformation*, 2)—and so he is, as such highly allusive passages demonstrate.

78 "By God's grace I seem to be doing better in the good hope of recovering my health if a doctor is with me, skilled in art [*siquidem mecum est medicus arte peritus*], master Georgius Obsinger ..., [who] takes care of me and assigns daily medicines to me with good discretion [*curam mei agit et medicinas quottidianas michi tribuit cum bona discrecione*]." This is letter 23 in Kolde, *Die deutsche Augustiner-Congregation*, 448. Dated 14 April 1524. See also Steinmetz, *Misericordia Dei*, 15 n. 4.

79 Steinmetz, *Misericordia Dei*, 15 n. 5. A picture of the epitaph on Staupitz's grave, St. Mary's Chapel at St. Peter's Archabbey, Salzburg, appears in Posset, *Front-Runner of the Catholic Reformation*, xxii.

were placed on the index of prohibited books by Pope Paul IV: "Even in death he continued to pay the cost of supporting Luther."[80]

The last several paragraphs have charted how Staupitz and Luther parted company. One would have to say that it happened gradually, over the course of several chaotic years, nor did their increased physical distance help the relationship. In short, Luther "grew into" his role as the leader of the Reform movement in Germany (cf. 1 Cor 13:11), whereas Staupitz—several years Luther's senior (and perhaps more "set in his ways"?)—could not follow his understudy for several reasons that need not be considered here.[81] Franz Posset makes a strong case for the possibility that Staupitz served as "the front-runner of the Catholic Reformation."[82] He documents at least that during his final preaching as abbot over the Benedictines Staupitz never lost his pastoral and evangelical focus—that justification happens through the sacraments, and that heart contrition should precede oral confession.[83] When Luther reported news of Staupitz's passing to Nicholas von Amsdorf, the abbot's nephew, he wrote: "Staupitz has withdrawn from the living [*Staupitius excessit e vivis*], having occupied himself with a brief tyranny [*brevi functus potentatu*]" (WA Br 3, no. 821, line 5; dated 23 January 1525). Probably Luther meant Staupitz's living conditions at Salzburg under Cardinal Lang, as he imagined them.[84]

3 Conclusion

One sees in the preceding pairing of Archias/Cicero and Staupitz/Luther the supreme devotion of a younger student to a teacher—and also joyfulness in literary pursuits shared; the identification of a student's talents, and diligence needed to bring these to perfection; patience on the part of a student with an older teacher's inevitable foibles; and—sometimes—the attainment of even greater accomplishment by a student than possibly could have been imagined by either the teacher or the student originally. For my part, I shall remain ever

80 Rossall, "The Cost of Supporting Luther," 22. Cf. Steinmetz, *Misericordia Dei*, 15 n. 7.

81 "There are, doubtless, many reasons why Staupitz did not follow Luther in his path as Reformer. It is likely that he chose the path of least resistance; or that, like Erasmus, he did not feel himself fitted for a martyr's role" (Schwiebert, *Luther and His Times*, 294).

82 See his Introduction in *Front-Runner of the Catholic Reformation*, 1–5; zu Dohna likewise mentions ("Staupitz and Luther," 119) that through monkish preaching and pastoral care the monastery was turned into "a leaven for the reform of Christendom."

83 Posset, *Front-Runner of the Catholic Reformation*, 284–85.

84 So Posset, *Front-Runner of the Catholic Reformation*, 335 n. 185.

grateful for the wisdom that was bequeathed to me by own beloved mentor Gottfried Krodel. As perhaps the most profound writer of wisdom literature once wrote, "Listen to your father who gave you life, and do not despise your mother when she is old" (Prov 23:22 ESV).[85] Certainly Cicero and Luther did just that; may that tradition continue.

85 Cited approvingly in *Luther's Small Catechism* (St. Louis: Concordia Publishing House, 1986), 72.

Bibliography

Abert, Hermann. *W.A. Mozart*. Translated by Stewart Spencer. Edited by Cliff Eisen. New Haven and London: Yale University Press, 2007.

Aland, Kurt. *95 Theses: With Pertinent Documents from the History of the Reformation*. St. Louis: Concordia, 1967.

Albrecht, O. "Bemerkungen zu Medlers Naumburger Kirchenordnung vom Jahre 1537." *Neue Mitteilungen aus dem Gebiet historisch-antiquarischer Forschungen* 19 (1898): 570–636.

Althaus, Paul. *The Theology of Martin Luther*. Translated by Robert Schultz. Philadelphia: Fortress, 1966.

Ameln, Konrad, ed. *Documenta musicologica* 1.38. Kassel: Bärenreiter, 1988.

Anderson, James Francis. *Reflections on the Analogy of Being*. The Hague: Martinus Nijhoff, 1967.

Annas, Julia. "Epicurus on Pleasure and Happiness." *Philosophical Topics* 15 (1987): 5–21.

Antiphonale Pataviense (Wien 1519): Faksimile. Edited by Karlheinz Schlager. Das Erbe Deutscher Musik 88. Kassel: Bärenreiter, 1985.

Anttila, Miikka E. *Luther's Theology of Music: Spiritual Beauty and Pleasure*. Berlin: De Gruyter, 2013.

Aquinas, Thomas. *Summa Theologiae*. Black Friars Edition. 60 vols. New York and London: McGraw-Hill, 1964–.

Asheim, Ivar. "Lutherische Tugendethik." *Neue Zeitschrift fur Systematische Theologie und Religionsphilosophie* 40.3 (1998): 239–60.

Ashworth, E.J. *Language and Logic in the Post-Medieval Period*. Boston: Reidel, 1974.

Augustine of Hippo. *Confessions*. Translated by Henry Chadwick. Oxford: Oxford University Press, 1991.

Bagchi, Davis. "Luther's Ninety-Five Theses and the Contemporary Criticism of Indulgences." In *Promissory Notes on the Treasury of Merits: Indulgences in Late Medieval Europe*, edited by R.N. Swanson, 331–55. Leiden: Brill, 2006.

Bailey, D.R. Shackleton, ed. and trans. *Valerius Maximus, Memorable Doings and Sayings*. LCL. Cambridge, MA and London: Harvard University Press, 2000.

Bainton, Roland H. *Here I Stand: A Life of Martin Luther*. Nashville: Abingdon Press, 1950.

Baker, Patrick, Johannes Helmrath, and Craig Kallendorf, editors. *Beyond Reception: Renaissance Humanism and the Transformation of Classical Antiquity*. Berlin: De Gruyter, 2019.

Balge, Richard D. "Martin Luther, Augustinian." In *Luther Lives: Essays in Commemoration of the 500th Anniversary of Martin Luther's Birth*. Edited by Edward C. Fredrich,

Siegbert W. Becker, David P. Kuske, 7–20. Milwaukee, WI: Northwestern Publishing House, 1983.

Balthasar, Hans Urs von. *The Glory of the Lord: A Theological Aesthetics*. 7 vols. San Francisco: Ignatius, 1982–1991.

Barber, Charles, and David Jenkins, eds. *Medieval Greek Commentaries on the Nicomachean Ethics*. Leiden: Brill, 2009.

Baschera, Luca. *Tugend und Rechtfertigung: Peter Martyr Vermiglis Kommentar zur Nikomachischen Ethik im Spannungsfeld von Philosophie und Theologie*. Zürich: TVZ, 2008.

Baschera, Luca. "Zwischen Philosophie und Theologie: Aspekte der Aristoteles-Auslegung Peter Martyr Vermiglis." In *Konfession, Migration und Elitenbildung: Studien zur Theologenausbildung des 16. Jahrhunderts*, edited by Herman Selderhuis and Markus Wriedt, 85–98. Leiden: Brill, 2007.

Bäsecke, Georg. *Luther als Dichter. Hallische Universitätsreden* 65. Halle: Niemeyer, 1935.

Baur, August. *Zwinglis Theologie: Ihr Werden und ihr System*. 2 vols. Zürich: Georg Olms, 1983–1984.

Bavinck, Herman. *Reformed Dogmatics*. Volume 1, *Prolegomena*. Grand Rapids: Baker Academic, 2003.

Bayer, Oswald. *A Contemporary in Dissent: Johann Georg Hamann as a Radical Enlightener*. Translated by Roy Harrisville and Mark Mattes. Grand Rapids: Eerdmans, 2012.

Beer, Susanna de. "Elegiac Poetry." *Brill's Encyclopaedia of the Neo-Latin World*. Leiden: E.J. Brill, 2014.

Ben-Tov, Asaph. *Lutheran Humanists and Greek Antiquity: Melanchthonian Scholarship between History and Pedagogy*. Leiden: Brill, 2009.

Bennet, Charles E. *Cicero's Selected Orations*. Boston, New York, Chicago: Allyn and Bacon, 1904.

Besier, Gerhard. "Myth Creation and Projections: From the Luther Myth to the Luther Campaign." *Kirchliche Zeitgeschichte* 26.2 (2013): 422–36.

Beutel, Albrecht. *The Cambridge Companion to Martin Luther*. Edited by Donald K. McKim. Translated by Katharina Gustavs. Cambridge: Cambridge University Press, 2003.

Beza, Theodore. *Psalmorum Davidis et aliorum prophetarum libri quinque, argumentis et Latina paraphrasi illustrati, ac etiam vario carminum genere Latine expressi*. Geneva, 1579.

Blair, Ann. *Too Much to Know: Managing Scholarly Information before the Modern Age*. New Haven: Yale University Press, 2011.

Boehmer, Heinrich. *Martin Luther: Road to Reformation*. Translated by John W. Doberstein and Theodore G. Tappert. Cleveland and New York: World Publishing, 1965.

Boersma, Hans. *Heavenly Participation: The Weaving of the Sacramental Tapestry*. Grand Rapids: Eerdmans, 2011.

Bömer, Heinrich. *Luthers Romfahrt*. Leipzig: Deichert, 1914.

Bonner, S.F. *Education in Ancient Rome*. Berkeley and Los Angeles: University of California Press, 1977.

Bonnus, Hermann. *Hymni et seqventiae, tam de tempore quam de Sanctis, cum suis Melodijs, sicut olim sunt cantata in Ecclesia Dei, & iam passim correcta*. Lübeck, 1559.

Bornkamm, Heinrich. *Luther's World of Thought*. Translated by Martin H. Bertram. St. Louis: Concordia Publishing House, 1958.

Bos, Egbert P., editor. *John Duns Scotus: Renewal of Philosophy*. Amsterdam: Rodiopi, 1998.

Bose, Mishtooni. "The Issue of Theological Style in Late Medieval Disputations." In *Medieval Forms of Argument: Disputation and Debate*. Edited by Georgina Donavin, Carol Poster, and Richard Utz, 1–21. Eugene, OR: Wipf & Stock, 2002.

Botley, Paul. *Learning Greek in Western Europe, 1396–1529*. Philadelphia: American Philosophical Society, 2010.

Boyle, Marjorie O'Rourke. "Stoic Luther: Paradoxical Sin and Necessity." *Archiv für Reformationsgeschichte* 73 (1982): 69–93.

Brecht, Martin. *Martin Luther*. 3 vols. Translated by James L. Shaaf. Minneapolis: Fortress Press, 1985–1999.

Broadie, Alexander. *Introduction to Medieval Logic*. Oxford: Clarendon Press, 1987.

Brown, Clifford Malcolm. "The Church of Santa Cecilia and the Bentivoglio Chapel in San Giacomo Maggiore in Bologna, with an Appendix containing a catalogue of Isabella d'Este's correspondence concerning Lorenzo Costa and Francesco Francia." *Mitteilungen des Kunsthistorischen Institutes in Florenz* 13.3/4 (1968): 301–24.

Buchanan, George. *Poetic Paraphrase of the Psalms of David*. Edited and translated by Roger P.H. Green. Geneva: Librairie Droz, 2011.

Bühler, Paul. *Die Anfechtung bei Martin Luther*. Zürich: Zwingli-Verlag, 1942.

Bühmann, Henning. "The Wittenberg Disputation Culture and the Leipzig Debate." In *Luther at Leipzig: Martin Luther, the Leipzig Debate, and the Sixteenth-Century Reformations*, edited by Mickey L. Mattox, Richard J. Serina Jr., and Jonathan Mumme, 61–92. Leiden: Brill, 2019.

Burnett, Amy Nelson. *Debating the Sacraments: Print and Authority in the Early Reformation*. Oxford: Oxford University Press, 2019.

Burney, Charles. *The Present State of Music in Germany, the Netherlands, and United Provinces*. Reprint or London, 1775 edition. New York: Broude Brothers, 1969.

Buszewicz, Elwira. "Poetry and the *Respublica Literarum* in the Sixteenth Century. The Communication of Ideas: George Buchanan and Jan Kochanowski." *Renaissance and Reformation* 36 (2013): 53–80.

Buszin, Walter E. *Luther on Music*. Lutheran Society for Worship, Music and the Arts, Pamphlet Series 3. St. Paul, Minn.: North Central Publishing, 1958.

Butterfield, David. *The Early Textual History of Lucretius' De rerum natura*. Cambridge: Cambridge University Press, 2013.

Butzek, Monika. *Die kommunalen Repräsentationsstatuen der Päpste des 16. Jahrhunderts in Bologna, Perugia und Rom*. Bad Honnef: Bock und Herchen, 1978.

Cairns, Francis. "Fracastoro's Syphilis, the Argonautic Tradition, and the Aetiology of Syphilis." *Humanistica Lovaniensia* 43 (1994): 246–61.

Calvin, John. *The Bondage and Liberation of the Will: A Defense of the Orthodox Doctrine of Human Choice against Pighius*. Translated by G.I. Davies. Grand Rapids: Baker Academic, 2002.

Calvin, John. *Commentary on the Book of Psalms*. Translated by James Anderson. Edinburgh: Calvin Translation Society, 1845.

Cameron, Euan. *The European Reformation*. Oxford: Oxford University Press, 2012.

Cary, Philip. *Outward Signs: The Powerlessness of External Things in Augustine's Thought*. New York: Oxford University Press, 2008.

Catechism of the Catholic Church. Rome: Libreria Editrice Vaticana, 1994.

Catholisches Gesang-Buch zum Gebrauch der Römisch-Catholischen Gemeinde in Leipzig. First ed. 1715.

Chadwick, Owen. *The Reformation*. Baltimore: Penguin, 1964.

Chazelle, Celia. "The Eucharist in Early Medieval Europe." In *A Companion to the Eucharist in the Middle Ages*. Edited by Ian Levy, Gary Macy, and Kristen Van Ausdall, 205–50. Leiden: Brill, 2012.

Cicero. *Brutus. Orator*. Translated by G.L. Hendrickson and H.M. Hubbell. Cambridge, MA: Harvard University Press; London, UK: William Heinemann, 1952.

Cicero. *The Speeches: Pro Archia poeta, Post reditum in senatu, Post reditum ad Quirites, De domo sua, De haruspicum responsis, Pro Plancio*, 6–41. Translated by N.H. Watts. Cambridge, MA: Harvard University Press; London: William Heinemann, 1955.

Clark, W. Norris. *The One and the Many: A Contemporary Thomistic Metaphysics*. Notre Dame, IN: University of Notre Dame Press, 2016.

Cochran, Elizabeth Agnew. *Protestant Virtue and Stoic Ethics*. London: Bloomsbury; T & T Clark, 2018.

Colloredo, Hieronymus Joseph. *Der aufgeklärte Reformkatholizismus in Österreich*. Edited by Peter Hersche. Bern: Verlag Herbert Lang, 1976.

Colloredo, Hieronymus Joseph. "Hirtenbrief auf die am 1ten Herbstm. dieses 1782ten Jahrs, nach zurückgelegten zwölften Jahrhundert, eintretende Jubelfeyer Salzburgs." In *Der aufgeklärte Reformkatholizismus in Österreich*, edited by Peter Hersche, 45–101. Bern: Verlag Herbert Lang, 1976.

Comba, Emilio. "Luther à Rome." *Revue de Théologie et de Philosophie et Compte-rendu des Principales Publications Scientifiques* 33 (1900): 228–46.

Commission on Worship of the Lutheran Church—Missouri Synod. *Lutheran Service Book*. St. Louis: Concordia Publishing House, 2006.

Congar, Yves. *A History of Theology*. Translated by Hunter Guthrie. Garden City, NY: Doubleday, 1968.

Conrady, K.O. *Lateinische Dichtungstradition und deutsche Lyrik des 17. Jahrhunderts*. Bonn: Bouvier, 1962.

Coreth, Anna. *Pietas Austriaca*. Translated by William D. Bowman and Anna Maria Leitgeb. West Lafayette, IN: Purdue University Press, 2004.

Cornish, Francis Warre, trans. *Catullus, Tibullus, Pervigilium Veneris*. Edited by G.P. Goold. LCL. Cambridge, MA and London: Harvard University Press, 1988.

Cosenza, Mario Emilio. *Biographical and Bibliographical Dictionary of the Italian Humanists and the World of Classical Scholarship in Italy, 1300–1800*. 6 vols. Boston: G.K. Hall, 1962–67.

Cosma, Alessandro and Gianni Pittiglio. *Iconografia agostiniana: Il Quattrocento*. Roma: Città Nuova Editrice, 2015.

Courtenay, William J. *Schools and Scholars in Fourteenth-Century England*. Princeton: Princeton University Press, 1987.

Crook, David. "The Exegetical Motet." *Journal of the American Musicological Society* 68 (2015): 255–316.

Cross, Richard. "Duns Scotus and Suarez at the Origins of Modernity." In *Deconstructing Radical Orthodoxy: Post-Modern Theology, Rhetoric, and Truth*, edited by Wayne Hankey and Douglas Hedley, 65–80. Burlington, VT: Ashgate, 2005.

Cross, Richard. *Duns Scotus on God*. Burlington, VT: Ashgate, 2005.

Cross, Richard. *Duns Scotus*. New York: Oxford University Press, 1999.

Cummings, Anthony M. "The Motet." In *European Music, 1520–1640*, edited by James Haar, 130–56. Woodbridge, UK: The Boydell Press, 2006.

Cummings, Anthony M. "Toward an Interpretation of the Sixteenth-Century Motet." *Journal of the American Musicological Society* 34 (1981): 43–59.

Cummings, Brian. *The Literary Culture of the Reformation: Grammar and Grace*. Oxford: Oxford University Press, 2002.

Czapla, Ralf Georg. *Das Bibelepos in der Frühen Neuzeit: Zur deutschen Geschichte einer europäischen Gattung*. Berlin and Boston: De Gruyter, 2015.

Damschen, Gregor and Andreas Heil. *Epigrammaton liber decimus. Das zehnte Epigrammbuch. Text, Übersetzung, Interpretationen. Mit einer Einleitung, Martial-Bibliographie und einem rezeptionsgeschichtlichen Anhang*. Studien zur klassischen Philologie 148. Frankfurt: Peter Lang, 2004.

David, Hans. T. and Arthur Mendel, eds. *The New Bach Reader: A Life of Johann Sebastian Bach in Letters and Documents*. Revised and enlarged by Christoph Wolff. New York: W.W. Norton, 1998.

Denis, Michael. *Geistliche Lieder zum Gebrauche der hohen Metropolitankirche bey St. Stephan in Wien und des ganzen wienerischen Erzbistums*. Vienna: Scholz, 1774.

Denzinger, Heinrich. *The Sources of Catholic Dogma*. Translated by Roy Deferrari. St. Louis: Herder, 1957.

De Temple, Michael. *Univocity and Analogy of Being in the Latin Metaphysics of Avicenna*. Washington, D.C.: Catholic University of America Press, 1974.

Dewan, Lawrence. *Form and Being: Studies in Thomistic Metaphysics*. Washington, D.C.: Catholic University of America Press, 2006.

Dieter, Theodor. *Der junge Luther und Aristoteles: Eine historisch-systematische Untersuchung zum Verhältnis von Theologie und Philosophie*. Berlin and New York: De Gruyter, 2001.

Dieter, Theodor. "Martin Luther and Scholasticism." In *Remembering the Reformation: Martin Luther and Catholic Theology*, edited by Declan Marmion, Salvador Ryan and Gesa E. Thiessen, 55–74. Minneapolis: Fortress, 2017.

Ditters von Dittersdorf, Karl. *The Autobiography of Karl Ditters von Dittersdorf*. Translated by A.D. Coleridge, London: Bentley, 1896. Reprint, New York: Da Capo Press, 1970.

Ditters von Dittersdorf, Karl. *Lebensbeschreibung*. Leipzig: Breitkopf & Härtel, 1801.

Dodson J. and D. Briones, eds. *Paul and Seneca in Dialogue*. Leiden: Brill, 2017.

Donnelly, John Patrick. "Calvinist Thomism." *Viator: Medieval and Renaissance Studies* 7 (1976): 441–55.

Dragseth, Jennifer, ed. *The Devil's Whore: Reason and Philosophy in the Lutheran Tradition*. Minneapolis: Fortress, 2011.

Duffy, Kathryn Ann Pohlmann. "The Jena Choirbooks: Music and Liturgy at the Castle Church in Wittenberg under Frederick the Wise, Elector of Saxony." PhD diss., University of Chicago, 1995.

Edwards, Mark. *Aristotle and Early Christian Thought*. London and New York: Routledge, 2019.

Edwards, Mark U. *Luther's Last Battles*. Ithaca, NY: Cornell University Press, 1984.

Eisen, Cliff. "Salzburg under Church Rule." In *The Classical Era*, edited by Neal Zaslaw, 166–87. Englewood Cliffs, NJ: Prentice Hall, 1989.

Eisenstein, Elizabeth. *The Printing Press as an Agent of Change*. Cambridge: Cambridge University Press, 1979.

Elze, Theodor. *Luthers Reise nach Rom*. Berlin: Verlag von Alexander Duncker, 1899.

Erasmus, Desiderius. *Collected Works of Erasmus*. Toronto: University of Toronto Press, 1974–.

Ernst, Germana and Simona Foà. "Egidio da Viterbo." *Dizionario Biografico degli Italiani*. Roma: Istituto Treccani, 1993.

Eusterschulte, Anne, and Günter Frank, eds. *Cicero in der frühen Neuzeit*. Stuttgart-Bad Cannstatt: Frommann-Holzboog, 2018.

Feldherr, Andrew. "*Non inter nota sepulcra*: Catullus 101 and Roman Funerary Ritual." In *Catullus*, edited by Julia H. Gaisser, 399–426. Oxford Readings in Classical Studies. New York: Oxford University Press, 2007.

Flaminio, Marcantonio. *Carminum libri VIII*. Padua: Josephus Cominus, 1727.

Forde, Gerhard. *The Captivation of the Will: Luther vs. Erasmus on Freedom and Bondage*. Grand Rapids: Eerdmans, 2005.

Forde, Gerhard. *On Being a Theologian of the Cross: Reflections on Luther's Heidelberg Disputation, 1518*. Grand Rapids: Eerdmans, 1997.

Fordyce, C.J. *Catullus: A Commentary*. Oxford and New York: Oxford University Press, 1961; reprinted, 2006.

Fordyce, C.J. "Catullus, Gaius Valerius." In *Oxford Classical Dictionary*. 3rd ed. Oxford: Oxford University Press, 1996.

Frank, William A. and Allan Bernard Wolter. *Duns Scotus, Metaphysician*. West Lafayette, IN: Purdue University Press, 1995.

Freidensburg, Walter von. "Ein Brief an Matthäus Nägelin von Strassburg vom 22 Juni 1556." *Zeitschrift für die Geschichte des Oberrheins* 86 (1934): 387–92.

Friedrich, Julius A. "*Vita Mea*: Biographical Data of My Life." *Concordia Historical Institute Quarterly* 76, no. 1 (Spring 2003): 10.

Fries, Heinrich. *Fundamental Theology*. Translated by Robert Daly. Washington, D.C.: Catholic University of America Press, 1996.

Funkenstein, Amos. *Theology and the Scientific Imagination from the Middle Ages to the Seventeenth Century*. Princeton: Princeton University Press, 1986.

Gaertner, Johannes A. "Latin Verse Translations of the Psalms: 1500–1620." *Harvard Theological Review* 49 (1956): 271–305.

Gamberini, Elisa. "Il complesso di Santa Maria della Misericordia di Bologna attraverso i suoi documenti." *I quaderni del m.æ.s. = Journal of Mediæ Ætatis Sodalicium* 10 (2007): 141–61.

Garrison, Daniel H. *The Student's Catullus*. 2nd ed. Norman: University of Oklahoma Press, 1995.

Gasch, Stefan and Sonja Tröster. "Senfl, Ludwig." *Grove Music Online*, http://www.oxfordmusiconline.com/ (accessed June 12, 2016).

Gay, Peter. *The Enlightenment: The Rise of Modern Paganism*. New York: Knopf, 1966.

Geertz, Clifford. *The Interpretation of Cultures: Selected Essays*. New York: Basic Books, 1973.

Il genio di Francesco Francia. Catalogue of the exhibition. Venezia: Marsilio, 2018.

Gerhard, Johann. *On the Nature of God and on the Most Holy Mystery of the Trinity*. Translated by Richard Dinda. St. Louis: Concordia Publishing House, 2007.

Gerrish, B.A. *Grace and Reason: A Study in the Theology of Luther*. Eugene, OR: Wipf & Stock, 2005.

Giffen, Hubert van. *In decem libros Aristotelis ad Nicomachum*. Francofurti: Impensis Lazari Zetzneri, 1608.

Giglioni, Guido. "What's Wrong with Doing History of Renaissance Philosophy? Rudolph Goclenius and the Canon of Early Modern Philosophy." In *Early Modern*

Philosophy and the Renaissance Legacy, edited by Cecilia Muratori and Gianni Paganini, 21–39. Dordrecht: Springer, 2016.

Gilson, Étienne. *History of Christian Philosophy in the Middle Ages*. New York: Random House, 1955.

Gilson, Étienne. *Reason and Revelation in the Middle Ages*. New York: Charles Scribner., 1963.

Goclenius, Rudolph. *Übungen zur Ethik/Exercitationes Ethicae*. Translated by Hans Günter Zekl. Würzburg: Königshausen & Neuman, 2010.

Goclenius, Rudolph, Petrus Martyr Vermigli, and Andreas Hyperius. *Meditationes ethicae sive Aristotelis ethicorum Nikomacheion perspicua ac perquam erudita, cum moribus sacris, id est, in sacra pagina descriptis, collata explicatio*. Lich: Nikolaus Erben, 1598.

Godwin, John. *Catullus: The Shorter Poems*. Warminster: Aris & Phillips, Ltd., 1999.

GOTT, und der allerseeligsten Gottes-Gebährerin, und Jungfrauen MARIAE gewidmetes, Neues, verbessert- und vermehrtes Catholisch Paderbornisches Gesang-Buch. Paderborn, 1765.

Grane, Lief. *Contra Gabrielem: Luthers Auseinandersetzung mit Gabriel Biel in der Disputatio Contra Scholasticam Theologiam 1517*. Copenhagen: Gyldendal, 1962.

Grant, W. Leonard. "Neo-Latin Verse-Translations of the Bible." *Harvard Theological Review* 52 (1959): 205–11.

Green, Roger P.H. "Classical Voices in Buchanan's Hexameter Psalm Paraphrases." *Renaissance Studies* 18 (2004): 55–89.

Green, Roger P.H. "Davidic Psalm and Horatian Ode: Five Poems of George Buchanan." *Renaissance Studies* 14 (2000): 91–111.

Green, Roger P.H. "George Buchanan, Arthur Johnston, and William Laud." *Scottish Literary Review* 2 (2010): 5–21.

Green, Roger P.H. "George Buchanan's Psalm Paraphrases: Matters of Metre." In *Acta Conventus Neo-Latini Sanctandreani: Proceedings of the Fifth International Congress of Neo-Latin Studies*, edited by Ian D. MacFarlane, 55–89. Binghamton, NY: Center for Medieval and Renaissance Studies, 1986.

Green, Roger P.H. "Horace's Odes in the Psalm Paraphrases of Buchanan." In *Acta Conventus Neo-Latini Guelpherbytani: Proceedings of the Sixth International Congress of Neo-Latin Studies*, edited by Stella P. Revard, F. Rädle, and M.A. di Cesare. Binghamton, NY: Center for Medieval and Early Renaissance Studies, 1988.

Green, Roger P.H. "On Not Being Buchanan: Arthur Johnston's *Magnum Opus*." In *Acta Conventus Neo-Latini Upsaliensis*. Edited by Astrid Steiner-Weber, 443–53. Leiden: Brill, 2012.

Green, Roger P.H. "Poetic Psalm Paraphrases: Two Versions of Psalm 1 Compared." In *Acta Conventus Neo-Latini Budapestinensis: Proceedings of the Thirteenth*

International Congress of Neo-Latin Studies. Edited by Rhoda Schnur, 261–70. Tempe, AZ: Arizona Center for Medieval and Renaissance Studies, 2010.

Green, Roger P.H. "The Text of George Buchanan's *Psalm Paraphrases*." *The Bibliotheck* 13 (1986): 3–29.

Gregory, Brad. *The Unintended Reformation: How a Religious Revolution Secularized Society*. Cambridge, MA: Belknap, 2012.

Greschat, Martin. *Martin Bucer: A Reformer and His Times*. Louisville: Westminster/John Knox, 2004.

Grimald, Nicholas. *Nicolai Grimoaldi viri doctiss. In P.V. Maronis quatuor libros Georgicorum in oratione soluta paraphrasis*. London: George Bishop and Ralph Newbery, 1591.

Gritsch, Eric and Robert Jenson. *Lutheranism: The Theological Movement and Its Confessional Writings*. Philadelphia: Fortress, 1976.

Gruen, E.S. *The Last Generation of the Roman Republic*. Berkeley, Los Angeles, London: University of California Press, 1974.

Gutberleth, Henricus. *Ethicae liber unus*. Herborn: ex officina Christophori Corvini, 1612.

Gwynn, Aubrey. *Roman Education from Cicero to Quintilian*. Oxford: Oxford University Press, 1926. Reprint, New York: Teachers College Press, 1966.

Haga, Joar. *Was There a Lutheran Metaphysics? The Interpretation of the* Communicatio Idiomatum *in Early Modern Lutheranism*. Göttingen: Vandenhoek & Ruprecht, 2012.

Hagen, Kenneth. "An Addition to the Letters of John Lang: Introduction and Translation." *Archiv für Reformationsgeschichte* 60 (1969): 27–32.

Haile, H.G. *Luther: A Biography*. London: Sheldon Press, 1980.

Hall, Alex. *Thomas Aquinas and John Duns Scotus: Natural Theology in the High Middle Ages*. London: Continuum, 2007.

Halporn, James W., Martin Ostwald, and Thomas G. Rosenmeyer. *The Meters of Greek and Latin Poetry*. Rev. ed. Norman: University of Oklahoma Press, 1980.

Hanchey, Dan. "Typically Unique: Shared Strategies in Cicero's *Pro Archia* and *Pro Balbo*." *Classical Journal* 108.2 (2012/2013): 163–64.

Harran, Marilyn J. "Luther as Professor." In *Luther and Learning: The Wittenberg University Luther Symposium*, 29–51. London and Toronto: Associated University Presses, 1985.

Hausrath, Adolf. *Martin Luthers Romfahrt nach einem gleichzeitigen Pilgerbuche*. Berlin: Grote, 1894.

Hayburn, Robert F. *Papal Legislation on Sacred Music, 95 A.D. to 1977 A.D.* Collegeville, MN: The Liturgical Press. Reprint of 1979 edition, 2006.

Hazlitt, William. *The Table Talk of Martin Luther*. George Bell & Sons: London, 1884.

Healy, Nicholas. *Thomas Aquinas: Theologian of the Christian Life*. Burlington, VT: Ashgate, 2003.

Heidegger, Martin. "The Onto-theo-logical Constitution of Metaphysics." In *Identity and Difference*. Translated by Joan Stambaugh, 42–74. New York: Harper and Row, 1969.

Heiland, Samuel. *Ethica ad Nicomachum libri decem…, breviter et perspicue per quaestiones expositi*. Tubingae: Georg Gruppenbach, 1579.

Heine, Ronald E. *The Commentaries of Origen and Jerome on St. Paul's Epistle to the Ephesians*. Oxford: Oxford University Press, 2002.

Helmer, Christine. *The Trinity and Martin Luther: A Study on the Relationship between Genre, Language, and the Trinity in Luther's Works (1523–1546)*. Mainz: Philipp von Zabern, 1999.

Hemmingsen, Niels. *On the Law of Nature: A Demonstrative Method*. Translated by E.J. Hutchinson. Grand Rapids: CLP Academic, 2018.

Hendrix, Scott H. *Martin Luther: Visionary Reformer*. New Haven: Yale University Press, 2015.

Herl, Joseph. *Worship Wars in Early Lutheranism: Choir, Congregation, and Three Centuries of Conflict*. Oxford and New York: Oxford University Press, 2004.

Herreros, Alfonso. "A Case Study of the Reception of Aristotle in Early Protestantism: The Platonic Idea of the Good in the Commentaries on the Nicomachean Ethics." *Renaissance & Reformation* 43:3 (2020): 41–69.

Hettrick, Jane Schatkin. "Colorful Comments on Church Music in Vienna around 1780." *The American Organist* 34.5 (2000): 77–81.

Hettrick, Jane Schatkin. Review of *Johann Leisentrit's* Geistliche Lieder und Psalmen, 1567: *Hymnody of the Counter-Reformation in Germany* by Richard Wetzel and Erika Heitmeyer. The *American Organist* 49.6 (2015): 70–73.

Hettrick, Jane Schatkin. "A Lutheran Hymnal of the Enlightenment." In *More than Luther: The Reformation and the Rise of Pluralism in Europe*. Edited by Karla Boersma and J. Selderhuis, 113–30. Göttingen: Vanderhoeck & Ruprecht, 2019.

Hirst, Michael. *Michelangelo: The Achievement of Fame*. New Haven & London: Yale University Press, 2011.

Hoerber, Robert G., ed. *Concordia Self-Study Bible: New International Version*. St. Louis: Concordia, 1986.

Hollerweger, Hans. *Die Reform des Gottesdienstes zur Zeit des Josephinismus in Österreich*. Regensburg: Verlag Friedrich Pustet, 1976.

Honnefelder, Ludger Rega Wood, and Mechthild Dreyer, eds. *John Duns Scotus: Metaphysics and Ethics*. Leiden: Brill, 1996.

Horan, Daniel. *Postmodernity and Univocity: A Critical Account of Radical Orthodoxy and John Duns Scotus*. Minneapolis: Fortress, 2014.

Hotson, Howard. *Commonplace Learning: Ramism and Its German Ramifications 1543–1630*. Oxford: Oxford University Press, 2007.

Hutchinson, E.J. "Written Monuments: Beza's *Icones* as Testament to and Program for Reformist Humanism." In *Beyond Calvin: Essays on the Diversity of the Reformed Tradition*, edited by W. Bradford Littlejohn and Jonathan Tomes, 21–62. Lincoln, NE: Davenant Press, 2017.

Hunt, Jeffrey M., R.A. Smith, and Fabio Stok. *Classics from Papyrus to the Internet: An Introduction to Transmission and Reception*. Austin: University of Texas Press, 2017.

Huse, Norbert. "Ein Bilddokument zu Michelangelos 'Julius II' in Bologna." *Mitteilungen des Kunsthistorischen Institutes in Florenz* 12.3/4 (1966): 355–58.

Hyperius, Andreas. *In Aristotelis Ethica Nicomachica annotationes haud inutiles*. Basileae: ex officina Oporiniana, 1586.

Ingham, Mary Beth. *Scotus for Dunces: An Introduction to the Subtle Doctor*. St. Bonaventure, NY: The Franciscan Institute, 2012.

Ingham, Mary Beth and Mechthild Dreyer. *The Philosophical Vision of John Duns Scotus: An Introduction*. Washington, D.C.: Catholic University of America Press, 2007.

Iserloh, Erwin. *The Theses Were Not Posted: Luther between Reform and Reformation*. Translated by Martin E. Marty. Boston: Beacon Press, 1968.

Jaczn, Antonie Vos. *Johannes Duns Scotus*. Leiden: Groen & Zoon, 1994.

James, Carolyn. "The Palazzo Bentivoglio in 1487." *Mitteilungen des Kunsthistorischen Institutes in Florenz* 41 (1997): 188–96.

Janz, Denis. *Luther and Late Medieval Thomism: A Study in Theological Anthropology*. Waterloo: Wilfrid Laurier, 1983.

Janz, Denis. *Luther on Thomas Aquinas: The Angelic Doctor in the Thought of the Reformer*. Wiesbaden: Franz Steiner, 1989.

Jauss, Hans Robert. *Toward an Aesthetic of Reception*. Translated by Timothy Bahti. Minneapolis: University of Minnesota Press, 1982.

Jedin, Herbert. "Die römischen Augustinerquellen zu Luthers Frühzeit." *Archiv für Reformationsgeschichte* 25 (1928): 256–70.

Johnston, Arthur. *Psalmorum Davidis paraphrasis poetica et canticorum evangelicorum*. Aberdeen: Raban, 1637.

Jones, David Wyn. *Music in Vienna: 1700, 1800, 1900*. Woodbridge, UK: The Boydell Press, 2016.

Jorgensen, Alfred T. *Martin Luther: Reformer of the Church*. Minneapolis, MN: Augsburg Publishing House, 1953.

Junghans, Helmar. *Der junge Luther und die Humanisten*. Göttingen: Vandenhoeck & Ruprecht, 1985.

Just, Martin and Bettina Schwemer, eds. *Die Handschrift des Jodocus Schalreuter (Ratsschulbibliothek Zwickau Mus. Ms. 73)*. Das Erbe Deutscher Musik, Bd. 115–16. Wiesbaden: Breitkopf & Härtel, 2004.

Kaczor, Christopher. "Reading Aquinas's Commentary on Aristotle's Nicomachean Ethics: A Reply To Mark D. Jordan." In *Theology Needs Philosophy: Acting Against*

Reason Is Contrary to the Nature of God, edited by Matthew L. Lamb, 279–92. Washington, D.C.: Catholic University of America Press, 2016.

Kallendorf, Craig. *A Bibliography of the Early Printed Editions of Virgil 1469–1850*. New Castle, DE: Oak Knoll Press, 2012.

Kallendorf, Craig. *Printing Virgil: The Transformation of the Classics in the Renaissance*. Leiden: Brill, 2020.

Kallendorf, Craig. "Virgil in the Renaissance Classroom: From Toscanella's *Osservationi* [...] *supra l'opere di Virgilio* to the *Exercitationes rhetoricae*." In *The Classics in the Medieval and Renaissance Classroom: The Role of Ancient Texts in the Arts Curriculum as Revealed by Surviving Manuscripts and Early Printed Books*, edited by J.F. Ruys, J.O. Ward, and M. Heyworth, 309–28. Turnhout: Brepols, 2013.

Kaufmann, Thomas. "Bucers Bericht von der Heidelberger Disputation." *Archiv für Reformationgeschichte* 82 (1991): 147–70.

Kellerman, James A., E.J. Hutchinson, and Joshua J. Hayes, eds. *Ad Fontes Witebergenses: Select Proceedings of "Lutheranism and the Classics III: Lutherans Read History."* Minneapolis: Lutheran Press, 2017.

Kellerman, James and Carl Springer, eds. *Ad Fontes Witebergenses: Select Proceedings of "Lutheranism and the Classics II: Reading the Church Fathers."* Fort Wayne: Lutheran Legacy Press, 2014.

Kellman, Herbert, ed. *The Treasury of Petrus Alamire: Music and Art in Flemish Court Manuscripts, 1500–1535*. Ghent, Amsterdam: Ludion, 1999.

Kelly, Henry Ansgar. "Luther at Augsburg, 1518: New Light on Papal Strategies." *Journal of Ecclesiastical History* 70.4 (2019.): 805–22.

Kilcrease, Jack. "Johann Gerhard's Reception of Thomas Aquinas's *Analogia Entis*." In *Aquinas among the Protestants*. Edited by Manfred Svensson and David VanDrunen, 109–28. Oxford: Wiley-Blackwell, 2018.

King, Charles W. *The Ancient Roman Afterlife:* Di Manes, *Belief, and the Cult of the Dead*. Austin, TX: University of Texas Press, 2020.

Kirnberger, Johann Philipp. *The Art of Strict Musical Composition*. Translated by David Beach and Jurgen Thym. New Haven and London: Yale University Press, 1982.

Kittelson, James M. "Luther the Educational Reformer." In *Luther and Learning: the Wittenberg University Luther Symposium 1983*. Edited by Marilyn J. Harran, 131–78. Selinsgrove, PA: Susquehanna University Press, 1985.

Klubertanz, George Peter. *Saint Thomas Aquinas on Analogy: A Textual Analysis and Systematic Synthesis*. Chicago: Loyola University Press, 1960.

Knight, W.F. Jackson. *Accentual Symmetry in Vergil*. Oxford: Basil Blackwell, 1939.

Kolb, Robert. "Luther on the Two Kinds of Righteousness; Reflections on His Two-dimensional Definition of Humanity at the Heart of His Theology." *Lutheran Quarterly* 13.4 (1999): 449–66.

Kolb, Robert. "Luther's Theology of the Cross Fifteen Years after Heidelberg: Lectures on the Psalms of Ascent." *The Journal of Ecclesiastical History* 61.1 (2010): 69–85.

Kolb, Robert. *Martin Luther and the Enduring Word of God: The Wittenberg School and Its Scripture-Centered Proclamation.* Grand Rapids: Baker, 2016.

Kolb, Robert. *Martin Luther: Confessor of the Faith.* Oxford: Oxford University Press, 2009.

Kolb, Robert. *Nicholas von Amsdorf: Champion of Luther's Reformation.* St. Louis: Concordia Publishing House, 2019.

Kolde, Theodor. "Innere Bewegungen unter den deutschen Augustinern und Luther Romreise." *Zeitschrift für Kirkengeschichte* 2 (1977): 460–80.

Kolde, Theodore. *Die deutsche Austiner-Congregation und Johann von Staupitz. Ein Beitrag zur Ordens- und Reformationsgeschichte nach meistens ungedruckten Quellen.* Gotha: Friedrich Andreas Perthes, 1879.

Kongsted, Ole, ed. *Motetter af Ludwig Senfl.* Capella Hafniensis Editions A.1. Copenhagen: The Royal Library, 2001.

Kopff, Christian E. "Vergil and Augustine in Luther's *De servo arbitrio.*" In *Ad Fontes Witebergenses*, edited by James A. Kellerman and Carl P.E. Springer, 39–52. Fort Wayne, IN: Lutheran Legacy, 2014.

Köster, Carl Felix. "Die Naumburger Kirchen- und Schulordnung von D. Nicolaus Medler aus dem Jahre 1537." *Neue Mitteilungen aus dem Gebiet historisch-antiquarischer Forschungen* 19 (1898): 497–569, 637–68.

Kristeller, Paul Oskar. *Renaissance Thought: The Classic, Scholastic, and Humanist Strains.* New York: Columbia University Press, 1995.

Krop, Henri A. "Philosophy and the Synod of Dordt: Aristotelianism, Humanism, and the Case Against Arminianism." In *Revisiting the Synod of Dort* (1618–1619), edited by Aza Goudriaan and Fred van Lieburg, 49–80. Leiden: Brill, 2010.

Kruse, Jens-Martin. *Universitätstheologie und Kirchenreform: Die Anfänge der Reformation in Wittenberg 1516–1522.* Mainz: Philipp von Zabern, 2002.

Küng, Hans. *Great Christian Thinkers: Paul, Origen, Augustine, Aquinas, Luther, Schleiermacher, Barth.* London: Continuum, 1994.

Kuropka, Nicole. "Melanchthon and Aristotle." In *Philip Melanchthon: Theologian in Classroom, Confession, and Controversy*, edited by Irene Dingel, Robert Kolb, Nicole Kuropka, Timothy Wengert, 19–28. Göttingen: Vandenhöck & Ruprecht, 2012.

Kusukawa, Sachiko. *The Transformation of Natural Philosophy: The Case of Philip Melanchthon.* Cambridge: Cambridge University Press, 2006.

Lamo, Pietro. *Graticola di Bologna, ossia descrizione delle pitture, sculture e architetture della città, fatta l'anno 1560.* Bologna: Tipografia Guidi all'Ancora, 1844.

Lawn, Brian. *The Rise and Decline of the Scholastic 'Quaestio Disputata:' With Special Emphasis on Its Use in the Teaching of Medicine and Sciences.* Leiden: Brill, 1993.

Leaver, Robin A. "A Catholic Hymnal for Use in Lutheran Leipzig: *Catholisches Gesang-Buch* (Leipzig 1724)." In *Bach and the Counterpoint of Religion*. Edited by Robin A. Leaver, 36–62. Urbana: University of Illinois Press, 2018.

Leaver, Robin A. *Luther's Liturgical Music: Principles and Implications*. Grand Rapids, Mich.: Eerdmans, 2007.

Leinsle, Ulrich. *Introduction to Scholastic Theology*. Translated by Michael Miller. Washington, D.C.: Catholic University of America Press, 2010.

Leo XIII. *Aeterni Patris: On the Restoration of Christian Philosophy*. Boston: St. Paul Editions, n.d.

Leppin, Volker. "Disputation als Medium der Theologie- und Kirchenreform in der Reformation: Zur Transformation eines akademischen Mediums." In *Lehren und Lernen im Zeitalter der Reformation: Methoden und Funkionen*, edited by Gerlinde Huber-Rebenich, 97–139. Tübingen: J.C.B. Mohr, 2012.

Leppin, Volker. "Die Genese des reformatischen Schriftprinzips: Beobachtungen zu Luthers Auseinandersetzung mit Johannes Eck bis zur Leipziger Disputation." In *Reformatorische Theologie und Autoritäten: Studien zur Genese des Schriftprinzips beim jungen Luther*, edited by Volker Leppin, 97–139. Tübingen: Mohr Siebeck, 2015.

Leppin, Volker. "*Salve, Sancta Roma* Luthers Erinnerungen an seine Romreise." In *Martin Luther in Rom: die Ewige Stadt als kosmopolitisches Zentrum und ihre Wahrnehmung*, edited by Michael Matheus, Arnold Nesselreth, and Martin Wallraff, 35–42. Berlin: De Gruyter, 2017.

Leppin, Volker. "Zuspitzung und Wahrheitsanspruch: Disputationen in den Anfängen der Wittenberger reformatischen Bewegung." In *Reformation und Rationalität*, edited by Herman Selderhuis and Ernst-Joachim Waschke, 43–58. Göttingen: Vandenhoeck & Ruprecht, 2015.

Leppin, Volker and Timothy J. Wengert. "Sources for and against the Posting of the *Ninety-Five Theses*." *Lutheran Quarterly* 29.4 (2015): 373–98.

Lewis, Charlton T. *A Latin Dictionary*. Oxford: Oxford University Press, 1879; reprint, 1996.

Linder, Robert D. "Calvinism and Humanism: The First Generation." *Church History* 44 (1975): 167–81.

Lines, David A. "Giovanni Bernardo Feliciano and the Edition of 'Eustratius.'" In Eustratius, Aspasius, Michael Ephesius et al.: *Aristotelis Stagiritae Moralia Nicomachia*. Übersetzt von Johannes Bernardus Felicianus, v–xviii. Paris 1543. Reprint, Stuttgart/Bad-Cannstatt: frommann-holzboog, 2006.

Link, Wilhelm. *Das Ringen um die Freiheit der Theologie von der Philosophie*. Munich: C. Kaiser, 1955.

Loewenich, Walter von. *Luther's Theology of the Cross*. Translated by Herbert J.A. Bouman. Minneapolis: Augsburg, 1976.

Lohse, Bernard. *Martin Luther: An Introduction to His Life and Works*. Translated by Robert C. Schultz. Edinburgh: T & T Clark, 1987.

Lohse, Bernard. *Martin Luther's Theology: Its Historical and Systematic Development*. Translated and edited by Roy A. Harrisville. Minneapolis: Fortress Press, 1999.

Lonergan, Bernard. *Insight: A Study of Human Understanding*, vol. 1. Toronto: University of Toronto Press, 1958.

Long, Steven A. *Analogia Entis: On the Analogy of Being, Metaphysics, and the Act of Faith*. Notre Dame, IN: University of Notre Dame Press, 2011.

Lortz, Joseph. *Die Reformation in Deutschland*. 2 vols. Voraussetzungen: Herder, 1949.

Ludwig, Walther, ed. *Die Musen im Reformationszeitalter*. Leipzig: Evangelische Verlagsanstalt, 2001.

Lueker, Erwin L. "Heidelberg Disputation." In *Lutheran Cyclopedia*, 368. St. Louis: Concordia, 1975.

Lueker, Erwin L. "Luther, Martin." In *Lutheran Cyclopedia*, 483–85. St. Louis: Concordia, 1975.

Lull, Timothy F. "Luther's Writings." In *The Cambridge Companion to Martin Luther*, edited by Donald K. McKim, 39–61. Cambridge: Cambridge University Press, 2003.

Lull, Timothy F. and Derek R. Nelson. *Resilient Reformer: The Life and Thought of Martin Luther*. Minneapolis: Augsburg Fortress, 2015.

Lund, Eric. "Baltic and Nordic Lutheranism." In *Lutheran Ecclesiastical Culture: 1550–1665*, edited by Robert Kolb, 159–204. Leiden: Brill, 2008.

Luther, Martin. *American Edition of Luther's Works*. 75 vols. Edited by Jaroslav Pelikan, Helmut Lehmann, and Christopher Brown. Philadelphia and St. Louis: Fortress Press and Concordia Publishing House, 1957–86, 2009–.

Luther, Martin. *The Bondage of the Will, 1525*. Edited by Volker Leppin and Kirsi Stjerna. Minneapolis: Fortress, 2016.

Luther, Martin. *D. Martin Luthers Werke: Kritische Gesammtausgabe*. 120 vols. Weimar: Hermann Böhlau and H. Böhlaus Nachfolg, 1883–2009.

Luther, Martin. *Kirchen-Gesangbuch für Evangelisch-Lutherische Gemeinden ungeänderter Augsburgischer Confession*. St. Louis, Missouri: Concordia, 1892.

Luther, Martin. *Luther and Erasmus: Free Will and Salvation*. Edited by E. Gordon Rupp and Philip S. Watson. Philadelphia: Westminster John Knox, 1969.

Luther, Martin. *Luther's Correspondence and Other Contemporary Letters*. Vol. 1 and 2. Translated and edited by Preserved Smith. Philadelphia: Lutheran Publication Society, 1913–18.

Luther, Martin. *Luther's Small Catechism*, 72. St. Louis: Concordia Publishing House, 1986.

Lutheran Service Book. St. Louis: Concordia, 2006.

"Lutheranism and the Classics," a special issue of *Logia: A Journal of Lutheran Theology* (edited by Jon Bruss and Carl Springer) 21.2 (2012).

Luy, David. "Disputations." In *The Oxford Encyclopedia of Martin Luther*, edited by Derek R. Nelson and Paul R. Hinlicky, vol. 1. Oxford: Oxford University Press, 2017.

Macdonald, A.J. *Berengar and the Reform of Sacramental Doctrine*. London: Longmans, Green, 1930.

MacIntyre, Alasdair. *After Virtue: A Study in Moral Theory*. Notre Dame, IN: University of Notre Dame Press, 2007.

MacIntyre, Alasdair. *A Short History of Ethics: A History of Moral Philosophy from the Homeric Age to the Twentieth Century*. London: Routledge, 1998.

Mack, Peter. "Melanchthon's Commentaries on Latin Literature." In *Melanchthon und Europa II: Westeuropa*, edited by Günter Frank and Kees Meerhoff, 29–52. Stuttgart: Thorbecke, 2002.

Mack, Peter. *Renaissance Argument: Valla and Agricola in the Traditions of Rhetoric and Dialectic*. Leiden: Brill, 1993.

Malvasia, Carlo Cesare. *Le pitture di Bologna, che nella pretesa, e rimostrata sin'ora da altri maggiore antichità, e impareggiabile eccellenza nella pittura, con manifesta evidenza di fatto, rendono il passeggiere disingannato, ed instrutto*. Bologna: Stamperia Longhi, 1755.

Manetsch, Scott M. "Psalms before Sonnetts: Theodore Beza and the *Studia Humanitatis*." In *Continuity and Change: The Harvest of Late Medieval and Reformation History*, edited by Robert J. Bast and Andrew C. Gow, 400–416. Leiden: Brill, 2000.

Mann, Otto. *Deutsche Literaturgeschichte*. Gütersloh: Verlagsgruppe Bertelsmann GmbH, 1969.

Mann, Thomas. *Zauberberg*. Frankfurt: Fischer, 2004.

Marenbon, John. *Later Medieval Philosophy (1150–1350)*. London: Routledge, 1987.

Marion, Jean-Luc. *God without Being*. Translated by Thomas Carlton. Chicago: University of Chicago Press, 1991.

Marius, Richard. *Martin Luther: The Christian between God and Death*. Cambridge, MA and London: Harvard University Press, 1999.

Markos, Louis, *From Achilles to Christ: Why Christians Should Read the Pagan Classics*. Wheaton: IVP Academic, 2007.

Maron, Gottfried. *Martin Luther und Epikur: Ein Beitrag zum Verständnis des alten Luther = Berichte aus den Sitzungen der Joachim*. Hamburg: Jungius-Gesellschaft der Wissenschaften e.V. 6.1., Göttingen, in Kommission beim Verlag Vandenhoeck & Ruprecht, 1988.

Marsh, David. "Pastoral Poetry." In *Brill's Encyclopaedia of the Neo-Latin World*, 425–36. Leiden: E.J. Brill, 2014.

Marshall, Bruce. "Quod Scit Una Uetula: Aquinas on the Nature of Theology." In *The Theology of Thomas Aquinas*, edited by Rik Van Nieuwenhove and Joseph Wawrykow, 1–35. Notre Dame, IN: University of Notre Dame Press, 2010.

Martini, Jakob. *Partitiones & Quaestiones Metaphysicae*. Wittenberg, 1615.

Massing, Michael. *Fatal Discord: Erasmus, Luther and the Fight for the Western Mind*. New York: HarperCollins, 2018.

Matheson, Peter, ed. and trans. *The Collected Works of Thomas Müntzer*. Edinburgh: T&T Clark, 1988.

Mau, Rudolf. "Die Kirchenväter in Luthers früher Exegese des Galaterbriefs." In *Auctoritas Patrum II: Neue Beiträge zur Rezeption der Kirchenväter im 15. und 16. Jahrhundert*, edited by Leif Grane, Alfred Schindler, and Markus Wriedt, 117–27. Mainz: Philipp von Zabern, 1993.

McClelland, J.C. "Calvinism Perfecting Thomism: Peter Marytr Vermigli's Question." *Scottish Journal of Theology* 31.6 (1978.): 571–78.

McFarlane, Ian D. *Buchanan*. London: Duckworth, 1981.

McGrath, Alister. *The Intellectual Origins of the Reformation*. Malden, MA: Blackwell, 2004.

McInerny, Ralph. *Aquinas and Analogy*. Washington, D.C.: Catholic University of America Press, 1998.

McInerny, Ralph. *The Logic of Analogy: An Interpretation of St Thomas*. The Hague: Martinus Nijhoff, 1971.

McLelland, Joseph C. "Introduction." In *Commentary on Aristotle's Nicomachean Ethics*. Kirksville, MO.: Truman State University Press, 2006.

Melanchthon, Philip. *Corpus Reformatorum: Philippi Melanthonis Opera quae supersunt omnia*. Edited by C.G. Bretschneider and H.E. Bindseil. 28 volumes. Halle: Schwetschke, 1834–60.

Melanchthon, Philip. "Loci Communes: 1521." In *Melanchthon and Bucer*, edited by Wilhelm Pauck, 18–154. Philadelphia: Westminster, 1969.

Melanchthon, Philip. "Oratio de Aristotle." In *Melanchthons Werke*, edited by R. Stupperich, 3:122–34. Gütersloh: Gerd Mohn, 1951–55.

Melanchthon, Philip. *Principal Writings on Rhetoric*. Edited by William P. Weaver, Stefan Strohm, and Volkhard Wels. Volume 2, book 2 of *Opera omnia: Opera philosophica*. Berlin: De Gruyter, 2017.

Mercken, H.P.F. "The Greek Commentators on Aristotle's Ethics." In *Aristotle Transformed: The Ancient Commentators and Their Influence*, edited by Richard Sorabji, 407–44. London: Gerald Duckworth, 1990.

Metaxas, Eric. *Martin Luther: The Man Who Rediscovered the Gospel and Changed the World*. New York: Viking, 2017.

Milbank, John. *Being Reconciled: Ontology and Pardon*. London: Routledge, 2003.

Milbank, John. *Beyond Secular Order: The Representation of Being and the Representation of People*. Malden, MA: Wiley-Blackwell, 2013.

Milbank, John. *The Future of Love: Essays in Political Theology*. London: SCM Press, 2009.

Milbank, John. *The Religious Dimension in the Thought of Giambattista Vico, 1668–1744: The Early Metaphysics*. Lewiston, NY: Edwin Mellen, 1991.

Milbank, John. *The Suspended Middle: Henri de Lubac and the Debate Concerning the Supernatural*. Grand Rapids: Eerdmans, 2005.

Milbank, John. *Theology and Social Theory: Beyond Secular Reason*. Malden, MA: Blackwell, 2008.

Milbank, John. *The Word Made Strange: Theology, Language, Culture*. Malden, MA: Wiley-Blackwell,1997.

Monson, Craig A. "The Council of Trent Revisited." *Journal of the American Musicological Society* 55.1 (2002): 1–37.

Montagnes, Bernard and Andrew Tallon. *The Doctrine of the Analogy of Being According to Thomas Aquinas*. Milwaukee: Marquette University Press, 2004.

Mortensen, John. *Understanding St. Thomas on Analogy*. CreateSpace Independent Publishing, 2010.

Moser, Hans Joachim. "Johannes de Cleve als Setzer von zehn Lutherischen Melodien." *Tijdschrift van de Vereniging voor Nederlandse Muziekgeschiedenis* 16 (1946): 31–35.

Moss, Ann. "Latin Liturgical Hymns of the Reformation Crisis (1520–1568)." *Humanistica Lovaniensia* 40 (1991): 73–111.

Moss, Ann. *Renaissance Truth and the Latin Language Turn*. Oxford: Oxford University Press, 2003.

Mowrey, Hannah Hutchens. "The Alamire Manuscripts of Frederick the Wise: Intersections of Music, Art, and Theology." PhD diss., Eastman School of Music, University of Rochester, 2010.

Moynihan, Martin, transl. and ed. *The Latin Letters of C.S. Lewis*. South Bend: St. Augustine's Press, 1998.

Muller, Richard. "Not Scotist: Understandings of Being, Univocity, and Analogy in Early Modern Reformed Thought." *Reformation & Renaissance Review* 14.2 (2012): 127–50.

Muller, Richard. *Post-Reformation Dogmatics: The Rise and Development of Reformed Orthodoxy, ca. 1520 to ca. 1725*. 4 vols. Grand Rapids: Baker Academic, 2003.

Muller, Richard. *The Unaccommodated Calvin: Studies in the Foundations of a Theological Tradition*. Oxford: Oxford University Press, 2001.

Mumme, Jonathan. "The University of Wittenberg." In *Martin Luther in Context*, edited by David M. Whitford, 38–46. Cambridge: Cambridge University Press, 2018.

Mynors, R.A.B. *P. Vergilii Maronis Opera*. Oxford: Clarendon Press, 1969.

Nestingen, James, Robert Kolb, and Charles Arand. 2012. *The Lutheran Confessions: History and Theology of the Book of Concord*. Minneapolis: Fortress.

Nevin, John. *The Mystical Presence: A Vindication of the Reformed or Calvinistic Doctrine of the Holy Eucharist*. Eugene, OR: Wipf & Stock, 2000.

Nicolai, Friedrich Christoph. *Beschreibung einer Reise durch Deutschland und die Schweiz, im Jahre 1781, nebst Bemerkungen über Gelehrsamkeit, Industrie Religion und Sitte*. 12 vols. Berlin: Stettin, 1783–1796.

Nordling, John G. "The Catechism: The Heart of the Reformation." *Logia* 16.4 (2007): 5–13.

Novikoff, Alex J. *The Medieval Culture of Disputation: Pedagogy, Practice, and Performance.* Philadelphia: University of Pennsylvania Press, 2013.

Oakley, Francis. *Omnipotence, Covenant and Order: An Excursion in the History of Ideas from Abelard to Leibniz.* Ithaca, NY: Cornell University Press, 1984.

Oberman, Heiko A. *The Harvest of Medieval Theology: Gabriel Biel and Late Medieval Nominalism.* Durham, NC: The Labyrinth Press, 1983.

Oberman, Heiko A. "Headwaters of the Reformation: *Initia Lutheri—Initia Reformationis.*" In *Luther and the Dawn of the Modern Era*, edited by Heiko Oberman, 40–88. Leiden: Brill, 1974.

Oberman, Heiko A. *Luther: Man Between God and the Devil.* Translated by Eileen Walliser-Schwarzbart. New Haven: Yale University Press, 1989.

Oberman, Heiko A. *Luther: Mensch zwischen Gott und Teufel.* Berlin: Severin and Seidler, 1982.

Oberman, Heiko A. *Masters of the Reformation: The Emergence of a New Intellectual Climate in Europe.* Translated by Dennis Martin. Cambridge: Cambridge University Press, 1981.

Oberman, Heiko A. and Frank A. James, III, eds. *Essays in Honor of Damasus Trapp, O.S.A.* Leiden, New York, Kobenhavn, Köln: Brill, 1991.

O'Connell, Marvin. *Critics on Trial: An Introduction to the Catholic Modernist Crisis.* Washington, D.C.: Catholic University of America Press, 1994.

O'Daly, Gerard. *Augustine's Philosophy of Mind.* Berkley: University of California Press, 1987.

Ottavi, Cavina Anna. "La cappella Bentivoglio." *Il tempio di San Giacomo Maggiore in Bologna.* Edited by Carlo Volpe, 117–32. Bologna: Padri Agostiniani, 1967.

Overfield, James A. *Humanism and Scholasticism in Late Medieval Germany.* Princeton: Princeton University Press, 1985.

Ozment, Steven. *The Age of Reform, 1250–1550: An Intellectual and Religious History of Late Medieval and Reformation Europe.* New Haven: Yale University Press, 1981.

Ozment, Steven. *Protestants: The Birth of a Revolution.* New York: Image Books, 1991.

Paisey, David and Giulia Bartrum. "Hans Holbein and Miles Coverdale: A New Woodcut." *Print Quarterly* 26 (2009): 227–53.

"Palm Sunday." In *Oxford Dictionary of the Christian Church*, edited by F.L. Cross and E.A. Livingstone. 3rd ed. Oxford: Oxford University Press, 1997.

Parker, Robert Christopher Towneley. "Priapus." In *Oxford Classical Dictionary.* 3rd ed. Oxford: Oxford University Press, 1996.

Parrott, Andrew. *The Essential Bach Choir.* Woodbridge, UK: The Boydell Press, 2000.

Pater, Calvin. *Karlstadt as the Father of the Baptist Movement: The Emergence of Lay Protestantism.* Toronto: University of Toronto Press, 1984.

Pauly, Reinhard G. "The Reforms of Church Music under Joseph II." *The Musical Quarterly* 43 (1957): 372–82.

Payton, James, Jr. *Getting the Reformation Wrong: Correcting Some Misunderstandings.* Downers Grove: IVP Academic, 2010.

Pearlman, Barry. *A Certain Faith: Analogy of Being and the Affirmation of Belief.* Lanham, MD: University Press of America, 2011.

Pelikan, Jaroslav. *From Luther to Kierkegaard: A Study in Historical Theology.* St. Louis: Concordia Publishing House, 1963.

Pelikan, Jaroslav. *The Melody of Theology: A Philosophical Dictionary.* Cambridge, Mass. and London: Harvard University Press, 1988.

Pesch, O.H. *Martin Luther, Thomas von Aquin und die reformatische Kritik an der Scholastik: Zur Geschichte und Wirkungsgeschichte eines Mißverständnisses mit weltgeschichlichen Folgen.* Hamburg: Joachim Jungius-Gesellschaft der Wissenschaften, 1994.

Peters, Albrecht. *Commentary on Luther's Catechisms.* Edited by Charles P. Schaum. Translated by Holger Sonntag, Thomas Trapp, and Daniel Thies. St. Louis: Concordia Publishing House, 2009–2013.

Petersen, Peter. *Geschichte der aristotelischen Philosophie im protestantischen Deutschland.* Leipzig: F. Meiner, 1921.

Pettegree, Andrew. *Brand Luther.* New York: Penguin, 2015.

Pezzl, Johann. *Skizze von Wien: Ein Kultur- und Sittenbild aus der josefinischen Zeit.* Edited by Gustav Gugitz and Anton Schlossar. Graz: Lehkam Verlag. 1923.

Pfatteicher, Philip H. *Festivals and Commemorations: Handbook to the Calendar in Lutheran Book of Worship.* Minneapolis: Augsburg, 1980.

Pfeiffer, Heinrich. "La Stanza della Segnatura sullo sfondo delle idee di Egidio da Viterbo." *Sodalizio tra studiosi dell'arte: Colloqui del Sodalizio* 3 (1970): 31–43.

Pfeiffer, Heinrich. *Zur Ikonographik von Raffaels "Disputa": Egidio da Viterbo und die christlich platonische Konzeption der Stanza della Segnatura.* Rome: Pontificia Università Gregoriana, 1975.

Pflug, J. *Correspondence.* Leiden: E.J. Brill, 1982.

Phelan, Gerald B. *St. Thomas and Analogy.* Milwaukee: Marquette University Press, 1941.

Pickstock, Catherine. *After Writing: On the Liturgical Consummation of Philosophy.* Malden, MA: Wiley-Blackwell, 1998.

Poblete, José Antonio. "El papel de la traducción latina de Roberto Grosseteste en la transmisión medieval del pasaje aristotélico sobre lo justo natural (Ethica Nicomachea 1134b18–35a5)." Diss., Universidad de los Andes, Santiago de Chile, 2019.

Poli, Marco and Simona Costato. "Martin Lutero in un affresco alla Misericordia? Ipotesi per una ricerca storico-artistica." *Strenna Storica Bolognese* 47 (1997): 425–38.

Porter, James. "The Geneva Connection: Jean Servin's Settings of the Latin Psalm Paraphrases of George Buchanan." *Acta Musicologica* 81 (2009): 229–54.

Posset, Franz. *The Front-Runner of the Catholic Reformation: The Life and Works of Johann von Staupitz*. Aldershot, UK: Ashgate, 2003.

Posset, Franz. "Luther's Journey to Rome 1511–12." *Luther Digest* 21 (2012): 9–14.

Potter, G.R. 1976. *Zwingli*. Cambridge: Cambridge University Press.

Praetorius, Michael. *Gesamtausgabe der Musikalischen Werke*, 11–14. Edited by Friedrich Blume. Wolfenbüttel: Georg Killmeyer, 1928–40.

Praetorius, Michael. *Syntagma musicum*. Bd. 1: *Musicae artis Analecta* Wittenberg 1614/15, Faksimile-Nachdruck. Edited by Wilibald Gurlitt. Basel: Bärenreiter Kassel, 1959. Originally published as *Syntagmatis Musici Tomus Primus*.

Praßl, Franz Karl. "Luther in Graz, oder: Die *Gesang Postill* des Andreas Gigler (1569/1574), ein fast vergessenes hymnologisches Kleinod." In *Hymnody and Hymnology in Times of Transformation, Part II: Proceedings of the 29th Biennial IAH Conference, in Logumkloster DK 2017*, IAH Bulletin No. 46 (2018), edited by Martin J.M. Hoondert, 35–49. Tilburg, 2019.

Prescott, Anne Lake. "English Writers and Beza's Latin Epigrams: The Uses and Abuses of Poetry." *Studies in the Renaissance* 21 (1974): 83–117.

Preus, Robert. *The Theology of Post-Reformation Lutheranism*. 2 vols. St. Louis: Concordia Publishing House, 1970–1972.

Provan, Iain. *The Reformation and the Right Reading of Scripture*. Waco: Baylor University Press, 2017.

Przywara, Erich. *Analogia Entis. Metaphysics: Original Structure and Universal Rhythm*. Translated by John Betz and David Bentley Hart. Grand Rapids: Eerdmans, 2013.

Pünjer, Georg Christian Bernhard. *History of the Christian Philosophy of Religion from the Reformation to Kant*. Translated by W. Hastie. Edinburgh: T&T Clark, 1887.

Quinn, Kenneth. *Catullus: An Interpretation*. New York: Barnes and Noble, 1973.

Quinn, Kenneth. *Catullus: The Poems*. 2nd ed. New York: St. Martin's Press, 1973.

Raath, Andries. "Stoic Roots of Early Reformational Resistance Theory." *Studia Historiae Ecclesiasticae* 35 (2009): 303–22.

Rachelius, Samuel. *Aristotelis ethicorum ad Nicomachum libri decem, cum Dionysii Lambini versione Latina a Matthia Bergio interpolata*. Helmstedt: Typis et sumptibus Henning Muller, 1660.

Rautenstrauch, Johannes. *Luther und die Pflege der kirchlichen Musik in Sachsen*. Leipzig, 1907.

Rehnman, Sabastian. "Virtue and Grace." *Studies in Christian Ethics* 25.4 (2012): 481–88.

Rhau, Georg. *Symphoniae jucundae, 1538*. Edited by Hans Albrecht. Musikdrucke aus den Jahren 1538 bis 1545 in praktischen Neuausgabe 3. Kassel: Bärenreiter; St. Louis: Concordia Publishing House, 1959.

Rhein, Stefan. "Melanchthon and Greek Literature." In Wengert and Graham, *Philip Melanchthon (1497–1560) and the Commentary*, edited by Timothy J. Wengert and Patrick M. Graham, 149–70. Sheffield: Sheffield Academic Press, 1997. Richter, Joseph. *Bildergalerie katholischer Missbräuche. Mit Kupfern und anpassenden Vignetten*. Frankfurt und Leipzig, 1784.

Rohling, Geraldine M. "Exequial and Votive Practices of the Viennese Bruderschaften: A Study of Music and Liturgical Piety." Ph.D. diss., Catholic University, 1996.

Rohls, Jan. *The Reformed Confessions: Theology from Zurich to Barmen*. Louisville: Westminster/John Knox, 1998.

Roper, Lyndal. *Martin Luther: Renegade and Prophet*. New York: Random House, 2017.

Rosin, Robert. "Mathesius, Johannes." In *The Oxford Encyclopedia of the Reformation*. New York: Oxford University Press, 1996.

Rossall, Judith. "The Cost of Supporting Luther: The Role of Johann von Staupitz in the Early Reformation." *Lutheran Forum* 53.4 (2019): 16–22.

Rummel, Erika. *The Humanistic-Scholastic Debate in the Renaissance and Reformation*. Cambridge, MA: Harvard University Press, 1995.

Rupp, Gordon. *Luther's Progress to the Diet of Worms*. London: S.C.M.; reprint Harper and Row, 1964.

Saak, Eric. *High Way to Heaven: The Augustinian Platform Between Reform and Reformation, 1292–1524*. Leiden: Brill, 2002.

Saak, Eric. *Luther and the Reformation of the Later Middle Ages*. Cambridge: Cambridge University Press, 2017.

Salas, Victor M. *The Analogy of Being According to Thomas Aquinas: Its Twofold Character and Judgmental Method*. Saint Louis: Saint Louis University Press, 2008.

Sannemann, Friedrich. *Die Musik als Unterrichtsgegenstand in den evangelischen Lateinschulen des 16. Jahrhunderts*. Berlin and Leipzig, 1904.

Sasse, Herman. *This Is My Body: Luther's Contention for the Real Presence in the Sacrament of the Altar*. Eugene, OR: Wipf & Stock, 2001.

Sassu, Giovanni. "Appunti per uno studio del Sant'Agostino e quattro monaci nella chiesa della Misericordia." *Strenna Storica Bolognese* 47 (1997): 439–43.

Satterlee, Craig Alan. *Ambrose of Milan's Method of Mystagogical Preaching*. Collegeville, MN: The Liturgical Press, 2002.

Scaglietti, Daniela. "La Cappella di Santa Cecilia." In *Il tempio di San Giacomo Maggiore in Bologna*, edited by Carlo Volpe, 133–46. Bologna: Padri Agostiniani, 1967.

Schilling, Heinz. *Martin Luther: Rebel in an Age of Upheaval*. Translated by Rona Johnston Gordon. Oxford: Oxford University Press, 2017.

Scotus, John Duns. *Omnia Opera*. 14 vols. Civitas Vaticana: Typis Polyglottis Vaticanis, 1950–2013.

Schäfer, Christiane. "Die Lieder Martin Luthers in der deutschsprachigen katholischen Gesangbuchrezeption." *Internationale Arbeitsgemeinschaft für Hymnologie Bulletin* 45 (2017): 85–86.

Schalk, Carl F. and William H. Braun. *Lutheran Choral Anthology: The 16th Century*. St. Louis: Concordia Publishing House, 2010.

Scheel, Otto. *Dokumente zu Luthers Entwicklung*. 2nd ed. Tübingen: Mohr Siebeck, 1929.

Scheible, Hans. "Die Universität Heidelberg und Luthers Disputation." In *Melanchthon und die Reformation: Forschungsbeiträge*, edited by Rudolf May and Rolf Decot, 371–91. Mainz: Philipp von Zabern, 1996.

Schleusner, Georg. *D. Martin Luthers Dichtungen in gebundener Rede mit den nötigen Anmerkungen*. Wittenberg: P. Wunschmanns Verlag, 1892.

Schmeisser, Martin. "Johann Crells aristotelische Ethik und die Moralphilosophie an der Academia Norica in den ersten Jahrzehnten des 17. Jahrhunderts." In *Religiöser Nonkonformismus und frühneuzeitliche Gelehrtenkultur*, edited by Friedrich Vollhardt, 101–20. Berlin: Akademie Verlag, 2014.

Schneider, Hans. "Luthers Romreise." In *Martin Luther in Rom: die Ewige Stadt als kosmopolitisches Zentrum und ihre Wahrnehmung*, edited by Michael Matheus, Arnold Nesselrath, and Martin Wallraff, 12–21. Berlin: De Gruyter, 2017.

Schneider, Hans. *Martin Luthers Reise nach Rom neu datiert und neu gedeutet*. Studien zur Wissenschaft und zur Religionsgeschichte. Series edited by Werner Lehfeldt. Berlin: De Gruyter, 2011.

Schubert, Anselm. "Libertas Disputandi: Luther und die Leipziger Disputation als akademisches Streitgespräch." *Zeitschrift für Theologie und Kirche* 105 (2008): 414–19.

Schulze, Manfred. "Martin Luther and the Church Fathers." In *The Reception of the Church Fathers in the West: From the Carolingians to the Maurists*, edited by Irena Backus, 1: 573–626. Leiden: E.J. Brill, 1997.

Schwarz, Reinhard. "Disputationen." In *Lutherhandbuch*, edited by Albrecht Beutel. 2nd ed. Tübingen: Mohr Siebeck, 2010.

Schwarz, Reinhard. *Martin Luther Lehrer der christlichen Religion*. Tübingen: Mohr Siebeck, 2015.

Schwarz, Waltraut. *Bologna ja Bologna nein: La città nella letteratura tedesca dal medioevo ad oggi*. Bologna, Cappelli, 1975.

Schwemer, Bettina. *Mehrstimmige Responsorienvertonungen in Deutschen Quellen des 15. und 16. Jahrhunderts*. Collectanea Musicologica 8. Augsburg: Wißner, 1998.

Schwiebert, E.G. *Luther and His Times: The Reformation from a New Perspective*. St. Louis: Concordia, 1950.

Scribonius, Wilhelm. *Ethica ex Aristotele et aliis summis philosophis repetita*. Francofurti: Johann Wechel, 1589.

Scullard, H.H. "The Political Career of a *Novus Homo*." In *Cicero*, 1–25. Edited by T.A. Dorey. London: Routledge and Kegan Paul, 1964.

Sehling, Emil. *Die evangelischen Kirchenordnungen des XVI. Jahrhunderts*. Volumes 1–9, 11–20, 24 in 23 physical volumes to date. Leipzig: O. R. Reisland, 1902–13; Tübingen: J.C.B. Mohr/Paul Siebeck, 1955–.

Serina, Jr., Richard J. "Luther's Doctorate and the Start of the Reformation." *Lutheran Forum* 56.3 (2017): 53–57.

Seymour, Laura. *An Analysis of Roland Barthes's The Death of the Author.* London: Macat International Limited, 2018.

Shackleton Bailey, D.R., ed. and trans. *Martial Epigrams: Books 6–10.* LCL 95, vol. 2; Cambridge, MA and London: Harvard University Press, 1993.

Shircel, Cyril L. *The Univocity of the Concept of Being in the Philosophy of John Duns Scotus.* Washington, D.C.: Catholic University of America Press, 1942.

Siemon-Netto, Uwe. *The Fabricated Luther: Refuting Nazi Connections and Other Modern Myths.* 2nd ed. St. Louis: Concordia Publishing House, 2007.

Simon, John Hedley and Dirk Obbink. "Tullius Cicero, Marcus." In the *Oxford Classical Dictionary*, 1515. Oxford: Oxford University Press, 2012.

Simonius, Simon. *Commentariorum in ethica Aristotelis ad Nicomachum liber primus.* Geneva: Apud Ionnem Crispinum, 1567.

Sinnema, Donald. "The Discipline of Ethics in Early Reformed Orthodoxy." *Calvin Theological Journal* 28 (1993): 10–44.

Smalley, Beryl. *The Study of the Bible in the Middle Ages.* Notre Dame, IN: University of Notre Dame Press, 1964.

Smith, Preserved. *The Life and Letters of Martin Luther.* New York: Barnes & Noble, 1911.

Smith, R.A. "*Deipnosophistae* Reformed: Classical Intertexts in Luther's *Tischreden.*" *Logia* 21 (2012): 19–23.

Smith, R.A. *Poetic Allusion and Poetic Embrace in Ovid and Virgil.* Ann Arbor: University of Michigan Press, 1997.

Sparn, Walter. *Wiederkehr der Metaphysik: Die Ontologische Frage in der Lutherischen Theologie des frühen 17. Jahrhunderts.* Stuttgart: Calwer, 1976.

Spitz, Lewis W. "Luther and Humanism." In *Luther and Learning: the Wittenberg University Luther Symposium 1983*, edited by Marilyn J. Harran, 69–94. Selinsgrove, PA: Susquehanna University Press, 1985.

Spitz, Lewis W. and Barbara Sher Tinsley. *Johann Sturm on Education: The Reformation and Humanist Learning.* St. Louis: Concordia Publishing House, 1995.

Springer, Carl P.E. "Ambrose's *Veni Redemptor Gentium:* The Aesthetics of Antiphony." *Jahrbuch für Antike und Christentum* 34 (1991): 76–87.

Springer, Carl P.E. "Arms and the Theologian: Martin Luther's *Adversum Armatum Virum Cocleum.*" *International Journal of the Classical Tradition* 10 (2003–04): 38–53.

Springer, Carl P.E. *Cicero in Heaven: The Roman Rhetor and Luther's Reformation.* Leiden and Boston: Brill, 2018.

Springer, Carl P.E. "Death and Life after Death in Martin Luther's Latin Elegies." In *Acta conventus neo-latini upsaliensis: Proceedings of the Fourteenth International Congress of Neo-Latin Studies (Uppsala 2009)*, edited by Astrid Steiner-Weber, 1049–59. Leiden, Boston: Brill, 2012.

Springer, Carl P.E. *The Hermeneutics of Hell: Devilish Visions and Visions of the Devil in World Literature*. Cham: Palgrave Macmillan, 2017.

Springer, Carl P.E. *Luther's Aesop*. Kirksville, MO: Truman State University Press, 2011.

Springer, Carl P.E. "Luther's Latin Poetry and Scatology." *Lutheran Quarterly* 23.4 (2009): 373–87.

Springer, Carl P.E. *Luther's Rome, Rome's Luther*. Minneapolis: Fortress Press, 2021.

Springer, Carl P.E. "Macarius Mutius' *De Triumpho Christi*: Christian Epic Theory and Practice in the Late Quattrocento." In *Acta Conventus Neo-Latini Torontonensis*, Medieval and Renaissance Texts and Studies 86, Edited by Alexander Dalzell, Charles Fantazzi, and Richard J. Schoeck, 739–46. Binghamton, NY: SUNY-Binghamton Press, 1991.

Springer, Carl P.E. "Martin's Martial: Reconsidering Luther's Relationship with the Classics." *International Journal of the Classical Tradition* 14 (2007): 23–50.

Springer, Carl P.E. "Pious Mirth: Poetry and Theology in Luke 2:13–14." *Faith-Life* 86.4 (2013): 2–10.

Springer, Klaus-Bernward. "Luther als Student der Artes und stundentisches Leben in Erfurt im Spätmittelalter und zu Beginn der Frühen Neuzeit," *Mitteilungen des Vereins für die Geschichte und Altertumskunde von Erfurt* 72 (2011): 72–97.

Stayer, James. *Luther's House of Learning: Indoctrination of the Young in the German Reformation*. Baltimore: Johns Hopkins University Press, 1978.

Stayer, James. *Martin Luther, German Saviour: German Evangelical Theological Factions and the Interpretation of Luther, 1917–1933*. Montreal: McGill-Queen's University Press, 2000.

Steinmetz, David Curtis. *Luther and Staupitz: An Essay in the Intellectual Origins of the Protestant Reformation*. Duke Monographs in Medieval and Renaissance Studies 4. Durham, NC: Duke University Press, 1980.

Steinmetz, David Curtis. *Misericordia Dei: The Theology of Johannes von Staupitz in Its Late Medieval Setting*. Leiden: Brill, 1968.

Stephans, W.P. *Huldrych Zwingli*. New York: St. Martin's Press, 1977.

Stephans, W.P. *The Theology of Huldrych Zwingli*. Oxford: Clarendon, 1986.

Stephans, W.P. *Zwingli: An Introduction to His Thought*. Oxford: Clarendon, 1992.

Stephanus, Henricus, ed. *Davidis psalmi aliquot Latino carmine expressi a quatuor illustribus poetis: quos quatuor regiones, Gallia, Italia, Germania, Scotia, genuerunt*. 1556.

Stephens, William O. *Stoic Ethics: Epictetus and Happiness as Freedom*. London: Bloomsbury, 2007.

Stolt, Birgit. *Martin Luthers Rhetorik des Herzens*. Tübingen, Mohr Siebeck, 2000.

Stroh, Wilfried. *Latein ist tot, es lebe Latein*. Berlin: Ullstein, 2007.

Sullivan, J.P. *Martial: The Unexpected Classic. A Literary and Historical Study*. Cambridge: Cambridge University Press, 1991.

Summers, Kirk. *Morality after Calvin: Theodore Beza's Christian Censor and Reformed Ethics*. New York: Oxford University Press, 2017.

Summers, Kirk. "Theodore Beza's Classical Library and Christian Humanism." *Archiv für Reformationsgeschichte* 82 (1991): 193–208.

Summers, Kirk, ed. *A View from the Palatine: The* Iuvenilia *of Thédore de Bèze*. Tempe: Arizona Center for Medieval and Renaissance Studies, 2002.

Svensson, Manfred. "Aristotelian Practical Philosophy from Melanchthon to Eisenhart: Protestant Commentaries on the Nicomachean Ethics 1529–1682." *Reformation and Renaissance Review* 21:3 (2019): 218–38.

Sweetman, Robert. "Univocity, Analogy and the Mystery of Being According to John Duns Scotus." In *Introducing Radical Orthodoxy: Mapping a Post-Secular Theology*, Edited by James K.A. Smith, 73–88. Grand Rapids: Baker Academic, 2005.

Talon, Omer. *In primum Aristotelis ethicum librum explicatio*. Paris: Mathieu David, 1550.

Thomas, Richard F., ed. *Virgil: Georgics*. Cambridge: Cambridge University Press, 1988.

Thomas, Richard F. "Virgil's *Georgics* and the Art of Reference." *Harvard Studies in Classical Philology* 90 (1986): 171–98.

Thomson, D.F.S. *Catullus*. Toronto: University of Toronto Press, 1997.

Till, Nicholas. *Mozart and the Enlightenment: Truth, Virtue and Beauty in Mozart's Operas*. New York and London: W.W. Norton, 1992.

Tinctoris, Johannes. *The Art of Counterpoint* (*Liber de arte contrapuncti*). Translated and edited by Albert Seay. Musicological Studies and Documents 5. Rome: American Institute of Musicology, 1961.

Tittel, Ernst. *Österreichische Kirchenmusik: Werden, Wachsen, Wirken*. Vienna: Verlag Herder, 1961.

Torrell, Jean-Pierre. *Saint Thomas Aquinas: Spiritual Master*, vol. 2. Washington, D.C.: Catholic University of America Press, 1996.

Trout, Dennis. *Paulinus of Nola*. Berkeley, CA: University of California Press, 1999.

Trygophorus, Johannes. *Concertationes ethicae ex Aristotelis X. libris Nicomachiis, una cum applicatione ad ethicam Christianam*. Gryphiswaldiae: Ferber, 1606.

Urban-Godziek, Grazyna. "*Patrum erga filiam amor luctuosus*. L'espressione funebre dell'amore familiare nella poesia di Giovanni Pontano e Jan Kochanowski: Paralleli e ispirazioni." *Studi Slavistici* 3 (2006): 65–80.

Vasari, Giorgio. *Lives of the Most Eminent Painters, Sculptors and Architects* (1568). Translated by G. De Vere. London: Macmillan, 1912–1915.

Velde, Rudi te. *Aquinas on God: The 'Divine Science' of the Summa Theologiae*. Burlington, VT: Ashgate, 2006.

Vermigli, Petrus Martyr. *Commentary on Aristotle's Nicomachean Ethics*. Kirksville, MO.: Truman State University Press, 2015.

Vermigli, Petrus Martyr. *In primum, secundum et initium tertii libri Ethicorum ad Nicomachum ... Commentarius doctissimus*. Tiguri: Apud Christophorum Froschoverum, 1563.

Vermigli, Petrus Martyr. *In primum, secundum et initium tertii libri Ethicorum Aristotelis ad Nicomachum commentarius doctissimus*. Edited by Guilio Santerenziano, Luca Baschera and Christopher Moser. Leiden: Brill, 2011.

Virgil. *Georgicorum Libri Quatuor Pub. Virgilij Maronis Commentarijs doctissimis illustrati*. Basel: Bartholomaeus Westheimer, 1539.

Virgil. *P. Vergilii Maronis Bucolica, Georgica, & Aeneis*. Venice, 1539.

Virgil. *P. Vergilii Maronis Bucolicon, Georgicon, & Aeneidos vocum omnium, ac sylvae rerum index*. Venice: Damiani Zenarii, 1587.

Virgil. *Vergilivs Philippi Melanthonis Scholiis doctissimis illustratus*. Mainz: Georg Wagner, 1556.

Virgil. *Virgilius, Philippi Melanchthonis Scholiis, ut brevissimis ita doctissimis, ubique exactissime adnotatus*. Cologne: Johann Gymnich, 1533.

Viroli, Marco. *I Bentivoglio Signori di Bologna*. Cesena: Il Ponte Vecchio, 2011.

Voßberg, Herbert. *Im Heiligen Rom: Luthers Reiseeindrücke 1510–1511*. Berlin: Heinrich Grote, 1966.

Vredeveld, Harry. "Eobanus Hessus." In *German Writers of the Renaissance and Reformation, 1280–1580*. Edited by James Hardin and Max Reinhart, 97–110. Detroit: Gale Research, 1997.

Vredeveld, Harry. "Hessus, Eobanus." In *The Oxford Encyclopedia of the Reformation*, edited by Hans J. Hillerbrand. Oxford: Oxford University Press, 1996.

Vredeveld, Harry. *The Poetic Works of Helius Eobanus Hessus*, vols. 1–2. Tempe, AZ: Arizona Center for Medieval and Renaissance Studies, 2004–08.

Vredeveld, Harry. *The Poetic Works of Helius Eobanus Hessus*, vols. 3–4. Leiden: Brill, 2012–16.

Wackernagel, Philipp. *Das deutsche Kirchenlied von der ältesten Zeit bis zu Anfang des XVII. Jahrhunderts*. Leipzig: B.G. Teubner, 1867.

Walaeus, Antonius. *Compendium ethicae aristotelicae ad normam veritatis christianae revocatum*. Lugduni Batavorum: Impensis Asingae Elhardi, 1625.

Wall, John. "The Latin Elegiacs of George Buchanan (1506–1582)." In *Bards and Makars: Scottish Language and Literature: Medieval and Renaissance*, edited by Adam J. Aitken, Matthew P. McDiarmid, and Derick S. Thomson. 184–93. Glasgow: University of Glasgow Press, 1977.

Walter, Johann. *Das geistliche Gesangbüchlein "Chorgesangbuch."* Documenta Musicologica, Erste Reihe: Druckschriften-Faksimiles, 33. Kassel: Bärenreiter, 1979.

Walter, Johann. *Geistliches Gesangbüchlein, Wittenberg 1551, zweiter Teil: Cantiones Latinae*. Sämtliche Werke, 2. Kassel: Bärenreiter; St. Louis: Concordia Publishing House, 1953.

Ward, Graham. *Barth, Derrida and the Language of Theology*. Cambridge: Cambridge University Press, 1995.

Ward, Graham. *Christ and Culture*. Malden, MA: Wiley-Blackwell, 2008.

Ward, Graham. *Cities of God*. London: Routledge, 2000.

Ward, Graham. *Cultural Transformation and Religious Practice*. Cambridge: Cambridge University Press, 2005.

Ward, Graham. *The Politics of Discipleship: Becoming Postmaterial Citizens*. London: SCM Press, 2009.

Ward, Graham. *Theology and Contemporary Critical Theory*. New York: St. Martin's, 2000.

Ward, Graham. *True Religion*. Malden, MA: Wiley-Blackwell, 2002.

Watson, Lindsay Cameron. "Priape(i)a." In *Oxford Classical Dictionary*. 3rd ed. Oxford: Oxford University Press, 1996.

Watson, Patricia. "Martial's Marriage. A New Approach." *Rheinisches Museum* 146 (2003): 38–48.

Weaver, William P. "A More Excellent Way: Philip Melanchthon's Corinthians Lectures of 1521–1522." *Renaissance and Reformation/Renaissance et Réforme* 37 (2014): 31–63.

Weber, Paul. "Josef Gabriel Rheinberger and the Reform of Catholic Church Music, Part I." *The American Organist* 48.10 (2014): 49.

Weber, Robert. *Biblia sacra iuxta vulgatam versionem*, vol. 1. Stuttgart: Deutsche Bibelgesellschaft, 1985.

Weijenborg, Reinould. "Neuentdeckte Dokumente im Zusammenhang mit Luthers Romreise." *Antonianum* 33 (1957): 147–202.

Weinacht, Harald, ed. *Melanchthon und Luther: Merkmal einer Kirchenreform; Martin Luthers Lebensbeschreibung durch Philipp Melanchthon*. Zurich: TVZ, 2008.

Wels, Volkhard. *Triviale Künste: Die humanistische Reform der grammatischen, dialektischen und rhetorischen Ausbilding an der Wende zum 16. Jahrhundert*. Berlin: Weidler, 2000.

Wengert, Timothy J. *A Formula for Parish Practice: Using the Formula of Concord in Congregations*. Grand Rapids: Eerdmans, 2006.

Wengert, Timothy J. *Human freedom, Christian righteousness: Philip Melanchthon's exegetical dispute with Erasmus of Rotterdam*. Oxford: Oxford University Press, 1998.

Wengert, Timothy J. *Philip Melanchthon's* Annotationes in Johannem *in Relation to its Predecessors and Contemporaries*. Geneva: Droz, 1987.

Wengert, Timothy J. "Philip Melanchthon's 1522 Annotations on Romans and the Lutheran Origins of Rhetorical Criticism." In *Biblical Interpretation in the Reformation: Essays Presented to David Steinmetz in Honor of his Sixtieth Birthday*, edited by R.A. Muller and J.L. Thompson, 118–40. Grand Rapids: Eerdmans, 1996.

Wengert, Timothy J. and Patrick M. Graham, eds. *Philip Melanchthon (1497–1560) and the Commentary*. Sheffield: Sheffield Academic Press, 1997.

Wernicke, Michael. "Egidio da Viterbo: Humanist und Reformer des Augustiner-Eremitenordens." In *Martin Luther in Rom: Kosmopolitisches Zentrum und seine Wahrnehmung*, edited by Michael Matheus, Arnold Nesselrath, and Martin Wallraff, 309–18. Berlin: De Gruyter, 2017.

West, Martin Litchfield. "Elegiac Poetry, Greek." In *Oxford Classical Dictionary*. 3rd ed. Oxford: Oxford University Press, 1996.

Westphal, Merold. *Overcoming Onto-theology: Toward a Postmodern Christian Faith*. New York: Fordham University Press, 2001.

Wetzel, Richard, and Erika Heitmeyer. *Johann Leisentrit's* Geistliche Lieder und Psalmen, 1567: *Hymnody of the Counter-Reformation in Germany*. Madison and Teaneck: Fairleigh Dickinson University Press; co-published with Rowman & Littlefield, 2013.

White, Thomas Joseph, S.J., ed. *The Analogy of Being: Invention of the Antichrist or Wisdom of God?* Grand Rapids: Eerdmans, 2010.

Wilkinson, L.P. *Golden Latin Artistry*. Cambridge: Cambridge University Press, 1963.

Williams, Peter. *Bach: A Musical Biography*. Cambridge: Cambridge University Press, 2016.

Williams, Thomas, ed. *The Cambridge Companion to Duns Scotus*. Cambridge: Cambridge University Press, 2003.

Williams, Thomas. "The Doctrine of Univocity Is True and Salutary." *Modern Theology* 21.4 (2005): 575–85.

Willich, Jodocus. *De methodo omnium artium et disciplinarum informanda opusculum*. Frankfurt an der Oder: Johann Eichorn, 1550.

Willich, Jodocus. *Dialysis quatuor librorum in Georgicis Virgilii*. Frankfurt an der Oder: Johann Eichorn, 1551.

Winkworth, Catherine. *Lyra Germanica: Hymns for the Sundays and Chief Festivals of the Church Year*. London: Longman, Green, and Longman, 1855.

Winterbottom, Michael. "Asianism and Atticism," 184. In the *Oxford Classical Dictionary*. Oxford: Oxford University Press, 2012.

Wippel, John. *The Metaphysical Thought of Thomas Aquinas: From Finite Being to Uncreated Being*. Washington, D.C.: Catholic University of America Press, 2000.

Wolf, Ernst. "Zur wissenschaftsgeschichtlichen Bedeutung der Disputationen und der Wittenberger Universität im 16. Jahrhundert." In *Peregrinatio: Studien zur reformatorischen Theologie, zum Kirchenrecht und zur Sozialethik*, edited by Ernst Wolf, 1:38–51. Munich: Ch. Kaiser, 1965.

Woodward, Avery. "The Fourth Foot in Vergil." *Philological Quarterly* 15 (1936): 126–35.

Wundt, Max. *Die deutsche Schulmetaphysik des 17 Jahrhunderts*. Tübingen: J.C.B. Mohr, 1939.

Zimmermann, Jens, ed. *Re-Envisioning Christian Humanism: Education and the Restoration of Humanity*. Oxford: Oxford University Press, 2017.

zu Dohna, Lothar Graf. "Staupitz and Luther: Continuity and Breakthrough at the Beginning of the Reformation." In *VIA AUGUSTINI: Augustine in the Later Middle Ages, Renaissance and Reformation*, edited by Heiko A. Oberman and Frank A. James, III, 116–29. Leiden, New York, Kobenhavn, Köln: E.J. Brill, 1991.

Zumkeller, Adolar. "Die Augustinertheologen Simon Fidati von Cascia und Hugolin von Orvieto und Martin Luthers Kritik an Aristoteles." *Archiv für Reformationsgeschichte* 54 (1963): 15–37.

Zwingli, Ulrich. "A Friendly Exegesis, That is, Exposition of the Eucharist." In *Huldrych Zwingli: Writings*. 2 vols. Translated by E.J. Furcha and H. Wayne Pipkin, 2:234–386. Allison Park, PA: Pickwick, 1984.

Index